BEST PRACTICES IN ELL INSTRUCTION

SOLVING PROBLEMS IN THE TEACHING OF LITERACY

Cathy Collins Block, Series Editor

Best Practices in ELL Instruction

Edited by
Guofang Li
Patricia A. Edwards

Foreword by Lee Gunderson

THE GUILFORD PRESS
New York   London

Library of Congress Cataloging-in-Publication Data

Li, Guofang, 1972–
    Best practices in ELL instruction / edited by Guofang Li and
Patricia A. Edwards.
        p. cm. — (Solving problems in the teaching of literacy)
    Includes bibliographical references and index.
    ISBN 978-1-60623-662-8 (pbk.: alk. paper)
    ISBN 978-1-60623-663-5 (hardcover: alk. paper)
    1. English language—Study and teaching—Foreign speakers.   2. English
language—United States.   3. Language and languages—United States.
I. Edwards, Patricia A.
    PE1128.A2L48 2010
    428.2′4—dc22

                                                        2010008326

To all teachers of ELLs, for their hard work and for their role in changing ELLs' lives every day in and out of school

About the Editors

Guofang Li, PhD, is Associate Professor in the Department of Teacher Education and Senior Researcher for the Literacy Achievement Research Center at Michigan State University, where she teaches undergraduate, graduate, and doctoral courses in second-language and literacy education. She specializes in ESL/ELL education, family and community literacy, and Asian American education, and has conducted research in these areas in international settings including China, Canada, and the United States. Dr. Li is a recipient of the Early Career Award from Division G, Social Context of Education, of the American Educational Research Association; the Edward B. Fry Book Award of the National Reading Conference; the Best Article Award from *McGill Journal of Education*; and the Young Investigator Achievement Award from the University at Buffalo. Her major publications include three authored books—*"East Is East, West Is West"?: Home Literacy, Culture, and Schooling*; *Culturally Contested Pedagogy: Battles of Literacy and Schooling between Mainstream Teachers and Asian Immigrant Parents*; and *Culturally Contested Literacies: America's "Rainbow Underclass" and Urban Schools*—and several edited volumes, including *Model Minority Myths Revisited: An Interdisciplinary Approach to Demystifying Asian American Education Experiences* and *Multicultural Families, Home Literacies, and Mainstream Schooling*.

Patricia A. Edwards, PhD, is Distinguished Professor of Teacher Education, Senior University Outreach Fellow, and Senior Researcher for the Literacy Achievement Research Center at Michigan State University, from which she received the prestigious Teacher–Scholar Award in 1994 and the Distinguished Faculty Award in 2001. Dr. Edwards served as an advisor to the First National Education Goal, "Readiness for School," and the Michigan State University Institute for Families, Youth, and Children, and currently serves as a family literacy expert for four Early Reading First grants. She has been a senior researcher at two nationally prominent and funded research institutes—the National Center for the Improvement of Early Reading Achievement (1997–2002) and the Center for the Study of Reading at the University of Illinois at Urbana–Champaign (1988–1989). She was a member of the Board of Directors of the International Reading Association from 1998 to 2001; she served as the Association's Vice President in 2008–2009, now serves as its President-Elect, and will serve as its President in 2010–2011. From 2006 to 2007, she served as the first African American President of the National Reading Conference, the world's premier reading research organization. Dr. Edwards is a pioneer in crossing boundaries that have traditionally constrained African American children and youth and has increased momentum in addressing the problems of educating the nation's culturally diverse children. Her publications are rich with evidence and insights into issues of culture, identity, equity, and power that affect families and schools. She is the author of two nationally acclaimed family literacy programs, *Parents as Partners in Reading: A Family Literacy Training Program* and *Talking Your Way to Literacy: A Program to Help Nonreading Parents Prepare Their Children for Reading.* Her books include *A Path to Follow: Learning to Listen to Parents*; *Children's Literacy Development: Making It Happen through School, Family, and Community Involvement*; and *Tapping the Potential of Parents: A Strategic Guide to Boosting Student Achievement through Family Involvement*; and two forthcoming books, *Change Is Gonna Come: Transforming Literacy Education for African American Students* and *It's Time for Straight Talk: Stories from the Field about the Real Reasons We Are Failing to Help African American Children Achieve.*

Contributors

Harriett Allison is Temporary Assistant Professor in the Teaching Additional Languages program and Foreign Language Education program at the University of Georgia. Her concentration is on qualitative inquiry on literacy development of and teacher training for U.S.-educated language-minority students. She has presented papers at conferences including Teachers of English to Speakers of Other Languages, the American Association for Applied Linguistics, the National Reading Conference, and the Conference on College Composition and Communication.

Alfredo J. Artiles is Professor of Special Education and Transborder Chicana/o Latina/o Studies at Arizona State University. His research foci are disability identification practices as a window into schools' cultural constructions and the precursors of educational inequity for racial-minority students through the examination of teacher learning for social justice. He is the 2009–2011 Vice President of the American Educational Research Association Division on the Social Contexts of Education and the coeditor of the *International Multilingual Research Journal* and the book series *Disability, Culture, and Equity*.

Kathryn H. Au is Chief Executive Officer of SchoolRise, LLC. A former elementary school teacher and professor at the University of Hawai'i, her research centers on school change and the literacy achievement of culturally and linguistically diverse students. Her latest book is *Multicultural Issues and Literacy Achievement*. She has served as President of the International Reading Association, President of the National Reading Conference, and Vice President of the American Educational Research Association.

Diane M. Barone is Foundation Professor of Literacy at the University of Nevada, Reno. Her research focuses on young children's literacy development and instruction in high-poverty schools. She has conducted two longitudinal studies of literacy development. She is widely published in journals and has authored many books, among them *Resilient Children* and *Literacy and Young*

Children: Research-Based Practices. She was a board member of the International Reading Association and the National Reading Conference.

Kristen Paratore Bock is a doctoral student in Curriculum and Instruction at the Lynch School of Education at Boston College. For the past 2 years, she has served as Family Literacy Coordinator for the Kindergarten Language Study, research that aims to improve the language and literacy skills of Spanish-speaking bilingual families. Her research interests focus on home–school connections, language and literacy acquisition among immigrants and other English language learners, and federal education policy.

Cynthia H. Brock is Professor of Literacy Studies in the Department of Educational Specialties at the University of Nevada, Reno. A former classroom teacher and current teacher educator and researcher, her interests include how children from linguistically diverse backgrounds learn literacy in upper elementary classrooms and how preservice and inservice teachers approach literacy instruction in diverse settings. She is the author of books, articles, and book chapters that focus in particular on how preservice and inservice teachers learn to teach children from nondominant backgrounds.

Ester J. de Jong is Associate Professor in Bilingual Education/ESOL at the College of Education, University of Florida, Gainesville. She has served as Assistant Director of Bilingual Education in the Framingham Public Schools, Massachusetts. Her research interests include bilingual education, with a particular focus on two-way immersion programs; educational language policy; and teacher preparation for standard-curriculum K–12 teachers working with bilingual students. She collaborated on the book *Educating Immigrant Children: Schools and Language Minorities in Twelve Nations* with Charles Glenn.

Patricia A. Edwards (*see* "About the Editors").

Carol Sue Englert is Professor in the Department of Counseling, Educational Psychology, and Special Education in the College of Education at Michigan State University. Her research interests include reading and writing interventions, text structure instruction, literacy across the curriculum, evidence-based practices for struggling readers and writers, and the role of technology in scaffolding and advancing literacy performance. Her current research focuses on instructional methods that help struggling middle school and junior high students to develop effective read-to-learn and write-to-learn strategies.

Kathy Escamilla is Professor in Education at the University of Colorado, Boulder. She does research on biliteracy development and assessment of Spanish-speaking Latino children. She has over 35 years of experience in the field of bilingual/ESL education as a teacher, researcher, and school administrator. She served two terms as the President of the National Association for Bilingual Education.

Erminda H. García is Instructional Coach at the University Public School in Phoenix, Arizona. She has taught for over 30 years, mostly in bilingual programs.

Eugene E. García is Professor of Education and Vice President for Education Partnerships at Arizona State University (ASU). He joined ASU from the University of California, Berkeley, where he was Professor and Dean of the Graduate School of Education from 1995 to 2001.

Claude Goldenberg is Professor of Education at Stanford University. He has taught both junior high school and first grade. Dr. Goldenberg was a recipient of the Albert J. Harris Award from the International Reading Association. He is author of *Successful School Change: Creating Settings to Improve Teaching and Learning* and coauthor of the forthcoming book *Promoting Academic Achievement among English Learners.*

Linda Harklau is Professor in the Teaching Additional Languages program and Linguistics program at the University of Georgia. Her research and teaching focus on second-language literacy development and qualitative research on adolescent and young adult immigrants. Her work has appeared in *TESOL Quarterly*, *Linguistics and Education*, and *Educational Policy*, among other journals.

Susan Hopewell is a PhD candidate in the division of Education Equity and Cultural Diversity at the University of Colorado, Boulder. Her research focuses on strengthening biliteracy education for Spanish–English bilingual children in the United States. She is currently examining the strategic use of Spanish during ESL literacy. She has spent 8 years as a classroom teacher in a dual-language elementary school and 4 years as the literacy coach in a maintenance bilingual program.

Barbara Krol-Sinclair is Director of the Intergenerational Literacy Program, a collaborative effort of the Chelsea Public Schools and Boston University. She also serves as adjunct faculty at Boston University and Granite State College. She has worked extensively in adult, secondary, and elementary education in a variety of schools and community education settings. Dr. Krol-Sinclair has authored and coauthored several publications in the area of home–school collaborations.

Guofang Li (*see* "About the Editors").

Troy V. Mariage is Associate Professor in the Department of Counseling, Educational Psychology, and Special Education in the College of Education at Michigan State University. His research interests include literacy interventions and the role of semiotic mediation to support teachers and learners. His current research examines teaching learning-to-learn and cognitive strategies in a Web-based environment. He is the current Program Coordinator of the Special Education Program at Michigan State University.

Sarah McCarthey is Professor of Language and Literacy in the Department of Curriculum and Instruction at the University of Illinois at Urbana–Champaign. Her research focuses on students' identities as writers, writing instruction, and the role of staff development in writing. She teaches undergraduate courses in reading and writing methods, and graduate courses in children's writing and classroom discourse. She is coeditor of *Research in the Teaching of English.*

Ellen McIntyre is Professor and Department Head of Elementary Education at North Carolina State University. Her research focuses on literacy learning of young children historically disenfranchised from schools and teacher preparation practices. Her studies have taken her into classrooms serving students of poverty, and into homes and communities to understand student learning from a sociocultural perspective. Her publications include the book *Six Principles for Teaching English Language Learners* and articles in *The Reading Teacher* and *School Community Journal*.

Eleni Oikonomidoy is Assistant Professor of Multicultural Education at the University of Nevada, Reno. Her research interests include academic identity construction of immigrant/refugee students; globalization, culture, and education; and culturally responsive teaching and research. She immigrated to the United States from Greece and has taught Greek as a foreign language and English as a second language in the past.

Alba A. Ortiz is Director of the Office of Bilingual Education in the College of Education at the University of Texas at Austin, where she is also Professor in the Department of Special Education and Coordinator of the Bilingual/Bicultural Education Program. She is a nationally recognized expert on the education of ELLs with language and learning disabilities. Dr. Ortiz is a Past President of the Council for Exceptional Children and a recipient of the National Association for Bilingual Education's President's Achievement Award.

Mariela Páez is Associate Professor at the Lynch School of Education, Boston College. Her primary research interests include bilingualism, literacy development, children's early language and literacy learning, and early childhood education.

Jeanne R. Paratore is Associate Professor and Coordinator of the Reading Education and Literacy and Language Education Programs at Boston University. She was part of the Boston University/Chelsea, Massachusetts, School Partnership, a comprehensive urban school reform effort, for 9 years. Her areas of interest include issues related to family literacy, classroom grouping practices, and interventions for struggling readers. Her most recent book is *Classroom Literacy Assessment: Making Sense of What Students Know and Do* (coedited with Rachel L. McCormack). She is presently co-curriculum director of the award-winning children's television series *Between the Lions*.

Julie L. Pennington is Associate Professor of Literacy Studies in the Department of Educational Specialties at the University of Nevada, Reno. She has focused on the areas of literacy and diversity throughout her career as a classroom teacher and currently as a teacher educator and researcher. Her research interests include pursuing questions related to how teachers approach literacy instruction in linguistically and culturally diverse settings. She is the author of *The Colonization of Literacy Education* and many articles and book chapters.

Maria Selena Protacio is a doctoral student in the Curriculum, Instruction, and Teacher Education program at Michigan State University. She serves as a research assistant for the Literacy Achievement Research Center, and is currently working on a professional development program for content-area and ESL high school teachers. Her research interests are in the areas of reading motivation, bilingualism, and biliteracy.

Taffy E. Raphael is on the Literacy, Language and Culture faculty at the University of Illinois at Chicago. Her research has focused on strategy instruction in comprehension and writing, and frameworks for literacy curriculum and instruction (e.g., Book Club Plus). She directs Partnership READ, a school–university partnership to improve literacy instruction through professional development, recognized by the American Association of Colleges for Teacher Education's 2006 Best Practices Award for Effective Partnerships. Dr. Raphael has published several books and over 100 articles and chapters in respected refereed journals. She currently serves on the Board of Directors of the International Reading Association (2007–2010).

Mary Eunice Romero-Little is Assistant Professor in the Division of Advanced Studies in Education Leadership, Policy, and Curriculum in the Mary Lou Fulton Institute and Graduate School of Education at Arizona State University. She recently served as a Co-Principal Investigator for the Native Language Shift and Retention Project, a 5-year research study funded by the U.S. Institute of Educational Sciences and sponsored by Arizona State University. Her professional and research interests are child language socialization, Indigenous language maintenance and revitalization, second-language acquisition, applied linguistics, and Native American and bilingual education. She is a member of Cochiti Pueblo, New Mexico.

Lucinda Soltero-González is Assistant Professor in the Division of Educational Equity and Cultural Diversity at the University of Colorado, Boulder. She was an elementary school teacher and a bilingual special education teacher for several years before earning her doctorate in language, reading, and culture from the University of Arizona. Her research interests include the development of bilingualism and early biliteracy in young Spanish-speaking children and biliteracy practices in U.S. schools.

Dianna R. Townsend is Assistant Professor of Literacy Studies in the Department of Educational Specialties at the University of Nevada, Reno. Her research focus is the literacy development of adolescent English learners, with specific attention to vocabulary development and academic English. She has had articles published in *Topics in Language Disorder* and *Reading and Writing: An Interdisciplinary Journal*, among other journals.

Xun Zheng is a PhD candidate in the Department of Curriculum and Instruction at the University of Illinois at Urbana–Champaign. Her research concentrates on writing instruction, writing practice at the elementary level, and the writing development of English language learners.

Foreword

Guofang Li and Patricia Edwards have been masterful in guiding the development of this book. It is extraordinary in its depth and breadth of coverage of important issues and concerns. To say that it is overdue is an understatement. The state of the art of teaching English language learners (ELLs) and English as a second language (ESL) is scandalous and is rapidly reaching the point of total disaster and no return. But this should be no surprise to the reader.

This foreword does not include comments and observations concerning how poorly ELL (ESL) students are doing in schools in North America. These stories are told every day in newspapers, in editorial columns, and in news commentaries, on television, on the Internet, and in everyday conversations in grocery store checkout lines. Recently, at an International Reading Association conference in Arizona, I heard a teacher conclude, "There are too many ESL students. They just bring down everything and everybody in my class." This blame-the-victim view seems widespread. It is an outrageous view in a country that promotes the notion that diversity represents strength.

The promise of a free, comprehensive education is that it allows human beings who would otherwise not have a chance to participate fully in society the knowledge and skills to do so. There are millions of human beings who are successful because they were given the social capital they needed to succeed as a result of their studies in public school, even though they were from poor or disadvantaged homes (Gunderson, 2007). The promise seems to have been lost, however. Instead, there appears to be a pervasive view that public education is culpable in terms of lowered standards, reduced possibilities, and overall failure. And in many cases the active perpetrators of the perceived failure are identified as the teachers or the students themselves, particularly ELL students.

A major suspect identified by many in lower scores and dropout rates is the ELL population (Gunderson, 2008a). It has been concluded, for instance, that California's dismal achievement scores were due, in part, to the fact that "vast numbers of students speak little English, and one in four lives in poverty" (Asimov, 1997). ELL students have had difficulties learning to speak, read, and write English at least for the last 50 years or so (Gunderson, 2008b). Why has the new millennium begun with the same poor results? Is it not the basic goal of public schools to provide programs that account for the skills, abilities, and needs of all students, including those who speak languages other than English? There appear to be a number of factors that account for this sad state of affairs, but two seem most relevant here: (1) the rapid increase in the ELL population, and (2) the lack of teacher knowledge and skills related to the teaching and learning of ELL students. The lack of knowledge about designing and implementing appropriate literacy programs for ELL students is a significant problem, and it will get worse as this population increases.

The number of ELL students enrolled in North American schools has risen dramatically. The National Clearinghouse for English Language Acquisition and Language Instruction Educational Programs (2007) reported that the percentage of ESL (ELL) students in America's schools has risen by 57.17% since 1995–1996. A local school district that had 1% ELL students in 1988 had 60% in 2007 (Gunderson, 2007). There are pockets of ELL students in locations such as Idaho and Wisconsin where there were few previously. The growth of ELL brings incredible diversity to schools and school districts. Unfortunately, it also finds teachers, through no fault of their own, unprepared to deal with the diversity, because ELL methodology, unfortunately, is not a feature of many teacher training programs. Mature teachers have seen ELL students for the first time in their classrooms and do not know how to plan and implement appropriate teaching and learning programs for them. ELL expertise and knowledge is significantly missing from many mainstream classrooms across North America. Many schools have ELL students but no trained literacy teachers to teach them. This book is an excellent resource for knowledge and expertise to help teachers plan appropriate programs for their ELL students and to serve as coaches for other teachers from kindergarten to secondary school levels. As a matter of convenience, I am using the abbreviation ELL in this foreword, but the category ESL or ELL is deceptively complex. As I (Gunderson, 2008a) have noted:

The label ESL or English-language learner (ELL) or whatever acronym is used is problematic because it masks significant underlying differences that have serious consequences. There are also many negative features associated with the label. There are ESL students who have never learned to read in their first language and those who have never attended school prior to immigrating. On the other hand, there are those who have attended school and who have learned to read some English. There are those who have learned to read and have studied advanced academic subjects in their L1s [first languages]. There are those who have entered as poor refugees and those who have entered as rich refugees. There are those who have entered when they were 6 years old and those who have entered at age 14 and higher. (p. 186)

There are ELL students who were born in the United States. There are students born in the United States who are native English speakers, but their English is often a dialect not represented in classrooms. An extremely complex and difficult issue is the identification of ELL students who have learning disabilities (Gunderson, D'Silva, & Chen, in press). It is a serious problem for teachers to design and implement teaching and learning programs for ELL students who have identified learning disabilities. Another significant problem for school personnel involves the assessment of ELL students (Gunderson, Murphy Odo, & D'Silva, in press). It is not clear that measures designed for native English speakers are appropriate for ELL students. Issues, for instance, related to accommodations (e.g., giving ELL students more time to complete an assessment) are both complex and contentious.

Issues are incredibly complex and so are the answers to myriad dilemmas that confront teachers and other school personnel. This book is an extraordinary resource that addresses many of the complexities and issues faced by teachers in grades K–12. Li and Edwards understand well the importance of professional development. As noted by Li and Protacio (Chapter 15, this volume), "A focus on a specific content area or a particular pedagogical strategy enables teachers to take this new knowledge from the professional development session and integrate it with their classroom practice" (p. 356). The range of content and author expertise in this book is impressive. There is likely no other book available that connects research and practice in so many areas and with such expertise.

The authors are experts in their areas. The coverage includes topics such as a review of related research, discussions of dual-language and bilingual instruction, principles of teaching young ELL students, strategies for teaching adolescent ELL students, teaching ELL students content-area reading, ELL student assessment, teaching Native American language learners, best practices in professional development, and an approach to include ELL students with learning disabilities. There is no doubt that this book will become a classic. It will provide both the research and practical strategies teachers need to design and implement teaching and learning programs for their ELL students. As you read this book, I am convinced it will help to address a terrible problem faced by schools and teachers across the continent: a significant lack of knowledge about ELL students at all levels. Over the last half-century teachers have not had access to the research and practical classroom knowledge provided in the various chapters in this book. I hope the contents of this book will provide teachers with the knowledge and expertise they need to integrate ELL students fully into their teaching and learning programs. Finally, it is my sincere hope that the contents of this book will show teachers that the diversity represented by ELL students can be a positive feature of their classrooms. We are in the 21st century, and it is time that we as teachers help all students, including ELL students, to meet their full potential. It is both our duty and our privilege to do so.

LEE GUNDERSON, PhD
University of British Columbia

REFERENCES

Asimov, N. (1997, January). California schools rate D-minus in report: Exhaustive study blames Prop 13 for the damage. *San Francisco Chronicle,* p. A2.

Gunderson, L. (2007). *English-only instruction and immigrant students in secondary school: A critical examination.* Mahwah, NJ: Erlbaum.

Gunderson, L. (2008a). Commentary: State of the art of secondary ESL teaching and learning. *Journal of Adolescent and Adult Literacy, 52*(3), 184–188.

Gunderson, L. (2008b). Bilingual education. In S. Mathison & E. W. Ross (Eds.), *Battleground schools* (pp. 57–64). Westport, CT: Greenwood Press.

Gunderson, L., D'Silva, R., & Chen, L. (in press). Second language reading disabilities: International themes. In D. Allington & A. McGill-Franzen (Eds.), *Handbook of reading disability research.* New York: Routledge.

Gunderson, L., D'Silva, R., & Murphy Odo, D. (in press). Assessing English language learners. In P. Afflerbach (Ed.), *Handbook of language arts.* New York: Routledge.

National Clearinghouse for English Language Acquisition and Language Instruction Educational Programs. (2007). *National and regional data and demographics.* Retrieved April 10, 2008, from *www.ncela.gwu.edu/stats/2_nation.htm.*

Acknowledgments

We are deeply indebted to Craig Thomas, Senior Editor at The Guilford Press, who took a strong interest in this book. We are grateful for his enthusiasm, his confidence, and his belief in us. We also would like to thank the chapter authors for their invaluable contributions. Their exemplary work and their passion to improve ELL instruction is reflected throughout this volume. Finally, we would like to thank two graduate students, Selena Protacio and Autumn Dodge, for their editorial assistance in this project.

Contents

BEST PRACTICES IN ELL INSTRUCTION

Introduction

Guofang Li and Patricia A. Edwards

In 2007, the U.S. Census Bureau reported that the number of people in the United States from ethnic or racial minorities has risen from 47 million in 2000 to more than 100 million, or around one-third of the population. The fastest growing groups are the Hispanic population, at a rate of 3.4% annually, and the Asians, at an annual rate of 3.2% (Reuters, 2007). The growth in immigrant populations or language minorities has drastically changed the student compositions in U.S. schools. There were about 1.3 million language-minority students, accounting for approximately 3% of the school student population in 1990. In 2001, it increased to 4.5 million, taking up approximately 9.6% of the total PreK–12 enrollment (Kindler, 2002). It is projected that by 2015 about 30% of the school-age population in the United States will be language minorities.

The changing demographics have posed unprecedented challenges for the public school system to accommodate a variety of needs for English language learners (ELLs) including their sociolinguistic, sociocultural, and socioemotional development (Li & Wang, 2008). To date, consensus among educators is that to address successfully the increasingly diverse student populations and ensure language-minority students' academic achievement, school instruction must be culturally responsive or reciprocal to students' linguistic and cultural backgrounds (Au, 1993, 2006; Gay, 2000; Li, 2006, 2008). For teachers and schools to be culturally reciprocal to students' diverse backgrounds, it is essential that they learn who the students are, what factors influence

1

their learning inside and outside school, what kinds of resources are available to these learners, and what strategies facilitate their academic achievement. To this end, in this edited volume, we provide up-to-date, research-informed best practices in teaching ELLs in K–12 public school settings. We focus on best strategies that work for multilingual students and those with special needs at both elementary and secondary levels. We address not only pedagogical issues concerning reading, writing, oracy, vocabulary, grammar teaching, assessment, and strategies to connect with students' cultural backgrounds but also programmatic and sociocultural issues, such as how to build school–home–community partnerships, ELL program models, and professional development models for teachers of ELLs. This comprehensive approach will help inservice and preservice teachers and educators who are interested in better serving culturally and linguistically diverse students to become informed of these research-based practices and be well prepared to teach our ever-growing ELL population.

Given the need in the field for work that bridges research and practice, this book will be an important resource for current and future educators. The book is divided into five parts: I. Perspectives on ELL Instruction, II. Strategies for Teaching Young ELLs, III. Strategies for Teaching Adolescent ELLs, IV. Best Practices in ELL/Bilingual Programs and Approaches, and V. Critical Issues Concerning ELL Instruction. In Part I, the authors situate the issues concerning the language and literacy instruction for ELLs within the context of research findings, and the specific social and economic conditions that ELLs face in education. Key research findings such as the importance of primary language in supporting English as a second language (ESL) learning and the need to accommodate ELLs' diverse needs in instruction, are emphasized. Part II addresses the principles for teaching ELLs in elementary schools, including guidelines for teaching ELLs across the curriculum and specific strategies for teaching oracy, reading, and writing, and conducting assessments. Whereas Part II focuses on young ELLs, Part III attends to the principles of teaching ELLs in secondary schools. Topics in this section include an overview of academic literacies instruction, specific strategies on teaching vocabulary, grammar and reading comprehension, and approaches to apprentice students into using cognitive strategies to learn content information. Part IV turns to programmatic issues and innovative models and approaches to teaching ELLs. Topics in this section include principles for designing quality programs for bilingual learners, bilingual framework in writing assessment, and a workshop approach to educate ELLs effectively. Part V addresses several current issues in the field of ELL education. Two chapters address issues related to two special subgroups within the ELL population, namely, the education of ELLs with learning disabilities and that of Native American ELLs. One chapter focuses on the issue of building school–home partnerships for ELLs. Last, two chapters discuss issues related to the process of teacher change and growth, and teacher professional development.

Part I: Perspectives on ELL Instruction

In Chapter 1, Claude Goldenberg presents key findings from two major syntheses of research published in 2006 on the education of ELLs: one by the National Literacy Panel, and the other by researchers associated with the Center for Research on Education, Diversity and Excellence (CREDE). The findings suggest that though ELLs learn in much the same way as non-ELLs and good instruction for students in general tends to be good instruction for ELLs, it is important to teach students to read in the first language and modify instruction to accommodate the diverse needs of ELLs. Goldenberg also raises several critical issues concerning ELLs' English language development, including oral language development, programmatic structure of English language development, and cultural responsiveness in instruction.

Following Goldenberg's call for emphasis on research about what really works for teaching ELLs, Eugene E. García and Erminda H. García discuss in Chapter 2 the state of education for such learners, and examine programs and best practices that are combating the achievement gap between ELLs and their English-speaking peers. The authors begin with a demographic overview of the growing dual-language-learning (DLL) population. DLLs who speak a first language other than English make up one in five children ages 0–8 years in the United States, resulting in educational skills and achievement that lag significantly in comparison to their non-ELL, native English-speaking peers. These ELLs start kindergarten behind their peers, and their gap in achievement grows even worse by the end of grade 3. The authors describe the varied language and cultural environments in which ELL children are raised. García and García entreat practitioners to address the basic questions related to language, culture, cognition, and educational opportunity for the growing young ELL population. In their review of best practices, they emphasize teacher competencies, instructional strategies, curricular content, programs, parent involvement, and related policy, and offer specific pedagogical alternatives that have demonstrated success in reducing the achievement gap among young ELLs.

Part II: Strategies for Teaching Young ELLs

Many best programs and practices discussions are aimed at teachers who already have ESL training. In Chapter 3, Ellen McIntyre addresses how traditional classroom teachers who have little or no training with ELLs can adapt instruction to make it more comprehensible to ELLs in their classrooms. McIntyre draws on multiple models of ELL instruction (e.g. Sheltered Instruction Observation Protocol [SIOP®], CREDE, culturally responsive instruction), outlining six principles for adapting instruction: (1) including more paired and group work; (2) making explicit connections between content taught and students' background experiences; (3) including oral language development as both an integral and separate part of each lesson; (4) keeping instruction rigorous; (5) using the instructional conversation as a tool for learning; and (6) involving families. McIntyre exemplifies these six principles by drawing on observation of teachers in two professional development studies she conducted. The participants in McIntyre's studies included traditional elementary and middle school teachers with ELLs in their classrooms. McIntyre discusses the challenges these teachers encountered while trying to make their instruction compatible with the needs of their ELLs. With the experiences of these teachers in mind, McIntyre proposes a developmental sequence for implementing these six principles in ways that recognize the challenges of instructional change and the demands of teaching.

Although the chapters thus far have focused on best programs and practices for ELLs in an overarching sense, Diane M. Barone, in Chapter 4, centers on beginning reading and writing instruction. Barone addresses concepts such as phonemic and phonetic awareness, various language forms (i.e., logographic vs. syllabic and right-to-left vs. left-to-right reading or writing), word decoding, comprehension, prior language knowledge, genre and content knowledge, and student engagement. For each of these concepts, the author provides several specific activities aimed at building competence and student interaction. Examples of activities are also provided that help teachers more fully visualize how to implement them. When addressing genre knowledge, for instance, Barone describes specific text constructions and how these texts can be used to scaffold ELL's understanding varying text structures (those of informational vs. narrative texts, etc.). Barone takes a cohesive approach to comprehension by detailing strategies for developing reading comprehension, as well as illustrating how a focus on writing can support reading comprehension. The activities, strategies, and teaching practices that Barone introduces all emphasize the importance of pair and/or group work, movement, variation, and communication to creating a learning environment where ELL students become engaged in learning to read and write in English.

Building on the prior chapter by Barone, Sarah McCarthey and Xun Zheng present in Chapter 5 details from their studies focused specifically on developing ELLs' writing skills. McCarthey and Zheng's studies demonstrate that to improve their writing, ELLs need many opportunities to write in a variety of genres and settings, as well as written and oral feedback to their writing. McCarthey and Zheng draw on their own and others' research to elaborate on six principles for ELL writing instruction: (1) Providing students with opportunities to write about their experiences enhances their development as writers; (2) providing opportunities to keep open-ended journals allows students to develop critical awareness of who they are; (3) providing opportunities to write in multiple genres across the school day is key to enhancing students' development as writers; (4) responding to students' writing is essential; (5) helping students become strong writers in their native language allows them to become more successful writers in English; and (6) talking to students about similarities and differences between their native language and English facilitates their metalinguistic awareness. The authors use examples from their own research to illustrate their six principles for ELL writing instruction. McCarthey and Zheng follow up with advice for teachers on how to tailor these principles to their own ELL populations.

Part III: Strategies for Teaching Adolescent ELLs

Turning to adolescent ELLs in Chapter 6, Harriett Allison and Linda Harklau provide an overview of best practices in teaching academic literacy to ELLs at the secondary level, drawing on insights from researchers in the United States and internationally. They begin by discussing various definitions of *academic language* and *literacy*, and pointing out controversies. They then articulate general principles of instruction gleaned from the research. The authors emphasize the need to have appropriate program models, explicit and targeted academic literacy instruction, and instruction on higher-level skills to ensure the success of adolescent ELLs' academic literacy learning. Given the complexity of the task of teaching academic literacy, the authors also make specific recommendations for best practices that address linguistic, cognitive, and sociocultural aspects of ELL academic literacy development.

Also focusing on academic literacy learning, in Chapter 7, Troy V. Mariage and Carol Sue Englert tackle one of the great challenges in secondary education—helping bilingual students and students with language/learning disabilities in inclusive social studies and science classrooms acquire the necessary learning-to-learn skills to support their understanding and production of informational texts. Drawing on their research known as Project ACCEL (*Acc*elerating *E*xpository *Lit*eracy), they offer a sociocognitive apprenticeship approach for teachers to use as they attempt to apprentice their middle school or junior high students into the learning-to-learn, cognitive, and metacognitive strategies that support all phases of an inquiry process. They emphasize the important role that teachers play in orchestrating classroom dialogues about learning-to-learn strategies, while they engage their students as active participants enroute to developing their mastery of the core literacy processes (e.g., comprehension, writing, text structures), and at the same time deepened their understanding of the disciplinary content.

Part IV: Best Practices in ELL/Bilingual Programs and Approaches

There is sometimes a foggy area between ELL program models and actual principles, policies, and practices that exist in the classroom. In Chapter 8, Ester J. de Jong helps teachers navigate this difficult region and find best practices for their ELL and bilingual students. As a starting point, de Jong addresses the often-confusing terminology used when discussing ELLs, in the hope that a more congruent understanding of terms can lead to more effective dialogue about what works for ELLs. For example, de Jong clarifies program models labels, giving examples of those that are commonly implemented and specifying each model's target population (minority–majority speakers), language distribution in the curriculum (native language, English, other languages), and program goals (additive bilingualism, subtractive bilingualism, monolingualism).

de Jong reiterates that when considering what works for ELLs, program model selection is important but not sufficient to ensure positive outcomes. Policies, practices, and principles enacted at the school and classroom level play an important role in ensuring that schools reach their academic, language, and sociocultural goals for all students, including ELLs. Additionally, de Jong discusses how program models and principles can work in tandem to create quality schooling for ELLs. In particular, de Jong uses a framework of commitment to educational equity to consider three key principles that can guide school- and classroom-level decision making: (1) affirming identities, (2) additive bilingualism, and (3) integration.

In Chapter 9, Kathryn H. Au and Taffy E. Raphael propose workshop approaches that offer the flexibility ELLs need to engage in higher-level thinking with text in meaningful projects, including the writing process and reading comprehension, while receiving necessary support and extensive instruction to complete each phase of the work. The authors suggest that authenticity involves four key concepts related to the language of literacy practices, the classroom community of practice, meaningful tasks, and routines. Through examples from two classrooms that use workshop approaches, they provide specific guidelines for teachers of ELLs on how to use these approaches in instruction.

In Chapter 10, Lucinda Soltero-González, Kathy Escamilla, and Susan Hopewell advance a theoretical framework of bilingualism and biliteracy in which the two languages of the bilingual individual are viewed holistically. Through this perspective, the authors promote the belief that languages should be separated for both instructional and assessment purposes. Soltero-González et al. call for an ideological transformation from a monolingual to a bilingual perspective through which to understand bilingual and biliteracy development. To illustrate the advantages of a bilingual–biliterate perspective, they present data from their study called Literacy Squared® that compares different aspects of a child's bilingual writing in both languages (e.g., bilingual strategies, student's voice, and unconventional segmentations), thus exemplifying how both of an individual's languages influence each other, as well as how the transfer of his or her writing abilities and knowledge occurs bidirectionally. Such theory and research perspectives support the notion of bidirectional transfer in the literacy development of bilingual writers and expand the predominant view on transfer from the first language to the second language. Finally, the authors discuss the theoretical and pedagogical implications of this perspective, and identify future directions for biliteracy research.

Part V: Critical Issues Concerning ELL Instruction

Whereas other chapters have detailed the demographic details of the U.S. ELL population, in Chapter 11, Alba A. Ortiz and Alfredo J. Artiles offer a picture of the a significant and growing segment of this population—ELLs with special needs. Indeed, 50% of ELLs with special needs have learning disabilities, most often reading difficulties. To this end, the authors present guidelines for designing and implementing programs that service this ELL population. For example, the authors call for collaboration between special language (i.e., bilingual education and ESL) and special education programs to identify ELLs whose language and literacy achievement may suggest the presence of a language or learning disability. For these students, special education assessments must be appropriate to their linguistic, cultural, and other background characteristics. Additionally, measures of student performance must account for ELLs' proficiency in both their native language and English, as well as the extent and nature of the native language and ESL instruction they have received up to that point. Ortiz and Artiles assert that, for eligible students, individualized education plans (IEPs) must simultaneously address students' language- and disability-related needs, and provide a continuum of instructional arrangements such that ELLs with disabilities have access to effective instruction in bilingual education, ESL, and special education programs that span multiple contexts, and are coordinated and coherent. The authors examine roles of administrators, teachers of bilingual education, ESL, and special education, and related services personnel (e.g., speech/language pathologists) in bringing about such collaboration.

A frequently underresearched ELL population is that of Native Americans (or American Indians). In Chapter 12, Mary Eunice Romero-Little focuses on Native American Indian language learners, beginning with a look at the impacts of early English-only schooling, and concluding with a discussion of contemporary language education, including community and school-based efforts to reclaim Indigenous languages and cultures. To lay the foundation for this chapter, the author introduces several key realities, including (1) the immense linguistic, cultural, social, and political diversity among over 500 Native nations; (2) the fact that Native American Indian language learners possess a range of multidimensional linguistic competencies and abilities; (3) the home language and literacy practices for teaching young children, including the expectations and roles of Indigenous families and communities; (4) the teaching and learning similarities and differences between the Indigenous home and community and those of mainstream schools; and (5) the theoretical and pedagogical issues of language and literacy learning for Native American Indian children and/or adults proven to be most effective and successful for academic achievement and Native language and culture learning.

With that foundation, Romero-Little discusses how the lessons from early English-only initiatives for Native Americans and the evolving field of language education have provided some valuable insights into best practices for meeting the dual challenge of maintaining or revitalizing the heritage language, while simultaneously learning English and English literacy. The author illustrates how this challenge has required reexamination and rethinking of education for Native American Indian children as associated with Indigenous sovereignty and social justice. The author's conversation is buoyed by the inclusion of sociocultural and sociolinguistic perspectives of language and literacy, and focuses on the dynamics of Indigenous and English language and literacy for young Native American Indian ELLs, including the early language and cultural socialization that occurs in their homes and communities.

Another critical issue concerning ELLs' education is the role parents play in their children's literacy development. Here, in Chapter 13, Jeanne R. Paratore, Barbara Krol-Sinclair, Mariela Páez, and Kristen Paratore Bock review best practices aimed at improving the literacy learning of non-native English-speaking families. The authors begin by discussing the role that parents play in their children's education, which has long been a focus of study by educators and policymakers, particularly in relation to efforts to understand high rates of failure among children who are acquiring English as an additional language. Paratore et al. draw special attention to the relationship between children's school success and two parent-related factors: parental education and home literacy practices. The authors give special focus to an intervention called *Lectura en Familia,* which is unique, the authors explain, because it uses the same children's books in both home and classroom contexts, therefore matching English language and literacy development in classrooms with Spanish language and literacy development at home. Paratore et al. discuss how evidence from many such studies has led to an ever-growing number of family literacy and home–school partnership initiatives, most often implemented in urban settings where there are many immigrant families. Despite the proliferation of such programs, however, the authors note that few reviews of family literacy programs and home–school partnerships have looked specifically at the types of practices that "pay off" when parents and children are acquiring English as an additional language. To address this gap in the research, Paratore et al. review theory and research that informs planning and implementation of programs and practices intended to bring parents, children, and teachers together in literacy learning.

Turning to the issues concerning teachers of ELLs, Cynthia H. Brock, Julie L. Pennington, Eleni Oikonomidoy, and Dianna R. Townsend attempt to answer the critical question in Chapter 14: In what ways can White teachers become better equipped to work with students who are different from themselves in culture, ethnicity, language, and other ways? Brock et al. posit that to be better able to work with children who are culturally and linguistically different from themselves requires that educators explore and examine their own situated racial, cultural, and linguistic identities, as well as best instructional practices. The authors situate their conversation by focusing on the growth of one

White teacher, Helen, and her journey of discovering and incorporating best practices to teach students from nondominant backgrounds. The authors document Helen's growth as she takes the first of a three-course series of professional development classes. In this first class, Helen focuses on learning about racial and linguistic diversity, examining her own racial and linguistic identity, and how her understanding of her own racial and linguistic identity impacts her work with students in her classroom. During the course of this first class, Helen examines her own identity as a person and as a teacher, makes a shift of focus from "self" to "others," views herself racially and linguistically, sees her own White privilege, comes to view her teaching differently based on her evolving identity, begins to see and value "others" differently, and forms a new outlook about institutional contexts.

Also focusing on teachers of ELLs, in Chapter 15, Guofang Li and Maria Selena Protacio address the issue of providing best practices in professional development for teachers of ELLs in light of the current educational crisis, with a seriously underprepared teaching force to meet the demands of the rapid growing ELL population. Li and Protacio point out that though there is an urgent need to prepare teachers of ELLs to meet the double challenge of teaching both content and ESL literacy to ELLs, relatively little scholarship has been devoted to address effective professional development practices to help teachers of ELLs to meet the varied and challenging academic, cultural, and linguistic needs of ELLs. To address this gap in literature, the authors set out to describe guidelines for effective practices of professional development for teachers of all students and proceed to offer specific principles for professional development with teachers of ELLs. In designing professional development for these teachers, Li and Protacio emphasize the need to include language-related knowledge and skills, and effective teaching strategies for ELLs; to promote collaboration between mainstream content-area teachers and ESL specialists; to help teachers address cultural diversity; and to engage teachers in inquiry-based, reflective professional learning. They illustrate how these principles can be applied by highlighting an ongoing professional development program that they implemented in a local school district, in which teams of content teachers and ESL specialists conduct action research projects to address their own professional development needs. Li and Protacio conclude by calling for new ways to help teachers implement their professional learning in their classrooms and change in both preservice teacher education programs and inservice teacher professional development programs to transform an underprepared teaching force and close the achievement gaps between ELLs and their peers.

REFERENCES

Au, K. H. (1993). *Literacy instruction in multicultural settings.* Fort Worth, TX: Harcourt Brace.

Au, K. (2006). *Multicultural issues and literacy achievement.* Mahwah, NJ: Erlbaum.

Gay, G. (2000). *Culturally responsive teaching: Theory, research, and practice.* New York: Teachers College Press.

Kindler, A. L. (2002). *Survey of the states' limited English proficient students and available educational programs and services: 2000–2001 summary report.* Washington, DC: National Clearinghouse for English Language Acquisition and Language Instruction Educational Programs.

Li, G. (2006). *Culturally contested pedagogy: Battles of literacy and schooling between mainstream teachers and Asian immigrant parents.* Albany: State University of New York Press.

Li, G. (2008). *Culturally contested literacies: America's "rainbow underclass" and urban schools.* New York: Routledge.

Li, G., & Wang, W. (2008). English language learners. In T. Good (Ed.), *21st century education: An encyclopaedia.* Thousand Oaks, CA: Sage.

Reuters. (2007). *U.S. minority population tops 100 million: Hispanics are largest and fastest growing ethnic population, census reports.* Retrieved May 10, 2008, from *www.reuters.com/article/idUSN1627210820070517.*

PART I

PERSPECTIVES ON ELL INSTRUCTION

CHAPTER 1

Improving Achievement for English Learners

Conclusions from Recent Reviews and Emerging Research

Claude Goldenberg

This chapter will:

1. Present key findings from two major syntheses of research published in 2006 on the education of English language learners (ELLs).

2. Identify and summarize relevant recent research published after the years reviewed by the research syntheses.

3. Explain how instruction and support in ELLs' primary language can help them develop literacy skills (and possibly other academic skills) in English.

4. Compare and contrast "generic" effective instruction with instruction that has been adjusted to the needs of ELLs.

Imagine that you are a second-grade student. During reading and language arts you will be faced with an ambitious learning agenda. It will likely include irregular spelling patterns, diphthongs, syllabication rules, regular and irregular plurals, common prefixes and suffixes, or what we have traditionally called structural analysis. It also includes how to follow written instructions, to interpret words with multiple meanings, to locate information in expository texts, and to use comprehension strategies and background knowledge to understand what you read, cause and effect, and features of texts, such as theme, plot, and setting. You will be expected to read fluently and correctly at least 80 words per minute, adding approximately 3,000 words to your vocabulary each year from different types of texts. And you'll be expected to write narratives and friendly letters using appropriate forms, organization, critical elements, capitalization, and punctuation, revising as needed.

You will have a similar agenda in math. And if you are fortunate enough to attend a school where all instruction has not been completely eclipsed by reading and math, you'll be tackling topics such as motion, magnetism, life cycles, environments, weather, and fuel; the physical attributes of objects; family histories and time lines; labeling continents and major landmarks on maps; and learning how important historical figures made a difference in the lives of others. The expectations created by state and district academic standards can be a bit overwhelming both for students and teachers.[1]

If you don't speak English very well, your job will be to learn what everyone else is learning—and learn English as well. And not just the kind of English you will need to talk with your friends and teacher about classroom routines, what you like to eat, what you are having for lunch, where you went over the weekend, or who was mean to whom on the playground. You will also need what is called *Academic English,* a term that refers to more abstract, complex, and challenging language that will eventually permit you to participate successfully in mainstream classroom instruction. Academic English involves things such as relating an event, or a series of events, to someone who was not present; being able to make comparisons between alternatives and to justify a choice; knowing different forms and inflections of words and their appropriate use; and possessing and using content-specific vocabulary and modes of expression in different academic disciplines, such as mathematics and social studies. As if this were not enough, you eventually need to be able to understand *and produce* Academic English, both orally and in writing (Scarcella, 2003). If you don't, there is a real chance of falling behind your classmates, making poorer grades, getting discouraged, falling further behind, and having fewer educational and occupational choices.

This is the situation faced by millions of students in U.S. schools who do not speak English fluently. Their number has grown dramatically just in the past 15 years. In 1990, 1 of every 20 public school students in grades K–12 was an English language learner (ELL), that is, a student who speaks English either not at all or with enough limitations that he or she cannot fully participate in mainstream English instruction. Today the figure is 1 in 9. In 20 years demographers estimate that it might be 1 in 4. The ELL population has grown from 2 to 5 million since 1990, a period when the overall school population increased relatively little. States not typically associated with non-English-speakers—South Carolina, North Carolina, Tennessee, Georgia, Indiana—each saw an increase in the ELL population of at least 400% between 1993 and 1994 and 2003 and 2004.

ELL students in the United States come from over 400 different language backgrounds; however, by far the largest proportion—80%—is Spanish speakers. This is an important fact to bear in mind, since Spanish speakers in the United States tend to come from lower economic and educational backgrounds than either the general population or other immigrants and language-minority populations. Consequently, most ELLs are at risk for poor school outcomes because of not only language but also socioeconomic factors. Speakers of Asian languages (e.g., Vietnamese, Hmong, Chinese, Korean, Khmer), who generally, although certainly not uniformly, tend to be of higher socioeconomic status, comprise the next largest group—about 8% of the ELL population.

In what sort of instructional environments are these students included? The question is difficult to answer, partly because of definitional and reporting inconsistencies from state to state (U.S. Department of Education, 2005; Zehler et al., 2003). The most recent national data come from a 2001–2002 school year survey (Zehler et al., 2003). To the extent that the portrait is still accurate 9 years later, a majority of English learners—approximately 60%—are in essentially all-English instruction. Beyond this, it is impossible to say what is typical. If anything, the picture has gotten more complex. Three states have over the past decade enacted laws that curtail bilingual education: California in 1998, Arizona in 2000, and Massachusetts in 2002; the number of students receiving bilingual education has steadily declined in those states. But even in states that require bilingual education—New Jersey, Texas, Illinois, New York, and New Mexico—the trends vary. In Texas, the number of students in bilingual education has gone up a bit; in Illinois, it has stayed about the same; in New York and New Jersey, it has gone down (Zehr, 2007a).

The shifting landscape is partly due to the accountability requirements of the No Child Left Behind Act of 2001 (particularly in basic skills such as reading and math) and how individual states interpret them. No Child Left Behind permits assessment of ELLs in their primary language for up to 3 years, and in some cases for an additional 2 years. But most states do not take advantage of this flexibility. The pressures on educators to immerse students in English are thus nearly overwhelming (Zehr, 2007a). This is ironic, since the best evidence we have shows that instruction in the primary language makes a positive contribution to academic achievement (particularly in reading) *in the second language*. I discuss this point at length in the following section.

About 12% of ELLs apparently receive no services or support at all related to their limited English proficiency. This might be a violation of the 1974 Supreme Court decision in *Lau v. Nichols* (414 U.S. No. 72-6520, pp. 563–572), requiring schools to teach ELLs so that they have "a meaningful opportunity to participate in the public educational program" (p. 563). Somewhat fewer than half of ELLs receive all-English instruction with some amount of "LEP services." (ELLs were formerly called LEP, or *limited English proficient*; the term is sometimes still used.) LEP services can include aides or resource teachers specifically for ELLs, instruction in English as a second language (ESL), and/or content instruction specially designed for students with LEP. The remaining ELLs—about 40%—are in programs that make some use of their primary language. Here, again, there is a wide range, with nothing being typical. In some cases, the native language is used extensively and students are taught academic skills in that language, for example, how to read and write in Spanish. In other cases, students are taught academic skills in English, but their primary language is used only for "support," for example, to translate, explain, or preview material prior to an all-English lesson (Zehler et al., 2003). There is no way to know the amount of support students receive or, most critically, the quality of the instruction and whether it is helpful for student achievement.

There are numerous program models that states report using with ELLs (U.S. Department of Education, 2005; see Genesee, 1999, for a description of the different program alternatives for ELLs, ranging from all-English instruction to different forms of bilingual education). Variability is again the rule. All 50 states (plus Washington, DC, and Puerto Rico) report some type of ESL instruction, but no state uses only one program model. Some states have as many as eight or nine different programs; New Mexico reports 10 (U.S. Department of Education, 2005). Clearly, it is difficult to generalize about the varied and complex instructional landscape for ELLs.

Regardless of the instruction ELLs are receiving, however, we have not done a particularly good job of promoting high levels of achievement among this fast-growing segment of the K–12 population. On state and national tests, students who are learning English consistently underperform in comparison to their English-speaking peers. In California, for example, approximately 50% of students who are fluent in English score as proficient or advanced on the California Standards Test in English language arts (the actual percentage of proficient or advanced students ranges from a high of 68% in grade 4 to a low of 46% in grade 11). In contrast, among ELLs *who have been enrolled in school for 12 months or more*, the percentage that is proficient or advanced in English language arts ranges from a high of 28% in second grade to a dreadfully low

4% in 10th and 11th grades (data are from the California Department of Education website *cde.ca.gov*). The national picture shows the same discrepancies. On the 2005 National Assessment of Educational Progress (NAEP; *nces.ed.gov/nationsreportcard*), fourth-grade ELLs scored 35 points below non-ELLs in reading, 24 points below non-ELLs in math, and 32 points below non-ELLs in science. These are very large gaps—on fourth-grade NAEP, 10 points is roughly equivalent to a grade level. Similar gaps have also been found in reading, math, and science among eighth graders.

These discrepancies should be no surprise, of course, since ELLs—even if they have been in the United States for a year—are limited in their English proficiency, and the tests cited here are *in* English. This points, again, to the important and very complex question of how and particularly in what language ELLs should be assessed. If ELLs are assessed in English, we are almost certain to underestimate what they know and put them at even greater risk of poor achievement. This is problematic both from a policy perspective and instructionally: How can we design effective policies and practices if we systematically misjudge the knowledge and skills of a large number of students? There is no way to know whether ELLs tested in English score low because of lagging content knowledge and skills or because of limited English proficiency or some other factor, or a combination of factors. Unfortunately, many states do not take advantage of even the modest provisions in the No Child Left Behind Act that permit assessing ELLs in their primary language for up to 3, possibly 5, years. Recently a group of school districts sued to force the state of California to allow Spanish-speaking ELLs to take state-mandated tests in Spanish. Plaintiffs in *Coachella Valley Unified School District v. California* argued that the state "violated its duty to provide valid and reliable academic testing" (King, 2007). However, in a preliminary ruling, the judge indicated that the court lacked the jurisdiction to decide the case (Zehr, 2007b).

Whatever the explanation for these achievement gaps, they bode ill for English learners' future educational and vocational options. They also bode ill for the society as a whole, since the costs of large-scale underachievement are very high (Natriello, McDill, & Pallas, 1990). Passage of No Child Left Behind in 2001 raised the stakes higher than ever for educators. Schools cannot meet their adequate yearly progress (AYP) goals unless all major subgroups at the school—including ELLs—meet achievement targets. Teachers of ELLs, as well as their site and district administrators, are thus under tremendous pressure. It is imperative that teachers, administrators, other school staff, and policymakers understand the state of our knowledge regarding how to improve the achievement of these students.

Unfortunately, the state of our knowledge is very modest. This is true for several reasons, among them that debates over language of instruction—the so-called "bilingual education" question—have historically dominated this field and, as a result, there has been relatively little solid research on many other important topics. *Bilingual education* is a term used to describe any instructional approach that teaches academic skills, such as reading, in the native language, in addition to teaching students academic skills in English. (For descriptions of the various approaches that fall under the bilingual umbrella, see Genesee, 1999.) The preeminent question in the education of ELLs has historically been whether student achievement is better when students are in some form of bilingual education, or whether achievement is superior when students are taught using only English.

Research and policy affecting ELLs have historically been fueled by ideological and political considerations (Crawford, 1999), often with less attention to coherent programs of research that could shed light on ways to improve these students' educational outcomes. The net result has been an inadequate research base for informing comprehensive policies and practices—including, very critically, guidelines for determining the skills and knowledge teachers need to be effective with ELLs. As if this were not enough, the research is practically nonexistent at the secondary level. Almost all the research we have is at the elementary level, with a handful in middle school. But the issues change as children go through school, so findings from elementary school might not be particularly useful in high school. In higher grades, the learning is more complex and the achievement gaps are wider. Adolescence ushers in questions of identity, motivation, peer groups, and a wide range of other factors that change in fundamental ways what teachers and parents must address. Although the picture is slowly changing, the research we have offers precious little guidance.

Studies Agree on Key Findings

Two major reviews of the research on educating English learners were completed in 2006, one by the National Literacy Panel (NLP; August & Shanahan, 2006), the other by researchers associated with the Center for Research on Education, Diversity and Excellence (CREDE; Genesee, Lindholm-Leary, Saunders, & Christian, 2006). The NLP comprised 18 researchers with expertise in literacy, language development, education of language-minority students, assessment, and quantitative and qualitative research methods. The NLP, whose work took nearly 3 years, identified over 3,000 reports, documents, dissertations, and publications, produced from approximately 1980 to 2002, that were candidates for inclusion in its review. Fewer than 300 met the criteria for inclusion: They were *empirical* (that is, they collected, analyzed, and reported data rather than stated opinions, advocated positions, or reviewed research) and dealt with clearly identified language-minority populations, and studied children and youth ages 3–18. The CREDE report was produced over 2 years by a core group of four researchers (and three coauthors), all of whom had been engaged in language-minority and language research for many years. Like the NLP, the CREDE panel conducted literature searches to identify candidate empirical research reports on language-minority students from preschool to high school, but their searches were not as extensive as the NLP's. Approximately 200 articles and reports comprised the final group of studies the CREDE panel reviewed and upon which they based their conclusions. The studies the CREDE panel reviewed were published during approximately the same period as the studies the NLP reviewed.

Although they covered a lot of the same terrain, the CREDE and NLP reports differed in some ways. For example, the CREDE report only examined research conducted in the United States and only took into consideration outcomes in English; the NLP included studies conducted anywhere in the world (as long as they were published in English) and took into consideration outcomes in children's first or second language. The CREDE panelists only included quantitative studies (experiments or correlational research) almost exclusively, whereas the NLP also included quite a few qualitative studies.[2] The CREDE panel reviewed research that addressed children's English language development, literacy development, and achievement in the content areas (science, social studies, mathematics). In contrast, the NLP only looked at influences on literacy development (and aspects of oral language that are closely related to literacy; e.g., phonological awareness and vocabulary). A final and very important difference between the two reports was the criteria used to determine whether to include studies of bilingual education. The NLP used more stringent criteria, resulting in a difference in the two reports' findings about how long ELLs should receive bilingual instruction. I describe this difference in the section that follows.

These two reviews used various methods to synthesize the research and draw conclusions that would be helpful to educators and that would also identify areas for additional future study.[3] In doing their reviews, both sets of panelists paid particular attention to the quality of the studies and the degree to which reported findings were adequately supported by the research undertaken. The reports warrant our attention, since they represent the most concerted effort to date to identify the best knowledge available and set the stage for renewed efforts to find effective approaches to help English learners succeed in school. It would be impossible to summarize fully the reports here, and educators are encouraged to obtain and study them. But their key conclusions can help us forge a new foundation for improving the education of children from non-English-speaking homes. The findings can be summarized in three major points, which I discuss in the sections that follow:

1. Teaching students to read in the first language promotes higher levels of reading achievement *in English*.
2. What we know about good instruction and curriculum in general holds true for English learners as well.
3. English learners require instructional modifications when instructed in English.

Teaching Students to Read in the First Language Promotes Higher Levels of Reading Achievement in English

To date, five meta-analyses[4] have concluded that bilingual education promotes academic achievement in students' *second* language (Greene, 1997; August & Shanahan, 2006; Rolstad, Mahoney, & Glass, 2005; Slavin & Cheung, 2005; Willig, 1985). This finding most clearly applies to learning to read. Findings for other curricular areas are much more equivocal. Nonetheless, this is an extraordinary convergence. To appreciate the strength of the finding, readers should understand how unusual it is even to have five independent meta-analyses on the same issue conducted by five independent researchers from diverse perspectives. The fact that they all reached essentially the same conclusion is noteworthy. With the exception of one, none of the meta-analysts have or had any particular investment, professionally or otherwise, in bilingual education. They were completely nonpartisan, methodologically rigorous, and independent researchers. (The one exception, Willig, was also rigorous, but had worked in the field of bilingual education, so skeptics might suspect a probilingual education agenda.) I know of no other finding in the entire educational research literature that can claim to be supported unanimously by five independent meta-analyses conducted over a 20-year span. In fact, this might be one of the strongest findings in the entire field of educational research. Period. Although many questions remain about the role of the primary language in educating English learners, the consistent findings from these meta-analyses should put to rest the idea that English-only instruction is preferable.

Approximately two or three dozen experiments conducted and reported over the past 35 years have compared reading instruction that uses students' primary and secondary languages with second-language immersion (which in the United States would, of course, be English). The NLP conducted a meta-analysis of 17 of these studies—the others did not meet their stringent methodological criteria—and concluded that teaching ELLs to read in their primary language, compared with teaching them to read in their second language only, boosts their reading achievement *in the second language.* In other words, students' second language reading achievement will be higher if they are first taught to read in their home language, compared to being taught to read in the second language right off the bat. And the higher-quality, more rigorous studies showed the strongest effects of all.

Although there are other possible explanations, the key to explaining how primary language instruction results in higher achievement in English is probably what educational psychologists call "transfer." Transfer is one of the most venerable and important concepts in education. With respect to English learners, a substantial body of research reviewed by both CREDE and NLP researchers suggests that literacy and other skills and knowledge transfer across languages; that is, if you learn something in one language, such as decoding, comprehension skills, or a concept such as "democracy," you either already know it in (i.e., transfer it to) another language, or you can more easily learn it in another language. Transfer also explains another important finding first pointed out in the meta-analysis by Slavin and Cheung (2005), published a year before the NLP report appeared[5]: ELLs can be taught to read in their primary language and in English simultaneously (at different times in the school day), with mutual benefit to literacy development in both languages. Teachers cannot assume that transfer is automatic, however. Students sometimes do not realize what they know in their first language (e.g., the cognates *elefante* and *elephant*; or *ejemplo* and *example*). Jiménez (1997) puts it this way: "Less successful bilingual readers view their two languages as separate and unrelated, and they often see their non-English language backgrounds as detrimental" (p. 227). It is necessary that teachers be aware of what students know and can do in their primary language, so they can help them apply these skills and knowledge to tasks in English.

Transfer of reading skills across languages appears to be true even if languages use different alphabetic systems, although the different alphabets probably diminish the degree of transfer. For example, studies of transfer between English and Spanish find relatively high correlations on measures of word reading and spelling. Some studies of English and non-Roman alphabets (e.g., Arabic or Persian) in contrast find much lower correlations. However, comprehension skills appear to transfer readily between languages with different alphabets, such as English and Korean.

"Transfer" is a critical point, since opponents of primary language instruction often argue that time spent in the first language is wasted from the standpoint of promoting progress in the second. The opposite is actually true: Productive learning in one language makes a positive contribution to learning in the second language. Since academic learning—with which schools and teachers must be most concerned—is most efficient and productive in the language one knows best, the clear conclusion from this research is that teaching academic skills (keeping in mind that research is strongest with respect to teaching reading) in the learner's stronger language is the most efficient approach to take.

The effects of primary language instruction are modest—but they are real. Researchers gauge the effect of a program or an instructional practice in terms of an *effect size* that tells us how much improvement can be expected from using the program or practice. The average effect size of primary language reading instruction over 2 to 3 years (the typical length of time children in the studies were followed) is around 0.35– 0.40; estimates range from about 0.2 to about 0.6, depending on how the calculation is done. What this means is that teaching students to read in their home language can boost achievement in the second language by a total of about 12–15 percentile points (in comparison to students who do not receive primary language instruction) over 2–3 years. This is not a huge amount, but neither is it trivial. These effects are reliable, and they apply to both elementary and secondary school students (although only two of the 17 studies the NLP included in the meta-analysis were with secondary school students, both produced positive effects). To provide some perspective, the National Reading Panel (2000), which reviewed experimental research on English speakers only, found that the average effect size of phonics instruction is 0.44, a bit larger than the likely average effect size of primary language reading instruction. Primary language reading instruction is clearly no panacea, just as phonics instruction is no panacea. But, relatively speaking, it makes a meaningful contribution to reading achievement *in English*.

Beyond the finding that primary language instruction promotes achievement in English, however, there are a great many unknowns: Is primary language instruction more beneficial for some learners than for others (e.g., those with weaker or stronger primary language skills? Weaker or stronger English skills?) Is it more effective in some settings than others? What should be the relative emphasis between promoting knowledge and skills in the primary language and developing English language proficiency? What level of skill in the students' primary language does the teacher need to possess to be effective? In an English immersion situation, what is the most effective way to use the primary language to support children's learning? We cannot answer these questions with confidence. Individual studies might point in certain directions, but we lack a body of solid studies that permit us to go beyond the general finding about the effects of primary language instruction on achievement in English.

We also cannot say with confidence how long students should receive instruction in their primary language. On the one hand, the CREDE synthesis concluded that more primary language instruction over more years leads to higher levels of ELL achievement in English. On the other hand, the NLP's meta-analysis of language of instruction did not support any conclusion about optimal number of years of primary language instruction. The reason for the discrepancy lies in the different criteria CREDE and NLP researchers used for including studies in their syntheses: The CREDE report included studies and evaluations of *two-way bilingual education*. Two-way models involve some combination of first (e.g., Spanish) and second language (e.g., English) instruction throughout elementary school; some go through middle and high school. Their goal is bilingualism and biliteracy for all students in the program. Evaluations have been very positive, but these studies do not control for preexisting differences or population differences between students in the two-way programs and students in comparison programs. Because of this limitation in the research designs, the NLP did not include two-way programs in its meta-analysis. The NLP included only programs of relatively short duration—1 to 3 years—among which there were no differences in student outcomes in relation to years in primary language instruction.

Despite these many unknowns, there is another reason to consider bilingual instruction for English learners. And that is the inherent advantage of knowing and being literate in two languages. It should come as no surprise that the meta-analyses found that in addition to promoting achievement in the second language, bilingual instruction also promotes achievement in the primary language. In other words, it helps students become bilingual. Knowing two languages confers numerous obvious advantages—cultural, intellectual, cognitive (e.g., Bialystock, 2001), vocational, and economic (Saiz & Zoido, 2005), although readers should note that the populations studied to support these conclusion are different from the population of ELLs addressed in this chapter. Regardless, many would argue that bilingualism and biliteracy ought to be our educational goal for English learners (see, most recently, Gándara & Rumberger, 2006). I would agree but take it a step further: It should be a goal for all students.

Questions of how long and to what extent bilingual instruction should be used and the benefits of bilingual instruction do not even arise in many schools. Instruction in the primary language is sometimes not feasible, either because there are no qualified staff or because students come from numerous language backgrounds or, sadly, because of uninformed policy choices or political decisions, such as California's Proposition 227. English learners can still be helped to achieve at higher levels. Although the research here is not as solid as the research on primary language instruction, which itself is incomplete in many respects, educators have two other important principles, supported by research to varying degrees, on which to base their practice. We turn to them now.

What We Know about Good Instruction and Curriculum in General Holds for ELLs

Both the CREDE and NLP reports conclude that ELLs learn in much the same way as non-ELLs (although modifications are almost certainly necessary, as discussed in the next section). Good instruction for students in general tends to be good instruction for ELLs in particular. If instructed in the primary language, the application of effective instructional models to English learners is transparent; all that differs is the language of instruction. But even when instructed in English, effective instruction for ELLs is similar in important respects to effective instruction for non-ELLs.

As a general rule, all students tend to benefit from clear goals and learning objectives; meaningful, challenging, and motivating contexts; a curriculum rich with content; well-designed, clearly structured, and appropriately paced instruction; active engagement and participation; opportunities to practice, apply, and transfer new learning; feedback on correct and incorrect responses; periodic review and practice; frequent assessments to gauge progress, with reteaching as needed; and opportunities to interact with other students in motivating and appropriately structured contexts. Although these instructional variables have not been studied with ELLs to the degree they have with English speakers, existing studies suggest that what is known about effective instruction in general ought to be the foundation of effective teaching for English learners. There are, of course, individual or group differences: Students might require or benefit from more or less structure, practice, review, autonomy, challenge, or any other dimension of teaching and learning. This is as likely to be true for English learners as it is for English speakers.

The NLP found that ELLs learning to read in English, just like English speakers learning to read in English, benefit from explicit teaching of components of literacy (e.g., phonemic awareness, phonics, vocabulary, comprehension, and writing). Particularly with respect to phonological and decoding skills, ELLs appear to be capable of learning at levels comparable to those of English speakers, if they are provided with good, structured, explicit teaching. Some of the studies supporting this conclusion were conducted with ELLs in Canada, so we must be cautious in interpreting them for the U.S. context. The ELL population in Canada is very different from the ELL population in the United States. Because of highly restrictive immigration laws, the Canadian ELL population is from families with higher income and education levels. Nonethless, the NLP reviewed five studies that, as a group, showed the benefits of structured direct instruction for the development of these early literacy skills. A study in England, for example, found that Jolly Phonics had a stronger effect on ELLs' phonological awareness, alphabet knowledge, and their application to reading and writing than did a Big Books approach.

Other studies also showed similar effects of directly teaching the sounds that make up words, how letters represent those sounds, and how letters combine to form words. In fact, studies published since the NLP and CREDE reports completed their reviews continue to show the positive impact of structured, explicit instruction on beginning reading skills. Vaughn et al. (2006) have shown the benefits of small-group, explicit instruction for at-risk first-grade readers. The intervention was conducted in either English or Spanish, depending on children's instructional language. In both languages, the intervention consisted of explicit phonological and phonics (decoding) instruction, fluency, oral language, vocabulary, and comprehension. Compared to children who received their school's existing intervention, children in the Vaughn et al. program scored higher on multiple measures of reading and academic achievement. In a study conducted solely in English, Roberts and Neal (2004) also showed that ELLs were more likely to learn what they were explicitly taught: Preschool children in a "comprehension-oriented" group learned more vocabulary and print concepts than children in a "letter/rhyme-focused" group. In contrast, children in the letter/rhyme-focused group learned more letter names and how to write letters.

Studies of vocabulary instruction for ELLs also show that students are more likely to learn words when they are directly taught. Just as with English speakers, ELLs learn more words when the words are embedded in meaningful contexts and students are provided ample opportunities for their repetition and use, in contrast to looking up dictionary definitions or presenting words in single sentences. In a preschool study, Collins (2005) showed that explaining new vocabulary helped Portuguese-speaking children acquire vocabulary from storybook reading. Although children with higher initial English scores learned more words, explaining new words was helpful for all children, regardless of how little English they knew. Similarly, a study reviewed by the NLP involving fifth-graders showed that explicit vocabulary instruction, using words from texts appropriate for and likely to interest the students, combined with exposure to and use of the words in numerous contexts (reading and hearing stories, discussions, posting target words, and writing words and definitions for homework) led to improvements in word learning and reading comprehension (Carlo et al., 2004). These principles of effective vocabulary instruction have been found to be effective for English speakers (e.g., Beck, McKeown, & Kucan, 2002).

Other types of instruction that the NLP review found to be promising with ELLs include *cooperative learning* (students working interdependently on group instructional tasks and learning goals), encouraging reading in English, discussions to promote comprehension (*instructional conversations*), and mastery learning. A *mastery learning study* reviewed by the NLP was particularly informative, because the researchers found this approach (which involves precise behavioral objectives permitting students to reach a "mastery" criterion before moving to new learning) more effective in promoting Mexican American students' reading comprehension than an approach that involved teaching to the students' supposed "cultural learning style."

The CREDE report concludes that "the best recommendation to emerge from our review favors instruction that combines interactive and direct approaches" (Genesee, 1999, p. 140). *Interactive* refers to instruction with give-and-take between learners and the teacher, where the teacher is actively promoting students' progress by encouraging higher levels of thinking, speaking, and reading at their instructional levels. Examples of interactive teaching include structured discussions (*instructional conversations*), brainstorming, and editing/discussing student or teacher writing. *Direct approaches* emphasize explicit and direct teaching of skills or knowledge, for example, letter–sound associations, spelling patterns, vocabulary words, and mathematical algorithms. Typically, direct instruction uses techniques such as modeling, instructional input, corrective feedback, and guided practice to help students acquire knowledge and skills as efficiently as possible. The CREDE report notes that "direct instruction of specific skills" is important to help students gain "mastery of literacy-related skills that are often embedded in complex literacy or academic tasks" (Genesee, 1999, p. 140).

In contrast to interactive and direct teaching, the report found at best mixed evidence supporting what it termed *process approaches,* in which students are exposed to rich literacy experiences and literacy materials but receive little direct teaching or structuring of learning. In one study, for example, students were exposed to alternative reading and writing strategies on wall charts, but this was insufficient to ensure the strategies would be employed. In another study, Spanish-speaking ELLs who received structured writing lessons outperformed students who received extended opportunities to do "free writing." The CREDE report concludes that process strategies are "not sufficient to promote acquisition of the specific skills that comprise reading and writing. . . . [F]ocused and explicit instruction in particular skills and subskills is called for if ELLs are to become efficient and effective readers and writers" (Genesee, 1999, pp. 139–140).

English Learners Require Instructional Modifications

The NLP review showed that in the earliest stages of learning to read, when the focus is on sounds, letters, and how they combine to form words that can be read, English learners can make comparable progress to that of English speakers, provided that the instruction is clear, focused, and systematic. In other words, when the language requirements are relatively low, as they are for learning *phonological skills* (the sounds of the language and how words are made up of smaller constituent sounds), letter–sound combinations, decoding, and word recognition, it is possible for ELLs to make the sort of progress we expect of English speakers, although they still probably require some additional support due to language limitations. But as content gets more challenging and language demands increase, more and more complex vocabulary and syntax are required, and the need for modifications to make the content more accessible and comprehensible increases accordingly.

ELLs' language limitations begin to slow their progress as vocabulary and content knowledge become more relevant for continued reading (and general academic) success, around third grade. Learners who know the language can concentrate on the academic skills they are to learn. But learners who do not know the language, or do not know it well enough, must devote part of their attention to learning the skills, and part of their attention to learning and understanding the language in which those skills are taught. This is why it is critical that teachers work to develop ELLs' English oral language skills, particularly vocabulary, and their content knowledge from the time they start school, even before they have learned the reading "basics." Vocabulary development is, of course, important for all students; but it is particularly critical for ELLs. There can be little doubt that explicit attention to vocabulary development—everyday words, as well as more specialized academic words—needs to be part of English learners' school programs. What constitutes effective vocabulary instruction for ELLs, and how does it differ from effective instruction for English speakers?

As I have already discussed, there are probably many similarities. Collins (2005), cited earlier, found that preschool English learners acquired more vocabulary when the teacher explained words contained in a storybook read to them. ELLs benefit from clear explanations, just as English speakers do. But Collins also found that children who began with lower English scores learned less than children with higher English scores; that is, knowing less English made it harder to learn additional English. What might have helped the children with lower initial English proficiency gain more English vocabulary? Another preschool study (Roberts & Neal, 2004) revealed that pictures helped children with low levels of oral English learn story vocabulary (e.g., *dentist, mouse, cap*). The *visual representation* of concepts, not just a language-based *explanation*, provided children with additional support in learning the vocabulary words. There is scant research on this topic, but we would also expect that songs, rhymes, chants, and additional opportunities to use and repeat words would help build vocabulary among young English learners.

It is a good bet that effective strategies for English speakers will involve some sort of modifications or adjustments to make them as effective as they are with English learners. Roberts and Neal (2004) provide an example related to the critical issue of assessment, which I mentioned earlier in the chapter. Roberts and Neal attempted to teach preschool ELLs rhyming skills, an important aspect of phonological awareness. The way they assessed rhyming skills was by prompting the children with a word and asking them to provide a word that rhymed. If the tester said *lake,* the child would be expected to produce, for example, *cake.* As it turned out, regardless of instructional group, *all* the children did very poorly on the assessment. The average score on the rhyming test was less than 1, meaning that a lot of children simply did not respond. Why? Probably because the task demand was simply beyond the children; they were unable to *produce* a rhyming word, since their vocabularies were so limited. The children were, in essence, given a test that measured their productive vocabularies as much as it measured their rhyming skills. The study would probably have obtained different results if the researchers had presented pairs of words and asked the children to distinguish between rhyming and nonrhyming pairs, or else had children select the rhyming word from several possible choices.

This example suggests two things: First, it is essential that ELLs be assessed in a way that uncouples language proficiency from content knowledge; language limitations can obscure an accurate picture of what children actually know and can do. Second, and directly following from this, an important instructional modification for ELLs might be to tailor task demands to children's English language proficiency. Teachers should not expect children to produce language beyond their level of English proficiency; conversely, they should provide language-learning and language-use tasks that challenge children and stretch their language development.

What about older children? Some clues for vocabulary instruction are offered in a study also cited earlier, by Carlo et al. (2004), who examined the effects of a vocabulary instruction program on Spanish-speaking ELL and English-speaking fifth graders. Their approach was based on principles of vocabulary instruction found to be valid for children who already speak English (e.g., explicit teaching of words, using words from texts likely to interest students, multiple exposures to and uses of the words in numerous contexts). The researchers included additional elements: activities such as charades that got learners actively involved in manipulating and analyzing word meanings; writing and spelling the words numerous times; strategic uses of Spanish (e.g., previewing lessons using Spanish texts, providing teachers with translation equivalents of the target words, using English–Spanish cognates, such as *supermarket* and *supermercado*); and selection of texts and topics on immigration that were expected to resonate with the Mexican and Dominican immigrant students. Overall, the experimental program produced relatively strong effects in terms of students learning of the target vocabulary. It produced much smaller, but still significant, effects on reading comprehension. Particularly noteworthy is that the effects of the program were equivalent for ELLs and English-speaking students. Thus, although the researchers acknowledged that they could not determine which of the extra ELL supports explained the program's impact on these students, their demonstration that, with additional support, a program can have a similar impact on both ELLs and English speakers is very important.

Below is a possible list of supports or modifications for ELLs receiving English-only instruction. Some of these are only now starting to be investigated empirically; others have data from studies that fail to control for important variables, therefore limiting our conclusions; still others have no supporting data.

Modifications Using Students' Primary Language

The first group of modifications involves use of the primary language. Readers should note the contrast between the use of the native language in bilingual instruction and in an English immersion context. In bilingual education, students are taught language arts, and sometimes math and other subjects, such as social studies, in their primary language. In contrast, when the primary language is used as an instructional modification in an English immersion context, instruction is basically in English, but the primary language is used to make the instruction more meaningful or comprehensible. This does not involve teaching children academic skills in their primary language or attempting to promote primary language development per se. Instead, the primary language is used as an bridge, or "scaffold," to learning the content in English. There are several possible examples of using the primary language as a support for ELLs:

- Use of the primary language for clarification and explanation. This can be done by the teacher, classroom aide, a peer, or a volunteer in the classroom. While this approach makes intuitive sense, I know of no research that actually gauges its effectiveness. It is easy to see how explaining or clarifying concepts in the home language can help provide ELLs with access to what is going on in the classroom. But it is also not difficult to imagine downsides; for example, if anyone but the teacher provides the explanations (e.g., a peer), he or she might not be accurate; or students can become dependent on a "translator," who provides a crutch for them and as a result do not exert themselves to learn English; or if translations or periodic explanations in the primary language are offered throughout lessons, students can "tune out" during the English part.

- Introducing new concepts in the primary language prior to the lesson in English, then reviewing the new content again in the primary language (sometimes called *preview–review*; see Ovando, Collier, & Combs, 2003). This is different from clarification and explanation, since what this does is "front-load" the new learning in the student's primary language, then review it after the lesson. There is no ongoing explanation or translation. When the real lesson is delivered in English, the student already is somewhat familiar with the content, but he or she has to concentrate to get the message as it is delivered in English. Because of the previewing, the language used in the lesson should be more comprehensible and, in principle at least, the student will walk away knowing more content *and* more language (vocabulary, key phrases). Then, by reviewing lesson content afterward, the teacher checks to see whether students accomplished the lesson objective. The NLP reviewed a study that provided some support for the effectiveness of this approach. Prior to reading a book in English, teachers previewed difficult vocabulary in the primary language (Spanish), then reviewed the material in Spanish. This produced better comprehension and recall than the control conditions: reading the book in English and doing a simultaneous Spanish translation while reading.

• Other primary language support. One can imagine numerous variations on the "primary language support" theme. A study not included in the NLP provides a creative example. Fung, Wilkinson, and Moore (2003) found that introducing reciprocal teaching strategies in students' primary language improved reading comprehension in the second language. *Reciprocal teaching* is a technique for promoting reading comprehension. Students are taught four strategies—asking questions about the text, summarizing what they have read, clarifying the text's meaning, and predicting what will come next. This set of strategies has been found to promote reading comprehension among students who are adequate decoders but poor comprehenders. Fung et al. taught middle school ELLs reciprocal teaching strategies in their primary language and in English. They then found that students used more reading comprehension and monitoring strategies, *and* their reading comprehension improved when they read in English. Although the authors suggest that teaching reading strategies in students' home language can be an effective form of primary language support, the study did not compare home-language-assisted reciprocal teaching with English-only reciprocal teaching; thus, we do not really know the role that primary language support itself played in improving student comprehension.

• Another type of primary language support consists of focusing on the similarities–difference between English and students' native language (e.g., if using the Roman alphabet, letters represent the same sounds in English and other languages, but others do not). In addition, languages have *cognates*, that is words with shared meanings from common etymological roots (e.g., *geography* and *geografía*). Calling students' attention to these cognates could help extend their vocabularies and improve their comprehension. However, we do not know the effect of cognate instruction per se. The Carlo et al. (2004) vocabulary program described earlier used cognates as one strategy to help ELLs develop their vocabularies and improve comprehension; but, as previously discussed, the intervention comprised many elements, and it is impossible to know the effect of any single element. Nonetheless, there are a number of useful sources of Spanish–English cognates that teachers of ELLs can consult (e.g., Calderón et al., 2003). Nash (1999) offers an exhaustive, book-length list, but also see Prado (1996) for false cognates that can cause problems, such as (my personal favorite) *embarrassed* and *embarazada*. The latter means "pregnant." When put in the masculine form *embarazado*, it can really light up a classroom of Spanish-speaking adolescents.

Modifications Using Only English

In addition to modifications that make use of students' primary language, a number have been suggested that use only English. All of the following appear to be "generic" scaffolds and supports; that is, there is little obviously tailored to ELLs. They might, in fact, be effective strategies for many students, particularly those who need more learning support than is typically provided in teaching–learning situations where verbal exchanges of information predominate. These modifications include the following:

• Predictable and consistent classroom management routines, aided by diagrams, lists, and easy-to-read schedules on the board or on charts, to which the teacher refers frequently.

• Graphic organizers that make content and the relationships among concepts and different lesson elements visually explicit.

• Additional opportunities for practice during the school day, after school, or for homework.

• Redundant key information (e.g., visual cues, pictures, and physical gestures) about lesson content and classroom procedures.

• Identifying, highlighting, and clarifying difficult words and passages within texts to facilitate comprehension and, more generally, greatly emphasizing vocabulary development.

• Helping students consolidate text knowledge by having the teacher, other students, and ELLs themselves summarize and paraphrase.

• Giving students extra practice in reading words, sentences, and stories to build automaticity and fluency.

• Providing opportunities for extended interactions with teacher and peers.

• Adjusting instruction (teacher vocabulary, rate of speech, sentence complexity, and expectations for student language production) according to students' oral English proficiency.

• Targeting both content and English language objectives in every lesson.

• Use of reading materials that take into account students' personal experiences, including relevant aspects of their cultural background, which aids their reading comprehension (although proficiency in the language of the text has a stronger influence on comprehension than familiarity with passage content).

The modifications that students need will probably change as they develop increased English proficiency. Students who are beginning English speakers will need a great deal of support, sometimes known as *instructional scaffolding*. For example, at the very beginning levels, teachers have to speak slowly and somewhat deliberately, with clear vocabulary and diction; use pictures or other objects to illustrate the content being taught; and ask students to respond either nonverbally (e.g., by pointing or signaling) or in one- or two-word utterances. As they gain in proficiency, students need less modification; for example, teachers can use more complex vocabulary and sentence structures, and expect students to respond with longer utterances; visual information can be presented in written form, as well as in pictures. On the other hand, more modification may be needed when completely new or particularly difficult topics are taught. It might also be that some students in some contexts require more modifications than others. We utterly lack the data necessary to offer such guidelines. In any case, proficiency in Academic English (as distinct from conversational English, which can be acquired to a reasonably high level in approximately 2–3 years) can require 6 or more years (Genesee et al., 2006), so some degree of support is probably required for a substantial portion of ELLs' schooling.

Why does proficiency in Academic English take 4–5 or more years than proficiency in conversational English? There are several possible reasons. Conversational English is probably used more and is fairly limited in the vocabulary and forms of expression it requires. It is also almost always contextualized by gestures, intonation, and references to familiar and concrete situations. In contrast, Academic English is generally not used outside of school and tends to present new vocabulary, more complex sentence structures, and rhetorical forms not typically encountered in nonacademic setting. "Academic" forms of the language are also used to refer to abstract and complex concepts in subject-matter disciplines (science, literature, mathematics, social studies, the arts), particularly as students progress through the grades. Knowing conversational English obviously helps in learning Academic English, but the latter is clearly a more challenging task.

English Language Development and Other Considerations

It should be apparent that providing English language development (ELD) instruction to ELLs is critically important. Unfortunately, and surprisingly, the CREDE report reveals that research can tell us very little about how or even whether we can accelerate progress in oral English language development. Studies have shown that specific aspects of language can be taught at least in terms of short-term learning effects (e.g., vocabulary, listening comprehension, grammatical elements; see meta-analysis on second-language teaching in Norris & Ortega, 2000), but we do not really know how to accelerate the overall process of language learning.

A study that appeared after the CREDE report was published, however, suggests that a comprehensive and structured approach to teaching English directly and explicitly can help accelerate young children's English language development. Tong, Lara-Alecio, Irby, Mathes, and Kwok (2008) found that providing kindergarten and first-grade students with an "English-oracy intervention" resulted in accelerated ELD growth (as measured by tests of vocabulary and listening comprehension). The intervention was equally effective with students in English immersion and bilingual education. Some of the elements it comprised included: daily tutorials with a published ELD program; story telling and retelling with authentic, culturally relevant literature and questions leveled from easy to difficult; and an academic oral language activity using a "question of the day." Students with lowest levels of English proficiency received 10–20 minutes of instruction in addition to the 75–90 minutes/day of the base intervention program. Because the experimental group received more ELD instructional time than the control group, it is impossible to rule out the effects of additional time. In addition, the measures of oral language used were very limited and did not gauge many important dimensions of language proficiency, Nonetheless, the study is important in demonstrating the possibility of accelerating English language development, at least in the early grades and on some aspects of language, through intensive, organized instruction.

Based on descriptive studies of ELLs in the United States, the CREDE report concluded that it takes at least 6 years for most students to go from being a nonspeaker to having native-like proficiency (e.g., from kindergarten to grade 5 or later). Even students in all-English instruction do not begin to show advanced intermediate levels—which are still short of native-like proficiency—for at least 4 years (i.e., grade 3 or later). The idea that children will quickly become fluent in English if immersed in all-English instruction is contradicted by the research literature. Certainly, exceptions can be found, but fluency within a year of English immersion in school is not the norm among the ELL population in the United States. Can the process be meaningfully sped up so that ELLs can benefit from mainstream English instruction earlier in their educational careers? We don't really know. The near absence of such research, combined with the obvious need to develop English proficiency as students acquire knowledge and skills across the curriculum, places a huge burden on both students and teachers.

One question that frequently arises is whether ELD should be taught separately or integrated with the rest of the curriculum. A recent study suggests that English language achievement is somewhat enhanced by a separate ELD period. Saunders, Foorman, and Carlson (2006) found that when a separate ELD block was used, teachers spent more time on oral English, and were more efficient and focused in their use of time. The ELD block, by design, targeted ELD, and students who received a separate ELD block scored somewhat higher than students who did not. When there was no ELD block, less time was spent focusing on English per se and more on other language arts activities, such as reading. It is important to bear in mind that this study was limited to kindergarten, and the effect was small. But if the findings are accurate, the cumulative effect of a separate block of ELD instruction over many years could be substantial. At the moment, however, this is speculation.

Some educators have also suggested that instruction for ELLs must also be tailored to students' culture. This suggestion is based on the observation that because different cultural groups speak, behave, and interact differently, educators should use instructional approaches that are "culturally compatible" (that build upon or complement students' behavioral and interactional patterns). Many readers will be surprised to learn that the NLP concluded that there is little evidence to support the proposition that culturally compatible instruction enhances the actual achievement of English learners (although materials that take into account students' background knowledge and personal experiences can aid in reading comprehension and development of literacy skills; see "Modifications Using Only English"). In fact, as mentioned earlier, a study reviewed by the NLP found that a mastery learning–direct instruction approach produced better effects on Mexican American students' reading comprehension than did an approach tailored to their "cultural characteristics." Some studies, most of which are methodologically very weak, have indicated that culturally accommodated instruction can promote engagement and higher-level participation during lessons. This is a meaningful finding, but it is not the same as establishing a connection between culturally accommodated instruction and measured achievement. The hypothesis is certainly plausible, and future research might establish such a connection. But for now it appears that developing lessons with solid content and clearly structured instruction is a better use of teachers' time.

Another proposition with dubious research backing is that grouping ELLs and English speakers during instruction will, in itself, promote ELLs' oral English proficiency. (Simply grouping or pairing students together should not be confused with well-implemented "cooperative learning," for which we have evidence of positive effects on ELLs' learning, discussed earlier.) Teachers sometimes assume that pairing ELLs and English speakers will provide ELLs with productive language learning opportunities, but the CREDE synthesis casts doubt on this. One study described the case of an ELL whose teacher relied almost exclusively on classmates to support the student's classroom participation. Because the assignments were far beyond this child's language and academic skills, her peers "were at a loss as to how to assist her" (Genesee, 2006, p. 28). Another study, an examination of cooperative learning in one 6th-grade classroom, found that English speaking students and ELLs rarely engaged in interactions that we might expect to promote learning. More typically, English speakers cut the interactions short in order to finish the assignment, as did this student: "Just write that down. Who cares? Let's finish up." (p. 28). If teachers use coooperative or peer learning activities, they must ensure that English speakers be grouped with ELLs who are not so lacking in English skills that meaningful communication and task engagement become problematic. In addition, tasks that students engage in must be carefully designed to be instructionally meaningful and provide suitable opportunities for students to participate at their functional levels. Simply pairing or grouping students together and encouraging them to interact or help each other is not sufficient.

Implications for Improving Instruction

Practically, what do these findings and conclusions mean? The following is the sort of instructional framework to which our current state of knowledge points:

- If feasible, children should be taught reading, and possibly other basic skills, in their primary language. Primary language instruction (1) develops first-language skills, thereby promoting bilingualism and biliteracy, (2) promotes learning (particularly learning to read) in English, and (3) can be carried out as children also learn to read (and learn other academic skills) in English. We lack definitive studies on whether there are optimal lengths of time for ELLs to receive primary language instruction; however, the answer to this question will partly depend upon our goals for the education of ELLs.

- As needed, students should be helped to transfer what they know in their first language to learning tasks presented in English; teachers should not assume that transfer is automatic.

• Teaching in the first and second languages can be approached similarly; in fact, what we know about effective instruction in general should be the foundation for how we approach instruction of ELLs; direct and explicit instruction is probably especially helpful. However, ...

• Adjustments or modifications will be necessary, probably for several years and at least for some students, until students reach sufficient familiarity with Academic English to permit them to be successful in mainstream instruction; more complex learning might require more modifications.

• ELLs need intensive ELD instruction (especially targeting Academic English), but we have little data on how, or even whether, the process of English language acquisition can be accelerated.

• ELLs also need academic content instruction, just as all students do; although ELD is crucial, it should not completely supplant instruction designed to promote academic content knowledge.[6]

Local or state policies, such as those in California, which block use of the primary language and limit instructional modifications for English learners, are simply not based on the best scientific evidence. Moreover, these policies make educators' jobs more difficult, which is unconscionable under any circumstance but especially egregious in light of increased accountability pressures they and their students face. Despite many remaining questions, we have useful starting points for renewed efforts to improve the achievement of this fastest growing segment of the school-age population. If educators and their students are to be held accountable, practice and policy must be based on the best evidence we have. Otherwise, claims of "scientifically based practice" are simply hollow slogans.

ENGAGEMENT ACTIVITIES

1. In your own words, identify and explain what you think are the key findings from the CREDE and National Literacy Panel reports.

2. Explain how ELLs' primary language can help them develop literacy skills (and possibly other academic skills) in English. Discuss primary language *instruction* and primary language *support* separately.

3. Describe how instruction that has been adjusted to the needs of ELLs differs from "generic" effective instruction.

4. Describe (in about a paragraph) a lesson for English speakers that uses ele-

ments of effective instruction identified in this chapter. Discuss the adjustments you would incorporate into the lesson if you were to teach it to class with ELLs (assume approximately intermediate English proficiency).

ACKNOWLEDGMENTS

This chapter is adapted with permission from Goldenberg, C. (2008). Improving achievement for English language learners. In S. Neuman (Ed.), *Educating the other America: Top experts tackle poverty, literacy, and achievement in our schools* (pp. 139–162). Baltimore: Paul H. Brookes Publishing Co., Inc.; and Goldenberg, C. (2008). Teaching English language learners: What the research does—and does not—say. *American Educator, 32*(2), 8–23, 42–44.

NOTES

1. Most of the preceding list is derived from content standards for second grade adopted by the California State Board of Education available at *www.cde. ca.gov*. The reading fluency figure is from Behavioral Research and Teaching (2005); vocabulary from Lehr, Osborn, and Hiebert (n.d.).

2. Experimental studies are considered the "gold standard" if one wants to determine the effect of a particular program or type of instruction. Experiments include treatment and comparison groups, as well as other controls designed to ensure that any impacts found can be attributed to the treatment (e.g., as opposed to differences between two groups of students). Correlational studies can establish that there is a relationship between two things (e.g., an instructional method and student achievement), but they cannot indicate that one thing caused another. Qualitative studies generally attempt to describe and analyze rather than measure and count. Precise and highly detailed qualitative studies can establish causation (e.g., a part of a lesson that led to student learning), but because the number of subjects in a qualitative study is typically low, they are not good for establishing generalizability.

3. Readers should be aware of the dramatic discrepancy between the research base for English speakers and English learners. For example, the National Reading Panel (2000) synthesized findings from over 400 experimental studies of instruction in phonological awareness, phonics, vocabulary, reading fluency, and reading comprehension. In contrast, the NLP could identify only 17 experimental studies of instructional procedures, even though the NLP considered more topics and used looser inclusion criteria.

4. A *meta-analysis* is a statistical technique that allows researchers to combine data from many studies and calculate the average effect of an instructional procedure. It is useful because studies often reach conflicting conclusions. Some find positive effects of a program; others find negative effects of the same type of program, and still others find no effects. Even among studies that report positive findings, the effects can be small or large. The questions a meta-

analysis addresses are these: Taking into account all the relevant studies on a topic *overall,* is the effect positive, negative, or zero? And if overall it is positive or negative, what is the magnitude of the effect—large, and therefore meaningful; small, and therefore of little consequence; or something in between? Are there additional factors (e.g., student characteristics) that influence whether effects are large or small?

5. Robert Slavin was a member of the NLP and worked on the meta-analysis of instructional language. He resigned to publish his review before the Panel's work was completed.

6. Starting in fall 2007, ELLs in Arizona spend 4 hours per day learning exclusively English (Kossan, 2007; Small, 2010). This virtually guarantees they will not receive instruction to promote academic content knowledge, which is no less necessary than English proficiency for school success.

REFERENCES

August, D., & Shanahan, T. (Eds.). (2006). *Developing literacy in second-language learners: Report of the National Literacy Panel on language-minority children and youth.* Mahwah, NJ: Erlbaum.

Beck, I., McKeown, M., & Kucan, L. (2002). *Bringing words to life: Robust vocabulary instruction.* New York: Guilford Press.

Behavioral Research and Teaching. (2005, January). Oral reading fluency: 90 years of assessment (BRT Technical Report No. 33). Eugene, OR: Author. Available online at *www.jhasbrouck.com.*

Bialystock, E. (2001). *Bilingualism in development: Language, literacy, and cognition.* New York: Cambridge University Press.

Calderón, M., August, D., Durán, D., Madden, N., Slavin, R., & Gil, M. (2003). *Spanish to English transitional reading: Teacher's manual.* Baltimore: Success for All Foundation. Adapted version available online at *www.ColorinColorado.org.*

Carlo, M. S., August, D., McLaughlin, B., Snow, C. E., Dressler, C., Lippman, D., et al. (2004). Closing the gap: Addressing the vocabulary needs of English language learners in bilingual and mainstream classrooms. *Reading Research Quarterly, 39,* 188–215.

Collins, M. (2005). ESL preschoolers' English vocabulary acquisition from storybook reading. *Reading Research Quarterly, 40,* 406–408.

Crawford, J. (1999). *Bilingual education: History, politics, theory, and practice* (4th ed.). Los Angeles: Bilingual Education Services.

Fung, I., Wilkinson, I., & Moore, D. (2003). L1–assisted reciprocal teaching to improve ESL students' comprehension of English expository text. *Learning and Instruction, 13,* 1–31.

Gándara, P., & Rumberger, R. (2006). *Resource needs for California's English learners.* Santa Barbara, CA: UC Linguistic Minority Research Institute. Available online at *www.lmri.ucsb.edu/publications/jointpubs.php.*

Genesee, F. (Ed). (1999). *Program alternatives for linguistically diverse students*

(Educational Practice Report 1). Santa Cruz, CA: Center for Research on Education, Diversity and Excellence.

Genesee, F., Lindholm-Leary, K., Saunders, W., & Christian, D. (2006). *Educating English language learners*. New York: Cambridge University Press.

Greene, J. (1997). A meta-analysis of the Rossell and Baker review of bilingual education research. *Bilingual Research Journal, 21,* 103–122.

Jiménez, R. (1997). The strategic reading abilities and potential of five low-literacy Latina/o readers in middle school. *Reading Research Quarterly, 32,* 224–243.

King, M. (2007, May 22). English-only tests, judge rules. Available at *www.santacruzsentinel.com/archive/2007/May/22/local/stories/04local.htm*.

Kossan, P. (2007, July 14). New learners must spend 4 hours a day on English. Available at *www.azcentral.com/arizonarepublic/news/articles/0714english0714.html*.

Lehr, F., Osborn, J., & Hiebert, E. (n.d.). *A focus on vocabulary*. Honolulu: Pacific Resources for Education and Learning.

Nash, R. (1999). *Dictionary of Spanish cognates thematically organized*. Sylmar, CA: NTC.

National Reading Panel. (2000). *Report of the National Reading Panel–Teaching children to read: An evidence-based assessment of the scientific research literature on reading and its implications for reading instruction* (Report of the subgroups). Washington, DC: National Institute of Child Health and Human Development. Available at *www.nichd.nih.gov/research/supported/nrp.cfm*.

Natriello, G., McDill, E., & Pallas, A. (1990). *Schooling disadvantaged students: Racing against catastrophe*. New York: Teachers College Press.

Norris, J., & Ortega, L. (2000). Effectiveness of L2 instruction: A research synthesis and quantitative meta-analysis. *Language and Learning, 50,* 417–528.

Ovando, C., Collier, V., & Combs, M.C. (2003). *Bilingual and ESL classrooms: Teaching in multicultural contexts* (3rd ed.). Boston: McGraw-Hill.

Prado, M. (1996). *Dictionary of Spanish false cognates*. Sylmar, CA: NTC.

Roberts, T., & Neal, H. (2004). Relationships among preschool English language learners' oral proficiency in English, instructional experience and literacy development. *Contemporary Educational Psychology, 29,* 283–311.

Rolstad, K., Mahoney, K., & Glass, G. (2005). The big picture: A meta-analysis of program effectiveness research on English language learners. *Educational Policy, 19,* 572–594.

Saiz, A., & Zoido, E. (2005). Listening to what the world says: Bilingualism and earnings in the United States. *Review of Economics and Statistics, 87,* 523–538.

Saunders, W., Foorman, B., & Carlson, C. (2006). Do we need a separate block of time for oral English language development in programs for English learners? *Elementary School Journal, 107,* 181–198.

Scarcella, R. (2003). *Academic English: A conceptual framework* (Technical Report 2003–1). Santa Barbara, CA: Linguistic Minority Research Institute. Available at *lmri.ucsb.edu*.

Slavin, R., & Cheung, A. (2005). A synthesis of research on language of reading instruction for English language learners. *Review of Educational Research, 75*, 247–281.

Small, J. (2010, February 1). Unanimous vote moves ELL opt-out bill through committee. AzCapitolTimes.com. Retrieved February 17, 2010, from *azcapitoltimes.com/blog/2010/02/01/unanimous-vote-moves-ell-opt-out-bill-through-committee/*

Tong, F., Lara-Alecio, R, Irby, B., Mathes, P., & Kwok, O. (2008). Accelerating early academic oral English development in transitional bilingual and structured English immersion programs. *American Educational Research Journal, 45*, 1011–1044.

U.S. Department of Education. (2005). *Biennial evaluation report to Congress on the implementation of the State Formula Grant Program, 2002–2004: English Language Acquisition, Language Enhancement and Academic Achievement Act (ESEA, Title III, Part A)*. Washington, DC: Author.

Vaughn, S., Mathes, P., Linan-Thompson, S., Cirino, P., Carlson, C., Pollard-Durdola, S., et al. (2006). Effectiveness of an English intervention for first-grade English language learners at risk for reading problems. *Elementary School Journal, 107,* 154–180.

Willig, A. (1985). A meta-analysis of selected studies on the effectiveness of bilingual education. *Review of Educational Research, 55*, 269–317.

Zehr, M. (2007a, May 8). *NCLB seen a damper on bilingual programs*. Retrieved April 30, 2007, from *www.edweek.org.*

Zehr, M. (2007b, May 23). Another take on Coachella Valley Unified School District v. California. *Learning the language.* Blog available at *blogs.edweek.org/edweek/learning-the-language.*

Zehler, A. M., Fleischman, H. L., Hopstock, P. J., Stephenson, T. G., Pendzick, M. L., & Sapru, S. (2003). *Descriptive study of services to LEP students and LEP students with disabilities: Vol. I. Research report.* Arlington, VA: Development Associates.

CHAPTER 2

Language Development and the Education of Dual-Language-Learning Children in the United States

Eugene E. García and Erminda H. García

This chapter will:

1. Provide a brief overview of the demography of English language learners (ELLs) in U.S. schools.
2. Describe the educational circumstances of our youngest ELLs.
3. Provide a review of programs and best practices demonstrated as effective in enhancing overall development and early academic achievement.

Some 2–3 million children, ages 0–8, in the United States are learning English as a second language (Garcia & Jensen, 2007). How we define these children and the labels we ascribe can be confusing. Several terms are used in the literature to describe U.S. schoolchildren whose native language is one other than English including the term *language minority* (García, 2005). In this chapter, we utilize a variant of this term, *dual-language learner* (DLL), as a way of emphasizing students' learning and progress in two languages at early ages of language development. A recent analysis of young children identified as speaking a language other than English in the United States indicates that most children under the age of 8 (85%) who live in predominantly non-English environments are also exposed in a substantial manner to English (Hernán-

44

dez, Denton, & Macartney, 2008). The term identifies, emphasizes, and strategically recognizes that integrating children's knowledge, skills, and abilities related to two languages is central to the educational practices needed in schools and classrooms to improve educational opportunities for youngest language-minority children.

The Demographic Reality

The common phrase "demography is destiny" is applicable to the present educational circumstances of young DLLs (García & Jensen, 2007). Currently, at least 1 in 5 children ages 5–17 in the United States has a foreign-born parent (Capps et al., 2005), and many, though not all, of these children learn English as their second language. It is important to note that DLL students and children from immigrant families (i.e., children with at least one foreign-born parent) are not the same populations, but certainly they are closely related. Most children from immigrant households are considered English language learners (ELLs) at some point in their lives. Yet, according to the Census 2000 data, a majority (74%) of school-age children (5–17 years) from immigrant families speak English exclusively or very well.

The overall child population speaking a non-English native language in the United States rose from 6% in 1979 to 14% in 1999 (National Clearinghouse for English Language Acquisition, 2006), and the number of language-minority students in K–12 schools has recently been estimated to be over 14 million. The representation of DLLs in U.S. schools has its highest concentration in early education, because DLL children from preschool or kindergarten tend to develop oral and Academic English proficiency by third grade. The number of DLL students from prekindergarten to grade 5 rose from 4.7 to 7.4% from 1980 to 2000, while the numbers of DLL students in grades 6–12 rose from 3.1 to 5.5% during the same time period (Capps et al., 2005). Young ELLs (ages 0–8 years), therefore, have been the fastest growing student population in the country over the past few decades, due primarily to increased rates in (legal and illegal) immigration, as well as high birthrates among immigrant families (Hernández et al., 2008).

Although the majority comes from Spanish-speaking immigrant families, DLLs represent many national origins and more than 350 languages. In 2000, over half of DLLs came from Latin American immigrant families (Capps et al., 2005). Mexico led the way, with nearly 40% of children from immigrant families (Hernández et al., 2008), and nationwide Spanish was the native language of some 77% of ELLs during the 2000–2001 school year (Hopstock & Stephenson, 2003). Following Mexico, DLL students' origins cover the globe. The Caribbean, East Asia, and Europe (combined with Canada and Australia) each account for 10–11% of the overall population of children from immigrant families, while Central America, South America, Indochina, and West Asia each account for 5–7% of the total; the former Soviet Union and Africa account for 2–3% each. At least 3 in 4 children in immigrant families are born in the United States, though U.S. nativity is higher among elementary school-age children of immigrant families than among those attending secondary schools (Capps et al., 2005).

Because immigrant families are settling in new destinations in response to labor demands (Zúñiga & Rubén, 2005), DLL students are increasingly attending school in districts and states that previously served few or no DLL children in the 1980s and previous decades. While immigrant families continue to be concentrated in California, Texas, New York, Florida, Illinois, and New Jersey (Capps et al., 2005), several states have witnessed rapid increases in their immigrant populations. Indeed, seven states experienced over 100% increases in the number of children from immigrant families attending PreK–grade 5 from 1990 to 2000, including Nevada, North Carolina, Georgia, Nebraska, Arkansas, Arizona, and South Dakota (from greatest to least percentage increases; Capps et al., 2005). Nevada, Nebraska, and South Dakota saw increases of 354, 350, and 264% respectively, in their young DLL populations.

Educational Circumstances

The academic performance patterns of DLL students as a whole cannot be adequately understood without considering their social and economic characteristics in comparison with native English speakers, in addition to the institutional history of U.S. schools (Jensen, 2008a). While a great deal of socioeconomic variation exists among DLLs, they are more likely than native English-speaking children, on average, to live in poverty and to have parents with limited formal education (García & Cuellar, 2006). In addition, DLL students are more likely to belong to an ethnic/racial minority (Capps et al., 2005). Each of these factors—low income, low parent education, and ethnic/racial minority status—decreases group achievement averages across academic areas, leading to the relatively low performance of DLL students.

In their analyses of a national dataset of academic performance in early elementary school, Reardon and Galindo (2006) found that reading and mathematics achievement patterns from kindergarten through third grade varied by home language environments among Hispanic students. Those living in homes categorized as "primarily Spanish" or

"Spanish only" lagged further behind White children than did Hispanics who lived in homes in which primarily English or English only was spoken. Given the associations among educational risk factors for DLL students, the impact of language background on achievement outcomes should be contextualized. The interrelationship of risk variables has been documented in several reports (Collier, 1987; Jensen, 2007). In a separate analysis of the same national dataset, Jensen compared Spanish-speaking kindergartners to their general education peers on a number of outcomes, including socioeconomic status (SES), parent education, and mathematics achievement. He found that Spanish-speaking kindergartners, on average, scored four-fifths of a standard deviation lower than the general body of kindergartners in mathematics. They also scored an entire standard deviation below their peers in terms of SES and maternal educational attainment. Nearly half of the kindergartners from Spanish-speaking homes had mothers who had not completed high school.

Thus, rather than pointing to one or two student background factors that account for the low achievement of DLL students, it should be understood that educational risk in general is attributable to myriad interrelated, out-of-school factors, including parent education levels, family income, parent English language proficiency, mother's marital status at the time of the child's birth, and single- versus dual-parent homes (National Center for Educational Statistics, 1995). The more risk factors to which the child is subject, the lower the probability that the child will do well in school in terms of learning and attainment in the standard educational environment. Because DLL children on average exhibit three of the five risk factors at higher rates than do native English speakers, they are generally at greater risk for academic underachievement (Hernández et al., 2008). Using Census 2000 data, Capps and colleagues (2005) found that 68% of DLL students in PreK through grade 5 lived in low-income families, compared to 36% of English-proficient children. The percentages changed to 60 and 32%, respectively, for sixth- to 12th-grade students. Moreover, 48% of DLL children in PreK–grade 5 and 35% of ELLs in the higher grades had a parent with less than a high school education, compared to 11 and 9% of English-proficient children in the same grades (Capps et al., 2005).

Language, Schooling, and Best Practices

Best-Fit Program Features for DLLs

There are many possible program options for young bilingual students and children learning English as a second language. These carry various titles, including transitional bilingual education, maintenance bilingual education, 90–10 bilingual education, 50–50 bilingual education, developmental bilingual education, dual-language, two-way immersion, English as a second language, English immersion, sheltered English, structured English, submersion, and so forth. These programs differ in the way they use the native language and English during instruction (Ovando, Collier, & Combs, 2006). They also differ in terms of theoretical rationale, language goals, cultural goals, academic goals, student characteristics, ages served, entry grades, length of student participation, participation of mainstream teachers, teacher qualifications, and instructional materials (García, 2005; Genesee, 1999). The extent to which a program is successful depends on local conditions, choices, and innovations.

Because sociodemographic conditions differ, and local and state policies demand assorted objectives from their schools and teachers, no single program works best in every situation. When selecting a program, one of the most fundamental decisions should be whether bilingual proficiency is an objective. Clearly, given the cognitive and economic advantages of bilingual proficiency in a world that is becoming increasingly globalized, promoting bilingualism is an intuitive ambition (García & Jensen, 2006). However, the development of balanced bilingualism depends on state and local policies, as well as the availability of teachers and course curricula to meet the need. Indeed, the feasibility of bilingual promotion varies among schools.

A critical feature that should be considered when selecting a program designed for DLLs is optimizing individual achievement and literacy development. Academic performance continues to be the driving force behind educational policy reform and practice in the United States, and programs developed for young DLLs should strive to reduce achievement gaps. It is additionally important, however, that programs support the development of the whole child, simultaneously sustaining the child's cognitive, social, emotional, and psychological development. Therefore, a holistic approach is especially important during the early years (i.e., PreK–3) of schooling (Zigler, Gilliam, & Jones, 2006).

Heritage, Language, and Culture

Decades of research support the notion that children can competently acquire two or more languages. The acquisition of these languages can but need not be parallel; that is, the qualitative character of one language may lag behind, surge ahead, or develop equally with the other language. Moreover, the relationship of linguistic properties between languages is quite complex. Several theories have been put forward to explain how language and literacy develop for young children managing two or more linguistic systems. Currently, among the available theoretical approaches, *transfer theory* is most widely accepted to explain the language development of DLLs. This theoretical position asserts that language skills from the first language transfer to the second. In like manner, errors or interference in second-language production occur when grammatical differences between the two languages are present. However, not all aspects of second-language development are affected by the first language. Language that is contextually embedded and cognitively undemanding—or automatic, overlearned interaction—does not lend itself well to transfer. This is the language involved in day-to-day interpersonal communication. Research shows that contextually reduced and cognitively demanding linguistic skills, on the other hand, transfer between languages (Genesee, 1999; August & Shanahan, 2007). Higher-order cognitive skills relevant to academic content are more developmentally interdependent and, therefore, amenable to transfer.

Bringing together the disciplines of psychology, semiotics, education, sociology, and anthropology, sociocultural theory has become an important way of understanding issues of language, cognition, culture, human development, and teaching and learning (García, 2005). This approach posits that a child's linguistic, cognitive, and social characteristics are fundamentally connected and interrelated. A child's basic cognitive framework is shaped by his or her native language, early linguistic experiences, and cultural context. Children from non-English-speaking homes often must adjust their cognitive and linguistic representations to negotiate social exchanges within the school environment. Though research in this area is limited, extant best practices (Goldenberg, Rueda, & August, 2006) suggest that bridging home–school sociocultural differences can enhance students' engagement and level of participation in classroom instruction. As home linguistic interactions (which vary by SES indicators, e.g., parent education) and teacher practices, perspectives, and expectations influence the development of literacy skills, children whose teachers recognize and take full advantage of home resources (including home language and cultural practices) and parental supports tend to experience more optimal outcomes.

Given the demographic circumstances of young DLL children in the United States, the development of school programs and practices that recognize the conditions and strengths of DLL children and families is crucial. Because three out of four young Hispanic children are exposed to Spanish in the home, and even more are exposed to Spanish through relatives and/or neighbors, ways in which these programs integrate language in teaching and learning are important. Currently, young Hispanic children, on average, lag substantially behind their

Asian American and White peers in terms of academic achievement; differences are quite large at the beginning of kindergarten, and the gap closes very little thereafter. Within the Hispanic population, first- and second-generation children and those of Mexican and Central American origins demonstrate the lowest achievement levels, influenced by multiple out-of-school factors, including SES, low parent education, limited English proficiency of parents, and other home circumstances (García & Miller, 2008).

It is important to evaluate children's culture and related educational practices in the home, because they bear on children's early cognitive development and, therefore, influence school readiness and sustained academic performance (García & Cuellar, 2006). The amount of language (regardless of the particular linguistic system) used in the home has been found to be strongly associated with early literacy and cognitive development. More specifically, research indicates that the amount of "extra" talk between caretakers and their children, book reading, and parent–child interactions (i.e., reading, telling stories, singing) influence early development. This is an important consideration, because low-income families are less likely, on average, to engage in these activities; DLLs' parents are less likely than non-DLLs' parents to read, tell stories, and sing to their children (García & Miller, 2008).

Schooling program options for young DLLs differ in terms of their goals, requirements for staff competency, and the student populations they are meant to serve. The effectiveness of a given program depends on local conditions, choices, and innovations. In terms of student achievement outcomes, meta-analyses and best evidence syntheses suggest that programs supporting bilingual approaches to curricula and instruction are favorable to English-only or English immersion programs. These programs provide sound instruction in both Spanish and English (García, 2005).

Driven by sociocultural notions of language and learning, dual-language (or two-way immersion) programs—a particular approach to bilingual education—integrate language-minority and language-majority students in the same classroom. Educators in DLL programs use English plus Spanish (EPS) approaches to teach both languages through course content. Studies suggest that students (from multiple-language backgrounds) in DLL programs perform at equal levels as their peers and, in many cases, outperform those in other programs (García & Jensen, 2006). Preliminary evidence suggests that prekindergarten programs (for 3- and 4-year-old students) can increase early learning for young DLL children (García & Miller, 2008). High-quality PreK programs can improve school readiness for young Hispanic children and decrease achievement differences between racial/ethnic groups at kindergarten entry (García & Miller, 2008).

Rich Language Environments

Because DLLs are highly likely to be raised in multilingual homes, ways in which language is used at home and in preschool and early elementary settings will continue to be important. Moreover, the compatibility or cultural congruence of home and school language environments is relevant, as preliminary research reveals associations among literacy outcomes for Hispanic DLLs and the extent to which teachers' discourse and interaction patterns resemble those found in the home (Goldenberg et al., 2006). In terms of frequency, research on cognitive development, language, and early experiences shows that the amount of talk and conversational exchange between adults and young children is strongly associated with school readiness and academic success in formal schooling (García, 2005).

High-Quality Teachers

The provision of rich language environments and high-quality dual-language programs across the PreK–3 spectrum requires high-quality teachers. This means teachers are bilingual/multilingual to the extent that they can communicate with children and families, and knowledgeable regarding the cultural and linguistic circumstances of these children and families (García, 2005). Indeed, research shows that the transfer of academic skills between languages is heightened, and early achievement outcomes are increased for young bilingual and emergent bilingual students when teachers use Spanish in the classroom (Jensen, 2007). The most successful teachers are fluent in both languages, understand learning patterns associated with second-language acquisition, have a mastery of appropriate instructional strategies (i.e., cooperative learning, sheltered instruction, differentiated instruction, and strategic teaching), and have strong organizational and communication skills. With these skills, teachers are able to interact with parents appropriately, to encourage them to engage in literacy activities with their children at home, to find out as much detail as possible about the linguistic backgrounds of their students, and to develop creative and accurate assessments of children's linguistic ability and development.

Best Practices

Instructors of young DLLs need the very best information regarding the development of the children they serve. Teachers need to gain specific information about how much English their ELLs use, when they use English, and with whom they use English. Teachers can create notes and rubrics around what they want their students to be able to know and do by the end of the year. García (2005) had teachers use such a note-taking and rubric analysis to determine baseline use of English by students at the beginning of the year and to assess growth throughout the year. Teachers began to realize that in all classroom contexts there were constant opportunities for listening to language (any time they were exploring, playing house, painting, looking through books). These teachers also created Talk to the Teacher (5 minute) conversations, so that each student could demonstrate language proficiencies over time and in the same context.

A central feature of the largest and fastest growing ethnic/minority population in the United States—young Hispanic children ages 0–8—is their complex/academic language development (García & Miller, 2008). A diverse population in terms of their national origins, geographical location, and home circumstances, a majority of Hispanic children grow up in homes in which Spanish is spoken regularly, and the most are exposed to Spanish through relatives and/or neighbors. Recent figures suggest that approximately three out of four young Hispanic children in the United States are influenced at some level by Spanish in the home (García & Miller, 2008). The extent to which children speak Spanish in the home and maintain bilingual proficiency over time varies by national origin, generation status, and between states and regions. Moreover, Spanish maintenance is influenced by a combination of personal, familial, educational, and societal factors. Importantly, the amount of parental educational attainment is associated with the quality of native Spanish proficiency, with more formal parental education associated with the maintenance, proficiency, and literacy in Spanish.

Sociocultural educational contexts need to be planned and created for our youngest students. With regard to the initial stages of reading, for example, exposure to the "skill" of reading means sitting together and looking (and not yelling out) at pictures, and having teachers demonstrate "what they do when they read." This is much more than just "skills" building. Instead, this approach augments the "skills" activities with issues related to the sociocultural importance of reading—who reads, why they read, when they read, and so forth. It becomes a social activity, with a focus on children thinking out loud about why they looked at pictures first (picture walks) and why they chose the words that did or did not work, and predicting that something would happen, because that was what happened when the teacher was in the same situation. During all this time, teachers need to accept multilingual interactions that are appropriate for advancing communication between teacher and child, and child and child. This means always planning for the kind of language one needs to operate effectively in various sociocultural contexts and drawing on the linguistic assets of the child to do so.

Vocabulary Development— the Key to Academic Comprehension

Snow, Burns, and Griffin (1998) concluded that academic language is learned in *only* two ways: from teachers and from academic text. If this is true, what, where, how, and when can teachers engage young learners in academic language?

Vocabulary learning, front-loading academic language, reading, and writing with young children support academic language learning. It is important to begin by identifying the academic words that learners will hear and see during the "teaching event" (reading a book, observing, and writing down the observation with help of the teacher). We have a good idea of what vocabulary is associated with academic achievement in the early grades (Miller & García, 2008). We also know that DLL children come to the academic enterprise with significant gaps in that vocabulary (García & Miller, 2008). Addressing this vocabulary gap requires some utilization of best practices. For example, in the García (2005) study, after a field trip to observe an ant farm, students shared what they saw with the teacher and the teacher included the academic talk in connected text: "The ant, or we can call it the insect, was transporting food on its back." This enriches the opportunity to construct academic phrases that the culture of school requires. On another occasion, during a math exploration, students were encouraged by the teacher to name the shapes and also describe corners and lines, and maybe "parallel" lines. This is an example of further elaboration on vocabulary that enriches students' opportunities to gain academic "talk."

Included in this practice should be vocabulary pictures and words. Examples are large posters that use the four-square format in which the teacher either draws or finds pictures of the word to place on the first square, writes the word in the second square, and writes a student-friendly meaning in the third square. Sometime during the same day, as the word is used, the teacher writes down the word and notes what the student said.

Always include as the "the golden rule" the opportunity to assess what learning students bring to the classroom, before you begin any teaching. A KWL (what we know, what we want to find out, and what we have learned) should precede any lesson with lots of pictures, so that other students who might "know" but not have the language to share will be able to access the new words using the pictures. Often teachers just ask about what the students might know about insects, yet if they write the word down and include pictures, other students may begin to label their own knowledge.

Teachers need to be cognizant of what words they choose to emphasize. Tier 1 words are day-to-day words we use; Tier 2 words are about the content being taught, but they also might be used in a number of contexts (parallel in math, in science, in art); Tier 3 words are unique to a particular story or content area. Teachers of young learners need to be careful what words they choose as academic language. For example, in *Little Red Riding Hood, woods, grandmother,* and *cabin* are Tier 2 words, while *woodcutter* is a Tier 3 word. Tier two words are more likely to generate comprehension around multiple teaching contexts. Moreover, in many content areas, English language acquisition can be bolstered through the use of cognates.

Another promising practice for vocabulary development in content areas is the development of ABC charts around the "content" that students are learning. For example, pictorial ABC charts are sent home with a request that parents "talk" to their child about six to eight insects, help the child draw the insects, and label the insects with the correct letters. This involves the parents in academic talk, writing, and more importantly, it validates parents as teaching partners. The charts should be large and colorful, but more importantly, be created with students to be reviewed and revisited many times during the learning context.

Think about an ABC chart that focuses on writing, about what a parent might include in an ABC word chart on writing: pencils, letters, erasers, computers, stamps, spelling, and so forth. And as the teacher teaches about organization, it is added to the chart. Thus, the ABC chart becomes a learning chart throughout the year and also the academic language keeper around writing. These are all examples of academic language development that is important to building high vocabulary portfolios that enhance comprehension of the academic material that students are asked to read and digest.

Reading Practices

With young learners, reading needs to be modeled. Recall that many DLLs come from homes in which reading my not be the norm. As teachers begin reading events, they review with the students the words they will hear (do not forget the pictures) and ask questions about the subject of the story or text. One practice that supports students in thinking about what they might hearing is to cover the book with paper and have students guess what the picture or book will be about. For example, if the book is about sharks, then the teacher could first tear off a piece of the paper from the book cover to show the ocean, then tear off a piece to show a shark's fin. Within a few minutes, the students begin to share what they know about oceans and sharks.

During reading "lessons," teachers need to ask children about how to predict what they might hear next. This can effectively be done with "think–pair–share" in a cooperative structure. The key here is that teachers ask higher-order questions, such as "What do you think she will see next and why do think that?" Students then think–pair–share their ideas. This allows students who might not be able to understand the story/text to listen while peers share their ideas and perhaps recall why they are predicting that answer. It also creates a context where students share in their first language with each other. This kind of practice helps DLLs develop the complex academic discourse that is a staple in schools. Teachers need to listen in and never ask individuals to call out answers, because, as the teacher turns the page, the answer is built into the pictures or the text he or she reads.

After reading any text, teachers need to engage students in creating a graphic organizer about the text. The graphic organizer needs to reflect the writing genre. A storyboard that shows character and setting is part of the board. As children retell the story, the teacher once again writes and draws pictures to retell the story using the graphic organizer. (Example: Metamorphosis would be part of a cycle graphic organizer with lots of room for academic words and pictures.) These best practices are particularly important to enhance DLL children's access to academic language.

Writing

There is so much more about to writing than "skills" development. Children need to have opportunity in planned time to explore letters, words and pictures, with a focus on the social nature of the writing process (García, 2005). Teachers can use a large whiteboard on which a topic is placed every morning to give students opportunities to share their thoughts about the topic in writing. The important component of this exercise is that they share these thoughts.

Names activities (use of children's first and last names) are so important because they are about the children. Examples include identifying *V* for Vicente. The child takes this letter home and the parents find words with *V* and circle them from logos found on things they have bought, or on food cans or cereals. They then cut out the logo and glue it on the large letter and bring it to class. These letters become the first ABC chart about children's names that serves as a basis for other writing and reading during the year.

Writing Journals

Because students are already "writing" in their heads, create pictures of what they are "talking" about, as well as what they have just seen, for example, the balloons in the movie *Up*. Writing journals creates a permanent record for both the student and the teacher of how each child is learning how to write. In the early grades, these journals need to include a place for pictures. We often forget that students create pictures of what they will write, and how much doing so supports them when they do write. We also need to consider that children might create and draw a picture about an event that happened in their first language. After drawing it, they can begin to think about second-language words they might need.

Conclusion

For our youngest language-minority children, the ages 3–8 years, are critically important for building a solid foundation for educational success. These DLL children offer us not only unique challenges but also the greatest opportunities to intervene with families as partners in ways that will enhance their present educational circumstances (García & Miller, 2008). We have attempted to review these educational circumstances, to provide some clear direction with regard to programs and program attributes that "work" for these children, and to identify what we believe are promising best practices.

ENGAGEMENTS ACTIVITIES

1. *Reflection on "rich" language development in academic contexts:* Identify and describe at least three different instructional strategies meant to enhance vocabulary development directly that are likely to assist students in addressing educational language demands. Consider the role of the teacher, the student, and materials that can be made available.

2. *Parents/families as partners:* Parents/families of DLLs can be critical partners in the education of their children. What specific recommendations and related activities would you give to both teachers and parents to enhance the educational partnership for young DLLs?

3. *Vocabulary enrichment:* English and Spanish (and many other languages) have common roots in numerous content areas, such as mathematics (*matematicas* in Spanish) and science (*ciencias* in Spanish), known as *cognates*. Beginning with Spanish, how many content-specific vocabulary items can you gener-

ate that have roots similar to the English term? Feel free to use Web-based resources to assist with this exercise.

REFERENCES

August, D., & Shanahan, T. (Eds.). (2006). *Developing literacy in second-language learners: Report of the National Literacy Panel on language minority youth and children.* Mahwah, NJ: Erlbaum.

Capps, R., Fix, M. E., Murray, J., Ost, J., Passel, J. S., & Hernández, S. H. (2005). *The new demography of America's schools: Immigration and the No Child Left Behind Act.* Retrieved from *www.urban.org/url.cfm?ID=311230.*

Collier, V. P. (1987). Age and rate of acquisition of second language for academic purposes. *TESOL Quarterly, 21,* 617–641.

García, E. (2005). *Teaching and learning in two languages: Bilingualism and schooling in the United States.* New York: Teachers College Press.

García, E. E., & Cuellar, D. (2006). Who are these linguistically and culturally diverse students? *Teachers College Record, 108,* 2220–2246.

García, E. E., & Jensen, B. T. (2006). Dual-language programs in the U.S.: An alternative to monocultural, monolingual education. *Language Magazine, 5*(6), 30–37.

García, E. E., & Jensen, B. (2007). Helping young Hispanic learners. *Educational Leadership, 64*(6), 34–39.

García, E. E., & Miller, L. S. (2008). Findings and recommendations of the National Task Force on Early Childhood Education for Hispanics. *Child Development Perspectives, 2*(2), 53–58.

Genesee, F. (Ed.). (1999). *Program alternatives for linguistically diverse students.* Berkeley Center for Research on Education, Diversity and Excellence, University of California.

Goldenberg, C., Rueda, R., & August, D. (2006). Synthesis: Sociocultural contexts and literacy development. In D. August & T. Shanahan (Eds.), *Report of the National Literacy Panel on language minority youth and children.* Mahwah, NJ: Erlbaum.

Hernández, D. J., Denton, N. A., & Macartney, S. E. (2008). Children in immigrant families: Looking to America's future. *Social Policy Report: A publication of the Society for Research in Child Development, 22*(3), 1–24.

Hopstock, P. J., & Stephenson, T. G. (2003). *Native languages of LEP students: Descriptive study of services to LEP students and LEP students with disabilities* (Special Topic Report No. 1). Arlington, VA: Development Associates, Inc., U.S. Department of Education, Office of English Language Acquisition.

Jensen, B. T. (2007). The relationship between Spanish use in the classroom and the mathematics achievement of Spanish-speaking kindergartners. *Journal of Latinos and Education, 6*(3), 267–280.

Jensen, B. T. (2008a). Immigration and language policy. In J. González (Ed.), *Encyclopedia of bilingual education* (pp. 372–377). Thousand Oaks, CA: Sage.

Jensen, B. T. (2008b). Meta-linguistic awareness. In J. González (Ed.), *Encyclopedia of bilingual education* (pp. 551–554). Thousand Oaks, CA: Sage.

Miller, L. S., & García, E. (2008). *A reading-focused early childhood education research and strategy development agenda for African Americans and Hispanics at all social class levels who are English language speakers or English language learners.* Tempe, AZ: Office of Vice President for Education Partnerships.

National Center for Education Statistics. (1995). *Approaching kindergarten: A look at preschoolers in the United States* (National household survey). Washington, DC: U.S. Department of Education, Office of Educational Research and Improvement.

National Clearinghouse for English Language Acquisition. (2006). *The growing numbers of limited English proficient students: 1993/94–2003/04.* Washington, DC: Office of English Language Acquisition (OELA), U.S. Department of Education.

Ovando, C., Collier, V., & Combs, M. (2003). *Bilingual and ESL classrooms: Teaching in multicultural contexts* (3rd ed.). New York: McGraw-Hill.

Reardon, S. F., & Galindo, C. (2006). *Patterns of Hispanic students' math and English literacy test scores* (Report to the National Task Force on Early Childhood Education for Hispanics). Tempe: Arizona State University.

Snow, C., Burns, M. S., & Griffin, P. (Eds.). (1998). *Preventing reading difficulties in young children.* Washington, DC: National Academies Press.

Zigler, E., Gilliam, W. S., & Jones, S. M. (2006). *A vision for universal preschool education.* New York: Cambridge University Press.

Zúñiga, V., & Rubén, H. (Eds.). (2005). *New destinations: Mexican immigration in the United States.* New York: Russell Sage Foundation.

PART II

STRATEGIES FOR TEACHING YOUNG ELLs

CHAPTER 3

Principles for Teaching Young ELLs in the Mainstream Classroom
Adapting Best Practices for All Learners

Ellen McIntyre

This chapter will:

1. Identify six principles derived from sociocultural theory and research for teaching English language learners (ELLs).
2. Illustrate these principles through transcripts and observations of a variety of teachers who work to implement these principles.
3. Explain the challenges teachers face in attempting to adapt their instruction to be more inclusive and responsive to ELLs.

Sometimes students, including English language learners (ELLs), are the best persons to articulate just what it is their teachers do that helps them learn best. As part of a research study that extended from a professional development project on sheltered instruction, we asked a group of ELLs the question "How does your teacher help you learn?" Some of the responses included:

> "[The teacher] sat down [with us] and explained many times. If we don't know [understand], she tell us in a new way."
> "We work together and help each other."
> "We do things [projects, activities] about our own country."

The students in the class were mostly Spanish speakers and their teacher was native Cuban, an advantage for those students. But the class spoke of a new student from Russia and how the teacher helped her in particular:

> "We have this girl, she from Russia, and [the teacher] she have to explain her with her hands. . . . She asked girl to draw a picture for her and [the teacher] explain with her hands."
> "[The teacher] get a dictionary in Russia for her."
> "Some of us [the other students], we can sit with her and explain like that too. We try to do the same thing [the teacher] do."

When prompted, the students mentioned their opportunities for group work as a tool for learning, and one student said their teacher often gave more time to them than to the native English speakers to complete work. These students said their teacher used many visual aids, such as pictures from magazines, books, posters, and the Internet. One student said the teacher often drew pictures for them. The students also said their teacher reads directions to them and then follows by asking them to read the directions themselves. One student explained that the teacher brings in many pictures about what they are studying and has students use tape recorders to practice speaking and reading.

The students also spoke about how meaningful the classroom activities were because they connected to their background experiences. For instance, they all chimed in to discuss their individual research projects on their home countries "using the computer" (likely the Internet), a play in which they acted, poster presentations they made of their country, and a fair in which they displayed what they knew about their countries. Finally, some responses indicated the deep caring the teacher has for her students. The teacher often asks them whether they need help, even if the students do not request it. One said, "She also helps us [the students] sound like Americans" by teaching local language and pronunciation.

The students in this classroom were experiencing instruction from a teacher who had participated in professional development on sociocultural approaches to teaching. The facilitators of the project focused on the standards for teaching developed by the Center for Research on Education, Diversity and Excellence (CREDE), formerly known as the Center for Research on Second Language Learning, which is grounded in the famous sociocultural work of Roland Tharp and Ron Gallimore (1988). The facilitators also taught the teachers about the Sheltered Instruction Observation Protocol (SIOP®) model (Echevarria, Vogt,

& Short, 2004) which is also grounded in CREDE principles. Finally, the facilitators used the vast body of research and practitioner literature on instruction for ELLs (August & Shanahan, 2006) and culturally responsive instruction (Dalton, 2007; Foster & Peele, 2001; Gay, 2000; Irvine, 2006; Ladson-Billings, 1994; McIntyre, Kyle, Chen, Kraemer, & Parr, 2008; McIntyre, Rosebery, & González, 2001; Nieto, 1999; Tharp, Estrada, Dalton, & Yamauchi, 2000) to help the teachers make explicit connections from their curriculum to students' cultural and linguistic backgrounds.

Sociocultural Approaches to Teaching

Sociocultural theory and practice is marked by the discovery of the work in the 1930s by Russian psychologist Lev Vygotsky (1978, 1987), who emphasized the importance of both history and culture in how and what is learned. Many researchers from the fields of anthropology, linguistics, psychology, and sociology have built on Vygotskian theory to illustrate how learners affect their surroundings as much as their surroundings affect them, and that a learner's academic success or failure is grounded in the child's history, culture, and environment, including schooling and instructional interactions within the school (Rogoff, 2003; Wells, 1999; Wertsch, 1991). Sociocultural theory posits a few assertions that are especially relevant for the teaching of ELLs, and each of these is discussed: (1) Outdated assumptions that cast learners, their families, and their backgrounds as deficient are mistaken; (2) all learning is mediated by tools, of which language is the primary tool; and (3) a learner's development occurs through assisted performance.

Deficit Perspective Interrupted

When educators attempt to explain the failure of individuals or groups of students, historically they have suggested that some students are less capable than others, or that particular languages or dialects are barriers to learning (McIntyre, 2010). Some have suggested that children of immigrants lack the appropriate experiences (e.g., visiting museums) that are necessary to learn, or that the families of learners were themselves deficient parents and perhaps could not assist their children in learning. This deficit view has historically been present with immigrant children in U.S. schools as they struggled to learn a new language while learning new content in less than ideal conditions. While less prevalent today, many ELLs were assumed to be slow or to have learning disabilities when perhaps only language was a barrier. In other cases, students lacked extensive schooling and might not have been prepared for the content. In these cases, the unfortunate students were seen as deficient rather than as students with the ability to learn content through a foreign language.

Today, sociocultural theory and research dispute these deficit perspectives by describing and critiquing the misevaluation of learners (Heath, 1991, 1994; Michaels, 1981; Moll, 1994) and arguing for alternative ways of viewing what counts as knowing (Stone, 2004; Rogoff, 2003; Moll, 1994). Studies have shown that classroom practices can often constrain—and that educators often underestimate—what children are able to display intelligently (Heath, 1991; Moll, 1994). Moll suggests that the rejection of deficit views, particularly the view that the poor, minorities, and children with language differences are devoid of proper experiences necessary for learning is perhaps the most important construct that has governed a sociocultural view of learning.

Mediation and Tools

As learning began to be viewed as a social process, the study of social interactions and what mediates these interactions became prominent. Vygotsky had been interested in the use of signs and tools in mediating learning, including, and especially, the role of speech. He showed that a child who learns something uses signs and tools to accomplish tasks, such as reading a passage. Wertsch (1991, 1998) explained that a learner's cultural tools are mediators of action, and one cannot truly understand the learner or development without attention to the tools. Wertsch (1991) used the example of the pole for the pole vaulter to illustrate this relationship. For instance, there is a dynamic tension between a learner and an appropriate tool, in that certain tools necessarily affect the learner; the tool might "do some of the thinking" (1998, p. 29) involved in the activity. Vygotsky would have referred to mnemonics or a teacher's interactions as psychological tools or signs, and to a pole or a book as a technical tool. To learn a new language, students use a variety of tools, both material and linguistic, and the teachers involved in the project presented in this chapter mediated the students' learning through these tools.

Assisted Performance

Learning occurs when one's performance is assisted by someone more proficient in that particular skill, much as when a worker (baker, craftsperson, etc.) apprentices alongside someone with much more experience in that work (Lave & Wenger, 1991; Rogoff, 2003; Tharp & Gallimore, 1988). Assisted performance occurs naturally in all cultures as children grow and learn in their early years; novices learn from experts as they work together on meaningful, purposeful tasks. Tharp and Gallimore lamented that learning as assisted performance is easily identified in homes and communities, but less so in classrooms. Yet more researchers are illustrating how teachers can implement a "hybrid" (Gutiérrez, Baquedano-Lopez, & Alvarez, 2001; Manyak, 2001) form of teaching that makes teaching and learning reflect what occurs naturally in homes. The teachers in this project were taught to assist the performance of their ELLs as these students worked alongside native language–speaking students and their teachers.

Instructional Assessment

The three assertions of sociocultural theory explained earlier raise important questions for teachers as they plan instruction for ELLs. For example, teachers should learn as much as possible about their students in order to (1) value the students' background knowledge and skills to avoid a deficit view, (2) come to know the best tools for use with each learner, and (3) understand learners' developmental levels to assist performance. Perhaps the teacher might want to know about a student's cultural and historical background. There are numerous potential questions that teachers may ask in this regard:

- How does the child's race/ethnicity play a role in the child's life?
- What languages are spoken in the home and community?
- How do family members identify themselves semantically, culturally, socially, and through everyday routines?
- What is the family makeup, and what characteristics of the family are significant to the child?
- How much education does the child's family members or parents/guardians have?
- Who reads and writes in the family, and for what purpose?
- What do the parents do for a living?
- What do family members or parents/guardians do outside of work and school, and with whom do they do it?
- What sorts of material resources does the family have that affect academic development? What other interests do family members have?
- How does the child spend out-of-school time?

These sorts of questions assess the student's history and culture, including variables that have been shown to correlate with school success and failure (McIntyre, 2010).

The assertions from sociocultural theory described earlier and the examples provided by students that opened this chapter in part form the foundations for the instructional principles for teaching ELLs described here. These principles are defined below and later described more fully, with several examples.

Six Principles for Teaching ELLs: Sounds Easy; Is It?

The instructional principles described in this chapter were the focus of two professional development projects conducted by Ellen McIntyre and her colleagues. Drawn from the SIOP model (Echevarria et al., 2004), CREDE, and culturally responsive instruction (Foster & Peele, 2001; Gay, 2002; Moll & González, 2003; Irvine, 2006; Ladson-Billings, 1994; McIntyre et al., 2008; Moll, 1994; Nieto, 1999; Tharp et al., 2000), the six principles at the heart of the professional development work include:

- *Joint productive activity:* Providing an opportunity for group work in which there is a definite product, with participation and scaffolding by the teacher.
- *Language and literacy across the curriculum*: Providing opportunities to develop and use oral and written language in all content instruction, including mathematics, science, and art.
- *Curricular connections*: Building curriculum around students' backgrounds, cultures, interests, and linguistic strengths.
- *Rigorous curriculum and teaching*: Taking special care not to dumb down the curriculum for ELLs, but to keep the content at the grade level provided to other students through adapted texts, high-level questioning, multimodal texts, and more.
- *Instructional conversation*: Implementing carefully planned conversations around content, so that students have an opportunity to learn, develop, and practice the language of disciplines, while constructing new understandings about content.
- *Family involvement*: Findings ways to involve families in the education of their students, both in school and out.

Teachers who attempted to implement these principles in their mainstream classrooms that included ELLs for most of the day claimed that the principles reflect what they view as good practice for all students. However, in general, the students found some of these principles easier than others to implement fully. An example of a lesson that incorporates most of these principles follows.

A Lesson Connecting the Past to Present

The following lesson took place in an urban school district in a classroom with nearly all students of color and mostly ELLs. The teacher, Cori, a native English speaker, has excellent command of Spanish as well. Cori's lesson illustrates the classroom-based principles that all teachers, including kindergarten teachers, in the project worked to implement. Although Cori is a seventh-grade language arts and social studies teacher, this example is included because she drew on all principles simultaneously, unlike the examples collected from the elementary teachers. Not all standards need to be in evidence in all lessons, as you will see from the many examples from the elementary classrooms, but it helps to see how this might be possible in one lesson.

Cori's lesson (described more fully in McIntyre et al., 2008) occurred in her first-period social studies class of 25 students. Only six students are White, and 12 are ELLs, mostly Spanish speakers, but some are Bosnian, Russian, and German speakers. They have been studying ancient civilizations. On the chalkboard, Cori has listed the objectives for the lesson, which she reads aloud to the students. Then she asks them, "What area of the world did we talk about yesterday? You can check your notes."

"The Fertile Crescent."

"Why do we call it the Fertile Crescent?"

A girl answers in Spanish. Cori, who can speak Spanish (a convenient but not necessary skill for teaching Hispanic ELLs), responds briefly first in Spanish and then in English, slowly and deliberately, "Yes, it has a lot of rich soil—it is *fertile*. The land can grow a lot because of all of the water nearby." She asks, "What is another name we use?"

"Mesopotamia."

"Yes, what does this mean?"

"Land between the rivers."

Cori points to the map on the wall. "Would someone come up and show us on the map?" A student comes to the front and shows the area in the Middle East that they are studying.

"Who can remember the names of these rivers?"

Different students answer "Tigris" and "Euphrates."

Cori asks, deliberately, "What were the people called who lived there?"

"Sumerians."

The review from the previous day continues with a discussion of Sumerian agriculture. The students had read about frequent flooding of rivers and recalled that the Sumerians depended on irrigation systems to control the water around them. After about 15 minutes, Cori leads the students into today's topic. She says, "Maybe if you've been watching the news you will know what this is."

She invites the students to come up to the front of the room and surround her at a table, so that all can witness a demonstration. Cori has a large bowl, with one side of the bowl packed with dirt as if to demonstrate land. From a pitcher, Cori gently pours water into the bowl almost to the level of the "land." Using more dirt, she creates a "levee" on the land side of the bowl, and slowly pours more water. The students witness the water sitting slightly above the land. Cori explains that today's system of controlling water is both similar and different from what the Sumerians did. She asks, "What would happen if I poke a hole or two in the levee? What will happen if the levee breaks?"

"The water will go to the land," answers one English learner.

"There will be a flood," says another student.

"*Why* might a levee break?" Cori asks.

As the students begin to offer speculations about this question, Cori holds up one finger to indicate, "Don't speak, think." She has taught them this signal, and they have learned that some questions require more thinking time than others. After a few seconds, different students offer reasons why a levee might fail.

Cori then asks a student to cut the levee with a tool. He does. The water seeps onto the "land" portion of dirt in the bowl. The students watch, mesmerized.

"See the big mess we have here?" The students nod. Cori then turns on an overhead projector on which she has several photographs to show the students. First, she shows them pictures of broken levees after Hurricane Katrina. She asks students to turn to a partner and describe the similarities between the broken levee in the classroom bowl demonstration and what they see on the screen. The students begin to talk, their heads turning back and forth from bowl to photographs.

Then Cori puts up several textbook drawings of what land looked like in ancient Sumeria. She asks the students to turn to their partners and compare what they see in the photos of Sumeria with what they see in the photos of the New Orleans levees. Again, the students talk for a few minutes.

When the group convenes, one student explains in Spanish that he saw in a video about Katrina that there are two kinds of levees, those that are broken, and those that are about to break. Cori responds to him in Spanish, then said in English, "Can you say that again, this time in English?"

The student slowly explains in English what he had seen on the video. Cori asks the class, "What does that tell you about levees?" The discussion ensues.

Then Cori asks the students to go back to their desks for a longer discussion. In this part of the lesson, she asks the students to think about why cities might emerge so close to the land and why people would live next to a levee.

Cori asks the students to get out the textbooks from which they had been reading about Sumeria. She introduces a "cause–effect" activity that the students are to do in pairs. Each pair is given a "cause" of broken levees, and they are to look through their text and recall the newscasts about Katrina as sources for "effects." After the pairs work together, Cori asks the students to offer the responses they collected in pairs as she creates a summary diagram on the overhead projector. During the process of creating the diagram, a lively discussion occurs about the effects of hurricanes today in New Orleans and in the past in Sumeria. The students discuss the differences in civilization, buildings that would have been destroyed, and what gets killed. Cori asks, "What kinds of animals would survive?"

One child raises her hand, but even after a long "wait time" cannot respond. Cori says to her, "Would you like to ask someone in your group (with whom she is sitting) to respond?" The child says yes and asks her group in Spanish. Cori and the rest of the class wait. Then the child says, in English, "Birds."

"Yes, Juana, but why would birds survive?"

"Because they can fly away."

"What other animals can get away?"

Juana pauses, "I think . . . the ones in the zoo?"

Cori smiles. "Yes, I heard a story on the radio recently about how the animals in the New Orleans zoo survived because the zoo was on a hill."

When Cori revisits the topic about why cities emerge around water, the class gives excellent, historically based reasons why Sumeria emerged as a civilization, whereas other tribes may not have survived. The students have a harder time understanding why people live so near the water today. Unfortunately, this discussion has to be delayed until the next time. As the students leave her classroom, it is clear that they look forward to the next lesson [excerpted from McIntyre et al., 2008, pp. 15–18].

Adapting Instruction for ELLs in Mainstream Classrooms

Cori's lesson exemplifies the instructional principles defined earlier, as well as the sociocultural principles that undergird the instructional model. The instruction is not wildly unusual or remarkable. It is, however, extremely well planned, so that Cori maintains a rigorous curriculum that includes joint productive activity; multiple physical, linguistic, and pneumonic tools; oral language interaction time; and assisted performance with the literacy activity. Cori has taken special care to make small adaptations in her teaching that help to make the content more comprehensible. Her preparation for the lesson is elaborate and specific for ELLs, as well as for the other students in her class. As stated, Cori was trained in the SIOP model of instruction (Echevarria et al., 2004), which provides teachers ideas on how to prepare lessons when the classroom has ELLs. This SIOP feature, preparation, involves creating objectives for the lesson that include both the content of what it to be covered in the lesson and the language skills to be addressed by the lesson.

Cori also had her students participate in *joint productive activity* when they worked in pairs to make a list of causes and effects of some phenomenon. It is a simple product, yet in order for the students to be successful at this product, they need to see Cori's vivid demonstration and the many photographs and drawings. She made *connections to students' backgrounds* by beginning with an extensive review of the previous day's lesson and emphasizing key vocabulary, such as *fertile*. She linked past and new concepts by comparing ancient Sumeria to vivid, current photos of Katrina, a topic on the minds of all Americans at the time of this lesson. Cori also provided her students multiple opportunities for oral *language learning* in just one lesson. Simply, "Turn to a partner and compare . . . " offers an example of how a teacher can provide multiple opportunities for students to practice Academic English in a psychologically safe environment as they first rehearse their responses with peers. This simple strategy provides an efficient way to get many students to participate rather than simply to have one student offer a response to the whole class, which is highly inefficient (although necessary at times). Cori also had her students write in response to the readings they had done and the class lesson on the causes and effects of broken levees. Finally, Cori kept the curriculum *rigorous* by keeping the content of the lesson at a high level, using sophisticated vocabulary, and asking high-level questions. Her expectation that students make connections from ancient civilization to the current news about Hurricane Katrina illustrates her respect for them as learners and her expectation that they be engaged with current events.

In Cori's lesson, there was only the beginning of an *instructional conversation*, and there was no evidence of family involvement, although Cori was successful at implementing these principles as well in other lessons. Each of these principles is described further, with examples from other teachers. These sections are followed by recommendations for the gradual implementation of these principles.

Joint Productive Activity

The CREDE standard of *joint productive activity* (JPA) means that students work together in small groups to complete a task, with the involvement of the teacher at points along the way to assist the performance of the learners. JPA often shapes a lesson, because the product often drives the process in teaching. Teachers can use strategies, graphic organizers, and a variety of other tools to organize students for JPA. Also, to create opportunities for JPA successfully, teachers must also attend to grouping patterns. For example, ELLs should at times have opportunities to work with others who speak their language (when possible) and at other times work with native English speakers. ELLs should work in small groups, large groups, pairs, groups of their choice, and assigned groups. When students are provided the opportunity to work together, one or more students can *assist the performance* of others. The following JPA activity illustrates the *indicators* of this standard, as outlined on the CREDE website. It evolved from the professional development projects on the SIOP and CREDE instructional models.

Community Study

One fifth-grade teacher asked her students to work in pairs or groups of three to study the neighborhood of the school or the one in which they lived. The students were to take tape recorders and cameras into a designated section and (1) interview at least one businessperson in the community; (2) photograph the physical surroundings; (3) visit a public agency, such a library; and (4) create a map of the streets they studied. Then, they were to return to the classroom and use the Internet and other tools to create either an "improvable product" (Wells & Haneda, 2009), which in this case included either a short book of their neighborhood, a mural, a map, or a poster. The students worked in pairs and wrote a physical description and narrative about the neighborhood using the Internet and primary sources, such as the businessperson they had interviewed. The pairs of students included native English speakers with ELLs, when possible, and the teacher assisted each group with the final products.

Of course, this is only one example illustrating this principles or standard. JPA can take an infinite number of forms. From the CREDE perspective, though, key elements include the teacher planning the activity with the students. The teacher also gives input on the final product in ways that push students' thinking about the content of the lesson from which the product emanated; hence, the phrase coined by Wells and Haneda (2009), an *improvable product*, is apt.

Language and Literacy across the Curriculum

This principle established the need for teachers to create classroom opportunities for ELLs (indeed, all learners) to practice oral language, and reading and writing skills as often as possible, using the language of discipline (e.g., mathematics, biology); that is, it is not just enough to *talk*. Children get very good at that quickly. They must learn to talk, read, and write about the topics they are studying, using the language of the discipline as much as possible. In every subject area, oral language development and literacy learning serve as tools to help students learn the content. In Cori's lesson, she invited the children into a high-level discussion comparing ancient history to current events. Thus, rather than always just listening to her, they were participating and practicing, framing sentences about the topic under study. She also had the students work in pairs to complete the cause–effect activity that involved group composition. The example below is how one of the elementary school teachers routinely provided an opportunity for her students to do more talking, reading, and writing about content.

Talking Back

Fourth-grade teacher April has her students regularly "talk back" to books. The children work in small groups of three or four and read aloud a nonfiction book that corresponds to the social studies or science unit under study. After one child reads a section aloud, he or she talks back to the book, using one of the following prompts:

> "I find it interesting that you say . . . "
> "I do not understand what you mean when you say . . . "
> "I agree with you about . . . "
> "I disagree with you about . . . "
> "I want to know more about . . . "

Students are permitted to talk about the printed section for as long as they stay on the topic. Then, other children in the group are allowed to join in, adding, explaining, or questioning. April tries to assist each group, because many children seem to have little to say at first. At times, she assists a learner by reading a section aloud, but allowing the child to do the "talking back." Before she routinely implemented this strategy, April demonstrated it several times with texts she read aloud, showing all kinds of emotions a reader might have: curiosity, puzzlement, dismay, excitement.

As with all the principles, teachers should know multiple ways of organizing instruction to extend and build on students' oral and written skills. The CREDE principle emphasizes the importance of *academic* discourse, not simply the development of more social language. When students use academic language in either speech or writing, they have more opportunity to learn the content, as well as the language.

Curricular Connections to Students' Backgrounds

Connecting to students' backgrounds is often cited as the most important principle for culturally responsive teaching. It requires that teachers get to know their students and also allows students to share their lives through their classwork. Teachers also find ways to connect the already-planned lesson from the state curricular framework with students' past experiences at home, with peers, or from previous lessons. In Cori's lesson, she began with an extensive review of the previous day's lesson, emphasizing key vocabulary, such as *fertile*. She linked past and new concepts by comparing ancient Sumeria to vivid current photos of the aftermath of Hurricane Katrina, a topic on the minds of all Americans at the time. In the JPA "community study" example discussed earlier, the teacher built an activity from the students' own neighborhoods, incorporating language and literacy skills building throughout.

Building background is essential for all learners, but it takes the explicit linking of past to present for ELLs, because they are learning content and language simultaneously. Indeed, in some lessons that are contextualized relative to students' backgrounds, the lesson or activity also helps build skills such as writing. In other lessons, the goal is simply to learn new content. The example provided below illustrates one way a fifth-grade teacher linked a social studies lesson to students' lives and helped them develop literacy skills.

Then-and-Now Books

This teacher had her students create little books that compared their new country with their home country. On the left side of a page, they wrote something about "then"—what it was like in their home country.

On the right side of the page, they compared it to "now"—what it is currently like in the United States. The students compared their homes, friends, household family size, transportation, weather, and more. An example from one child's book is presented in Figure 3.1.

As a reader of this chapter, it is probably quite evident to you now that the principles for teaching ELLs outlined in this book are integrated. This activity certainly is one that can develop written language skills while connecting to backgrounds. A similar book-making activity can be done jointly, adhering to indicators of JPA. All such activities should be rigorous enough to push students' thinking, and one way to achieve this goal is through an instructional conversation. Many activities can include families in some ways. These latter principles are presented next.

Rigorous Curriculum and Instructional Conversation

The final CREDE principles are rigorous curriculum or complex thinking and instructional conversation. They are presented together, because instructional conversation is one of the primary tools for ensuring that instruction pushes students' thinking, that teachers reach students in their *zone of proximal development* (Vygotsky, 1978)—that place in a student's development where he or she can work on a task with the teacher but might not be able to do the task without assistance.

Another purpose for keeping the curriculum rigorous is that too many educators make the wrong assumption when they learn that students have limited English skills. There is evidence that many ELL students are put in remedial classrooms or taught content far below their level. Also, I have observed teachers using only simple vocabulary when talking with ELLs, when they could be using both simple and advanced vocabulary in an effort to extend the vocabulary of all students. Students need to be exposed to the content and vocabulary at their grade level and supported with adaptations in the pedagogy.

The *instructional conversation* (IC) is a structured form of dialogue that begins with teachers setting a goal about the content they want students to learn through the dialogic lesson (Goldenberg, 1993; Tharp & Gallimore, 1988). Not all academic talk is an IC. Classroom talk can be merely "dialogue" or "discussion" if it is not rigorous and does not advance the thinking of students (McIntyre, Kyle, & Moore, 2006). Researchers (Saunders & Goldenberg, 1996) who have studied the effects of IC on ELLs in classrooms define ICs as follows:

> Teacher and students engage in discussion about something that matters to the participants, has a coherent and discernible focus, involves a high

FIGURE 3.1. Example of a then-and-now book.

level of participation, allows teacher and student to explore ideas and thoughts in depth, and ultimately helps students arrive at higher levels of understanding about topics under discussion (e.g., content, themes, and personal experiences related to a story). (p. 142)

In the IC below, second-grade teacher Genna is leading a guided reading lesson on a children's book that portrays a bully. In the lesson, Genna teaches a reading strategy that asks the students to anticipate the story line and words they might come across as they read. After the reading lesson and the guided silent reading of the text, Genna leads an IC on the book. In an IC, the teacher has a definite goal for the content she wants the students to learn. An IC is not goal-less discussion about whatever the students feel about the book. It is intentional and guided, and pushes students' thinking. Yet even ICs do not always go as planned, as illustrated below. Teachers must be prepared to take advantage of teachable moments.

Genna's goal was for the children to understand that if they witness bullying, it is critical that they inform a teacher, because conflict can escalate and someone could get hurt. The students seemed to grasp that concept immediately; in the book, the bully was physically abusive, and a child was physically hurt. But the conversation turned to identification of bullying if no one gets "hurt." In the longer conversation, all seven children participated. In the excerpt below, only Genna (G) and three students participated, but the others chimed in with "Yeah!" from time to time. Alex (S3) is the ELL in this group. His first language is Spanish, although he was born in the United States. He is still acquiring English.

S1: I . . . I saw someone take [name]'s ?? [food item] and I told them.

G: You told? Who did you tell?

S2: That's not a bully . . . I mean, he's not a bully.

G: Why do you say that?

S2: He did something bad. I mean, he stole. But he didn't hurt someone.

S1 AND S3: He did! Yeah . . .

S2: Well, I mean . . .

G: What? What do you mean, Simon?

S2: Well, no one got *hurt* (*sarcastically*). Did he break her arm or something? Was he starving to death? I mean . . . what he did was bad . . . and [unintelligible] punished, but he didn't hurt anybody.

S3: I think . . .

S1: No . . .

S3: I think . . .

S2: What I am trying to say is . . .

G: (*to S3*): Alex, you are trying to say something? What do you think?

S3: I think maybe [name of child] was hurt. I think he was hurt because he wanted [unintelligible] and it was his own . . .

G: What do you mean by "hurt"?

S2: I mean . . .

G: Let's let Alex explain. He has an idea and he wants to explain. Being hurt doesn't always mean your body is hurt. Alex?

S3: Yeah. He was hurt *inside*. My . . .

S2 AND OTHERS: Yeah! (*Some unintelligible speech.*)

G: So, hurt can happen inside, like when you get your feelings hurt or you are upset about something.

KIDS: Yeah . . .

G: So, if someone hurts you on the inside, is that person a bully?

(*There is 3 seconds of silence.*)

KIDS: Yeah.

S3: Yes, he hurt him.

From here, Genna goes on to explain to the children that verbal bullying can be just as hurtful as physical bullying. She asks whether they have ever heard anyone called names, and soon a new discussion begins.

In this IC, the students do come to new understandings, even beyond Genna's goal of having them understand that bullying is wrong and should be reported. They come to understand that the concept of hurt can be emotional, as well as physical, and that bullying can come in multiple forms.

Genna was just learning how to conduct ICs. She illustrated some indicators of ICs quite well in this excerpt, while other parts of the IC show her beginning development. First, in this excerpt, she spoke fewer words than the combined amount the students spoke. In ICs, the students must speak more than the teacher; whoever is doing the speaking is doing the thinking. Surprisingly, in traditional discussions, the teacher (one person) does twice or even three times as much talking as all students in the class *combined*! In this excerpt, Genna was aware that there had to be some student-to-student interaction, and she was able to step back a bit and allow the children to respond to one another.

Genna also made sure that Simon did not dominate this conversation, and she jumped at the chance to involve Alex, the one ELL in the group. In typical class discussions, it is easy to permit the same children to contribute repeatedly. Genna also asked high-level, open-ended questions that pushed students' thinking. "Why do you say that?" and "What do you mean?" are scaffolding questions that ask students to dig a bit deeper, to use vocabulary they might not be used to, and to form thoughts while forming sentences.

Genna also made mistakes common to all teachers attempting rigorous ICs. At one point, when she saw where Alex was going and knew it was important, she said, "Let's let Alex explain. He has an idea and he wants to explain." Yet she went ahead and provided the answer for Alex! She said, "Being hurt doesn't always mean your body is hurt. Alex?" Well, he had little else to say, because his teacher had provided the words from his head. That moment would have been a perfect opportunity for Alex to practice explaining a difficult concept.

Still, this is the sort of conversation that teaches, and Genna conducted it quite well. It would be easy to see how this sort of conversation could extend from a JPA that also connected to students' background experiences. The integration of the principles can illustrate outstanding teaching of all students, not just ELLs.

Family Involvement

Much has been written about the importance of family involvement. Research has shown that family involvement in schools increases student engagement in school and, ultimately, student achievement (Epstein, Coates, Salinas, Sanders, & Simon, 1997; Hoover-Dempsy & Sandler, 1997; Kyle, McIntyre, Miller, & Moore, 2002). Many teachers know that connections with families can reap these positive results, but they struggle with how to make that happen. Some teachers wonder about whether their students' families care about education or would show up in schools if invited. Yet most studies of families of school-age children illustrate that parents and guardians care deeply about their children, want them to learn, and want something better for their children than what they have for themselves (Kyle et al., 2002). Many families see schools as the "ticket" for their children's entry into middle-class life, as well as the chance for them to grow into independent decision makers.

Yet this work is not easy for either families or teachers. Some parents or guardians may not know how to help their children succeed in school, and others may have different goals for their children than the schools have. Many teachers are reluctant to reach out to families due to several barriers. With respect to ELLs, language is the primary barrier for school–home communication and collaboration. Time is also a barrier, because both teachers and families work hard and find it difficult to schedule time together. Despite these issues, many teachers and whole schools have been successful in involving families in schools.

Family involvement of ELLs cannot be conducted in typical ways, such as through homework and at traditional parent conferences. The strategies must focus on connecting personally to the families and building from what they know. A few ideas follow:

- Get to know your students' outside-of-school interests and passions, their families, family members' jobs and interests, and home routines and literacy practices, then use this information to connect your curriculum to what students already know.
- Use family knowledge to invite speakers into your classroom, especially when the family knowledge builds on the curriculum.
- Have students study their own community, as in the example in this chapter.
- Have students interview their elders and compare life in this country with life in their home country.
- Plan a family night in which families and students work together on a project. Be sure to have interpreters there to assist with the language.

These ideas are only a beginning. Details on planning family events are beyond the scope of this chapter. However, specific examples from the projects mentioned in this chapter have been described (Epstein et al., 1997; Kyle et al., 2002, 2005; McIntyre et al., 2008).

Reflections and Future Directions

It takes a career to learn to teach. Change in instructional practice must be based on new students, new contexts, new learning opportunities, and new technologies. The job of teachers is to assess their practice continually to see whether it is working with their current students in the current context. No doubt, the principles and practices you read about in this chapter and book are already somewhat familiar to you. Adapting these familiar practices for ELLs will take some trial and reflection.

The principles described in this chapter are intended to be intertwined across all teaching activities. For example, a community study that involves families can be contextualized in the background knowledge of the students and can include a written product jointly created by students, assisted by the teacher, and a rigorous instructional conversation about the improvable product. Thus, all principles described in this chapter are included.

However, some teachers prefer to work on one principle at a time, attending to each of the specific *indicators* (Dalton, 2007) of that principle. Teachers often begin by planning a joint activity that addresses the core content they intend to teach, ensuring that all students participate and that teachers assist in scaffolding the product. Becoming expert at IC, too, takes dedicated attention to assess whether students are constructing new understandings through teacher questioning. And teachers of ELLs often need to pay special attention to building in classroom interaction time, so that students have increasing amounts of time to discuss the academic content in safe places, where their oral language can be scaffolded by their peers and the teacher. Thus, it is recommended that teachers tackle one or two of the principles described here at a time. These principles are a guide for teachers' constant reflection, tweaking instruction for the population of students in their classrooms. When teachers see that learning to teach is a career-long endeavor, they often become the sort of reflective practitioners (Ross, Bondy, & Kyle, 1993) who can adapt to any learner.

The education of ELLs in the future must rely more on educational research from multiple paradigms. Studies from a sociocultural perspective often focus on student engagement and teacher–student connections. These are critical studies, and many more are needed to understand what engages students, what keeps them in school, and what links home to school. Equally important, however, are large-scale, comparative studies of instructional approaches that measure student learning. With advanced statistical procedures, it has become more possible to link teacher behaviors and/or socioeconomic or cultural variables to student achievement, while controlling for confounding variables.

ENGAGEMENT ACTIVITIES

1. Ask yourself the following questions: Why do some children fail in schools while others succeed? Why do some populations of children succeed more than others? Then ask yourself how you came to believe these assumptions about learners. Were they ideas passed down to you from parents or guardians? Were they ideas you developed through popular media sources? Were they ideas you learned from books? Which of your viewpoints reflect a deficit perspective and which reflect a culturally respectful perspective? Why?

2. Choose an ELL in your school, one you do not yet know well, one you are responsible for teaching. Invite the child and a parent or guardian to an interview. Tell them you are trying to learn more about the child so you can better teach him or

her. Ask the following questions and others that come to mind. Some questions are most appropriate for the child. Others might be best for the adult. The idea is to learn as much as you can about the child, so you can improve your own instruction. Take notes, so that you remember everything.

- ■ "Do you have a country you call 'home country' other than the United States?"
- ■ "Some people whose parents were born outside the United States call themselves by their two home countries, like 'Mexican American.' What do you call yourselves?"
- ■ "What languages are spoken in the home and community?"
- ■ "Tell me about you and your family. What do you like to do after school and on weekends? What work and play are important to you?"
- ■ "What sorts of reading, writing, and mathematics do you do at work or at home?"
- ■ "What other interests do you have?"
- ■ "What goals do you have for schooling?"
- ■ "What do you like and dislike about school?"
- ■ "How can I help you learn best?"

3. Use the information you learned from your interview with the student and guardian to plan a lesson, or series of lessons that includes as many of the following instructional principles as possible: JPA, language and literacy development, linking home to school, rigorous curriculum, and IC. Invite others who have similar backgrounds, interests, or needs to join the lesson. Videotape yourself teaching to analyze your interactions. Most importantly, ask your students: What do I do that helps you learn the most? What should I do more of? What does not help you learn so much? You may be surprised at how astute your students are at determining what effective instruction is.

REFERENCES

August, D., & Shanahan, T. (2006). *Developing literacy in second-language learners: Report of the National Literacy Panel on Language Minority Children and Youth.* Mahwah, NJ: Erlbaum.

Dalton, S. S. (2007). *Five standards for effective teaching: How to succeed with all learners.* San Francisco: Jossey-Bass.

Echevarria, J., Vogt, M. E., & Short, D. (2004). *Making content comprehensible for English language learners: The SIOP model* (2nd ed.). Boston: Pearson.

Epstein, J. L., Coates, L., Salinas, K. C., Sanders, M. G., & Simon, B. S. (1997). *School, family, and community partnerships: Your handbook for action.* Thousand Oaks, CA: Corwin Press.

Foster, M., & Peele, T. (2001). Ring my bell: Contextualizing home and school in an African American community. In E. McIntyre, A. Rosebery, & N.

González (Eds.), *Classroom diversity: Connecting curriculum to students' lives* (pp. 27–36). Portsmouth, NH: Heinemann Educational Books.

Gay, G. (2000). *Culturally responsive instruction: Theory, research, and practice.* New York: Teachers College Press.

Goldenberg, C. (1993). Instructional conversations: Promoting comprehension through discussion. *Reading Teacher, 46,* 316–326.

Gutiérrez, K. D., Baquedano-Lopez, P., & Alvarez, H. H. (2001). Literacy as hybridity: Moving beyond bilingualism in urban classrooms. In M. L. Reyes & J. J. Halcon (Eds.), *The best for our children: Critical perspectives on literacy for Latino students* (pp. 212–230). New York: Teachers College Press.

Heath, S. B. (1991). The sense of being literate: Historical and cross-cultural features. In R. Barr, M. L. Kamil, P. Mosenthal, & P. D. Pearson (Eds.), *Handbook of reading research* (Vol. II, pp. 3–25). Mahwah, NJ: Erlbaum.

Heath, S. B. (1994). The children of Trackton's children: Spoken and written language in social change. In R. B. Rudell, M. R. Rudell, & H. Singer (Eds.), *Theoretical models and processes of reading* (pp. 208–230). Newark, DE: International Reading Association.

Hoover-Dempsey, K. V., & Sandler, H. M. (1997). Why do parents become involved in their children's education? *Review of Educational Research, 67,* 3–42.

Irvine, J. J. (2006). *Educating teachers for diversity: Seeing with a cultural eye.* New York: Teachers College Press.

Kyle, D., McIntyre, E., Miller, K., & Moore, G. (2002). *Reaching out: A K–8 resource for connecting families and schools.* Thousand Oaks, CA: Corwin Press.

Kyle, D. W., McIntyre, E., Miller, K., & Moore, G. (2005). *Bridging school and home through family nights.* Thousand Oaks, CA: Corwin Press.

Ladson-Billings, G. (1994). *The dreamkeepers: Successful teachers of African American children.* San Francisco: Jossey-Bass.

Lave, J., & Wenger, E. (1991). *Situated learning: Legitimate peripheral participation.* New York: Oxford University Press.

Manyak, P. S. (2001). Participation, hybridity, and carnival: A situated analysis of a dynamic literacy practice in a primary-grade English immersion class. *Journal of Literacy Research, 33,* 423–465.

McIntyre, E. (2010). Sociocultural perspectives on children with reading difficulties. In R. Allington & A. McGill-Franzen (Eds.), *Handbook of research on children with reading disabilities.* New York: Routledge.

McIntyre, E., Kyle, D. W., Chen, C., Kraemer, J., & Parr, J. (2008). *Six principles for teaching English language learners.* Thousand Oaks, CA: Corwin Press.

McIntyre, E., Kyle, D. W., & Moore, G. (2006). A teacher's guidance toward small group dialogue in a low-SES primary grade classroom. *Reading Research Quarterly, 4*(1), 36–63.

McIntyre, E., Rosebery, A., & González, N. (2001). *Classroom diversity: Connecting curriculum to students' lives.* Portsmouth, NH: Heinemann.

Michaels, S. (1981). "Sharing time": Children's narrative styles and differential access to literacy. *Language in Society, 10,* 423–442.

Moll, L. C. (1994). Literacy research in community and classrooms; A sociocultural approach. In R. B. Rudell, M. R. Rudell, & H. Singer (Eds.), *Theoreti-*

cal models and processes of reading (pp. 22–43). Newark, DE: International Reading Association.

Moll, L. C., & González, N. (2003). Engaging life: A funds of knowledge approach to multicultural education. In J. Banks & C. A. Banks (Eds.), *Handbook of multicultural education* (pp. 699–715). New York: Jossey-Bass.

Nieto, S. (1999). *The light in their eyes: Creating multicultural learning communities.* New York: Teachers College Press.

Rogoff, B. (2003). *The cultural nature of human development.* New York: Oxford University Press.

Ross, D., Bondy, E., & Kyle, D. W. (1993). *Reflective teaching for student empowerment: Elementary curriculum and methods.* New York: Macmillan.

Saunders, W. M., & Goldenberg, C. (1996). Effects of instructional conversation and literature logs on limited and fluent English proficient students' story comprehension and thematic understanding. *Elementary School Journal, 99,* 277–301.

Stone, C. A. (2004). Contemporary approaches to the study of language and literacy development: A call for the integration of perspectives. In C. A. Stone, E. R. Silliman, B. J. Ehren, & K. Apel (Eds.), *Handbook of language and literacy: Development and disorders* (pp. 3–24). New York: Guilford Press.

Tharp, R. G., Estrada, P., Dalton, S., & Yamauchi, Y. (2000). *Teaching transformed: Achieving excellence, fairness, inclusion, and harmony.* Boulder, CO: Westview.

Tharp, R., & Gallimore, R. (1988). *Rousing minds to life: Teaching, learning and schooling in social context.* Cambridge, UK: Cambridge University Press.

Vygotsky, L. S. (1978). *Mind in society: The development of higher psychological processes.* Cambridge, MA: Harvard University Press.

Vygotsky, L. S. (1987). *Thought and language* (Ed. Alex Kozulin, 2nd printing). Cambridge, MA: MIT Press.

Wells, G. (1999). *Dialogic inquiry: Toward a sociocultural practice and theory of education.* Cambridge, UK: Cambridge University Press.

Wells, G., & Haneda, M. (2009, April). *Authority and equality in instructional conversation.* A presentation at the annual meeting of the American Educational Research Association, San Diego, CA.

Wertsch, J. V. (1991). *Voices of the mind: A sociocultural approach to mediated action.* Cambridge, MA: Harvard University Press.

Wertsch, J. (1998). *Mind as action.* New York: Oxford University Press.

CHAPTER 4

Engaging Young ELLs with Reading and Writing

Diane M. Barone

> In all discoveries about exemplary teachers, especially
> exemplary teachers of ELLs, one central discovery is that
> they provide language-rich classrooms where children have
> opportunities to talk about and write about their learning.
> —BARONE AND XU (2008, p. 17)

This chapter will:

1. Highlight appropriate instruction for English language learners (ELLs) in learning about sounds, letters, and words.

2. Share ideas to support ELLs in learning to read and write, with a focus on comprehension.

3. Provide suggestions to support students when they are not working directly with the teacher.

4. Highlight engagement strategies to maximize instruction.

The preceding quote shares an important understanding about instruction, in that all discussion about reading and writing instruction is grounded in the idea that the classroom is rich in language, mainly student language. While language-rich classrooms are valuable for all students, they are critically important for young children who are learning a new language as they learn to read and write for the first time (Goldenberg & Patthey-Chavez, 1995). English language learners (ELLs), in order to practice new oral and receptive language skills, require multiple opportunities to engage in discussion. Central issues surrounding language-rich classrooms are management and time constraints. These concerns are attended to throughout the chapter as reading and writing strategies are shared.

Learning about Sounds, Letters, and Words

Children new to English come to school knowing words in their home language. While they are also familiar with letters and sounds, they may not be aware of this knowledge explicitly. For instance, they can pronounce the word *cat* as *el gato*, and while they can make the /l/ and /g/ sounds, they may not have an understanding of the letters or the sounds matched to these letters. When teachers of young children begin formally to develop this knowledge, they are not starting as if an ELL has no background knowledge about letters and sounds. Just like English-only children, they are taking the child's implicit knowledge about letters and sounds and making it explicit.

Although making the implicit explicit is the fundamental learning issue with phonemic awareness, there are related concerns for teachers to consider when supporting letter and sound knowledge of English for children new to English (August, 2003; Barone & Xu, 2008). First of all, not all languages have phonemes. For instance, Cherokee is a syllabic language in which each syllable is pronounced. Chinese and Japanese are logographic languages, because they rely on characters; however, in Japanese, there are syllabic elements as well. Second, not all languages are read from left to right and top to bottom. Chinese readers read down a column, moving from right to left. Hebrew is another language that does not use the English left-to-right, top-to-bottom line structure. Third, there are home language pronunciations that may influence English pronunciation. For instance, Spanish speakers pronounce *d* for *th* or *dey* for *they*, *y* or *ch* for *j*, so they may say *chuice* for *juice*, or substitute *b* for *v*, and say *ban* for *van* (Helman, 2004). Moreover, few words in Spanish end with *t*. When thinking about beginning reading instruction in English and how many core reading programs begin with the *at* word pattern, reading of these words can be particularly difficult for children whose home language is Spanish (Rodríguez-Galindo & Wright, 2006). Important for teachers to remember is that even though students may have difficulty with pronunciation, it does not mean they are not aware of the correct sound–symbol representations. Finally, some young children have already started to learn English in their home country. English lessons are common in Taiwan, among other countries (Oladejo,

2006). These children may bring explicit understandings of the sounds of letters in English to instruction in U.S. classrooms.

Phonemic Awareness

Children learning English may acquire literacy skills in English in a similar manner as native speaking children, although their alphabetic knowledge may precede and facilitate the acquisition of phonological awareness in English.
    —CHIAPPE, SIEGEL AND, WADE-WOOLEY (2002, p. 369)

A fundamental step in development of understanding about the sounds within words or phonemes begins with oral manipulation of sounds. Unlike the typical instruction for English-only students, where phonemic awareness instruction precedes phonics learning, for ELLs this instruction often occurs simultaneously (Chiappe et al., 2002) because phonemic awareness in English may take longer to develop. While teachers may worry about the appropriateness of phonemic awareness and phonics instruction for ELLs, it is beneficial to their learning to read and write (Manyak, 2007). Important for teachers to remember, however, is that while this instruction about the structure of words provides support for beginning reading, it does not necessarily promise long-term reading achievement (Lesaux, Koda, Siegel, & Shanahan, 2006).

Following are a few activities to support phonemic awareness with young ELLs:

1. *Picture Sorts.* Children sort pictures based on the initial consonant sound. They can find pictures that begin with *b*, for instance. When this process is easy, children can move to finding pictures for two or more initial consonants. For ELLs, careful selection of pictures is important. Preference should be given to pictures that show only one item. For example, a picture of a bird on a tree may be confusing, as the child may focus on the bird or the tree.

2. *Move It.* Children are given approximately three markers (chips, game pieces). As the teacher says a three-phoneme word, the child moves a chip to a line on a paper or whiteboard for each one. For *bat*, the teacher says: *b-a-t*. For each phoneme, the child moves a chip to a line in a left-to-right progression. Having the child move a chip helps the teacher to assess quickly each child's phonemic awareness knowledge.

3. *Name Comparisons.* Children can compare the first sound of their names with those of other children. Children whose names begin with *C* stand together, and the remaining children give a thumbs up if they were correct, or down if incorrect. Because a child's name is important, children are easily engaged with this activity.

Phonics

Children must gain control of the print-to-speech mapping
system early if they are to become successful readers.
　　　　　　　　　　　　—BECK (2006, p. 12)

The importance of sound–symbol relationship knowledge, the alphabetic principle, is critical to early reading success (Beck, 2006). Learning to become automatic in decoding words requires that children (1) know the speech sounds associated with written letters; (2) put these sounds together, or blend them to form a word; (3) have a sense of English orthography; and (4) complete the previous three items quickly or automatically (Beck, 2006). If a child is hesitant in being aware of sound–symbol relationships, for instance, then decoding is slowed, with a limiting effect on comprehension.

Most teachers begin the process of phonics instruction with a focus on initial consonants. Following this instruction, they bring children's attention to short vowels and word families (*bat, can*). Building on this instruction, the focus becomes blends and digraphs. Finally, teachers move to exploration of long-vowel patterns (Peregoy & Boyle, 2005).

Following are a few activities to support phonics instruction and learning for ELLs:

1. *Picture Sorts.* Children once again use pictures to sort for words that begin with a particular initial consonant or have a specific short vowel. For these sorts, children are encouraged to write the word. For instance, a child sorting for initial *r* words might record r_____. This writing shows the child knew that *rabbit* starts with an *r*, but he or she was unsure of what followed. As children build knowledge of the alphabetic principle, they record more phonemes within words.

2. *Word Sorts.* This activity is the same as that described for picture sorts. Here children sort words rather than pictures. For instance, a group of children might generate words with *short a* in them, like *cat*. As the teacher records these words on chart paper, each child writes a word on a small card. Then the teacher models a sort for these words. For example, he or she sorts *short a* words by the initial consonant, the vowel and what follows, among other ways. The focus is for children to use what they know (initial consonants) and move to the central focus for learning—the vowel and what follows. Children can be dismissed and asked to resort the words. Many teachers use word sort notebooks, where the child can record the way he or she sorted for later conversation (Bear, Helman, Invernizzi, Templeton, & Johnston, 2007). See Figure 4.1 for an example.

3. *Making Words.* Cunningham (1991) developed a method to

M	at	ag	an
man	mat	rag	man
mat	rat	tag	ran

FIGURE 4.1. Sorting example.

engage students with learning phonics. When teachers use this strategy, they identify letters that can be used to build simple to complex words. Each child receives letters on small cards. Children begin creating words, following their teacher's directions. For instance, they may create *bat, sat, ask*, and so on, at first. Teachers challenge children with longer words, such as *base*. Finally, children create the word *basket*, which includes all of the letters. Sometimes teachers find this strategy difficult to use, because they must prepare the letters for each student. An easy way to solve this dilemma is to utilize the table function on a computer. The teacher then places one letter in each cell. Following this process, a copy is printed for each student then students just quickly cut between each cell, and they have their own copies of the letters. See Figure 4.2 for an example.

Each of the activities shared for phonemic awareness and phonics require active participation of students. As teachers engage students in this learning, they can easily see and hear how students are making decisions about sounds and blending sounds to form words. These observations guide future instruction.

Focusing on Reading Comprehension

When children have abundant opportunities to talk about books, when classroom discussion in small and large groups is encouraged, comprehension improves.
—KEENE AND ZIMMERMANN (2007, p. 40)

Comprehension relies on all students having sufficient knowledge of decoding, background knowledge of the topic or genre, and strategies to support comprehension, such as clarification when confusion occurs

b	k	e	t	a	s

FIGURE 4.2. Table to create alphabet cards.

(Barone & Xu, 2008). Added to this list for children who are learning English is their proficiency with English (Peregoy & Boyle, 2000). The strategies suggested to support ELLs in comprehension are similar to those for English-only students, although more time and attention are given to developing background knowledge through student talk, drawing, and writing.

Prior Knowledge

Prior Knowledge of Topic

One huge issue for ELLs is making sense of a text if they lack background knowledge about its topic (Fitzgerald & Graves, 2004; Hickman, Pollard-Durodola, & Vaughn, 2004). For instance, if children are reading the book *Little Beauty* (Browne, 2008), they are expected to know about gorillas, sign language, and zookeepers on the very first page of the book. If, as young children often do, they rely on the illustration for clues to meaning, they see a gorilla sitting in a chair with coffee and a hamburger as he manipulates a remote control for the television. As is typical of Anthony Browne and other writers and illustrators of books for young children, the illustration does not always relate directly to the text. Further into the book, the gorilla gets angry because he watched the movie *King Kong* on television and saw what happened to King Kong. If children have no understanding about this popular culture figure, they will not understand why he was angry and broke the television.

To support students with this particular text, teachers might share a few photos of gorillas in the wild, then photos of gorillas in a zoo. In the discussion centered on these photos, teachers would bring in pertinent vocabulary, such as *zookeepers*. A second topic that is necessary to understanding how the gorilla communicates is sign language. There is an abundance of material that shows children how to sign letters and a few words (e.g., *www.iidc.indiana.edu/cedir/kidsweb/amachart.html*). Again, this background would not take extensive time to share with students, and it would support them as they gain understanding of this text. The last area of background necessary for this story is the movie *King Kong*. Certainly there is no reason to share this movie with children, but teachers need to provide a brief explanation of King Kong and the central plot of the movie, or children will not understand the behavior of the gorilla. Other elements within this story are interesting but not central to understanding. For instance, Browne has included a replica of a painting on one page. While children may want to investigate the painting and perhaps why it is included, not knowing these details will not hamper comprehension.

Little Beauty (Browne, 2008) is a narrative, and most children are familiar with its structure of beginning, problem, resolution, and end. Unlike narratives, informational texts are less familiar to young readers and also require support with background knowledge. When young children experience a book like *Flashy Fantastic Rain Forest Frogs* (Patent, 1997), they bring to the text general information about frogs, so they can better understand the frogs that live in rain forests. But if teachers realize that their students do not have this information, it is important to develop it before engaging with this text. Teachers often use KWL (Ogle, 1986) to support this background knowledge attainment; during this process, students identify what they already know, what they want to learn, and what they learned after reading. The difficulty with KWL is that often ELLs identify misinformation about what they know. If teachers record these misperceptions, children come to believe them as facts, simply by the fact that they were placed on a chart. Stead (2006) developed a variant of KWL called Reading and Analyzing Nonfiction (RAN). Using this strategy, students first identify what they think they know, then during or after reading they decide which of these facts were confirmed in reading and which were misconceptions. They also record new information and "wonderings" for further reading. By using RAN, teachers validate students' current knowledge, although it is not accepted as fact until confirmed in reading. Another strength of this strategy is it is extended to further reading through the wonderings category.

This discussion of supporting and extending background knowledge has relied on discussion and guided chart creation. Photos have been used to support students with visual information. Other ways to support students in gaining content knowledge might be with short video clips, reading from other texts, writing investigations, and so on. Before any of these supportive instructional techniques can be used effectively, teachers must carefully preread the text students will encounter to determine content with which they may not be familiar. Then teachers can make appropriate decisions on how best to share this information with students before or during reading.

Prior Knowledge of Genre

Most young children are familiar with narrative structure, because their parents and teachers have read narratives to them. Even preschool teachers have nudged their students to understand the beginning, middle, and end of a story. However, it is important for teachers to tease out the variations of narrative text for children (Barone & Xu, 2008). As teachers bring a new genre to children or relabel a familiar narrative with a more precise title, students and teachers can create charts with important characteristics of the genre. For instance, young children can categorize fables, folktales, myths, legends, and so on. Figure 4.3 shares the beginning of a genre study of folktales in which children are noting important features.

As children continue to read folktales, they add to this chart, thus expanding and refining their knowledge of this genre.

Similar to narrative text, informational text has structures that, if known, facilitate comprehension. For example, in *Flashy Fantastic Rain Forest Frogs*, Patent (1997) uses a descriptive structure. Each page shares description of rain forest frogs. On page 1, he writes about their colors and sizes. The next page describes where they live. To support children with this text, they could have a paper on which they record details about the rain forest frogs. The paper might be divided into important categories, such as what they look like, where they live, what they eat, and so on. Through this process, children can use their notes to chat about the rain forest frog, and they become familiar with this structure in other informational books.

Other typical structures in informational text include cause–effect, sequence, problem–solution, and compare–contrast (Barone & Taylor, 2006). Teachers need explicitly to share these structures with young students. As with the descriptive structure, note taking to match the structure helps students acquire these understandings. Figure 4.4 shares note-taking structures to support understanding informational text.

Teachers first model these structures with children by completing the graphic organizer with student input. As children gain facility with reading and writing, they can begin organizing the structure with the teacher, then work on it independently. As children become familiar with these structures, they develop sophisticated knowledge of them and how many authors of informational books combine them. This

---

Folktales

Begin with "Once upon a time."

Have really nice and really mean characters.

There is magic.

Animals can be characters that talk, and they can be scary like wolves.

Have a happy ending.

FIGURE 4.3. Folktale genre chart.

Structure	What is learned	Note-taking structure
Description	Details about something	Web, cluster, list
Compare–contrast	How two or more things are alike or different	Venn diagram, T-chart
Cause–effect	How something is connected to something else	Tree diagram, matching lines with arrows
Problem–solution	How something is solved	Tree diagram, matching lines with arrows
Sequence	How things happen in order	List, folded paper

FIGURE 4.4. Understanding text structures.

knowledge of structure helps children understand how information is shared in books and how better to learn what is important.

Strategies to Support Comprehension

Most core reading programs identify a set of comprehension strategies that are taught at each grade level. The strategies group around prediction, monitoring and clarifying, questioning, summarizing, and visualizing (Smith & Read, 2009). These strategies are explicitly taught, so that students automatically use them when they read independently. Even if teachers do not organize part of their reading curriculum around a core reading program, these strategies are important to student comprehension. Following are brief descriptions of each strategy:

1. *Prediction.* Students use background knowledge, cover illustration, and/or text to predict what might happen in a story. For informational text, students may peruse illustrations, maps, charts, and so on, to get a sense of the topic before reading.

2. *Monitoring and Clarifying.* Students realize when they are confused by text and reread to clarify passages that do not make sense. The important part of monitoring and clarifying is rereading to fix up comprehension issues.

3. *Questioning.* Students spontaneously form questions about the content of text before, during, and after reading. These questions are not the typical comprehension questions to which the teacher already has the answer. These are questions that help the reader focus closely

on text in response to his or her question. For instance, in *Little Beauty* (Browne, 2008), readers want to read on to find out where the keepers are taking Beauty and what might happen to the gorilla.

4. *Summarizing*. Students understand the most important content shared in a passage or text. Summarizing is not easy, because most students often get caught up in the numerous details in a story or informational text. Teachers might ask students to step back from the details and decide what is important about them. In this stepping back, students begin to understand that summarizing is not a listing of details.

5. *Visualizing*. Students create mental images of the text during and after reading. Teachers often use this strategy to help students better understand the setting in a story, for instance. However, if students quickly draw a character, setting, or detail from an informational book, they better understand each element.

These strategies certainly work for ELLs, although they may need additional support with them. For instance, while ELLs can certainly predict what a book may be about from the cover illustration, they may not be as fast with a response as English-only children. If the teacher calls on an individual student to share a prediction, the ELL is often left out of the conversation. However, if the teacher allows students to talk with a partner or in small groups first, ELLs can participate successfully. Furthermore, if the teacher carefully listens to these conversations, he or she can summarize to the group the important ideas of students, thus relieving the pressure for an ELL to share this information with a whole group (August, 2003).

In classrooms where ELLs are successful with comprehension, teachers are thoughtful in their organization and the way they scaffold instruction for students. Teachers think carefully about the target strategy they model in whole-group instruction. If the strategy is monitor and clarify, they share this process with students as they read the selection from the anthology or any read-aloud with a think-aloud (Barone & Xu, 2006). They stop purposefully as they read to highlight what part of text was confusing, and they reread to clarify the comprehension problem. Teachers preview the read-aloud material to determine potential comprehension issues for ELLs, as well as information that may be culturally unfamiliar to students, and choose these places for think-alouds (Hickman et al., 2004). For instance, if there is an idiom in the text (e.g., *easy as pie* or *quick as a fox*), they explain what this phrase means, so that children do not try to comprehend it literally. Following whole-group instruction, guided reading groups target the same comprehension strategy. Now ELLs read the text, and with teacher modeling, practice the strategy. Later, the teacher will expect these students to practice the same strategy during independent reading. Through this careful structuring of instruction, grouping, and materials, ELLs are offered consistent practice of a new strategy to support their comprehension.

To support ELLs' comprehension, teachers preview texts to determine what extra support they may need. They may bring in *realia*, real objects, shared in text so students can see what they are. When bringing an object is not appropriate, they find photos of the object, event, or setting to help children visualize these important elements in text. Teachers often use *googleimages.com* to find these photos, although this is not an Internet site where children should be free to explore, because some photos are inappropriate for them.

Teachers also act out vocabulary words that students might find difficult, and that interfere with comprehension. They quickly share a movement, such as making a fierce face, when the word *fierce* occurs in text. Through this process, students quickly understand a word and can move back to comprehension of text.

Key to supporting ELLs in gaining comprehension is engagement. If a single child is called upon, then others do not have to pay attention or respond. When teachers use whole-group responses for simple, one-word responses, all children participate. For example, if a teacher wants to know whether students know the name of a character, all students say the name aloud. Teachers can also use cards with *yes* on one side and *no* on the other for yes–no responses. However, if the answer is more complex, students form partners and discuss the potential answer. If the teacher notices that some children never participate in the partner discussion, then each child is given a number or letter. The teacher can request Partner A to share with Partner B. Following this sharing, Partner B shares with Partner A. Importantly, this partner process allows all students to participate, not just one. This expectation that *all* students will participate in learning events facilitates the development of comprehension for all students, and especially ELLs.

Focusing on Writing to Support Reading Comprehension

Writing about learning is a key component to supporting comprehension. Writing to learn is grounded in first-draft writing where the goal is to share ideas, confusions, or connections (Barone & Taylor, 2006; Gersten, Baker, Haager, & Graves, 2005). Students write using what they know about conventionally representing words and ideas, although there are often numerous errors in this writing. Teachers may find it hard to look beyond the errors, but the focus needs to be on ideas, not mechanics. Other writing opportunities offer children the chance to move from ideas to conventional representation. Typically, teachers are more familiar with having students write informally in content areas such as math or science. However, students can easily write about narrative text as well.

Writing to Learn with Narrative Text

Having students write about their reading is most successful if it is a daily expectation. Children may start the day by completing an entry task as they enter the classroom, in which they write about the book they will read (Barone & Taylor, 2006). The teacher has the cover projected on a screen, and as children come into the room, they receive a small piece of paper, where they list three things they think the book will be about. Later, on their way to recess, the teacher checks to see that each child accomplished this writing as an entry ticket to recess. Through the use of an entry task, students focus on learning from the moment they enter the room. Very young children may be asked to draw three things about the book, but the rest of the process is the same. Entry tasks on other days can be varied to meet the expectations of a later, whole-class reading experience. If children are learning about genre, they might write one new thing they discovered about a certain genre, record a new word to describe the main character, or add a fact they learned (e.g., about frogs). The opportunities for topics in entry tasks are endless, but they should be targeted to later instruction.

Students may also be asked to write about their reading through the use of graphic organizers. Young children may fold a paper in half and on one side write about and draw the beginning of a story, and on the other, the end of the story. As their understanding of story develops, more folds can be made in the paper, so they move to the beginning, middle, and end. Later they can add other details, such as other events in the plot.

If teachers are working on prediction, students can respond to "I wonder what will happen next." Using this format, they write their prediction, then draw a quick sketch of it. Or if teachers are working on building connections across characters or text, they can use a form that asks children to draw and then explain a connection (McLaughlin & Fisher, 2005). Important when using these kinds of forms is follow-up discussion, in which children explain their choices. The organizer should serve as a foundation for ongoing discussion about a book or character, for instance; it should not be the end of an instructional event that is just graded and returned. This follow-up conversation is very important, because most graphic organizers are centered in literal comprehension and do not extend to inferential understandings.

To support children as they read through a text, teachers might use bookmarks or reading journals. When using a bookmark, teachers highlight an expectation. Children might look for interesting words, details about a character or setting, questions that they form as they read, and so on. It makes most sense to match the expectations highlighted in the bookmark with the strategy or target of instruction to maximize the effect of the bookmark. Similar to a bookmark for recording ideas is a reading journal. In the journal, children record similar ideas. For instance, the teacher can ask that they write about the setting, or their predictions, or interesting words. What is important about a notebook is that students record ideas in it daily as they read, then, following several days of reading and note taking, they reread their notes to determine what they thought was most important and why. Similar to graphic organizers, the writing is a way of remembering, but to take the notes to a more sophisticated level, conversation is necessary. Sharing these conversational events with others nudges students to consider ideas they may not have thought about, or in ways they had not considered. The writing serves as a foundation for conversational events that deepen comprehension.

Writing to Learn with Informational Text

Figure 4.4 lists different organizational structures within informational text. Each structure requires a different graphic organizer that matches the structure of text. For descriptive text a web, cluster, or list works fine. This structure allows students to share aspects of the description without other organization. Once students are comfortable with general webs, lists, or clusters, teachers can nudge them toward more organized representations of information. They might create an organized web, as seen in Figure 4.5. The organized, or semantic, web allows descriptive information to be clustered around topics. Following from the creation of the web, children might write about a spider, using the graphic organizer structure, or they might just share one aspect about a spider and why it is important to know.

The compare–contrast structure is more difficult to teach than just description. It requires students to be familiar with basic facts about two things and to compare them. So, if the earlier spider description is used, children might compare two different spiders, or they might compare a spider to an insect. To support children in this process, teachers might begin with two organized webs, as in Figure 4.5, before moving to a format for comparison, such as a Venn diagram or a T-chart. In watching teachers support students using comparison organizational charts, the T-chart proves easiest. Using this chart, children do not directly write about two things that are the same, but the format offers an easy struc-

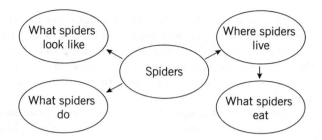

FIGURE 4.5. Organized web.

ture for this discussion as students write about one topic at a time. Following this note taking, they are ready to make comparisons. See Figure 4.6 for an example.

Cause–effect and problem–solution structures are supported by similar organizational charts. A tree diagram is similar to a computer flowchart that starts with one box from which other boxes descend. In the top box is placed a cause or a problem, then effects or solutions are placed in the other boxes. The structure allows a student to see easily the effects or possible solutions offered. Using lines with arrows is similar to the tree diagram, except that they are horizontal, with a phrase followed by an arrow that leads to the effect or solution. For example, the problem in *Little Beauty* is that Beauty was taken away because the gorilla became violent. An arrow from this statement of the problem can lead to the solution, where Beauty uses sign language to convince the zookeeper that she broke the television.

Time sequence is also matched with a graphic organizer that allows children to see the time sequence. Children can create a list to show events in order, or they might fold a paper into sections, with each section containing a date and description of its importance. At first, young children might form only four squares formed by folding a paper. Later the paper can be folded into six or eight squares for recording sequenced events.

Garden Spider	*Water Spider*
Harmless to people	Lives in ponds
Flies at night to catch insects	Eats water bugs
Builds an orb web	Builds a bell-shaped web

FIGURE 4.6. T-chart of spiders.

What is important is that each writing suggestion ties directly to the text selection and the focused-upon strategy. When students are expected to write about their reading, they take time to reflect on their reading, thus enhancing comprehension. Furthermore, the writing expectation supports students in rereading text and, once again, comprehension is deepened.

Writing also serves as a foundation for conversation about text. ELLs often require more thinking time to organize their thoughts in English. Through writing, they can rehearse their ideas and are much more prepared to share with their teacher and other students.

A Few Final Ideas about Engagement

> Just as speakers of a first language must engage
> in frequent, meaning-centered interactions
> with speakers of that language, so should ELLs.
> BAUER AND MANYAK (2008, p. 176)

Teachers who are ranked highest in effectiveness in teaching ELLs have students who are focused on instructional events and engaged (Gersten et al., 2005). Student engagement is especially important, so that ELLs don't move to the background during instruction. Following are several strategies to support ELLs:

1. *Sharing by Partners*. Students are formed into partners by the teacher to make sure the partnerships are appropriate. When there is an expectation of a lengthy response to a question, students talk together. To ensure that both students share, the teacher can label each partner (e.g., as the one closest to the door, or by letters or numbers). While individual students can be called on to share with the whole class, it is often more engaging for students when the teacher shares what he or she heard while listening to student conversations.

2. *Numbered Heads*. Students, sitting at tables, are each given a number. Teachers give students opportunities to talk about a topic, respond to a question, and so on. Then the teacher calls out a number. The student with that number in each grouping shares with the class.

3. *Whole-Class Response*. Students have whiteboards or yes–no cards for instance. If the teacher asks a question requiring a yes–no response, the students all show their cards. If the response is more complicated, students can write on a whiteboard, then show it to the teacher.

4. *Written Response.* Students have sticky notes or paper on which they write a response to a prompt from the teacher. Once students have written, they share comments with other students or with their partner.

5. *Four Corners.* When using four corners, the teacher indicates where children should go by the prompt in each corner. Children might choose corners based on different information about an animal. Children who want to share information about habitat would go to one corner, about description to another, about food to yet another, and the final corner would be for predators.

6. *Cast Your Opinion.* In the cast your opinion strategy, students decide their viewpoints on an issue. They move to either side of the room and share with like-minded people to convince the remaining students of their opinion. For instance, after reading *Little Beauty* (Browne, 2008), students might be asked to decide whether they think it was right for Beauty to lie to the zookeepers. Students who said yes would meet to think about why it was okay to lie. Those who said no would engage in the same process. Once discussion was complete, students would support their opinions to try to convince other students to change their opinions.

In all of these strategies, students are given time to compose their ideas. Moreover, the teacher does not call on individual children. When a teacher does call on one student, the other students do not have to pay attention. They know they can sit back and take a break. However, if all children are always expected to respond, then they are more fully engaged with instruction throughout the day.

Engagement also occurs when students are not working directly with their teacher. When teachers plan for independent work, it is beneficial to ELLs if engagement is built into the independent tasks. For instance, teachers can have students read and then complete a graphic organizer together. Or students can read together to complete a poster that describes the main character of a story. Or they can read together to complete a list of the important aspects of the setting. When teachers plan this way, students are involved with reading and writing as they work independently, and they have opportunities for conversations to further extend their comprehension.

Throughout all of the discussion about comprehension in this chapter, engagement of students is key to its success. To support engagement strategies, students just need to know the routines and expectations for these conversational events. Once the routine is in place, students and teachers are free to focus on content-rich discussions.

ENGAGEMENT ACTIVITIES

1. After reading this chapter, choose a favorite book for read-aloud. How might a teacher plan for a more engaging reading of a text that supports ELLs?

2. After reading this chapter, think about opportunities for instruction in which students' conversations support comprehension. How might a teacher build on these conversations during literacy instruction?

3. After reading this chapter, explore a favorite genre. What do ELLs need to know about this genre to comprehend it successfully?

4. Numerous activities are described throughout this chapter. Although reading aloud to students is implicit in this chapter, there is no direct discussion about it. So when preparing to read aloud to ELLs, a few suggestions make this experience more meaningful.

   ■ Preview the text to determine whether there is content or words that are unfamiliar to students.

   ■ Determine whether any vocabulary words need to be shared before reading, or whether any content is difficult for students. Decide how you will share this information.

   ■ Share the cover of the story or informational text. Share important vocabulary, fewer than five words, and photos or realia to support comprehension.

   ■ Be prepared to provide on-the-spot descriptions of words that may not be familiar to students as you read. Words like *delicious* just need a quick definition—"Delicious means a food is yummy"—and back to the reading.

   ■ Have students engage in discussion with a partner about the cover illustration.

   ■ Share a few of their suggestions.

   ■ Read to students, stopping where it seems appropriate. Either conduct a think-aloud or have students talk with a partner about something specific. They might talk about:

      a. Do you think Little Beauty did a good or bad thing? Why do you think so?

      b. The setting is a place where the story happens. So what is the setting of this story?

      c. This book is about horses, so what did you just learn about them?

   ■ At the end of the book, students might chat about what they noticed in the book, or what they thought was important. The teacher can share these ideas.

   ■ Following this first reading, students might create a quick drawing, then write about it. This drawing could be focused on the topic, plot, characters, and so on.

■ The teacher should find time to have students reread this book. On the second read, students can ponder what they notice on this reading that they did not on the first. What do they notice about the way the author crafted the book? Numerous questions can serve to guide discussion on a second or subsequent read.

REFERENCES

August, D. (2003). *Supporting the development of English literacy in English language learners: Key issues and promising practices.* Baltimore: Center for Research on the Education of Students Placed at Risk.

Barone, D., & Taylor, J. (2006). *Improving students' writing, K–8.* Thousand Oaks, CA: Corwin Press.

Barone, D., & Xu, S. (2008). *Literacy instruction for English language learners pre-K–2.* New York: Guilford Press.

Bauer, E., & Manyak, P. (2008). Creating language-rich instruction for English-language learners. *Reading Teacher, 62,* 176–178.

Bear, D., Helman, L., Invernizzi, M., Templeton, S., & Johnston, F. (2007). *Words their way with English learners: Word study for spelling, phonics, and vocabulary instruction.* Upper Saddle River, NJ: Prentice-Hall.

Beck, I. (2006). *Making sense of phonics: The hows and whys.* New York: Guilford Press.

Browne, A. (2008). *Little Beauty.* Cambridge, MA: Candlewick Press.

Chiappe, P., Siegel, L., & Wade-Wooley, L. (2002). Linguistic diversity and the development of reading skills: A longitudinal study. *Scientific Studies of Reading, 6,* 369–400.

Cunningham, P. (1991). *Phonics they use: Words for reading and writing.* New York: HarperCollins.

Fitzgerald, J., & Graves, M. (2004). *Scaffolding reading experiences for English language learners.* Norwood, MA: Christopher-Gordon.

Gersten, R., Baker, S., Haager, D., & Graves, A. (2005). Exploring the role of teacher quality in predicting reading outcomes for first-grade English learners. *Remedial and Special Education, 26,* 197–206.

Goldenberg, C., & Patthey-Chavez, G. (1995). Discourse processes in instructional conversations: Interactions between teacher and transition readers. *Discourse Processes, 19*(1), 57–74.

Helman, L. (2004). Building on the sound system of Spanish: Insights from the alphabetic spelling of English-language learners. *Reading Teacher, 57,* 452–460.

Hickman, P., Pollard-Durodola, S., & Vaughn, S. (2004). Storybook reading: Improving vocabulary and comprehension for English-language learners. *Reading Teacher, 37,* 720–730.

Keene, E., & Zimmermann, S. (2007). *Mosaic of thought* (2nd ed.). Portsmouth, NH: Heinemann.

Lesaux, N., Koda, K., Siegel, L., & Shanahan, T. (2006). Development of literacy. In D. August & T. Shanahan (Eds.), *Developing literacy in second-language learners: Report of the National Literacy Panel on Language-Minority Children and Youth* (pp. 75–122). Mahwah, NJ: Erlbaum.

Manyak, P. (2007). A framework for robust literacy instruction for English learners. *Reading Teacher, 6,* 197–199.

McLaughlin, M., & Fisher, L. (2005). *Research-based reading lessons for K–3.* New York: Scholastic.

Ogle, D. (1986). KWL: A teaching model that develops active reading of expository text. *Reading Teacher 39,* 563–570.

Oladejo, J. (2006). Parents' attitudes towards bilingual education policy in Taiwan. *Bilingual Research Journal, 30,* 147–170.

Patent, H. (1997). *Flashy fantastic rain forest frogs.* New York: Scholastic.

Peregoy, S., & Boyle, O. (2000). English learners reading English: What we know, what we need to know. *Theory Into Practice, 39,* 237–247.

Peregoy, S., & Boyle, O. (2005). *Reading, writing, and learning in ESL* (4th ed.). New York: Allyn & Bacon.

Rodriguez-Galindo, A., & Wright, L. (2006, July). *English language learners: Teach them and they will learn.* Paper presented at the annual Reading First Conference, Reno, NV.

Smith, J., & Read, S. (2009). *Early literacy instruction: Teaching reading and writing in today's primary grades* (2nd ed.). Boston: Allyn & Bacon.

Stead, T. (2006). *Reality checks: Teaching reading comprehension with nonfiction K–5.* Portland, ME: Stenhouse.

CHAPTER 5

Principles for Writing Practices with Young ELLs

Sarah McCarthey and Xun Zheng

The chapter will:

1. Identify and elaborate on six principles for writing instruction for English language learners (ELLs) in grades K–8.
2. Describe research from the literature that supports each principle.
3. Provide examples from our own studies of ELLs.
4. Elaborate on ways teachers can use these principles to address the needs of ELLs.

As the immigrant population and the number of students who are learning English as a second language (ESL) increase, teachers are seeking ways to support students' literacy acquisition. While emphasis has been placed on scaffolding students' reading, less emphasis has been placed on English language learners' (ELLs) writing development. Our studies of English language learners learning to write (McCarthey, 2009; McCarthey, García, López-Velásquez, Lin, & Guo, 2004; McCarthey & García, 2005; McCarthey, Guo, & Cummins, 2005; Zheng, 2010) have demonstrated that ELLs need many opportunities to write in a variety of genres and settings to develop as writers. In addition, students need written and oral responses to improve their writing. Allowing students to use their native language to support writing and engaging in discussions about the similarities and differences between languages promote metalinguistic awareness. Below we elaborate on these key ideas.

Principle 1: Providing Students with Opportunities to Write about Their Experiences Enhances Their Understanding of Themselves in New Contexts

Allowing students to write about their lives assists them in expressing their struggles and their successes, and validates their experiences as ELLs. Students write about their lives when provided an opportunity. Representing their experiences helps students to understand who they are as writers and as immigrants to a new country.

Ivanič (1998) proposed a model of the "autobiographical self" that takes into account the writers' encounters with others' interests, ideas, opinions, sense of self-worth, and literacy practices. She suggested that writers draw on aspects of others' identities and are influenced by their life experiences. Both direct and indirect encounters with people influence texts. She drew from Vygotsky (1978) and Bakhtin (1981, 1986) to suggest that "who we are" is a consequence of social class, ethnicity, gender, physical abilities, and the ways these are constructed within the sociocultural contexts in which we live. In our (McCarthey & García, 2005) study of ELLs' writing development, we found that students were willing to write about their life experiences in both their countries of origin and the United States, providing a picture of their developing identities. In his ESL writing journal, Carlos,[1] a fifth-grade ELL, wrote the following:

> I dislike saying goodbye to my family and friends in Nicaragua. Because is very hard. I been with them since I was a little kid. I don't like saing good-bye because is very hard for me to say goodbye to my best friends and they are: Carlos, Jean Carlos, Ariel, and Kevin. I will miss my friend because I been with them since I was three year old and this are my special friends: Eduardo, Sergio and Ana Laura.

In his text, Carlos reveals his identity as an ELL separated from friends and family in Nicaragua. Carlos embodies much of what Ivanič (1998) is suggesting—that writing is far from neutral, that who we are affects everything we write, and we are continually in the process of negotiating our past experiences within our new contexts.

Researchers have found that second-language learners draw upon linguistic, textual, and cultural resources to create themselves through writing (Vollmer, 2002). Shen (1989) found a shift in her identity as a writer between writing in English and in Chinese, and saw the emergence of two kinds of identity—ideological (social values from the Chinese culture) and logical (organization of writing drawn from both cultures). Although she wrote in English for her career, rather than eliminate her

Chinese identity, she adopted both identities and used them interchangeably. Jo (2001) found in her study that Korean American college students struggled with learning "standard" forms of Korean but were able to cross boundaries, constructing new expressions and hybrid identities.

Several studies have suggested that ELLs are in the process of constructing hybrid identities as they negotiate their new linguistic and cultural environments. For example, in a study of four bilingual elementary classrooms, Jiménez (2000) found that students experienced a blending of identities as they straddled two cultures and languages. Students saw literacy as a language-specific activity as they engaged in teaching younger siblings, translating for the family, and acting as "brokers" in Spanish and English. A young Latina interwove her home, school, and peer language practices to serve a variety of purposes in her first-/second-grade classroom, indicating an ability to develop a hybrid identity (Solsken, Willett, & Wilson-Keenan, 2000). Manyak (2001) found that primary-grade Spanish-speaking students successfully blended English and Spanish with home and school knowledge while engaged in producing "The Daily News," a class literacy project that involved sharing news from the students' lives in oral and written form. Students increasingly assumed roles and responsibilities that allowed them to take different positions, develop literacy practices, and establish bilingualism as an important ability and marker of academic competence. Many of these researchers agree that valuing hybridity in students' texts can create opportunities for students from diverse backgrounds to share aspects of their cultures and communities.

The ELLs in our study (McCarthey & García, 2005) wrote about topics of interest to them, as well as some of the challenges they had in adapting to U.S. culture. They often focused on their families, friends, home countries, and aspects of their culture when provided opportunities to write in their journals. For example, Hui Tzu not only related details of her daily life, but she began to evaluate her experiences within the text:

> Jan-1 is New Year day. I'm very happy. That evening, I ate a chicken. It's very good. And I ate some dry seaweeds. I like dry seaweeds.
> Night, I go to bed. I dream a sonwman play with me. I like my mother cooked chicken and seaweeds.

In her brief text, Hui Tzu incorporated aspects of her Chinese culture, eating seaweed, but she also wrote about a new aspect in her life, encountering snow and dreaming of snowmen. The next year, when she was in a middle school ESL class, Hui Tzu wrote about her mother in the following way:

> My mother is a very good mom. She always cooks for my dad and me.
> On one hand, she's a good mother, on the other hand she's a good
> wife. She always learn how to cook some food that she doesn't know.
> She study very hard, too. When she do her homework, she always let
> my dad check her spelling. She's a great mom.

Hui Tzu's texts show her admiration for her mother, providing insights about the value of hard work. She also reveals her family's literacy practices: Her mother had been a university professor in China and was now studying at a community college.

As students make the move from their home country to the United States, they often experience shifts in their identities. Igoa (1995) described stages that many immigrant children experience as they adjust to their new cultures in the United States. These include the silent stage and stages of uprooting, including mixed emotions, culture shock, and the pressure to *assimilate* (giving up values to become part of the mainstream) or *acculturate* (becoming part of the mainstream without having to give up cherished values). Children often experience isolation from their current surroundings, loneliness as a result of not having others who share their experiences, and exhaustion from immersion in a new language they do not understand. Several of the ELLs in our study (McCarthey & García, 2005) expressed their loneliness by writing about missing their friends in their home countries.

> (Yi Lin)
>
> In China I have many best friends. Sometimes I have secret I will tell
> my firend. I wish some day I sit with them and wach stars. Now I am
> in USA. I miss my friends. I want back to China a play with them. I can
> go to school in China.

> (Hui Tzu)
>
> Every night, on my bed, I always think about my best friends (In
> China). I miss them very much. Maybe sometimes I forgot them, but
> now I miss them. Sometimes I dreamed I play with them, study with
> them. In China, sometimes I fight with them, but now I know it's all my
> fault. I MISS THEM!!!!

A sense of loneliness and isolation, similar to what Igoa (1995) found, is expressed in the students' texts as they struggle to locate themselves in their new schools, communities, and cultures. Writing about their home countries helps students to mitigate their loneliness; several students combine their personal experiences with descriptions of the country in their writing. In the following example, the students' ESL teacher provided the prompt of "My Country" for students. Yi Lin combined her experiences as a student in China with a description of the country in a response to the prompt "My Country."

My Country

Almost everybody in the world have their own country every country have their own religen. Today, I'm going to talk about my country which in China. When I was in China I study very hard and sometimes I have to do homework to 2:AM then I don't even have time to eat dinner, And every time when I get home I quickly took my homework out and start to do it. Well, it doesn't matter sometimes I really like it. My country China have a lot of big mall. I love to go to all the malls. I love my country because is my country.

Students often highlighted the positive aspects of their home countries, such as the history, natural wonders, or memorable places (e.g., "big malls"). However, occasionally students wrote about their lives in previous countries as being less desirable than their current situations. In response to the prompt "T = Title. If you had a title instead of a name, what would it be?" Manuel wrote the following:

I would chose the boy that change his life for a title to my name because I was poor I lived in Peru. In Peru it was dangerous it was a city with a lot of roberts [robbers]. Here in [names town] is a town calm. There might be a little danger but is not compair to Peru.

Manuel implied that he moved from a more dangerous setting to a safe town in the United States. He also expressed an understanding that he had fewer economic opportunities in Peru than in the United States.

Students' writing often reflects their emerging identities as visitors or immigrants in a new country. For example, students wrote about cultural experiences from both U.S. and home cultures. They often wrote about enjoying American holidays and experiences. Halloween, Thanksgiving, and Valentine's Day (holidays that most of these students did not celebrate in their home countries) were topics of great interest. Students also inserted aspects of their culture that expressed some cultural identity. Here is an excerpt from Manuel's piece about his favorite holiday:

My favory holiday is Christmas because we share our food with our families. We get presents and god was born in that time. The houses get all cute, decorate, and at night they turn the light to decorated. We celebrate Christmas by putting up a Christmas tree and buy presents eat Pannetone. Pannetone is like a bread. We call some friends over to my house and celebrate with us.

Manuel described his family's experiences during Christmas but also seemed to direct his comments to an audience by informing us about *pannetone*. Students drew on their own experiences in their narratives, and positioned themselves as knowledgeable about their own cultures.

The texts just presented demonstrate how students represent features of their identities within their texts. Their texts express a range of feelings, from attachment to their friends and home countries to being able to articulate some of the differences between their cultures and U.S. customs. Students took advantage of opportunities to write about their identities, challenges, and interests when teachers provided the opportunities. Thus, we suggest that teachers provide regular opportunities for students to select their own topics and write about their experiences. Although many students initiate these opportunities, some ELLs may need more encouragement from teachers or peers to write about their lives. This is a significant change for many students who may not have been encouraged to write about their experiences in their previous classroom settings. For example, many students from Chinese cultures were not encouraged to write in first person; in their previous settings, teachers determined topics and encouraged students to write expository texts about nature (McCarthey, Guo, & Cummins, 2005). Teachers need to be familiar with the norms of students' cultures as they encourage students to write from their own experiences.

Principle 2: Providing Students with Opportunities to Keep Open-Ended Journals Allows Them to Develop Critical Awareness of Who They Are

Keeping journals can be the first step to students' development of critical awareness of identity (Ivanič, 1998). By keeping journals with dates, students and the teacher can see the progress they have made in developing their English writing skills, as well as gaining an understanding of how students position themselves in relation to audience and peers.

Bomer and Laman (2004) focused on two primary-grade students' spontaneous talk during writing. They found that students positioned themselves in multiple ways through their utterances and body language. Students drew upon cultural resources, such as home, school, and the media, to assign roles and story lines to themselves and to each other. In work in college classrooms with second-language learners, researchers found that writers positioned themselves in multiple ways: (1) demonstrating their interests through topics, stances, and knowledge, (2) conveying a sense of their own authority and relationship with reader, and (3) resisting or adopting features of a particular genre (Ivanič & Camps, 2001).

Our examination of students' texts revealed students' stances toward their native language and English, and aspects of their social class and political views. Clearly, one of the biggest challenges for these students is learning English. Not surprisingly, some students wrote about this topic, especially when they felt successful:

(Hui Tzu)

May 1, 2002

I'm so happy. Because my English is getting better better! When I came to United Stats, my English is so poor, I can't even speak. But now, I love to speak English and speak to teachers. When I came to United Stats, I was so shy, when teacher speak to me.

But I really need to study harder and harder.

Sometimes, I got a super Citizen, I'm really happy. But sometime I got a mistake, I'm really unhappy.

Anyways, I LOVE TO SPEAK English!!!!

In this text, Hui Tzu positions herself as a person who has been successful at learning English. She emphasizes her own efforts, and her text reflects how important success in school is to her self-esteem.

Luis showed sensitivity to issues of poverty when he referred to his home country of Mexico. Luis wrote the following in response to the prompt "M for magician: If you were a magician, what would you do?":

I want be an astarnot [astronaut] only for a little years and when I finish the work I going to try to buy a Lamborghini Diablo S. And with the other money I want to make a hospital for poor people. When I finish the hospital I going to help my friends.

I would change myselve into a billionaire and give 1 billion dollars to ophains [orphans] in Mexico. Because people there are so poor I will also give 1 thousand dollars to [?] hospitals in Mexico.

While Luis writes about the things he would like for himself, both career goals and acquiring symbols of wealth, he also shows an awareness of the poverty in his own country. He positions himself as a person who would like to help make conditions better, especially through health care.

Paul took a political stance in response to the prompt "N (noise): What kind of noises bother you most? What kind of noises do you enjoy?" He wrote:

I really hate the noises that are the ones you make when people are picking president. They all say, "Please vote for me" with all those bus [meaning unclear] they are just so loud. I bet they just want to be rich and president are all so rich.

Paul took the stance of a person who is dissatisfied with the noise caused by advertising. Yet he also seemed to position himself as a working-class student who views presidents as having money and power. His disapproval of wealthy people and people who hold political offices comes through in his text.

In contrast, Yi Lin expresses gratitude for a Chinese leader who was opening up her country. Yi Lin wrote in response to the prompt, "What are you most thankful for today?":

1/11/02

Chinese president
     If you ask me who I'm thank for today, I will say I thank for xiao ping deng because if China deosn't have him. Now China maybe so bad. But when he comes up China opened and China can learn the things from other Country. So that why I really thank him for.

Yi Lin's text reflects a belief that China has become more democratic under this leadership, and she shows an appreciation for the changes. Her texts, like many of the students' writing, suggest that ELLs are interested in taking political stances and communicating their understandings when provided with opportunities.

In our study, students experienced a wide variety of writing topics, genres, and types of instruction as the result of being in native language, all-English, and ESL classes (McCarthey et al., 2004). Some students had two different ESL teachers, one who focused more on a structured approach to writing, and another who emphasized more integration of writing into other subjects. While some teachers allowed students to choose genres and topics for their journal entries, others provided prompts. Given these different settings, almost all students preferred open-ended, first-person writing assignments over other genres and over teacher prompts. With the exception of Chun Ming, who chose to write summaries of books and television shows such as the *Three Stooges*, most students preferred to write first-person narratives without prompts. For example, Manuel said:

[a prompt] is a question you have to answer. I prefer to think about something. For example, sometimes I make up a story or I write whatever I want and I think about things, for example, about what I did over the weekend.

Luis found that his open-ended ESL journal allowed him to write more about himself in a short period of time; he said, "Time goes by fast because I am expressing myself, time goes by fast." Yi Lin also preferred selecting her own topic, without a prompt to assigned topics: "I like free writing. . . . I like to write something I like such as skiing."

The students in the study preferred "free writing" to responding to a prompt. They believed that they had more opportunities to write about topics of importance to them and to engage fully in the writing tasks when they had more choices. Journal writing provided students with opportunities to express who they are through their writing. Many of them took advantage of this genre to write about topics of personal interest and to explore their identities. Visiting museums in large cities or going to amusement parks was often highlighted in students' journals. Students also wrote about everyday activities they enjoyed, such as playing soccer, going to the park with their parents, going to Meijer's [a store], spending the night with friends, or playing computer games. These activities also provide a window into how the students were becoming acculturated into the United States.

Because our data suggest that students prefer open-ended assignments in which they choose their topics, we recommend that students have many opportunities for generating ideas and writing about experiences that interest them. Teachers may provide students with journals in which they generate their own topics and write about personal experiences. If a student has difficulty thinking of a topic, then the teacher might provide ideas or even prompts. However, we do not suggest that personal, open-ended writing is the only type of writing ELLs should do; rather, we recommend that ELLs have opportunities to write in a variety of genres throughout the school day.

Principle 3: Opportunities to Write in Multiple Genres across the School Day Are Key to Enhancing Students' Development as Writers

While the personal narrative can facilitate expression of students' identities, it is not the only genre in which this is possible. For example, students reveal who they are within all of their writing, because they take positions in relation to texts, readers, and the larger social context. Nieto (2002) suggests that students need opportunities to write essays in which they take positions about social and political issues, and shed light on issues that affect their everyday lives. Additionally, because of the focus on specific genres in state writing tests (Hillocks, 2002), students need to become successful in a variety of genres that can be made relevant to their lives.

Comber, Thomson, and Wells (2001) demonstrated that young writers are able to develop critical literacies through writing in various genres. In a second-/third-grade class of students from mostly socioeconomically disadvantaged families, students discussed, drew and wrote about an urban renewal project in their neighborhoods. Not only did the young authors extend their understanding of the city and their own place in the world, but they expressed their perspectives to a particular audience. Bomer and Bomer (2001) documented students' efforts to be engaged in their communities through their social action projects.

ELLs, although limited in English proficiency, can still become advocates for social changes given adequate opportunities and guidance. Coady and Escamilla (2005), in a study of fourth-/fifth-grade Mexican descendants in a transitional bilingual education program in Colorado, showed that teachers' assessment of writing focused mainly on the development of students' English-language literacy. However, the researchers found that the "problematic" writings of those students were actually very rich in content and details, and full of descriptions of their social lives. Instead of insisting on the original writing prompt "My best birthday ever," the researchers gave students another topic, "If I could be someone else for a day," to write in either English or Spanish according to their English proficiency. One student expressed his understanding of social systems and democracies through writing about being a king; another wrote about being a principal, by incorporating the school experience of management, discipline, and students' concerns. Other students' writings revealed concerns about poverty, freedom, and racial discrimination. These students were often regarded as poor writers because of their grammatical mistakes and Spanish-like spelling. However, if one looked deeper into the content, they revealed themselves as members of the society and expressed their views on various social realities. Coady and Escamilla promoted the notion of *transfer of self*, by which they meant a "transfer of self (that) encompassed both students' identities and life experiences" (p. 468) and highlighted students' identities as bilingual or multilingual.

Writing in a variety of genres also provides ELLs with many ways to explore writing and experience being writers. In the third-grade ESL class that Zheng (2010) observed, students had many different writing practices for a single project, the plant project. For instance, after reading books about plants, children used their new vocabulary to summarize the characteristics of plants. Once they had planted their own seeds, they recorded plant growth by making charts and giving descriptions the way that scientists record their observations. Students tasted the plants they had in everyday life and wrote about their favorite foods. Then they composed individual poems about the plants they grew and shared them with their peers. Through all these writing activities, students were able to practice different genres of writing, become familiar with the common vocabulary in plant science, and gain experience as young writers and scientists.

Donovan and Smolkin (2006) point out that early and continual experience with multiple genres can support a foundation for children's understanding of these genres in their later literacy lives. Providing primary-grade ELLs with many writing opportunities for different purposes is also beneficial. For example, many Chinese kindergartners in the Zheng (2010) study played with words for multiple purposes, such as inventing words that reflected the class content. They wrote letters to their friends about occurrences in their lives and created thank-you letters to class guests. These activities helped students gain an initial understanding of genres and gradually to build awareness of audience and purposes for writing.

Access to multiple genres, as well as instruction in different genres, helps both young students and older ELL writers in becoming successful writers. Since many state writing tests require students to write in a specific genre to a prompt, some opportunities to write in those genres are warranted (see Illinois Standards Achievement Test, 2009). However, we maintain that providing many opportunities to write for real audiences and purposes is the most important goal; occasional practice for state writing tests can support these overall goals of understanding different genres while preparing students for the reality of the tests.

Principle 4: Responding to Students' Writing Is Essential for Improving Their Writing and Validating Their Development

Responding to students' writing can be one of the most powerful ways to validate students. The variety of forms of responses that may occur in classrooms includes responding with comments on students' papers or conducting teacher–student conferences. Feedback or response can effectively engage the writer and provide the sense that the teacher is responding to an individual rather than to a script (Hyland & Hyland, 2006), and help the student understand that his or her writing has purpose and an audience (Calkins, 1986).

Written feedback is a common practice for teachers working with ELLs. Ferris (2003) created a list of types of helpful teacher feedback for students, including requesting more information, making suggestions, giving information, providing encouraging feedback, and commenting on grammar and mechanics. Though different researchers have produced different categories, they agree that teachers' feedback should not be limited to grammar but should instead offer more information about content to students. Students' responses to feedback may vary. In Hyland's (1998) study of college ELLs, students had distinctive responses to teachers' written feedback. For some, teachers' positive feedback served as a reminder to make more and better revisions. However, others interpreted positive comments as useless for their further development in writing. Such dilemmas need genuine dialogue between teacher and students to clarify the expectations of both sides, as well as interpretation of the comments within the frame of the teachers' intentions. In the McCarthey et al. study (2004), some teachers wrote questions or comments in students' journals. Occasionally, students did not understand the purpose of the comments and did not know whether they were expected to respond; this can be attributed to some cultural differences in the ways that students had been schooled in their former countries. However, even when students are writing in their native language, or when their English is difficult to decipher, it is worth the effort for teachers to talk to students about their writing. Once ELLs understand that the teacher is honestly interested in what they have to say, the process of engaging in dialogue can be rewarding for the teacher, as well as the students.

In the fourth-/fifth-grade ESL class that Zheng (2007) observed, written remarks were placed on the margin of students' writings. Instead of focusing on grammatical mistakes, the teacher emphasized the story line and the flow of ideas. These remarks helped her students to rethink their writings in a more critical manner. The teacher saw feedback as a way to scaffold students' writing development and to interact with students in a genuine manner. Many young authors welcomed comments that showed them where to improve. However, a student also expressed the concern that she did not want to confront the teacher:

> "You know, in Chinese culture, especially in my own family, it would be very rude to confront the teacher or the parents. I guess it is the cultural reason that I often don't want to dispute Mrs. Rose even though I know she would accept my suggestions."

Students also showed their emotional sides when looking at the comments on their writing:

"I almost felt like crying each time I saw those comments on my paper. They asked me to make huge changes to my original work. I think I have made great efforts, but still, every time I talked with the teacher, I have to change."

Comments such as these suggest that teachers and students sometimes misunderstand one another, or that students resist revising a text they have already spent a significant amount of time creating. Many students regard their ESL class as the only opportunity to practice writing and hear from the teacher about their writing; thus, it is particularly important to provide students with meaningful responses. Keeping in mind that students may not understand why they are being asked to revise their work is also important for teachers to consider as they write their comments.

Teacher–student conferences are another form of response that has an impact on students' writing development. Considerable research has been conducted about college-level ELLs. Patthey-Chavez and Ferris (1997), in their research on the writing conferences with international college students, found that different teachers had different approaches toward strong writers and weak writers, and students' cultural backgrounds affected interactions. It is relevant for elementary teachers to understand that while writing conferences can support students' writing, teachers' understanding of differences in students' cultural backgrounds is essential for effective conferences. In the fourth-/fifth-grade ESL class that Zheng (2007) researched, Mrs. Rose encouraged students to become aware of the importance of the writing process through writing conferences in which she offered oral feedback. During the conferences, the teacher used the strategies of negotiating with students, guiding them with more direct feedback, and asking for assistance from other adult helpers, who spoke the students' native language, to support students' writing skills.

Spontaneous responses to primary-grade ELLs' writing are especially valuable. Zheng's study (2010) of kindergarten ELLs showed that short teacher–student writing conferences often occurred when kindergartners started to think about their stories. As students planned their stories, they wrote a few letters or words down on the paper. The ESL teacher asked each writer what he or she was thinking and guided the student to sound the words out; students wrote even more than they had planned initially due to the teacher's immediate response and encouragement.

Both research and practice have demonstrated that it is important to respond to students' writings. By getting feedback, students become more aware of their audience and the expectations of the readers. ELLs learn writing through a gradual process in which both oral and written feedback play essential roles. At the same time, misunderstandings can occur between teacher and students. Whereas some of these misunderstandings come from the lack of effective dialogue between them, while others might arise due to different cultural expectations. These misunderstandings can be solved by open conversations between teachers and ELLs to clarify the purpose of revision and the process of drafting, revising, and editing for specific audiences.

Principle 5: Allowing Students to Write in Their Native Language Builds Successful English Writers

Research has indicated that students are more successful in developing literacy in a second language when they have a strong foundation in their first language (García, 2000). For example, Carlisle and Beeman (2000) found that Spanish-speaking students instructed in Spanish before English wrote more complex sentences than did students who did not receive this instruction. Edelsky (1982) found that Spanish-speaking students could transfer what they knew about writing from their first language into their second. The students in McCarthey et al.'s (2004) study enjoyed writing in their first language when allowed and were able to transfer their knowledge of writing in Spanish or Chinese to their English writing. In Buckwalter and Lo's (2002) study, the 5-year-old Mandarin-speaking child was able to transfer the concept of print from Chinese to English. Olsen (1999) found that students relied on their first language, using compensatory strategies, as they learned English as a foreign language. Woodall's (2002) study of 28 adult ELLs showed that writers who were less proficient in their second language (L2) might switch more often to their first language (L1) than did proficient learners. Unlike many studies that showed a decrease of L1 use as students' L2 proficiency increased, Wang (2003) discovered that the adult ELLs did not reduce their cross-language transfer when they developed English proficiency. While these studies show different findings about students' reliance on their first language, they demonstrate that it is important to consider the role of students' native language. Furthermore, it is important to recognize which aspects of children's writing might transfer between languages. Durgunoglu (2002) synthesized a group of research studies examining what aspects children may use for cross-linguistic transfer in literacy learning. One important transfer in writing, as Durgunoglu pointed out, is the knowledge of writing conventions and story grammar. For instance, Spanish- and English-speaking children from fourth grade were asked to write stories in Spanish and in

English based on two respective pictures. Results showed that children who produced rich, coherent story lines were able to do so in both languages; they were able to add details to the characters in the pictures, as well as give them names, conversation, and motivation.

In a study of U.S. college students in a paired writing group, De Guerrero and Villamil (2000) scrutinized the writing of two male ESL learners who spoke Spanish as their native language. They participated in revision sessions in which one was the reader and the other, the writer. L1 use in discussing writing helped each participant to comprehend more deeply the intentions of the other. In addition, the interaction between the two participants was built upon *intersubjectivity*; that is, each was willing to consider suggestions from the other and scaffolding for the partner to increase understanding and improve writing. Both the reader and the writer tried to negotiate their roles during the conversation by giving suggestions, scaffolding, and telling jokes. L1 use stimulates students' reflection, reconsideration, and restructuring of English during revision.

The findings of De Guerrero and Vallamil (2000) are inspiring for writing instruction in K–12 schools. While many people hold the viewpoint that native language may be a barrier for ELLs to learn English, much research has disputed this assumption. Based on her research of Spanish and Hmong students, Reyes (1992) challenged educators' assumptions, such as "Success comes from the immersion of linguistic minorities in English only class" (p. 433), "One size fits all" (p. 435), and "Error correction in writing process hampers learning" (p. 438). She noted that only by recognizing and relating to ELLs' linguistic and cultural backgrounds could teachers authentically improve instruction and help them succeed.

Understanding the benefits of transfer between two languages may help teachers to create more opportunities for ELLs to use their L1 knowledge to assist in developing their L2. Many students in the McCarthey et al. (2004) study used their L1 in the ESL classrooms at the beginning stage of their English learning. For example, the Chinese child Hui Tzu wrote Chinese in her ESL journal. She recorded her feelings about a particular day and how she spent her first Thanksgiving holiday in the United States. She was quite aware of the audience for her writings as well: To help her ESL teacher to understand the meanings, she drew pictures above the entries and used imagery for many words.

Similar features can be found in Zheng's recent study on elementary ELLs. Mei, a Chinese girl who recently came to America with her mother, was not yet able to write in English in her journal. The ESL teacher allowed both languages in class (see Figure 5.1) and encouraged her to use Chinese during the writing process of drafting and revising.

PLANT VOCABULARY

Plant 植物 Plant are living things.
Leaves 叶子 In the fall, leaves are falling.
Leaf 叶子 I find a beautiful red leaf.
Stem 茎 sunflower has a long stem.
Flower 花 Rose is a flower.
tree 树 Birds live on the tree.
Roots 根 Roots help plant get ...

FIGURE 5.1. Mei's (third grade) ESL note.

In the project where students learned about the characteristics of plants, Mei put the Chinese translation right beside her English words. The Chinese translations helped her not only to memorize English meanings but also to connect her previous knowledge about plants to the current class content. With encouragement from her ESL teacher, Mei also wrote a poem in Chinese next to the picture of her plant (see Figure 5.2).

Zheng (2010) found that ELLs as young as kindergartners could use their native language in their texts. Unlike third graders who were already literate in their native language, the 5- and 6-year-olds were beginning literacy learners in both languages. However, they were confident enough to try whatever they had learned in Chinese in their English writing. For instance, Elaine, a 5-year-old girl from China, wrote Chinese characters in her ESL journal (see Figure 5.3).

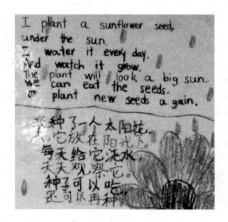

FIGURE 5.2. Mei's plant poem.

Using their L1 can also help ELL students to understand writing instruction and to help each other in literacy learning. In research focused on the writing activities in ESL classrooms, Zheng (2007) found that students used both languages to understand the school context and comprehend their identities in two different cultures. In the fourth- and fifth-grade classes, some Mandarin-speaking students were put in the same group. They spoke Chinese to help each other understand classroom instructions and writing tasks. In their writing, students used English or code-switched in the rest of their conversation for academic purposes. By using both languages, students were able to negotiate among audiences, contexts, and purposes of writing.

These examples show that by using their L1, students may have better understandings of the new literacy environments in the United States. Teachers need to value the native languages of ELLs and encourage them to use their L1 in English writing practices, because their native language is not only part of students' culture and social worlds, but it also has cognitive benefits. Samway (2006) claimed that it was an asset for ELLs to be taught in their native language. However, many teachers who have ELLs in their classes do not speak the same L1 as their students. Awareness that children need to use their L1 to understand English and the new context can help teachers who do not speak the native language of their students to support students' developmental stages in English. For students with no writing experience in their L1, teachers may need to consider encouraging the concept of print, while instructing students who have more experience with writing about the differences between languages. By being in contact with parents or the community, students' teachers may obtain important information regarding children's language backgrounds and writing stages.

The writers in the research of Brock, McVee, and Shojgreen-Downer (1998), Maguire and Graves (2001), Manyak (2001), and Moll,

FIGURE 5.3. Elaine's ESL journal.

Sáez, and Dworin (2001) all enjoyed using their native languages and transferred the knowledge of writing from one language to another. Employing their L1 was a way of participating in the social context of writing that helped them to make connections between their previous and current experiences. While some of the ELLs in McCarthey and García's (2005) study had parents or grandparents as audiences for their writing, students did not have an audience for their native language school writing in their ESL or all-English classes. When students have native language–speaking students in the same school, if not in the same classroom, teachers can identify students of the same linguistic background and have them serve as audiences for one another. Having peer audiences for their native language may keep students from experiencing total loss of their native language and show them that teachers value their linguistic abilities.

Principle 6: Talking to Children about Similarities and Differences between Languages Facilitates Metalinguistic Awareness

The students in the McCarthey et al. (2004) study recognized differences between their native language and English, and noted that there are different styles of writing in different languages. By asking students about the differences and similarities they see between their native language and English, teachers can facilitate cross-linguistic transfer and aid students in acquiring biliteracy (García, 2000).

Metalinguistic awareness (MA) is a term used to explain the ability to analyze language as an object, process, or system; it is most often applied to bilingual learners' literacy development (Bialystok, 2007). Cazden (1974) used the term to explain the transfer of linguistic knowledge and skills across languages. Mora (2008) argued that MA is helpful in learning a new language because it allows learners to monitor their production of correct forms. Research has shown MA can enhance bilingualism because of its positive effects on language ability and literacy skills.

Although code switching and translation are examples of bilinguals' MA, McCarthey et al. (2004) also found that children as young as fourth and fifth grade demonstrate MA through articulation of their writing processes. They asked Chinese and Spanish students to explain what language they preferred to write in and why, at different points during the 2-year study. Students demonstrated their awareness of the differences between languages as they discussed the topics they selected in each language, the differences between symbol systems, and the different strategies they used for each language. For example, one of the Mandarin speakers, Wen Hsien, said:

"Writing in Chinese is more difficult, because writing in Chinese has more requirements. You need to write person, thing, objects, scene, etc. I think writing about a thing is very difficult because you need to describe it very clearly. Writing in English here is easier, because the topics I write are easier. For example, making up a story based on the pictures given. This kind of story writing is easier."

Yi Lin, who was an average writer in both Chinese and English, noted that it was important to memorize phrases and idioms to be a good writer in Chinese; however, it was not necessary to memorize phrases for writing in English. Although a beginning Chinese writer and a competent English writer, Susie was able to express the differences in languages:

"And I like English because it's a lot easier, not like Chinese has so much words, and you have to remember so much words, like a zillion or something. But in English you only need to remember how to spell it."

While she did not say specifically that Chinese used characters, whereas English was an alphabetic language, Susie recognized that the languages differed and that she had to use different strategies to write in each language.

Chun Ming, an excellent writer in Chinese who was rapidly increasing his English skills, found that a writer in any language has to be clear about what he wants to say:

"Chinese writing is more difficult, because there are lots of phrases and vocabulary in Chinese. As for English, as long as you remember more words, writing also becomes easier. . . . A good writer states clearly what he attempts to write, and his writing always can connect with the topic. If you are clear about what you write, you know what conclusion you should make."

Later on, Chun Ming had developed an even more sophisticated view of the similarities and differences between writing Chinese and English:

"For Chinese, if you want to write, your level has to be high. As for English, as you learn some new words, you can write composition. When you learn some words, you can use them. For Chinese, some you still don't know their meanings, don't know how to use them. . . . English you write a little you finish it. Use a little English, write a few English words. But you have to write a lot of Chinese words about some major contents. If you write in English, it's shorter."

He knew that idioms were valued in Chinese and stated:

> "If you read the story about the words of wisdom, [you can] write some sentences, such as 'Don't catch the chicken until they are hatched,' like these."

He had an emerging understanding of the challenges in translation between the two languages: "Sometimes, one (English) word can be translated into four Chinese characters."

Several researchers have identified the similarities and differences between English and Spanish orthography (Mora, 2008). Comparing the alphabetic principle, spelling, and print conventions of both languages, Mora argues that bilingual readers can activate and apply the skill from one language to another once they have acquired MA. McCarthey et al. (2004) found that many of the Spanish-speaking students focused on accents in Spanish as a difference in the two languages; their Spanish teacher spent a great deal of instructional time teaching them where to put the accents, and students found this to be challenging. Ramón, for example, said that he tried "to get the accents right" and believed he could learn where the accent goes by writing the words repeatedly.

Reflections and Future Directions

The six principles presented are key to assisting ELLs develop their writing skills. By facilitating students' writing about their own experiences, keeping daily journals, and writing across the school day in multiple genres, teachers can come to understand ELLs' identities as writers and gain a deeper knowledge of students' backgrounds and cultures. Responding to students' writing both orally and through written comments can increase communication between teacher and students and help ELLs to become better writers. Understanding the role of the native language in learning English and assisting students in becoming aware of the similarities and differences between their native language and English help teachers to provide meaningful writing opportunities. Applying the six principles to writing instruction can provide opportunities for ELLs to become not only better writers but also bilingual–biliterate–bicultural learners.

While these six principles might provide a guide for teaching writing to ELLs, they are not exhaustive; other principles may arise as researchers and teachers work together to address the needs of these students. Each teacher and each group of students is unique, with its own successes and failures in teaching writing to ELLs, and these stories can continue to inform us about strategies for teaching them. More research is still needed to document students' learning and the most effective practices for teaching ELLs. For example, research is needed to understand young ELLs' perceptions of writing in both English and their native language, their use of technology for writing, and conditions that support students' maintenance of their native language. Research can contribute to the efforts of teachers, parents, schools, and policymakers to support English language writers.

Teaching writing has often been regarded as the most difficult aspect of literacy instruction. For ELLs, expressing ideas in a new language is even more challenging. Teaching writing is much more than having students memorize all the English words they did not know before; it involves scaffolding to help them to express themselves, to describe their lives, and to record their knowledge. To support students' writing, teachers need to understand the uniqueness of ELLs' language background and the challenges of learning a new language at the same time they are communicating their expectations for students' writing. The following ideas can help to deepen teachers' understanding of ELLs and provide opportunities to implement strategies for teaching writing to them.

ENGAGEMENT ACTIVITIES

1. Write about your experiences in teaching writing to ELLs. What stories do you have? Share both your successes and failures.

2. Keep an open-ended journal documenting your interactions with ELLs for a week, and reflect on your experiences at the end of the week. What patterns did you notice? How might you use those reflections to enhance students' writing?

3. With another teacher as a partner, share one piece of writing. Then conduct a conference with the writer, indicating the strengths of the piece as well as noting places for improvement. Switch roles, giving each person a chance to be both author and respondent. Use a digital camera to record the conferences. Watch the clips together and identify the strengths and weaknesses in the conference regarding expectations, tone, quality of responses, and so forth.

4. List several genres in which your students have written and think about other genres to include in your curriculum. Keep a record of the writing activities across the school day, and add a writing activity to one subject in which you have not generally used writing.

5. During parent–teacher conferences or other opportunities for discussions with parents, ask parents about their children's language backgrounds. Provide ideas

to parents about how to build a rich home literacy environment to maintain students' native languages. For example, parents might bring books or other literacy materials from their home countries; children can write letters or use e-mail to correspond with relatives and friends in their countries of origin; or parents can obtain native language materials from the Web or local sites to encourage students to value their native language.

6. Meet with a group of teachers to create lesson plans for incorporating students' native languages into instruction.

NOTE

1. All students' writing has been typed from the original; no corrections have been made to spelling, grammar, or punctuation. All students' names are pseudonyms.

REFERENCES

Bakhtin, M. (1981). *The dialogic imagination*. Austin: University of Texas Press.

Bakhtin, M. (1986). *Speech genres and other late essays* (V. W. McGee, Trans.; C. Emerson & M. Holquist, Eds.). Austin: University of Texas Press.

Bialystok, E. (2007). Acquisition of literacy in bilingual children: A framework for research. *Language Learning, 57*(1), 45–77.

Bomer, R., & Bomer, K. (2001). *For a better world: Reading and writing for social action*. Portsmouth, NH: Heinemann.

Bomer, R., & Laman, T. (2004). Positioning in a primary writing workshop: Joint action in the discursive production of writing subjects. *Research in the Teaching of English, 38*(4), 420–462.

Brock, C., McVee, M., & Shojgreen-Downer, A. (1998). *No habla Ingles*: Exploring a bilingual child's literacy learning opportunities in a predominantly English-speaking classroom. *Bilingual Research Journal, 22*(2–4), 175–200.

Buckwalter, J., & Lo, Y. (2002). Emergent biliteracy in Chinese and English. *Journal of Second Language Writing, 11*(4), 269–293.

Calkins, L. M. (1986). *The art of teaching writing*. Portsmouth, NH: Heinemann.

Carlisle, J. F., & Beeman, M. M. (2000). The effects of language of instruction on the reading and writing of first-grade Hispanic children. *Scientific Studies of Reading, 4*, 331–353.

Cazden, C. R. (1974). Play with language and metalinguistic awareness: One dimension of language experience. *Urban Review, 7*, 28–29.

Coady, M., & Escamilla, K. (2005). Audible voices, visible tongues: Exploring social realities in Spanish-speaking students' writing. *Language Arts, 82*(6), 462–471.

Comber, B., Thomson, P., & Wells, M. (2001). Critical literacy finds a "place":

Writing and social action in a neighborhood school. *Elementary School Journal, 101*(4), 451–464.

De Guerrero, M., & Villamil, O. S. (2000). Activating the ZPD: Mutual scaffolding in L2 peer revision. *Modern Language Journal, 84*(1), 51–68.

Donovan, C. A., & Smolkin, B. A. (2006). Children's understanding of genre and writing development. In C. McAurther, S. Graham, & J. Fitzgerald (Eds.), *Handbook of writing research* (pp. 131–143). New York: Guilford Press.

Durgunoglu, A. (2002). Cross-linguistic transfer in literacy development and implications for language learners. *Annals of Dyslexia, 52*, 189–204.

Edelsky, C. (1982). Writing in a bilingual program: The relation of L1 and L2 texts. *TESOL Quarterly, 16*, 211–228.

Ferris, D. R. (2003). *Response to student writing: Implications for second language students*. Mahwah, NJ: Erlbaum.

García, G. E. (2000). Bilingual children's reading. In M. Kamil, P. Rosenthal, P. D. Pearson, & R. Barr (Eds.), *Handbook of reading research* (Vol. 3, pp. 813–834). Mahwah, NJ: Erlbaum.

Hillocks, G., Jr. (2002). *The testing trap: How state writing assessments control learning*. New York: Teachers College Press.

Hyland, F. (1998). The impact of teacher written feedback on individual writers. *Journal of Second Language Writing, 7*(3), 255–286.

Hyland, K., & Hyland, F. (2006). Interpersonal aspects of response: Constructing and interpreting teacher written feedback. In *Feedback in second language writing: Contexts and issues* (pp. 206–224). New York: Cambridge University Press.

Igoa, C. (1995). *The inner world of the immigrant child*. Mahwah, NJ: Erlbaum.

Illinois Standards Achievement Test. (2009). Retrieved March 11, 2009, from *www.isbe.state.il.us/assessment/writing.htm*.

Ivanič, R. (1998). *Writing and identity: The discoursal construction of identity in academic writing*. Philadelphia: Benjamins.

Ivanič, R., & Camps, D. (2001). "I am how I sound": Voice as self-representation in L2 writing. *Journal of Second Language Writing, 10*(1/2), 3–33.

Jiménez, R. T. (2000). Literacy and the identity development of Latina/o students. *American Educational Research Journal, 37*(4), 971–1000.

Jo, H. Y. (2001). "Heritage" language learning and ethnic identity: Korean Americans' struggle with language authority. *Language, Culture, and Communication, 14*(6), 26–41.

Maguire, M. H., & Graves, B. (2001). Speaking personalities in primary school children's L2 writing. *TESOL Quarterly, 35*, 561–593.

Manyak, P. (2001). Participation, hybridity, and carnival: A situated analysis of a dynamic literacy practice in a primary-grade English immersion class. *Journal of Literacy Research, 33*, 423–465.

McCarthey, S. J. (2009). Understanding English language learners' identities from three perspectives. In G. Li (Ed.), *Multicultural families, home literacies, and mainstream schooling* (pp. 221–244). New York: Information Age.

McCarthey, S. J., & García, G. (2005). English language learners' writing practices and attitudes. *Written Communication, 22*(1), 36–75.

McCarthey, S. J., García, G. E., López-Velásquez, A. M., Lin, S., & Guo, Y. (2004). Understanding writing contexts for English language learners. *Research in the Teaching of English, 38*(4), 351–392.

McCarthey, S. J., Guo, Y., & Cummins, S. (2005). Understanding changes in elementary Mandarin students' L1 and L2 writing. *Journal of Second Language Writing, 14*(2), 71–104.

Moll, L. C., Sáez, R., & Dworin, J. (2001). Exploring biliteracy: Two student case examples of writing as a social practice. *Elementary School Journal, 101,* 435–449.

Mora, L. (2008). Metalinguistic awareness as defined through research. Retrieved March 10, 2009, from *coe.sdsu.edu/people/jmora/moramodules/metalingresearch.htm.*

Nieto, S. (2002). *Language, culture, and teaching: Critical perspectives for a new century.* Mahwah, NJ: Erlbaum.

Olsen, S. (1999). Errors and compensatory strategies: A study of grammar and vocabulary in texts written by Norwegian learners of English. *System, 27,* 191–205.

Patthey-Chavez, G. G., & Ferris, D. R. (1997). Writing conferences and the weaving of multi-voiced texts in college composition. *Research in the Teaching of English, 31*(1), 51–90.

Reyes, M. L. (1992). Challenging venerable assumptions: Literacy instruction for linguistically different students. *Harvard Educational Review, 62,* 427–446.

Samway, K. D. (2006). *When English language learners write: Connecting research to practice, K–8.* Portsmouth, NH: Heinemann.

Shen, F. (1989). The classroom and the wider culture: Identity as a key to learning English composition. *College Composition and Communication, 40,* 459–466.

Solsken, J., Willett, J., & Wilson-Keenan, J. (2000). Cultivating hybrid texts in multicultural classrooms: Promise and challenge. *Research in the Teaching of English, 35*(2), 179–212.

Vollmer, G. (2002). Sociocultural perspectives on second language writing. *ERIC Clearing House on Languages and Linguistics: News Bulletin, 25*(2), 1–3.

Vygotsky, L. (1978). *Mind in society* (M. Cole, Trans.). Cambridge, MA: Harvard University Press.

Wang, L. 2003. Switching to first language among writers with differing second-language proficiency. *Journal of Second Language Writing, 12*(1), 347–375.

Woodall, B. R. (2002). Language-switching: Using the first language while writing in a second language. *Journal of Second Language Writing, 11*(1), 7–28.

Zheng, X. (2007). *Bringing the initiatives of English language learners: Teacher strategies and students' resources in an elementary ESL writing class.* Unpublished manuscript, University of Illinois, Urbana.

Zheng, X. (2010). *Writing development of elementary ESL students from two grades.* Unpublished doctoral dissertation, University of Illinois at Urbana–Champaign.

PART III

STRATEGIES FOR TEACHING ADOLESCENT ELLs

CHAPTER 6

Teaching Academic Literacies in Secondary School

Harriett Allison and Linda Harklau

The chapter will:

1. Define academic literacy and what it means for English language learners (ELLs).
2. Provide general principles for academic literacy instruction for ELLs at the secondary level.
3. Outline linguistic, cognitive, and sociocultural aspects of exemplary academic literacy instruction for ELLs.
4. Identify best practices for educating secondary school content-area teachers to bring ELLs to high levels of academic literacy.

The United States is at an economic crossroads. With increasing globalization and dwindling employment for unskilled labor, business and educational leaders agree on the urgent need to prepare more students for college and a postindustrial workplace. Yet millions of the nation's secondary school students are not even reading at grade level (Kamil, 2003), and by some estimates only about half of high school graduates are ready for college-level reading (American College Test [ACT], 2005, 2006). Reading readiness scores for U.S. students actually diminish as they move from elementary to middle and high school (Perle & Moran, 2005). Even worse, this decline coincides with a widening achievement gap between majority and minority, and among higher- and lower-socioeconomic-status students (Snow & Biancarosa, 2003), just as school texts become more complex and require discipline-specific approaches to reading (Shanahan & Shanahan, 2008). Particularly hard hit is the nation's rapidly growing population of English language learners (ELLs), who face the dual task of learning sophisticated academic concepts and English at the same time. These students' scores are typically 10 or more percentage points below their English-first-language classmates compared with all U.S. students (Short & Fitzsimmons, 2007). Clearly there is a need to develop more effective and proactive approaches to ELL content area literacy in upper grades.

This chapter presents an overview of promising instructional practices in teaching academic literacy, and study strategies and skills, to ELLs at the secondary level.[1]

Defining "Academic Literacy" for ELLs

To contextualize best practices, it is first important to understand that the notions of "Academic English" and "academic literacy" have been subject to widely varying definitions and considerable critique (e.g., Faltis & Wolfe, 1999; Valdés, 2004). They have also been influenced by two distinct scholarly traditions that have rarely been in dialogue with each other. One of these traditions comes out of second-language acquisition and the teaching of English to speakers of other languages (TESOL or ESOL). The other major tradition of scholarly work on academic literacies originates from reading and literacy education, where there has been considerable variation in conceptualizations of academic literacy. Some scholars and educators emphasize discipline-specific language and task demands (Shanahan & Shanahan, 2008). Others highlight learner cognitive and academic concept development (Chall & Jacobs, 2003). Still others focus on school discourse conventions and/or settings (Gee, 1996). Moreover, notions of academic literacy have shifted and expanded over time, moving from comparatively decontextualized, cognitively focused views to broader, context-embedded perspectives that take into account sociocultural and affective factors (Bean, 2000; Bean & Readence, 2002). An initial focus on "content-area literacy" has given way to a focus on *academic literacy*, broadening the focus beyond discipline-specific reading and writing tasks (Alvermann & Eakle, 2003). More recently, the construct has often been folded into a broader focus on *adolescent literacy*, adding the significant and meaningful engagement students have with out-of-school literacies, and the sociocultural aspects of the environments within which adolescent literacies are enacted (Alvermann & Eakle, 2003; Bean, 2000). Social, cultural, and historical aspects of adolescent literacy have been at the forefront as our schools become more diverse (Alvermann & Eakle, 2003).

The focus here is on practices and interventions developed specifically for second language (L2) learners in academic settings. For the purpose of this discussion, we draw on the Short and Fitzsimmons (2007, p. 2) definition of *academic literacy* that

- Includes reading, writing, and oral discourse for school.
- Varies from subject to subject.
- Requires knowledge of multiple genres of text, purposes for text use, and text media.
- Is influenced by students' literacies in contexts outside of school.
- Is influenced by students' personal, social, and cultural experiences.

This view of adolescents' academic literacy encompasses individual learner characteristics, backgrounds, and knowledge; the discourse community and setting for academic, or school, literacy; and the discipline-specific nature of middle and secondary literacy tasks and skills.

In the following, we begin by articulating general principles of instruction gleaned from the research. We then address three main foci in the best practices literature: linguistically oriented work addressing the registers, genres, and characteristics of academic materials and subject areas; cognitively oriented work addressing the kinds of thinking and processing valorized in academic settings; and socioculturally oriented work that addresses the interconnection of ELL academic literacy achievement and motivation, family, identity, self-efficacy, and other factors that make for successful learners. Given that ELLs are found in a broad diversity of learning contexts, we provide examples from a range of settings and conditions, including both schools with small numbers of ELLs and others whose student bodies are largely made up of language-minority students, including ELLs. Some practices are aimed at students in separate, ESOL-only settings; others are intended for "sheltered" instruction classes; and still others are designed to be used with language-minority English learners in mainstream classes.

General Principles

Research suggests that bilingual education is ultimately the most successful educational model for ELLs (Thomas & Collier, 2002). One guiding principle, therefore, is that the first recourse for exemplary academic literacy instruction for ELLs should be a bilingual immersion or a dual-immersion model combining academic content in native language and L2. The recommendations in most of this chapter, however, also reflect the reality that a vast majority of U.S. ELLs and other language-minority students at the secondary level are educated in English-medium classrooms, in which instruction is designed for monolingual English speakers (Harper & de Jong, 2004),

A second guiding principle is suggested by Shanahan and Shanahan (2008), who note that educators often assume that extensive literacy instruction in early grades makes further instruction in middle or high school unnecessary. However, they find that "the idea that early teaching practices will continue to provide literacy advantages without continued enhanced teaching efforts—the so-called 'vaccination' conception of teaching (Shanahan & Barr, 1995, p. 982)—does not appear to hold" (p. 88). ELLs are especially hurt by the false presumption that they will continue developing advanced literacy skills in mainstream classrooms through mere exposure to classroom discourse and text reading, even without effective, ongoing language learning assistance (Allison, 2008; Callahan, 2005). It is therefore crucial for ELLs to continue to receive explicit and targeted academic literacy instruction at the secondary level.

Remedies for improving secondary literacy instruction have frequently depended on the "every teacher a teacher of reading," an approach "that has historically frustrated secondary content-area teachers" (Shanahan & Shanahan, 2008, p. 84). Teachers of mainstream classes frequently resist including more than mandated course content in their syllabi, no matter how worthy or beneficial the activities may be (Conley, 2008), for they typically view themselves as content instructors, not teachers of reading (Shanahan & Shanahan, 2008). Moreover, administrative pressures encourage "teaching to the test" (Allison, 2008) so that as many of their students as possible pass mandated end-of-course and graduation assessments; such a policy has clearly promoted a focus on content acquisition, not teaching of academic literacy skills (Conley, 2008). Another guiding principle for ELL academic literacy instruction is for prospective teachers to be prepared to look beyond content delivery and consider the literacy skills students need to integrate, analyze, evaluate, and critique course information independently.

Many proposals have concentrated on helping struggling readers, calling for more instruction in basic decoding skills (Conley, 2008). Shanahan and Shanahan (2008), however, point out that students' difficulties are more likely attributable to lack of instruction on more complex and more subject-specific reading skills in subject areas. They speculate that "the high-level skills and abilities embedded in these disciplinary or technical uses of literacy are probably not particularly easy to learn, since they are not likely to have many parallels in oral language use, and they have to be applied to difficult texts" (Shanahan & Shanahan, 2008, p. 88).

Another guiding principle, then, is that reading instruction for ELLs at the secondary level needs to go well beyond decoding or basic reading skills and include instruction on higher-level skills, such as summarizing and identifying key points, synthesizing across multiple sources, and reading critically.

Another erroneous assumption is that interventions designed for monolingual struggling readers will be effective for ELLs and multi-linguals (Harper & de Jong, 2004; Snow & Biancarosa, 2003). While L2 research and pedagogy have a long history of drawing productively on the literature of L1 literacy (Grabe & Stoller, 2002), they have also established that there are fundamental differences between literacy learning in an L1 and in an additional language (August, 2006; Grabe & Stoller, 2002) in terms of prior knowledge of culturally specific infor-mation, academic vocabulary beyond discipline-specific terminology, and language and discourse knowledge necessary for academic tasks (Harper & de Jong, 2004; Valdés, Bunch, Snow, Lee, & Matos, 2005). Therefore, what is pedagogically effective for monolingual struggling readers is often insufficient or inappropriate for ELLs and bilinguals (Harper & de Jong, 2004). Moreover, language-minority students are disproportionately tracked into noncollege preparatory classes, where they are less likely to participate in the kinds of language-rich activities that are most likely to contribute to academic literacy acquisition (Cal-lahan, 2005; Harper & de Jong, 2004). In all, then, although addressing ELLs' literacy learning by "tweaking" (Meltzer & Hamann, 2006, p. 33) methods for mainstream adolescents may sound reassuring to some educators, it is not sound practice. Instead, reading interventions need to be tailored for ELLs' specific needs, such as developing cultural back-ground knowledge, enriching and enhancing academic vocabulary, and developing a sense of academic genres.

We turn now to specific recommendations for best practices that address linguistic, cognitive, and sociocultural aspects of ELL academic literacy development.

Linguistic Aspects

Early methods for teaching ELLs in U.S. K–12 schools treated language as the object of instruction and focused on improving oral–aural com-munication without reference to discipline-specific academic content (Chamot & Stewner-Manzanares, 1985; Kaufman & Crandall, 2005).

Growing out of concerns about language-minority students' academic achievement, Cummins (1979, 1980) was among the first scholars to point out that ELLs could quickly develop proficiency in spoken English but nonetheless struggle with the demands of written, Academic English in school. He posited two distinct sets of language competencies, basic interpersonal communication skills (BICS) and cognitive academic language proficiency (CALP) (Cummins, 1979, 1984). Cummins (1980) further posited that BICS, language used more often in informal, face-to-face interactions, was acquired relatively quickly and easily, while the more decontextualized and cognitively demanding CALP would take much longer to acquire. While the Cummins model was subsequently subjected to considerable critique (Edelsky et al., 1983; Faltis & Wolfe, 1999; Troike, 1984) and reformulated by Cummins himself (1981), the terms BICS and CALP nonetheless remain widespread in educational parlance, perhaps because they capture a central insight: Developing the level of language proficiency necessary to function effectively in a monolingual English academic environment is a protracted, effortful process that may take 5, 7, or even 10 years. Chamot and O'Malley (1987) subsequently adopted and popularized Cummins's model in the widely known cognitive academic language literacy approach (CALLA).

Current linguistically oriented recommendations for best practices are guided by "a recognition of the importance of language structures, skills, or functions that are characteristic of different content areas" (Snow, Met, & Genesee, 1989, p. 203). Teachers identify "content-obligatory language objectives and content-compatible language objectives" (p. 205) and devise instruction that engages and challenges learners to expand subject matter and Academic English knowledge (Faltis & Wolfe, 1999; Kaufman & Crandall, 2005; Short, 1999; Snow et al., 1989). We look at two widely recognized language-based models here: content-based instruction (CBI) and sheltered instruction (SI).

CBI represented a significant move toward embedding L2 instruction in academic subjects areas across the curriculum (Faltis & Wolfe, 1999; Kaufman & Crandall, 2005; Short, 1999; Snow et al., 1989). CBI approaches have been used successfully in a variety of settings—ESOL-only classrooms, discipline-specific SI, and mainstream classes (Short, 1999). Ideally in CBI, ESOL teachers and content-area instructors collaborate closely to plan curriculum and day-to-day lessons. Instructors from language and content areas work together to (1) identify discipline-specific vocabulary and language structures likely to interfere with ELLs' academic progress and (2) devise lessons and on-the-spot interventions that introduce students to the language, content, and discourse practices they will encounter in mainstream classes (Kaufman & Crandall, 2005; Short, 1999; Snow et al., 1989). At the heart of most CBI best practices are lessons carefully scaffolded (Gordon, 2005). Teachers must continually reassess their students' evolving language competencies and challenges, then adjust language and content instruction accordingly (Bernache, Galinat, & Jiménez, 2005; Gordon, 2005).

In ESOL-only classrooms, CBI academic content is typically organized around cross-curricular themes (Kaufman & Crandall, 2005; Snow, 1998; Snow et al., 1989): for example, a unit for beginner ELLs on Martin Luther King, Jr. and the Civil Rights Movement (Bernache et al., 2005) or preservation of the rain forest (Short, 1999). The latter is also an example of a topic that lends itself to incorporating content objectives from several subject areas, including math, science, and history. Moreover, since the instructional focus in CBI classes goes beyond language learning, many tasks and strategies typical to each discipline ideally are included in CBI instruction, thereby easing students' transition into mainstream coursework (Bernache et al., 2005).

Whereas CBI focuses on content-based units within *a language course*, SI develops academic language through *subject-area courses* designed for ELLs (Echevarria, Vogt, & Short, 2008). SI courses are designed to meet grade-level content objectives, while providing ELLs with language-learning support and tasks made more understandable through "modified instruction" (p. 213). As with CBI, there is significant variation in SI programs. Perhaps the best known and most codified model is the Sheltered Instruction Observation Protocol (SIOP®) of Echevarria et al. (p. xi).

Another contemporary approach to facilitating academic language and literacy development draws from Hallidayan (Halliday & Matthiesen, 2004) systemic functional linguistics (SFL) (e.g., Bunch, 2006; Fang & Schleppegrell, 2008; Hammond, 2006; Mohan & Slater, 2006; Schleppegrell & Colombi, 2002). For example, Schleppegrell and colleagues (Fang & Schleppegrell, 2008; Schleppegrell & Colombi, 2002) have set the goal of *advanced literacy*, focusing on "the kind of meaning-making that is typical of secondary and postsecondary schooling and that is also required for participation in many of the professional, technical, and bureaucratic, and social institutions of our world" (Schleppegrell & Colombi, 2002, p. 1). This definition emphasizes that academic literacy must be learned by not only ELLs but also all students (Gebhard, Harman, & Seger, 2007). Educators in this tradition have also reversed a tendency in CALLA and CBI to focus on course content to define language and skills. Instead, their starting point is to analyze how language characteristics of a given content area's text serve as a means to understand its content and learn how language is used to accomplish desired results, both in and out of school. Hence, the focus is on meaning, not form (Schleppegrell & Oliveira, 2006). The approach also contrasts with SI, in that course language is not modified; rather, students examine how language in both primary sources and secondary texts is used to accomplish writers' objectives (Gebhard et al., 2007).

In contrast to more traditional approaches that tend to focus on word- and sentence-level grammatical form and correctness, SFL emphasizes the linguistic and stylistic choices speakers and writers make to convey their overall intentions, the relation between writers/speakers and their audience, and the topic of the discussion (Thompson, 2004). From this view, writers/speakers are not evaluated on how correctly they construct the syntactical components of a text; rather, teachers and students focus on making linguistic decisions about composing messages concerning unique subjects that most effectively inform or persuade their reader/listener. Similarly, teachers can employ this approach to examine and explore intended meanings of discipline-specific writing and the distinct ways authors in diverse subject areas construct texts according to the practices and goals of the content domain (Thompson, 2004).

An SFL approach has been used successfully in a variety of settings with diverse groups of students. Schleppegrell and Oliveira (2006), for example, describe a project in which mainstream history teachers learned to use SFL to analyze and teach their students how historians write and the sorts of language choices they make.

> History is about events though time and what brought them about or followed from them, and the fact that all events have multiple causes means that historians use language carefully when they are constructing explanations, often eliding agency to present events as a natural unfolding. (p. 256)

By examining content through the language used to present it, teachers can bring together form and meaning to demonstrate how historians select language to impart their interpretations.

Another example of the application of an SFL approach is provided by Gebhard et al. (2007), who describe how a mainstream fifth-grade teacher with many ELLs helped her class to understand and use the language of academia to persuade school authorities to reverse an onerous school policy, the taking away of a recess period to provide additional time for test preparation. Students in the class worked in mixed groups to compose persuasive letters to school administrators, laying out their arguments for restoring the daily break. Working through a series of drafts in which they considered purposes of different language choices, students wrote letters, laying out their arguments for the benefits of recess; after reading and considering their arguments, the school principal reinstated recess.

Yet another example is offered by Hammond (2006), who documented a first-year high school English literature program for a linguistically and culturally mixed group, in which SFL and scaffolded lessons were combined with challenging content and high expectations. Instead of diluting course content, instruction focused on "supporting-up" ELL and multilingual students in mainstream language arts classes through continuous instruction in the use of language in *Romeo and Juliet*. Through activities such as inquiries into academic language, " 'playing' with language across different registers" (p. 282), student-written and produced dramas, and numerous group discussions, the class, including ELLs, was able to access and engage with Shakespeare's writing.

Cognitive Aspects

Reading for academic study involves interweaving both cognitive and linguistic skills in complex and reciprocal ways (e.g., Guthrie, 2003; Pressley & Wharton-McDonald, 1997; Shanahan & Shanahan, 2008; Wittrock, 1985, 1990). Readers draw on cognitive resources, such as prior knowledge or schemas, cognitive strategies, and metacognitive approaches, to create meaning from texts (Alvermann & Eakle, 2003; Wittrock, 1985, 1990; Wittrock, Marks, & Doctorow, 1975).

As students navigate the critical transition from elementary to middle and high school, course concepts and school text materials become increasingly complex and cognitively demanding. At this point, in addition to knowledge of academic language, they are expected to learn— or somehow to already know—discipline-specific ways of reading for learning (Shanahan & Shanahan, 2008). Students also need an array of metacognitive thinking and learning strategies to decide how best to approach an assignment, to monitor how well they are reading and understanding relevant information sources, and to determine whether they have completed the assigned task (García & Godina, 2004). Finally, they are expected to develop more broadly applicable thinking skills and metacognitive strategies they will need for lifelong learning and civic participation after high school, in college and the workplace (Conley, 2008).

Direct instruction in subject-area strategies (Klingner & Vaughn, 2004; Snow & Biancarosa, 2003) and scaffolded learning coupled with ample course-related teacher and peer interactional opportunities (Langer, 2001) have been shown to be successful for all students. However, many mainstream secondary school classes fail to offer students enough opportunities to engage in the kinds of needed, scaffolded reading and learning experiences that develop the collaboration, problem-solving, and critical thinking skills valued in postsecondary school and workplace settings (ACT, 2006; Callahan, 2005).

Accordingly, ELL educators and researchers almost unanimously recommend direct instruction in reading and critical thinking skills (e.g., Banks, et al., 2005; Chamot & O'Malley, 1987; Conley, 2008; Klingner & Vaughn, 2004; Olson & Land, 2007; Snow & Biancarosa, 2003; van Gelderen, Schoonen, Stoel, de Glopper, & Hulstijn, 2007). For more than 25 years, a cognitive strategy (CS) instruction approach has been promoted for improving content and academic literacy learning of monolingual, as well as multilingual, students (e.g., Chamot, 2005; Chamot & O'Malley, 1987; Coady et al., 2003; Conley, 2008; Crandall, Jaramillo, Olsen, & Peyton, 2002; Gibbons, 2008; Snow & Biancarosa, 2003). Cognitive and metacognitive strategy instruction in individual content areas was foregrounded in the CALLA model (Chamot & O'Malley, 1987; Klingner & Vaughn, 2004); unfortunately, however, research evidence for the effectiveness of this approach is still lacking (García & Godina, 2004; Klingner & Vaughn, 2004). Sheltered instruction formats, such as SIOP, likewise include CS instruction as an important component (Echevarria et al., 2008). The approach has also been applied successfully for discipline-specific literacy learning in individual subject areas, such as social studies (Zwiers, 2006), language arts (Olson & Land, 2007), and science (Litman & Greenleaf, 2008). At times referred to as a learning strategies approach, this method characterizes cognitive strategies as compilations of the thinking and problem-solving actions that successful learners employ to accomplish individual learning tasks, a kind of "mental tool kit" (Olson & Land, 2007, p. 276) for task analysis and learning. Instead of proceeding linearly through a series of steps, learners "go back to go forward . . . [possessing] the knowledge and motivation to access their tool kit of cognitive strategies without being constrained by any fixed order" (p. 276).

Broadly speaking, curricula using this approach begin with the teacher presenting CSs by modeling discipline-specific strategies used by experts in the target content area, so that students can "see" how a method works (Brown, 2008; Conley, 2008). Activities for accomplishing literacy tasks are carefully scaffolded through guided exercises, with control of tasks gradually released to students (Brown, 2008; Chamot & O'Malley, 1987; Conley, 2008; Olson & Land, 2007; Paris, Wasik, & Turner, 1991). Self-regulation and comprehension monitoring are also key components in a CS approach (Brown, 2008).

Although many literacy educators regard CSs as critical for academic work, they also note a lack of adequate research on how strategies are best taught, and a resulting tendency toward reductionist thinking and pedagogy. Conley (2008), for example, points out that many materials and methods developed to teach CSs display a propensity for oversimplification, an "all you have to do is . . . " attitude, and may mislead students into applying a "one-strategy-fits-all approach" to learning and thinking (p. 100). For example, a lesson using graphic organizers with the intent of teaching critical reading strategies may instead devolve into a lesson on "doing graphic organizers" (p. 90). Conley therefore suggests that exemplary CS instruction needs to be combined with instruction in applying and managing these strategies for self-regulated learning and self-monitoring.

Conley (2008) lauds Olson and Land's (2007) research on the California Pathway Project as one example of the sound, research-based approach needed to develop effective CS instruction with adolescent students. The project combined concentrated professional development, pedagogy constructed around teaching CSs for academic work, and a highly challenging curriculum. Quantitative results included gains in participating students' average scores over those of the control group that were statistically significant for 7 years (Olson & Land, 2007).

Teachers worked with the research team to learn about, and at times help to develop, CS methods and materials for teaching reading and writing. This rigorous and challenging language arts curriculum focused on teaching cognitive and metacognitive strategies presented through explicit instruction, modeling, and guided exercises, with particular attention to learning *declarative* (what a strategy is), *procedural* (how to use it), and *conditional* (when to use it) knowledge (Olson & Land, 2007). Key components of Project Pathway for both teachers and students were (1) carefully scaffolded strategy instruction and (2) a gradual release of responsibility for learning. Qualitatively, participant interviews demonstrated that students were aware of differences in how they were being taught, and the pedagogical methods and expectations had positive effects on their attitudes toward learning and academic aspirations. Conley (2008) calls for other, similarly well-executed and documented efforts to teach cognitive and metacognitive strategies to adolescents.

Sociocultural Aspects

Research has amply demonstrated that social, cultural, and historical factors are key to reader comprehension, interest, investment, and success (RAND Corporation, 2002). Students' perception of their capability as scholars and readers has an impact on their willingness to take part in school literacy activities (Alvermann, 2003). In fact, students' sense of their own capabilities and skills, or *self-efficacy,* has a greater influence on their willingness to engage in a task than their actual skills level (Pajares, 1996). ELLs are no different from their peers, in that they fare best in classrooms where they are a part of the conversation; where their unique backgrounds, strengths, and learning characteristics are valued and respected; and where they receive affective support (Alvermann, 2003; Moje et al., 2004; Orellana & Gutiérrez, 2006; Valdés, 2004).

While ELLs' school environments may vary widely in student demographics and resources, examples of schools that bring ELLs to high levels of academic literacy through a focus on sociocultural factors can be found across the spectrum. Space allows only a brief review of two examples of educators' thoughtful and deliberate efforts to create real learning spaces in different settings. In one setting, ELLs are newcomers to schools that have little previous experiences working with students from home language backgrounds other than English (Kouritzin, 2004), whereas in the other (Gibbons, 2008) ELLs form the majority population.

Kouritzin's (2004) comparative case study examined how four Canadian high schools with "low incidence" or small populations of language-minority students (less than 6%) went about creating academic literacy and learning environments in which ELLs completed high school and moved into postsecondary education at higher than average rates. She found that "in low-incidence areas, schoolwide programs and attitudes more than specific pedagogical practices seemed to be correlated with student success" (p. 481). She identified three characteristics shared by these successful programs. One was supportive administrations, particularly principals who were persistent and creative in seeking funding to support ESOL programs. Successful principals were perceived by ESOL faculty as respectful of teachers' expertise and open to ESOL teachers' direction and suggestions. Interestingly, all four school principals were either speakers of a home language other than English or had lived outside Canada for a significant period.

A second characteristic of these schools was that educators made concerted, informed efforts to establish and maintain positive contacts with students and their families. They engaged families when possible in program planning and evaluation. Teachers were careful to monitor whether students and families understood the information included in report cards and ensured that comments from content-area teachers provided specific information about each student's progress. Administrators and teachers also devised ways to include the community in the school through incorporating the newer cultures in school activities. Finally, school faculty and staff concerned themselves with ELLs' non-school needs (Kouritzin, 2004).

A third characteristic of low-incidence schools that were successful in fostering high levels of ELL academic literacy was a schoolwide attitude of "respectful inclusion" (Kouritzin, 2004, p. 492). These schools not only provided high-quality ESOL academic literacy instruction that took away any association between ESOL instruction and remediation but they also facilitated ELLs in becoming school leaders and content-area experts who tutored other students in math and science. ESOL teachers at these four schools communicated continuously with content-area teachers, assisting them to adapt materials and methods for their language-minority ELLs. Schools' arrangement of the course schedule to optimize ELLs success included having ESOL teachers hand-schedule ELLs, setting up the school master calendar so that students could immediately repeat failed courses, and arranging with a university to accept credit for coursework completed in sheltered ESOL classes.

Gibbons (2008) provides an example of how exemplary academic literacy instruction can also be fostered in the very different context of a school where ELLs are in the majority. Gibbons's purpose was to investigate how "high challenge, high support classrooms" can build "'intellectual quality'" (p. 155) in pedagogy for ELLs. Through a series of socioculturally oriented action research projects in Australian primary and high schools, teachers and researchers jointly developed syllabi for intellectually challenging pedagogy across the curriculum—history, science, language arts, music, and mathematics—built around tasks and activities that facilitated intellectual quality and higher-order thinking. Like the low-incidence contexts investigated by Kouritzin (2008), the key to best practices was to engage the whole student in the sociocultural context and provide a challenging and receptive curriculum.

Gibbons found that one result of these projects was a shifting of classroom interactions from teacher-prompted displays of known information to encouraging learners to interrogate and investigate larger, discipline-specific questions. Students thus took on greater responsibility for their learning, thereby becoming "legitimate participants" (2008, p. 160) in their education. Researchers also found that by focusing on foundational discipline-specific concepts, students increasingly followed lines of reasoning that "`mirror[ed]' the ways of thinking and meaning of scientists, historians, or mathematicians" (p. 161). Gibbons describes other significant teaching methods and student responses:

> We noted the extensive use of message abundancy by teachers which amplified, rather than simplified, the curriculum; the use of many kinds of guiding mediating texts to create affordances for students to talk aloud about their reasoning in collaboration with others, and to prepare them for subsequent tasks; the sequences of talk between teachers and students

which allowed for sustained contributions from students and modeling by teachers; and the explicit teaching of disciplinary-related language and literacy. . . . Students learned *about* language in the context of *using* language, thus avoiding a disjunction between the teaching of language and the teaching of "content." (p. 171)

Most importantly, both students and teachers stressed that the supportive sociocultural atmosphere in the classes was fundamental to student engagement and academic success.

Reflections and Future Directions

In this section we consider (1) implications of this review for teacher preparation and (2) some cautions in using the term *academic literacy*.

Teacher Preparation

What can we distill and take away from this literature that informs teacher preparation? Conley (2008) provides a broad framework that can be applied to teacher training agendas for ELLs, whether the classrooms are ESOL-only or mainstream. In a discussion on CS instruction, Conley laments that too many teacher education programs direct students to focus on *what* prospective teachers are to teach—on content, instead of on *how* and *whether* students are learning. As a result, many teacher candidates view their primary task as transmitting knowledge to their students rather than building students' facility to learn. As Conley puts it, "State teacher-preparation standards that emphasize teaching activities, as in the content-area literacy textbooks, state tests, and core curricula, all conspire to keep the focus squarely on subject-matter and step-by-step pedagogy" (p. 98).

Moreover, little attention is given to how teachers might get to *know* their students and their existing capacities and knowledge, to "focus on understanding adolescents in rich ways by integrating goals for content learning with developing adolescents' capacities and identities" (Conley, 2008, p. 98). These remarks have particular resonance in the context of preparing teachers to work with ELLs and other language-minority students given the frequent lack of appreciation for and understanding of ELLs' unique characteristics and hidden skills.

Teacher candidates also need to be made aware of how language is used within their content areas, and how it frames domain knowledge to express discipline-specific modes of thinking. For example, if a prospective teacher is preparing to instruct students about history, how does he or she *talk about* history in ways that are different from how the biology teacher talks about biology?

In addition, developing understandings of the ways subject-area experts think and construct knowledge in their respective fields, and the approaches and strategies they take to problem-solving and explaining in their discipline, is also vital for teacher candidates to assist ELLs in learning how to read and respond to different subject-area concepts and texts. Not only do historians ask different questions than biologists about their subject area, but they also work toward answers differently in approaching issues and topics.

Finally, teacher candidates need to know that responsibility for their students' learning does not end with presenting course subject matter in a comprehensible format. Above all, the school setting should be one in which all students, ELLs included, are recognized and valued as equal participants and contributors to the learning environment. That means teachers-educators need to develop programs in which teacher candidates are encouraged to look beyond their particular school subject areas to engage their students as individuals, as well as parts of families and communities.

Cautions about "Academic Literacy"

In spite of the compelling arguments for academic literacy instruction for ELLs, it is important for educators and administrators to realize that the notion of "academic literacy" remains problematic, particularly when applied to ELLs. Orellana and Gutiérrez (2006), for example, point out that a focus solely on what ELLs can do in English and school-based language almost inevitably positions them as deficient, while ignoring that "if we look at what youth do outside of school we see a wide range of language and literacy practices that involve complex social, cultural, linguistic, and cognitive skills (e.g., translation and interpretation practices that involve many kinds of texts, domains, genres, and social relations)" (p. 120). This suggests that in developing students' academic literacy, educators must nonetheless realize that when students' competencies and strengths outside the classroom are considered, different images—of capable individuals navigating and negotiating meaning between two languages—can emerge (Alvermann, 2003; Bayley & Scheter, 2003; Gutiérrez & Orellana, 2006; Walsh, 1994).

Valdés (2004) highlights the lack of a commonly articulated and accepted definition of *academic language*, and a tendency for schools and universities to fall into definitions of *academic language* and *academic literacy* that conflate them with ELLs' ability to write error-free language, at the same time overlooking the point that "writing is about ideas, that presentations are about ideas" (p. 122). Valdés therefore suggests that academic language cannot be defined in terms of language alone. Rather, since language is only the by-product of academic experiences and interactions, providing those experiences and interactions is key to ELL and language-minority student success. Likewise, Bunch's (2006) study of the language seventh graders used to accomplish complex reading and writing assignments questions any dichotomy between school and social language. He proposes reframing school language use as "the language of ideas: answering questions by talking about them" (p. 293) and "the language of display: constructing 'answers' for the presentation" (p. 295). He notes that as these seventh graders worked with the assignment's concepts and content, their language could not unilaterally be described as either "decontextualized" or "literate" (p. 295), as academic language has at times been described. However, as students prepared their presentation, they gradually selected the kind of language they thought most appropriate for use in a formal setting.

Because of their focus on academic practices *using* language rather than on language itself, both Bunch (2006) and Valdés (2004) question whether "academic language" can be taught in ESOL-only classrooms. Bunch notes the need "to envision classrooms in which students can be *included in,* rather than *excluded from,* opportunities to participate in as wide a range of English for academic purposes as possible" (2006, p. 299). In all, then, we caution educators that academic literacy development for ELLs cannot be reduced to a formula or a narrow, reductionist curriculum. It is a protracted process and a moving target with considerable linguistic, cognitive, and sociocultural complexity.

Concluding Remarks

While a definition of *academic literacy* may remain elusive, there is nevertheless widespread agreement that there is an urgent imperative to develop more direct, intensive academic literacy preparation for ELLs at the secondary level. Almost one-fourth of high school students aspiring to higher education now speak a language other than English at home (College Board, 2008). Current academic literacy instruction at the secondary level arguably fails a significant proportion of even the monolingual students for which it was originally designed, and it is even less successful with ELL and other language-minority students for whom it is often ill-suited. Although more research remains to be done, we already have considerable information about how best to develop these students' academic literacy and further their academic success in high school, higher education, and the workplace.

ENGAGEMENT ACTIVITIES

1. What approaches to academic literacy and content instruction are used for working with ELLs at the secondary level in schools in your area? What strengths and weaknesses have been noted in these approaches by students and educators?

2. Pick a chapter in a secondary content-area history or language arts textbook and explain how you might adapt it for a sheltered instructional approach.

3. Take that same chapter and predict what cultural background knowledge and schemas might need to be taught to immigrant ELLs.

4. Identify an instructional theme or topic that could be used in a content-based instruction approach, and explain how you would incorporate multiple content areas.

5. Take the same instructional theme or topic identified earlier and explain what cognitive or learning strategies you could teach as part of the same content-based instruction unit.

6. Using the instructional theme you selected in item 4 and the learning strategies you identified for item 5, consider what kinds of information, both sociocultural and individual, from your students could enhance your lessons on this content. How would you go about acquiring this knowledge?

NOTE

1. While we recognize the essential interconnection of academic reading and writing, in this chapter we focus largely on reading and study skills. Those interested primarily in adolescent academic writing are directed to other recent reviews (see, e.g., Harklau & Pinnow, 2008; Leki, Cumming, & Silva, 2008).

REFERENCES

Allison, H. (2008). *Generation 1.5 readers in high school and college: Their challenges and accomplishments.* Unpublished dissertation, University of Georgia, Athens.

Alvermann, D. E. (2003). *Seeing themselves as capable and engaged readers: Adolescents and re/mediated instruction.* Retrieved March 28, 2006, from *www. learningpt.org/pdfs/literacy/readers.pdf.*

Alvermann, D. E., & Eakle, A. J. (2003). Comprehension instruction: Adolescent and their multiple literacies. In A. P. Sweet & C. E. Snow (Eds.), *Rethinking reading comprehension.* New York: Guilford Press.

American College Test (ACT). (2005). *Average national ACT Score unchanged in 2005; Students graduate from high school ready or not.* Iowa City: Author.

American College Test (ACT). (2006). *Reading between the lines: What the ACT reveals about college readiness in reading.* Iowa City: Author.

August, G. (2006). So, what's behind adult English second language reading? *Bilingual Research Journal, 30*(2), 245–264.

Banks, J., Cochran-Smith, M., Moll, L., Richert, A., Zeichner, K., LePage, P., et al. (2005). Teaching diverse learners. In L. Darling-Hammond & J. Bransford (Eds.), *Preparing teachers for a changing world: What teachers should learn and be able to do* (pp. 232–274). Indianapolis, IN: Jossey-Bass.

Bayley, R., & Schecter, S. R. (2003). *Language Socialization in Bilingual and Multilingual Societies. Bilingual Education and Bilingualism.* Tonawanda NY: Multilingual Matters.

Bean, T. W. (2000). Reading in the content areas: Social constructivist dimensions. In P. D. Pearson (Ed.), *Handbook of reading research* (Vol. III, pp. 629–644). Mahwah, NJ: Erlbaum.

Bean, T. W., & Readence, J. E. (2002). Adolescent literacy: Charting a course for successful futures as lifelong learners. *Reading Research and Instruction, 41*(3), 203–210.

Bernache, C., Galinat, K., & Jiménez, S. (2005). Coteaching in a sheltered model: Maximizing content and language acquisition for beginning-level English language learners. In D. Kaufman & J. Crandall (Eds.), *Content-based instruction in primary and secondary school settings* (pp. 67–80). Washington, DC: Teachers of English to Speakers of Other Languages (TESOL).

Brown, R. (2008). Strategy matters: Comprehension instruction for older youth. In K. A. Hinchman & H. K. Sheridan-Thomas (Eds.), *Best practices in adolescent literacy instruction* (pp. 114–131). New York: Guilford Press.

Bunch, G. C. (2006). "Academic English" in the 7th grade: Broadening the lens, expanding access. *Journal of English for Academic Purposes, 5*(4), 284–301.

Callahan, R. M. (2005). Tracking and high school English learners: Limiting opportunities to learn. *American Educational Research Journal, 42*(2), 305–328.

Chall, J. S., & Jacobs, V. A. (2003). The classic study on poor children's fourth-grade slump. *American Educator, 27*(1), 14–15, 44.

Chamot, A. U. (1985). *English language development through a content-based approach.* Washington, DC: National Clearinghouse for Bilingual Education.

Chamot, A. U. (2005). Language learning strategy instruction: Current issues and research. *Annual Review of Applied Linguistics, 25*(1), 112–130.

Chamot, A. U., & O'Malley, J. M. (1987). The cognitive academic language learning approach: A bridge to the mainstream. *TESOL Quarterly, 21*(2), 227–249.

Chamot, A. U., & Stewner-Manzanares, G. (1985). *A synthesis of current literature on English as a second language: Issues for educational policy. Part C Research Agenda.* Washington, DC: National Clearinghouse for Bilingual Education.

Coady, M., Hamann, E. T., Harrington, M., Pacheco, M., Pho, S., & Yedlin, J. (2003). *Claiming opportunities: A handbook for improving education for English language learners through comprehensive school reform.* Providence, RI: The Education Alliance, Brown University.

College Board. (2008). *2008 College-bound seniors: Total group profile report.* New York: Author.

Conley, M. W. (2008). Cognitive strategy instruction for adolescents: What we know about the promise, what we don't know about the potential. *Harvard Educational Review, 78*(1), 84–106.

Crandall, J., Jaramillo, A., Olsen, L., & Peyton, J. K. (2002). *Using cognitive strategies to develop English language and literacy.* Retrieved April 21, 2008, from *www.cal.org/ericcll.*

Cummins, J. (1979). Linguistic interdependence and the educational development of bilingual children. *Review of Educational Research, 49,* 222–251.

Cummins, J. (1980). The cross-lingual dimensions of language proficiency: Implications for bilingual education and the optimal age issue. *TESOL Quarterly, 14,* 175–187.

Cummins, J. (1981). The role of primary language development in promoting educational success for language minority students. In California State Department of Education, Office of Bilingual Bicultural Education (Ed.), *Schooling and language minority students: A theoretical framework* (pp. 3–49). Los Angeles: Evaluation, Dissemination, and Assessment Center, California State University.

Cummins, J. (1984). Wanted: A theoretical framework for relating language proficiency to academic achievement. In C. Rivera (Ed.), *Language proficiency and academic achievement.* Clevedon, Avon, UK: Multilingual Matters.

Echevarria, J., Vogt, M., & Short, D. J. (2008). *Making content comprehensible for English learners: The SIOP model* (3rd ed.). Boston: Allyn & Bacon.

Edelsky, C., Hudelson, S., Flores, B., Barkin, F., Altwerger, B., & Jilbert, K. (1983). Semilingualism and language deficit. *Applied Linguistics, 4*(1), 1–22.

Faltis, C. J., & Wolfe, P. (Eds.). (1999). *So much to say: Adolescents, bilingualism, and ESL in the secondary school.* New York: Teachers College Press.

Fang, Z., & Schleppegrell, M. J. (2008). *Reading in secondary content areas: A language-based pedagogy.* Ann Arbor: University of Michigan Press.

García, G. E., & Godina, H. (2004). Addressing the literacy needs of adolescent English learners. In T. L. Jetton & J. A. Dole (Eds.), *Adolescent literacy and practice.* New York: Guilford Press.

Gebhard, M., Harman, R., & Seger, W. (2007). Reclaiming recess: Learning the language of persuasion. *Language Arts, 84*(5), 419–430.

Gee, J. P. (1996). *Social linguistics and literacies: Ideology in discourses* (2nd ed.). New York: Routledge.

Gibbons, P. (2008). "It was taught good and I learned a lot": Intellectual practices and ESL learners in the middle years. *Australian Journal of Language and Literacy, 31*(2), 155–173.

Gordon, T. (2005). Working together to raise content-based instruction into the zone of proximal development. In D. Kaufman & J. Crandall (Eds.), *Content-based instruction in primary and secondary settings* (pp. 81–92). Washington, DC: TESOL.

Grabe, W., & Stoller, F. (Eds.). (2002). *Teaching and researching reading.* London: Longman.

Guthrie, J. T. (2003). Concept-oriented reading instruction: Practices of teaching reading for understanding. In A. S. Sweet & C. E. Snow (Eds.), *Rethinking reading comprehension* (pp. 115–140). New York: Guilford Press.

Gutiérrez, K. D., & Orellana, M. F. (2006). The "problem" of English learners: Constructing genres of difference. *Research in the Teaching of English, 40*(4), 502–507.

Halliday, M. A. K., & Matthiesen, C. (2004). *An introduction to functional grammar.* London: Arnold.

Hammond, J. (2006). High challenge, high support: Integrating language and content instruction for diverse learners in an English literature classroom. *Journal of English for Academic Purposes, 5*, 269–283.

Harklau, L., & Pinnow, R. (2008) Second language writing. In L. Christenbury, R. Bomer, & P. Smagorinsky (Eds.), *Handbook of adolescent literacy research* (pp. 126–139). New York: Guilford Press.

Harper, C., & de Jong, E. (2004). Misconceptions about teaching English-language learners. *Journal of Adolescent and Adult Literacy, 48*(2), 152–162.

Kamil, M. (2003). Adolescents and literacy: Reading of the 21st century [Electronic version]. Retrieved January 4, 2009, from *www.all4ed.org/files/adolescentsandliteracy.pdf.*

Kaufman, D., & Crandall, J. (2005). *Content-based instruction in primary and secondary school settings: Case studies in TESOL Practice Series.* Alexandria, VA: TESOL.

Klingner, J. K., & Vaughn, S. (2004). Strategies for struggling second-language readers. In T. L. Jetton & J. A. Dole (Eds.), *Adolescent literacy research and practice* (pp. 183–209). New York: Guilford Press.

Kouritzin, S. G. (2004). Programs, plans, and practices in schools with reputations for ESL student success. *Canadian Modern Language Review, 60*(4), 481–499.

Langer, J. A. (2001). Beating the odds: Teaching middle and high school students to read and write well. *American Educational Research Journal, 38*, 837–880.

Leki, I., Cumming, A. H., & Silva, T. (2008). *A synthesis of research on second language writing in English.* New York: Routledge.

Litman, C., & Greenleaf, C. (2008). Traveling together over difficult ground: Negotiating success with a profoundly inexperienced reader in an introduction to chemistry class. In K. A. Hinchman & H. K. Sheridan-Thomas (Eds.), *Best practices in adolescent literacy instruction* (pp. 275–296). New York: Guilford Press.

Meltzer, J., & Hamann, E. T. (2006). Literacy for English learners and regular students, too. *Principal Leadership, 6*, 32–40.

Mohan, B., & Slater, T. (2006). Examining the theory/practice relation in a high school science register: A functional linguistic perspective. *Journal of English for Academic Purposes, 5*(4), 302–316.

Moje, E. B., Ciechanowski, K. M., Kramer, K., Ellis, L., Carrillo, R., & Collazo,

T. (2004). Working toward third space in content area literacy: An examination of everyday funds of knowledge and discourse. *Reading Research Quarterly, 39*(1), 38–70.

Olson, C. B., & Land, R. (2007). A cognitive strategies approach to reading and writing instruction for English language learners in secondary school. *Research in the Teaching of English, 41*(3), 269–303.

Orellana, M. F., & Gutiérrez, K. D. (2006). What's the problem?: Constructing different genres for the study of English learners. *Research in the Teaching of English, 41*(1), 118–123.

Pajares, F. (1996). Self-efficacy beliefs in academic settings. *Review of Educational Research, 66*(4), 543–587.

Paris, S. G., Wasik, B. A., & Turner, J. C. (1991). The development of strategic readers. In R. Barr, M. L. Kamil, P. Mosenthal & P.D.Pearson (Eds.), *Handbook of reading research* (Vol. 2, pp. 609–640). New York: Longman.

Perle, M., & Moran, R. (2005). *NAEP 2004 Trends in Academic Progress: Three decades of student performance in reading, 1971–2004 and mathematics, 1973–2004.* Retrieved October 21, 2008, from *www.eric.ed.gov/ERICDocs/data/ericdocs2sql/content_storage_01/0000019b/80/29/da/3e.pdf.*

Pressley, M., & Wharton-McDonald, R. (1997). Skilled comprehension and its development through instruction. *School Psychology Review, 26*(3), 448–466.

RAND Corporation. (2002). *Reading for understanding: Toward an R&D program in reading comprehension* (No. 0-8330-3105-8). Santa Monica, CA: Science and Technology Policy Institute, RAND Corporation.

Schleppegrell, M. J., & Colombi, M. C. (Eds.). (2002). *Developing advanced literacy in first and second languages: Meaning with power.* Mahwah, NJ: Erlbaum.

Schleppegrell, M., & Oliveira, L. C. D. (2006). An integrated language and content approach for history teachers. *Journal of English for Academic Purposes, 5,* 254–268.

Shanahan, T., & Shanahan, C. (2008). Teaching disciplinary literacy to adolescents: Rethinking content-area literacy. *Harvard Educational Review, 78*(1), 40–59.

Short, D. (1999). Integrating language and content for effective sheltered instruction programs. In C. J. Faltis & P. Wolfe (Eds.), *So much to say: Adolescents, bilingualism, and ESL in the secondary school* (pp. 105–137). New York: Teachers College Press.

Short, D., & Fitzsimmons, S. (2007). *Double the work: Challenges and solutions to acquiring language and academic literacy for adolescent English language learners–a report to Carnegie Corporation of New York.* Washington, DC: Alliance for Excellent Education.

Snow, C. E., & Biancarosa, G. (2003). *Adolescent literacy: What do we know and where do we go from here?* New York: Carnegie Corporation of New York.

Snow, M. A., Met, M., & Genesee, F. (1989). A conceptual framework for the integration of language and content in second/foreign language instruction. *TESOL Quarterly, 23,* 201–217.

Thomas, W. P., & Collier, V. P. (2002). *A national study of school effectiveness for language minority students' long-term academic achievement: Executive sum-mary.* Santa Cruz, CA: Center for Research on Excellence and Diversity in Education.

Thompson, G. (2004). *Introducing functional grammar.* London: Hodder Arnold Press.

Troike, R. C. (1984). SCALP: Social and cultural aspects of language profi-ciency. In C. Rivera (Ed.), *Language proficiency and academic achievement* (pp. 44–54). Clevedon, Avon, UK: Multilingual Matters.

Valdés, G. (2004). Between support and marginalisation: The development of academic language in linguistic minority children. *International Journal of Bilingual Education and Bilingualism, 7,* 102–132.

Valdés, G., Bunch, G., Snow, C., Lee, C., & Matos, L. (2005). Enhancing the development of students' language(s). In L. Darling-Hammond & J. Bransford (Eds.), Preparing teachers for a changing world: What teachers should learn and be able to do (pp. 126é168). San Francisco: Jossey-Bass.

van Gelderen, A., Schoonen, R., Stoel, R., de Glopper, K., & Hulstijn, J. (2007). Development of adolescent reading comprehension in language 1 and language 2: A longitudinal analysis of constituent components. *Journal of Educational Psychology, 99*(3), 477–491.

Walsh, C. (1994). Engaging students in learning: Literacy, language, and knowledge production with Latino adolescents. In D. Spener (Ed.), *Adult biliteracy in the United States: Language in education: Theory and practice* (pp. 211–237). Washington, DC: ERIC Clearinghouse for ESL Literacy.

Wittrock, M. C. (1985). Teaching learners generative strategies for enhancing reading comprehension. *Theory into Practice, 24*(2), 123–126.

Wittrock, M. C. (1990). Generative processes of comprehension. *Educational Psychologist, 24*(4), 345–376.

Wittrock, M. C., Marks, C., & Doctorow, M. (1975). Reading as a generative process. *Journal of Educational Psychology, 67*(4), 484–489.

Zwiers, J. (2006). Integrating academic language, thinking, and content: Learning scaffolds for non-native speakers in the middle grades. *Journal of English for Academic Purposes, 5,* 317–332.

CHAPTER 7

Constructing Access and Understanding in Inclusive Middle-Grade Content Classrooms

A Sociocognitive Apprenticeship in Literacy with Bilingual Students and Those with Language/Learning Disabilities

Troy V. Mariage and Carol Sue Englert

This chapter will:

1. Provide practitioners with summary data and examples of middle-grade students' performance of learning to learn and cognitive strategies as they attempt to comprehend and compose expository texts in the content areas of social studies and science.

2. Present a curricular approach for apprenticing students into strategic processes before, during, and after they inquire about an informational topic in social studies and science.

3. Provide concrete instructional tools and scaffolds for supporting students as they plan, gather, comprehend, organize, and compose, while they inquire about an expository topic.

4. Present an example of how practitioners can view their role as supporting a sociocognitive apprenticeship in which they utilize cultural tools, including the academic discourses of reading, composing, and disciplinary content, to engage learners in thinking and understanding.

One of the great challenges in secondary education is helping all students acquire the necessary learning-to-learn skills to support their understanding and production of informational texts. Success in rigorous content areas is vital for graduation and postsecondary education, and writing is considered a "threshold" skill for many individuals who hope to advance their career in an increasingly global citizenry (National Commission on Writing, 2003). The cognitive demands of reading and writing in social studies and science require that students be able to synthesize information across multiple sources of information, summarize that information, clarify unclear concepts, utilize multiple text structures to organize information, identify key details, and compose texts in multiple genres (e.g., compare–contrast, explanation, argumentation, exposition, sequence, cause–effect, and problem–solution). Integrating reading and writing to support learning in the secondary content-area classroom is among the most complicated and multifaceted skills sets that students must develop to become independent learners (Alexander & Jetton, 2000; Baker, Gersten, & Scanlon, 2002).

Navigating this complexity can be particularly challenging for several groups of students in our classrooms, including bilingual students, who may be conversationally fluent English speakers but are still learning the unique academic languages associated with learning to learn, cognitive strategies, text structure, disciplinary processes, and content. A second group is students with language and learning disabilities, who represent the largest single group of included students who hold individualized education plans (IEPs) in general education classrooms. Approximately 80–90% of the IEP goals for students with learning disabilities are in the areas of reading (i.e., fluency, comprehension) and written expression (i.e., fluency, composition), making access to and expression of the content-area curriculum a great challenge. While these groups of students are clearly not identical (e.g., most bilingual students do not have learning disabilities) and have substantial between- and within-group diversity, the frequent attention in the literature on challenges related to both groups' comprehension, composition, and the need to learn the academic discourses related to understanding expository content (e.g., social studies and science processes, content) suggests that the instructional response for each may have many things in common (e.g., explicitness, intensity, instructional scaffolds, role of dialogue, apprenticeship). In response to the importance placed on comprehension and composition in accessing content curriculum in the middle grades, a time when students are supposed to be reading to learn and writing to learn, we believe that principles of sociocognitive apprenticeship can play a helpful role in guiding instructional practices. In addition to teaching students strategies for comprehending and composing, this view of learning also emphasizes the role of apprenticing students into the unique disciplinary discourses, processes, and ways of knowing that mark one as being competent in a discourse community (Gee, 2008; Wells, 1999).

Decades of research have illustrated the unique comprehension and composition challenges for learners related to expository texts. There is evidence that students with language and learning disabilities have difficulty in identifying main ideas (Graves, 1986, 1987; Taylor & Williams, 1983; Williams, 2003), distinguishing relevant from irrelevant information (Englert, Hiebert, & Stewart, 1987; Williams, Taylor, Jarin, & Milligan, 1983), categorizing and organizing expository ideas (Englert et al., 1987; Englert & Raphael, 1988; Wong & Wilson, 1984), following text structure in comprehension and composition (Graham & Harris, 1989; Meyer, Brandt, & Bluth, 1980; Wong & Wilson, 1984; Taylor & Samuels, 1983), summarizing expository text (Baumann, 1984; Gajria & Salvia, 1992; Malone & Mastropieri, 1992), monitoring their comprehension, and employing revision or fix-up strategies (Wong & Jones, 1982). They have been described as *passive learners* because they have frequent difficulties with metacognition and self-regulation (Wong, 1997; Wong & Jones, 1982; Wong & Wilson, 1984). The complexity of employing individual learning-to-learn and cognitive strategies increases when students are asked to direct and execute the strategies in a coordinated fashion as they plan, gather, synthesize, comprehend, interpret, organize, and compose expository information as part of an inquiry-driven process.

Graves and Rueda (2009) identified three broad areas that need to be unpacked to identify more accurately the unique needs of culturally and linguistically diverse learners, including factors related to (1) language, (2) culture, and (3) socioeconomics. In the area of language, students who are learning English are simultaneously being apprenticed into an "academic language" or "register" that enables them to talk, think, and communicate about expository topics, including the component processes related to reading (e.g., inferencing, summarizing, clarifying), writing (e.g., the processes of planning, organizing, revising), and interpreting topics in the content-area curriculum (e.g., photosynthesis, osmosis). While bilingual students may develop fluency in a second language that allows them to communicate effectively in social situations, the ability to utilize academic discourses to describe, communicate, or direct their own cognitive actions takes substantially longer to develop. In the content areas, precisely these unique academic discourses are implicated in the difficulties that students experience in comprehending and composing expository texts in the core disciplinary subjects of the school curriculum. At the same time, bilingual students bring language and cultural strengths that can enrich the content curriculum, if educators possess the cultural sensitivity and pedagogical knowledge to bridge the gap between school-based and culturally based experiences and discourses.

Instructionally, teachers' knowledge of language and culture also influences their ability to teach responsively and in culturally relevant ways (Ladson-Billings, 1992; Nieto, 1999; Purcell-Gates, 2002). In the area of culture considerations, Graves and Rueda (2009) note that it is important to differentiate between cultural practices and cultural models. *Cultural models* represent broader cultural beliefs and values, while *cultural practices* reflect what people actually do in their everyday lives. One of the risks noted by the authors is when educators attribute the broad labels of cultural models to particular ethnic or racial groups. A delicate balance exists between being informed by cultural models, while also ensuring that educators look at each individual as a participant in overlapping and embedded communities or practice, including classroom, school, family, community, country, and even global community. Understanding the rich nature of students' affiliation with multiple linguistic and cultural communities allows teachers to become more sensitive in accessing students' unique funds of knowledge (Moll, Amanti, Neff, & González, 1992) and making linkages between these experiences to the content of the academic curriculum. Finally, the importance of socioeconomic status is a variable that can impact all learners but may uniquely impact families where there are differences in schooling and English language fluency. Teachers need to be aware that socioeconomic conditions do not determine a family's course of action, but they may contribute to challenges that students bring to school, including differential access to life experiences, quality of nutrition, and access to health care and a variety of cultural models used in schools.

This chapter offers a framework of supports for teachers to use as they attempt to apprentice their middle school or junior high students into the learning-to-learn, cognitive, and metacognitive strategies that support all phases of an inquiry process. The supports are drawn from research known as Project ACCEL (*Acc*elerating *E*xpository *L*iteracy). Although the original project focused on supporting teachers and students in inclusive social studies and science classrooms, it became apparent that a sociocognitive apprenticeship approach to teaching reading and writing addressed the strategic needs of a majority of the adolescent students, including bilingual students in content-area classrooms. The explicit focus of the project on the development of academic discourses associated with reading to learn and writing to learn was associated with the growth of students as learners and communicators in content-area subjects.

In the first part of the chapter we report the results of our investigation into the performance of junior high students' in highlighting expository information, taking notes, synthesizing information across multiple sources, and developing a writing plan that informed an actual written report. The findings from this study suggested the complexities of supporting students in social studies and science curricula and, especially, the important role that teachers play in orchestrating classroom dialogues about learning-to-learn strategies, while they engage their students as active participants enroute to developing their mastery of the core literacy processes (e.g., comprehension, writing process, text structures) and deepen their understanding of the disciplinary content. The chapter then examines a curricular response that constituted the foundation of Project ACCEL, which combined teacher supports and student supports in a serviceable curricular approach based on a pedagogical model that viewed teaching and learning as a sociocognitive apprenticeship in which teachers were key knowledgeable others who over time ceded increasing control of all aspects of constructing meaning to students. The chapter concludes with a brief discussion of the need for a research agenda in the content-area writing for middle-grade bilingual students.

ACCEL Assessments: A Window into Students' Thinking-to-Learn and Learning-to-Learn Strategies

The ACCEL strategies were developed in response to problems we identified in the learning-to-learn strategies in the general population of adolescent students. The project assessed students' abilities to comprehend, compose, and perform learning-to-learn strategies related to effective reading and writing in content areas (see Englert et al., 2007). Comprehensive assessments were administered to over 1,000 sixth-, seventh-, and eighth-grade students over a period of 4 years (2004–2008). Students came from both an urban middle school (sixth, seventh, and eighth grade) and a suburban junior high school (seventh and eighth grade). Specific academic measures that were administered to students included the following (Englert et al., 2007):

- Highlighting information in a social studies passage (e.g., Battle of Trenton, Plains Indians).
- Taking notes on a social studies passage to study for a test.
- Having students retell what they remember from a social studies passage after reading.
- Writing a persuasive essay by taking a position on an issue.

- Synthesize information from multiple scientific sources (fact sheets, table, graph).
- Creating a plan, map, or organizer based on the content information.
- Writing an informational report about an animal (e.g., Canadian lynx, platypus).

In addition, students in a small group were interviewed individually to ascertain their knowledge of strategies they employed before, during, and after reading or writing. Thirty-six sixth-, seventh-, and eighth-grade students, several of whom were bilingual and had IEPs, were interviewed about their learning strategies.

The results of the assessment revealed that while general education students outperformed students with language/learning disabilities on virtually every learning-to-learn measure (e.g., highlighting, note taking, reading, and writing), the majority of students appeared to struggle in employing the learning-to-learn strategies, mentioned earlier, in the service of reading or writing expository texts.

Two case examples illustrate how learning-to-learn strategies may provide teachers with insight into the performance abilities and inner thinking of their students. In the first case, a summary of how students highlighted and summarized information is reported. Then the second case looks at students' ability to synthesize information from several sources to develop a writing plan for composing an informational report about an animal. The work of one student, Juan Rodriguez, a seventh grader identified as having a learning disability in the area of reading, serves to illustrate the complexity in attending to the learning zones of students' academic discourses around learning to learn, cognitive strategies, reading, and composition.

Case 1: Highlighting Information and Taking Notes as Learning-to-Learn Strategies

The results of the interview revealed some interesting teaching and learning dilemmas. All students reported that they were asked to highlight information or take notes in at least one or several of their content-area classes. However, when asked if their teachers had taught them how to highlight and take notes, only 50% reported being directly taught to perform these skills.

The gap between being asked to perform highlighting and note-taking tasks, but not being apprenticed in how to perform these tasks using learning-to-learn strategies was reflected in the student performance data. Examining highlighting performance revealed that many students did not know how to select important information effectively by highlighting main ideas and key details. Instead, these students tended to highlight excessively (i.e., highlighting everything) or too insufficiently to provide an adequate summary of the important ideas in the passage.

Similarly, when asked to take notes on the important information in a social studies passage, less than 13% of general education students and less than 5% of the special education students produced notes that were labeled or hierarchically organized to reflect the main ideas and supporting details of the passage. Furthermore, students tended to use one of three inefficient note-taking strategies: (1) a copy strategy, in which they rewrote the original source text verbatim; (2) a bullet strategy, in which they listed random facts in a bulleted but undifferentiated list; and (3) a copy/alt/delete strategy, in which they copied the text but left out connecting words, such as prepositions. However, none of the three note-taking strategies resulted in meaningfully chunked sets of ideas, with easily discernible categories of main ideas and supporting details, or sets of ideas with labels that conveyed the relationship among the ideas. The failure to create an organized and labeled set of ideas reduced the likelihood that the notes would be an effective way to rehearse, memorize, conceptualize, store, and retrieve information.

Juan Rodríguez is an example of a student who has appropriated several key ideas about highlighting information and note taking but could benefit from additional modeling and practice. As shown in Figure 7.1, Juan's highlighting of the social studies passage about the "Battle of Trenton" indicates that he appeared to have some selectivity in what ideas he highlighted, because no paragraphs were totally highlighted or left completely blank. Juan highlighted mostly complete sentences, but he did show an ability to highlight key vocabulary (e.g., *Hessians* and *American* in paragraph 6), sentence fragments (e.g., *shrink from the service of their country*), and key quotations (e.g., "Let the Americans come!"). A close look at what information is highlighted also reveals that Juan was not consistent in his ability to identify main ideas and key details in the passage. Juan highlights the first sentence in five of the seven full paragraphs on the page, some that contain the main ideas (e.g., "A second problem was the lack of trained men"), but an examination of the highlighted details following the main ideas do not demonstrate selection of key facts that support the main idea. When one rereads Juan's highlighted text, it typically does not provide an efficient summary of the main points and key supporting details. In some paragraphs, including paragraphs 3 and 4, Juan highlights extensively and only at the sentence level, making it just as efficient to read the entire paragraph as to read the highlighted information. Where Juan does provide more selectivity,

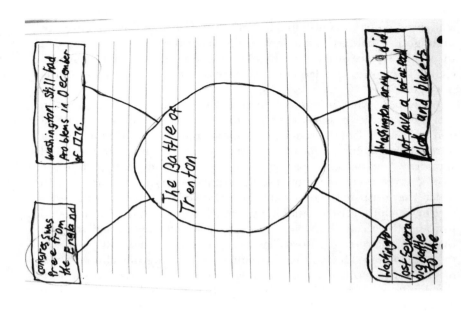

FIGURE 7.1. Juan's highlighting and note taking.

such as in paragraphs 6 and 7, highlighting does not provide a coherent summary of the paragraph: "Washington called together his soldiers on Christmas Eve . . . shrink from the service of the country . . . that a good soldier . . . The password was "Victory or death." Juan's highlighting provides one source of evidence in attempting to understand how he might be making sense of the expository passage.

When asked to take notes on the same passage, Juan drew a web, with the words "The Battle of Trenton" in the middle of the web and four boxes that projected out from the middle (see Figure 7.1). A separate and unique detail copied from the passage was written in each of the four boxes (e.g., "Washington still had problems in December of 1776"). Juan successfully recorded three main ideas in his web, but without any supporting details to illuminate the main idea; the four ideas that he recorded represent only 5% of the total number of ideas. Furthermore, although Juan attempted to produce a facsimile of a concept map, the superordinate categorical labels that he recorded did not allow him to represent or subordinate the key details according to their meaningful relationship with other ideas or their purpose in the passage. Without this hierarchical relationship, the notes were not an efficient tool for rehearsing the information. The consequences of this difficulty may be reflected in his written recall and a short multiple-choice assessment of the passage. While Juan copied texts verbatim from the information sheets into his maps and essay (see Figure 7.2 in next section), his written recall revealed a fairly limited understanding of the passage that included just three details: "We lead aboued the britis vs the Aarcans. The Amercu did not have a lot of men food clase shous and blaces (We learned about the British vs. the Americans. The Americans did not have a lot of men, food, clothes, shoes, and blankets). In a short, 10-question quiz following the written retelling, Juan correctly answered 3 of 10 multiple-choice questions correctly.

Juan's performance suggested that he has some partial understandings of possible learning-to-learn strategies. In examining his highlighting of the passage, it is evident that he would occasionally highlight the first sentence of a paragraph, then search for some additional key details, but not consistently or accurately, in cases where main ideas were not contained in the first sentence. He also demonstrates that he has seen graphic organizers being used (see also Figure 7.2 for Juan's writing plan for the platypus lesson) by organizing his notes in the form of a web. Particularly important is that Juan does identify three of four main ideas in his web, with each main idea and detail also highlighted in his text. However, Juan does not take advantage of these superordinate categorical labels to recall additional key details. Without this hierarchical relationship, the notes cannot be used as an efficient tool to rehearse information. Juan's highlighting and note taking provide teachers with ample information to see where to bridge new and known information. Juan's ability to identify some main ideas in highlighting and successfully pull main ideas into his note-taking web suggest that there are openings into a zone of development that relate to searching for main ideas, then finding key details that lend evidence to support that main idea. Over time, with repeated opportunities to participate in sociocognitive apprenticeship, where Juan can witness and coparticipate in instructional dialogues with knowledgeable others, a discourse space can be created to provide Juan with the cognitive and mediational tools to bridge these learning gaps.

Case 2: Synthesizing and Organizing Information to Develop a Writing Plan and Report in Science

Content-area teachers are increasingly engaging their students in inquiry around special topics in the curriculum. There is an expectation that students should be able to conduct an appropriate search for information pertaining to an assigned topic, independently comprehend that information using multiple source materials (e.g., texts, digital texts, media, primary/secondary artifacts), effectively reduce that information into main ideas/supporting details, organize that information, and then create a product that demonstrates understanding (e.g., a written report, a poster, or PowerPoint presentation). Many teachers do not contemplate the cognitive demands they place on their students when assigning these projects. While teachers have made important strides to improve clarity and accountability by assigning complex rubrics that highlight component standards, we seldom witness teachers providing explicit instruction to help students develop key learning-to-learn strategies that make accessing information possible.

To gain insight into whether students can synthesize and organize information from several sources about an endangered animal (e.g., platypus, wombat), middle-grade (sixth to eighth) students were provided two fact sheets that each contained 25 details, a graph, and a table with data about the animal they were to study. The facts were randomly distributed on the two sheets but corresponded to eight categories of information (e.g., how they hunt, appearance, care for young), with at least five details per category. Students were asked to look at the information across the four sources of information and develop a writing plan for a written report about their animal. Students were told that they could use any form of plan they wished, including web, outline, table, or organized notes. Day 1 was devoted entirely to planning the paper. Day 2 was devoted to writing the report.

Results of the data analysis revealed that the vast majority of students chose to utilize either a web or table to organize the information for their writing plans. Close inspection of the writing plans provided important insight into the inner thinking of students with and without disabilities:

- Writing plans often looked like a web, but many students struggled to identify a categorical label that would constitute the main idea for a set of ideas.
- Details were often grouped together in a random fashion rather than categorically linked and labeled.
- Few students identified even 75% of the available categories (i.e., six of eight items on fact sheets).
- Few students identified the majority of details within a category.
- Less than 10% of the students used information in the table and graph to inform their writing plan; only 5% used all four sources of information

In looking at Juan's writing plan and report (Figure 7.2), there is evidence that he has become aware of mapping as a strategy for organizing information, and this is supported by his note-taking web in Figure 7.1. Close examination of the content of his map reveals important insights about Juan's current learning zone. All four boxes include specific details ("Platypus lay 1–2 leather eggs"; "Platypus Belly is grey or golden," etc.) that are directly copied from the fact sheet, although Juan does not provide conceptual or categorical labels for the chunked ideas. There is also only a single level of information, with no evidence that there might be hierarchical relationships involving superordinate and subordinate ideas. Juan's selection of details represent four different categories, suggesting that he may indeed perceive or understand the importance of different categories of information (e.g., "what they eat," "predators," "appearance," and "care for young"). Juan's written report supports this claim, because he constructs two separate paragraphs containing four and three coherent details that conform to each of two categories, "care for young" and "predators," respectively. This indicates that Juan was able to read through the fact sheets and successfully identify details that support a category of information, even though that category was not labeled, and additional details used in the essay were not included in his writing plan. Juan's report illuminates several possible focus areas that may warrant instruction, including construction of introductory paragraphs, concluding paragraphs, and topic sentences; paraphrasing information; sentence combining; transition words; and strategies for making Juan's writing more sensitive to his audience.

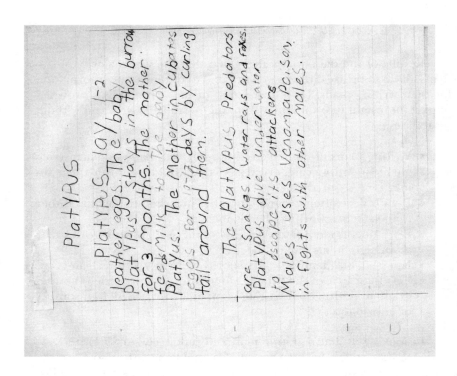

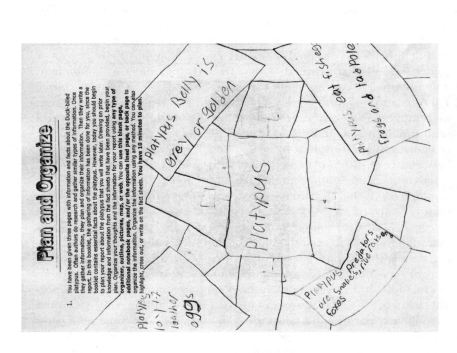

FIGURE 7.2. Juan's writing plan and written report.

These findings highlight some unique challenges for teachers. First, while there is reason to celebrate the unprecedented access to information in multiple modalities (Internet, text readers, video streaming), even when provided access to information from several sources, many students may not have the requisite skills to synthesize and organize that information in ways that can inform their writing. Second, the difficulty in organizing and representing information by constructing superordinate and subordinate categories illustrates some of the challenges that students face in comprehending and writing informational reports. Third, when presented with information that they might gather through their independent research of a topic, students may demonstrate some difficulties with both breadth of categories identified and depth of details to support a category of information. Finally, access to multiple sources does not ensure that students utilize information within those sources. In this study, students either chose not to use information in the tables and graphs or they had difficulty in interpreting these sources of information, a common expectation in today's Information Age. Interpreting and learning to "read" tables and graphs are important comprehension and interpretation (linking information to self, text, and world) skills that likely require direct and explicit instruction.

Examining students' notes, writing plans, and compositions provides teachers with a unique window on their students' thinking. Teachers can quickly examine the quality of students' notes or writing plans on several dimensions, including the ability to identify main ideas and key details, the breadth of students' categories as they research a topic, and the depth of details to support a category of information. The remainder of the chapter explores a curricular approach that attempted to support middle-grade content-area teachers as they taught their students learning-to-learn, comprehension, and composition strategies for interacting with informational texts. The following section briefly examines the theoretical and pedagogical backdrop that supported teachers and students on Project ACCEL. The next section then examines the ACCEL curricular approach for accessing content-area learning.

Teacher and Student Supports on the ACCEL Project

Catalyst Lessons to Support Teaching of Strategies

During the past 5 years of working with content-area teachers, we have repeatedly observed how difficult it is to teach students learning-to-learn strategies. Content-area teachers in our studies provided students with multiple opportunities to use reading and writing to support their instruction on a daily basis. We observed teachers having students highlight information, take notes, use graphic organizers to represent ideas, and engage in partner or small-group work. However, as Conley (2008) notes, there is a subtle but distinct difference in teaching activities and cognitive strategy instruction. Teachers engaged students in activities that had the potential to become useful learning strategies, but without making these strategies salient by helping students to become metacognitive relative to the strategy (what, when, where, why, how). Students appeared to be engaging in activity without the conscious realization of how the strategy might be a cognitive tool to accomplish learning goals.

Existing research on effective cognitive strategy instruction demonstrates the importance of having high levels of procedural fidelity to the intervention (Deshler et al., 2001; Mariage, 1995; Troia & Graham, 2003). One way we supported teachers when implementing new pedagogical practices was to provide direct modeling and a lesson script to help reduce the cognitive load related to grappling with content and pedagogy. In our project, doctoral students volunteered to model catalyst lessons in social studies and science classes, to allow the teacher to experience the lessons firsthand. Then, later, each project teacher identified and taught a lesson while their grade- and content-level colleagues observed the lesson. This classroom observation was then followed by a debriefing period of all grade-level content-area faculty (e.g., the five seventh-grade social studies teachers) and the researchers who viewed the lesson. To support debriefing of the lesson, a procedural facilitation tool that outlined a series of evidenced-based pedagogical practices supported a guided conversation. Rather than leave this shift toward metacognitive strategy instruction to chance, a series of catalyst lessons was created for teachers' use in whole or in part to introduce a strategy, or set of strategies, for the first time. Catalyst lessons included a lesson script, supporting materials (e.g., transparencies, posters, cue cards, procedural facilitation checklist), and attention to the principles of cognitive apprenticeship (see below). Contact us for copies of the lesson plans for teaching PLANS It, Highlights It, Marks It/Notes It, Maps It, and Writes It.

Making Visible the Invisible: Tools, Scaffolds, and Procedural Facilitation

Content-area learning places unique demands on learners, because students with limited background knowledge often must learn content (e.g., historical understanding, scientific method) and be introduced to expository texts that are vocabulary and conceptually dense. Students are learning the unique disciplinary processes, such as carrying out scientific investigations or creating claims and justifications related to historical evidence (Okolo, Ferretti, & McArthur, 2007; VanSledright, 2004), while also attempting to understand the content. These unique disciplinary ways of knowing require an approach to instruction that makes visible these often invisible mental representations. Fortunately, the field of special education has a long and rich history of helping to scaffold and support students as they increasingly take control of the learning process. An example of the ACCEL framework is shown in Figure 7.3. The tools remind teacher and students that they may need to call on different strategies and tools at different phase of the inquiry.

Cognitive Apprenticeship: Pedagogical Principles for Learning to Learn

The goal of helping students to access rigorous content-area curriculum required a theory of teaching and learning that emphasized the role of knowledgeable others in providing a social and cognitive apprenticeship in the unique content, processes, strategies, and discourses that define the content area. Collins, Brown, and Holum (1991) provided an architecture for thinking about engaging learners in cognitive apprenticeships. In their original article, they provided a series of design principles that included (1) *content* (the types of knowledge required for expertise), (2) *method* (the ways to promote the development of expertise), (3) *sequencing* (keys to ordering activities), and (4) *sociology* (the social qualities of learning environments).

The ACCEL project drew upon and combined aspects of sociocultural and cognitive theories of learning to inform the development of a pedagogical approach that emphasizes the teaching of content through a form of sociocognitive apprenticeship. Sociocultural principles of learning include the central importance placed upon (1) the role of knowledgeable others (e.g., teachers, peers) in apprenticing students in the discourse, tools, and processes of content-area learning; (2) the use of cultural artifacts and tools (e.g., cue cards, think sheets, graphic organizers, procedural facilitators) to mediate collaborative learning in various grouping arrangements; (3) work within students and teachers' zones of proximal development through responsive feedback and instructional scaffolds of all kinds (Stone, 2002); and (4) creation of

ACCEL Curriculum Framework

Phases of Inquiry	PLANNING	GATHERING	INTERPRETING		ORGANIZING	REPORTING
ACCEL Strategy Frameworks	**PLANS It**	**Highlight It**	**Reads It**		**Maps It**	**Writes It**
			Note It · Mark It	Respond to It		
Purpose	•Preview information •Brainstorm •Predict •Question •Connect •Structure of information	•Highlight information •Identify main ideas •Summarize ideas •Self question •Connect to self, text, and world	•Clarify unfamiliar vocabulary •Draw inferences •Self-questioning •Visualizing •Summarizing •Sequencing •Intertextuality	•Using evidence to support claims •Perspective taking •Critiquing ideas •Connecting to text, self, and world •Giving/receiving feedback	•Gather information •Integrate multiple sources •Note key ideas •Use multiple representations •Organize information from multiple sources •Record information on graphic organizer	•Generate a written report •Communicate findings •Multiple representations •Oral sharing/ discussion
Examples of Academic Discourses: Strategies, Processes, and Content	**P**urpose **L**ist topics and preview **A**ctivate prior knowledge by connecting to self, texts, world **N**ote your questions **S**tructure: What text structure? •Cause/Effect •Problem/Solution •Compare/Contrast •Time Sequence •Classification •Explanation	•Highlight main ideas •Highlight key details •Mark text with symbols: Cl–clarify PK–prior knowledge Q–question P–predict S–summarize I–imagery C–connect D–detail MI–main idea *–key point ?–confusing part		**Respond to it with Text Structure Tools:** •Cause/Effect •Problem/Solution •Compare/Contrast •Time Sequence •Classification •Explanation	**Map with Text Structure Tools:** •Cause/Effect •Problem/Solution •Compare/Contrast •Time Sequence •Classification •Explanation •Main Idea/details •Persuasion	•Oral sharing techniques •Writing genres •Using data to represent findings •Planning •Organizing •Writing •Editing •Revising
Teacher and Student Supports	•Lesson plan •PLANS It log	•Lesson plans •Cue cards (Reads It, Highlights It, Marks It, Notes It) •Local, interpretative, and global comprehension •Rubrics •Think-Pair-Share •Reads It Log			•Graphic organizers •Rubrics •Lesson plan •Text structure maps	•Writes It cue cards •Rubrics •Lesson plan •Text structures as rhetorical devices

FIGURE 7.3. ACCEL curriculum framework.

activity settings that position learners in new roles and responsibilities that foster strategic learning.

Creating Access to the Content Curriculum: Teaching Learning-to-Learn, Comprehension, and Composition Strategies as Academic Discourses in Content-Area Classrooms

In an inquiry process, students are asked to orchestrate strategies before, during, and after an investigation, including strategies related to (1) activating or building background knowledge about a topic; (2) generating questions to guide inquiry; (3) gathering information from multiple sources of information (e.g., texts, digital images, media); (4) comprehending information and organizing information through a process of synthesis; (5) interpreting information to make connections to the self, to other texts, and to the past/present/future worlds; and (6) making learning public through a process of demonstration. For teachers, the pedagogical challenge in middle-grade content-area inquiry is at least twofold: (1) helping to ensure that students have requisite strategies for each phase of the inquiry that are unique to the discipline (i.e., activating background knowledge, questioning, identifying main ideas and details, organizing information, and composition strategies), and (2) seeing that students have opportunities to orchestrate these strategies within and across an inquiry process, as opposed to learning cognitive strategies as isolated entities. Research suggests that for students to be successful in the richest forms of inquiry in content areas, teachers may need to adopt *advanced instructional features*—modifying the text, task, social support, and basic reading requirements (Englert & Dunsmore, 2004; Palincsar, Magnusson, Collins, & Cutter, 2001; Okolo et al., 2007).

The ACCEL approach to accessing the curriculum is organized around four areas that can either be focused on separately (e.g., teaching prereading strategies) or in combination to support thinking and understanding. These four areas include strategies related to (1) PLANS It, (2) Reads It (Highlights It, Marks It, Notes It, Responds to It), (3) Maps It, and (4) Writes It. The four areas, used together, are designed to provide supported instruction for an entire inquiry process as students plan, research, organize/map, write, and publish their work. Although individual teachers chose to use ACCEL in ways that suited their unique learners, subjects, and grade-level curriculum, a set of pedagogical features distinguished ACCEL instruction, including (1) explicit catalyst lessons for teaching each of the five areas within ACCEL; (2) tools, scaffolds, and procedural facilitation to support learners; and (3) pedagogical principles to guide instruction.

Planning for Learning: PLANS It

Effective and strategic learners take time to analyze their learning task, look at available information to determine the lay of the land, use information (pictures, graphs, tables, headings, subheadings, bolt text) to begin to anticipate what they will read, and may even draw on other sources of information to build sufficient background knowledge to make more sense of new information. On Project ACCEL, teachers drew on a framework of strategies that mirrored several of the mental actions of strategic learners. Cued by the acronym PLANS It, these strategies were prompted by key questions and actions to prepare students for learning new information. As shown in Figure 7.4, students first identified their *P*urpose for reading by asking themselves, "Why am I reading this?" Students were then asked to *L*ist topics and preview by moving through the material, skimming, scanning, and identifying key topics that might be cued by looking at major headings, subheadings, pictures, tables, graphs, or other clues. The third step in the PLANS It framework was to *A*ctivate prior knowledge by making connections to the self, other texts they had read, or experiences in the world. Students then *N*oted questions that they wanted or needed to answer. Questioning the text has been shown to be one of the most effective strategies that more able readers apply to self-monitor and evaluate their understanding (Pressley & Afflerbach, 1995). Finally, one of the most uncommon features of the PLANS It framework is asking students to identify the possible *S*tructures they might encounter in the text. Text structures are the ways that texts are organized to accomplish authors' goals, such as to demonstrate cause and effect, problems and solutions, explanations, time lines, or persuasion, among others. Rarely do teachers ask students to make these types of meta-level predictions about how the text might be structured or restructured to answer particular questions about expository content. While teachers often ask students to fill out graphic organizers after they begin reading information, they seldom ask students to consider how the author may use the text's structure to communicate information about the topic. For example, in a unit on wave types, a seventh-grade science teacher asked students what types of text structures the author might use to discuss different types of waves (e.g., sound, light). The students then predicted that the author might compare and contrast the different wave types on key dimensions.

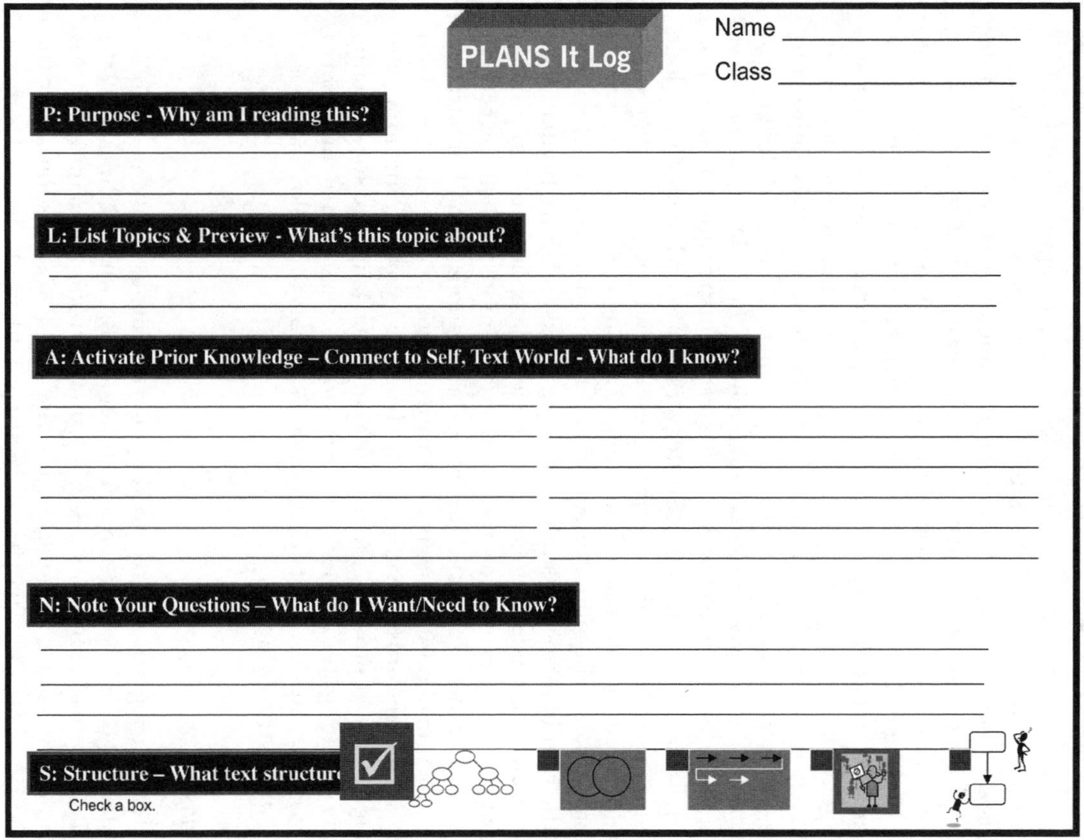

PLANS It Log

Name _____

Class _____

P: Purpose - Why am I reading this?

L: List Topics & Preview - What's this topic about?

A: Activate Prior Knowledge – Connect to Self, Text World – What do I know?

N: Note Your Questions – What do I Want/Need to Know?

S: Structure – What text structure

Check a box.

FIGURE 7.4. PLANS It log.

Reads It: A Suite of Learning-to-Learn and Comprehension Monitoring Strategies

A second area that warranted explicit social mediation involved a suite of learning-to-learn strategies that one could use to begin comprehending expository information from multiple sources, including texts, images, videos, tables, graphs, or historical documents. Five strategy frameworks were developed to interact with expository information within the information-gathering phase of the inquiry process: (1) Reads It logs, (2) Highlights It, (3) Marks It, (4) Notes It, and (5) Responds to It. Each strategy framework was prompted by a comprehensive lesson script, lesson materials, student materials (e.g., graphic organizers, think sheets, and text structure maps), and cue cards to facilitate collaborative practice using the strategies. Lesson scripts for teachers were designed to promote higher levels of procedural fidelity to the pedagogical practices that underlie more effective cognitive strategy instruction (Deshler et al., 2001; Troia & Graham, 2003). Strategy lessons were designed to include many features of cognitive apprenticeship (Collins et al., 1991), especially a focus on the role of modeling, thinking aloud, demonstration, coparticipation in guided practice, and the gradual ceding of control of the cognitive work as students assume more and more regulation of the strategies. Student cue cards extended the apprenticeship process, providing an intermediary tool between the more explicit instruction provided by the teacher and the independent application of the strategy in authentic expository texts. Cue cards were also differentiated, with one set of cue cards providing more structured support, including language stems to provide students with an inner language for directing and regulating strategy performance, and another, less structured set of cards that simply prompts or reminded students to employ the steps of the strategic routine.

Reads It Log

A Reads It log was created to support students as they engage in six evidenced-based comprehension strategies (Brown & Palincsar, 1989) while they read expository texts: (1) summarizing the main idea ("My summary is . . . "); (2) questioning the text ("My question about the topic is . . . "); (3) clarifying unclear vocabulary or ideas ("I am confused about . . . " or "A term that I don't know is . . . "); (4) connecting ideas in the text to self, text, or world ("This reminds me of . . . " or "I wonder if . . . "); (5) using text structure to understand the text (asking text structure questions); and (6) predicting what may come next ("I predict that . . . "). The Reads It log itself serves as a cue card that could guide a conversation with oneself or dialogue between students using the six strategies. Sentence stems that foster a specific language for talking about the content of the informational text were included on the log to support discussion about the meaning of the text. So, for example, the strategies of questioning and clarifying, the stems to prompt discussion included "My question about this topic is . . . " and "I'm confused about. . . . " Some teachers used a Reads It think sheet to capture students' inner thoughts and responses based on the strategy prompts, and these think sheets guided students' discussions and collaborations with a peer or small group. Built into the log were prompts with sentence stems that cued the type of self-talk associated with the effective application of each strategy. Students also were partnered in a think–pair–share format, where they were asked to share and discuss their logs and ideas with a partner. Hence, the specific language of comprehension was made visible and accessible to all students, including students with diverse language backgrounds; the procedure simultaneously privileged students who asked questions, clarified concepts or vocabulary, and connected ideas to themselves and their worlds. This provided a context wherein language learners could be recognized as leaders in the application of strategic knowledge to comprehend expository topics.

Highlights It and Notes It

A second set of strategies for supporting students' interaction with texts as they read is highlighting and noting key ideas and facts. Although highlighting can serve multiple purposes (e.g., highlighting key vocabulary, key dates, or facts), highlighting and note taking were used primarily to help students learn to identify and construct the meaning relationship among the main ideas and key details. The extensive literature on students' difficulties in identifying main ideas, summarizing information, and monitoring to understand as they read expository information indicated a need to teach students a way to monitor understanding as they extracted key information within a text (Klingner, Vaughn, Dimino, Schumm, & Bryant, 2001). Teachers modeled, thought aloud, and engaged students in highlighting and note taking as they made visible the cognitive routines for making textual decisions about the relative importance and relationship among sets of ideas.

Throughout their demonstrations, teachers emphasized the importance of reading and rereading text, carrying on an inner dialogue with the text and oneself while searching for the key ideas in a passage, and reducing the information to the essential main ideas as opposed to highlighting or copying extensive sections of text. Teachers also emphasized to students the importance of being able to "read" their own highlighting/note taking, so that the marked-up text and notes serve as a cognitive resource that can be used to locate key ideas rapidly or to study the information to prepare for a test or composition. Flexibility also was central to helping students understand how to take notes to achieve their own learning purposes and goals. For this reason, note taking was allowed to assume multiple forms in ACCEL classrooms to demonstrate the relationship between form and function, including (1) Cornell notes, where students divide their papers into two columns, with main topics or ideas noted in the left column, and corresponding facts or details in the right column; (2) text structure maps to organize ideas and notes into specific textual patterns and relationships (e.g., cause–effect, time line, compare–contrast, or main ideas/details); (3) tailored notes that use features of the content area for guiding note taking (e.g., using five themes of social studies to guide note taking on Roman civilization); and (4) using Post-it Notes to identify key facts that are later put into superordinate and labeled categories on a graphic organizer that outlines key information related to the topic.

A Highlights It and Notes It cue card is shown in Figure 7.5. The cue cards were designed to extend practice opportunities for students who need support as the teacher transfers increasing responsibility for directing the cognitive routine to students. Cue cards prompt the steps of the strategy, as well as scaffold the nature of the inner dialogue and regulatory processes that students are asked to apply to monitor their strategic performance. As shown in Figure 7.5, for example, the cue card prompts students to highlight or take notes on the important ideas and details, reread their highlighting/notes, conduct a self-check to see whether the recorded ideas make sense, engage in a think–pair–share activity with a partner, then be prepared to report as a partner or team to the whole class. All of these activities are designed to deepen students' abilities to communicate about the expository ideas related to the academic content of the disciplinary subject, with plenty of opportunities for feedback from peers and the teacher. The opportunity to communicate frequently about expository ideas is an important quality that supports students for whom the language of the textbook is unfamiliar or distant from their everyday experience.

Marks It

A third way to interact with written informational texts is the Marks It strategy. Similar to Highlights It and Notes It, the Marks It framework of strategies provides students with access to the thinking of knowledgeable others. The teacher typically models the Marks It strategy by identifying a passage or chapter in the content curriculum and conducting a think-

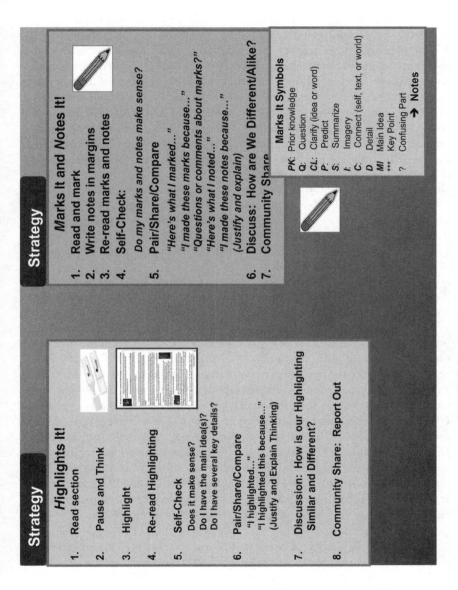

FIGURE 7.5. Highlights It and Notes It cue card.

aloud that incorporated a series of Marks It symbols corresponding to the strategies introduced and modeled as tools for comprehending and responding to the text. For example, the Marks It symbols include: CL (Clarify), BK (Background Knowledge), ? (Question), MI (Main Idea), P (Prediction), and I (Inference). Recording the symbols at the textual locations where students had particular strategic responses provided them, with a permanent record of their inner thoughts and interpretations, further deepened their own metacognitive knowledge of the strategies they were employing. The final marked-up text offered a record of students' literacy performance that could then be shared with partners and or the whole class in a community share (see Marks It cue card in Figure 7.5). Importantly, teachers also discussed the types of strategies that students applied to comprehend the passage and the features of the text or context that provoked the use of particular strategies. In this manner, talk about strategies, content, and literacy processes figured prominently in shaping the linguistic and cultural context for making meaning in the content-area classroom.

Responds to It

The final set of Reads It strategies includes two strategy frameworks for interpreting texts: (1) using text structures (sequence of events, cause–effect, compare–contrast, etc.) to identify the rhetorical goals of the author, and (2) using a set of critical literacy strategies to help students challenge, extend, and connect to the information. Historical and scientific inquiry both invite and even demand thinking beyond the text, though this type of critical discourse is absent in most classrooms. In ACCEL classrooms, it was important to prompt teachers to create discourse spaces that encouraged students to connect experiences to their own cultural life (Klingner & Vaughn, 2004), especially for students who may not share dominant cultural experiences and history. Equally important was the opportunity to encourage voices that might provide challenge to dominant discourses (Delpit, 1995). To create such spaces, teachers were encouraged to emphasize a series of strategies: (1) critique the author, (2) multiple perspectives, (3) sources of bias, and (4) personal connection.

The ACCEL project made visible and explicit in an apprenticeship process a number of evidence-based strategies for comprehending and interpreting informational text. One of the challenges leveled at content-area instruction, such as social studies and science, is the infrequent opportunities that immigrant, ELL, and bilingual students have to impose their own experiences, cultural values, or funds of knowledge

(Moll et al., 1992) on the meaning-making process. The opportunity to go beyond the text's literal meaning through both cognitive strategies and critical literacy demands the creation of inquiry spaces where students are apprenticed in language, using practices that support their initial attempts to connect their historical and scientific understandings with other texts, their experiences, and their understanding of the world. The Responds to It cue card was designed specifically to prompt teachers to create a discourse space where conventional knowledge could be challenged by allowing students to move through and beyond the text to bring other experiences to bear on constructing meaning, such as thinking about information from multiple perspectives.

Maps It and Writes It

Interacting with expository text through learning-to-learn strategies (e.g., marking text, noting text, highlighting), cognitive strategies (summarize, clarify, question, connect), and text structure provide students with tools to facilitate understanding of expository information as they participate with knowledgeable others in using the tools, sharing their thinking with partners, and working independently across content areas. Getting meaning from multimedia sources is an important first step in developing an inquiry-based approach to content learning. Increasingly, however, the goals of inquiry in a multimedia world require that students synthesize information from diverse sources and impose structures for understanding and representing that information. In fact, although the world has been opened up to students, research suggests that for students who struggle with organization and do not possess or utilize cognitive strategies to impose structures, such as categories, main ideas, summaries, or superordinate and subordinate ideas, may be denied access to rich learning (Chen, 2009; Swanson, Hoskyn, & Lee, 1999; Klingner et al., 2001). At a time in history when we trumpet "access" to the general education curriculum, it is likely that without principled sociocognitive apprenticeships provided by capable teachers, many students who have been most at-risk for problems with understanding and composing remain on the outside looking in. Creating access is a step on the inquiry path, not an end point.

The data generated from the ACCEL assessments demonstrate that middle-grade students, regardless of ability, status, gender, ethnicity, or language practices, struggle with precisely those skills needed to impose organization on data from multiple sources. Even when students were provided the data in a series of fact sheets, graphs, or texts (e.g., facts about the platypus), they had difficulty organizing the information into categories to plan an expository essay. These challenges in identifying and constructing categories or main ideas are also reflected in students' expository writing, whether it be report writing or persuasive writing.

Teachers in ACCEL classrooms provide explicit instruction in strategies that students can use to impose categories on information they have compiled through mapping. At one level, teachers utilized categories of information associated with a particular content area that often provided recurring themes across chapters. For example, the teachers used five recurring themes within social studies (economy, government, culture, movement, language) as they studied different civilizations (e.g., Roman, Greek), using the themes to organize the information, then comparing and contrasting different civilizations. In this sense, the themes served as a metacomprehension tool or heuristic for organizing large amounts of information as students studied different cultures over long periods of time. A second mapping technique was the use of text structure organizers, such as cause–effect maps, compare–contrast, category/details, problem–solution, and persuasion. Text structure organizers helped teachers demonstrate how authors used structures to convey meaning, especially as they connected to particular content. Identifying the underlying structures of texts allowed students to identify key information related to the text structure. Text structure organizers were used in at least two ways in ACCEL classrooms: Teachers used text structure maps as note-taking tools, whereas students interacted with expository text. The notes typically served as a strategy for interacting with the text and gleaning information for later rehearsal (e.g., studying for a quiz). A second use of text structure maps was as a location to store information from multiple sources in an inquiry process to support future writing. For example, in a unit on Kenya, a teacher utilized information from the course textbook, supplemental readings, streaming video, and a guest speaker. A category/detail map served as a site to add information continually throughout the unit. A final use of the text structure maps was to support compositions.

A final strategy framework on Project ACCEL was Writes It. While students used writing to learn in virtually every strategy framework on ACCEL (i.e., PLANS It log, Reads It log, Notes It, Marks It), there were occasions when content-area teachers extended their inquiry to include written compositions. Writes It, like all strategy frameworks on ACCEL, includes both teacher supports (e.g., scripted lesson plans for teaching writing via an apprenticeship approach; procedural fidelity checklists for teaching cognitive strategies) and student supports (e.g., Writes It cue card, rubrics). In early lessons, teachers provided much of the cognitive work, facilitating dialogue around each facet of the composition process, including planning the paper, modeling how to get meaning from textual sources (e.g., main ideas and details), and organizing information using text structure organizers that matched the goal of the composition (e.g., report writing, persuasion), then engaging students in making visible the inner dialogues of writers as they moved from their maps (Maps It) to constructing written prose.

An Example of ACCEL Supporting an Inquiry into a Topic

As an example of a sociocognitive apprenticeship in researching and writing on the ACCEL project, a seventh-grade social studies teacher, Mr. Altenburg, engaged his students in a 2-week exploration of the Middle Ages, including the role of the Black Death pandemic. Mr. Altenburg used the 2-week unit, early in school year, as a site to introduce a variety of learning-to-learn strategies as cognitive tools that students would use the remainder of the year. He introduced students to the ACCEL framework (PLANS It, Reads It, Highlights It, Notes It, Marks It, Maps It, Writes It) as a process that would support their study of the Middle Ages and culminate in a written research report that could be shared with an authentic audience—a special reading to the school principal. Mr. Altenburg viewed this early unit as the important first step of an apprenticeship process that would extend across the entire year and increasingly cede more control to students for leading the instructional dialogue (Pearson & Gallagher, 1983).

During the introduction of each strategy, Mr. Altenburg reminded students that they would engage in a process where they would learn to "crawl, walk, and run" as they grew more proficient and independent in their strategy use. Mr. Altenburg explained that as the students learned something as complicated as researching a topic they knew little about, such as the Middle Ages, they would be "crawling," because he would assume greater responsibility for the cognitive work in modeling, thinking aloud, and demonstrating each strategy as they interacted with the content. Each day of the unit, Mr. Altenburg introduced a different learning-to-learn strategy to his students, explaining the purposes of the strategy, then modeling it through the use of a think-aloud dialogue with his students. This direct, explicit instruction helped to ensure that students had access to the academic discourse of learning to learn, reading, synthesizing, and composing as the teacher engaged them in a dialogue in which they gained insight into the metacognitive processes of knowledgeable others.

For example, on the first day of the unit, Mr. Altenburg introduced Highlights It. To generate excitement and interest, Mr. Altenburg brought in his own college textbook to show his students how he had used highlighting in his master's class text. He then drew upon the

ACCEL lesson to engage students in a discussion about how they might use highlighting, thought aloud with students as he searched for main ideas and key details of a supplemental reading on the digital image projector, then used the ACCEL Highlights It cue card to allow students the chance to practice highlighting independently and with their peers. The students were then asked to report on their partners in community sharing, what Mr. Altenburg called "ratting out a partner" who had done a good job highlighting key information. This process was repeated with the Notes It, Marks It, and Reads It strategies as the class interacted with different texts each day.

Mr. Altenburg then introduced a Maps It organizer as a location to gather all of the research students had done throughout the unit. Students reread their highlighted text, their margin notes from Marks It, their Reads It logs, and the Post-it Notes were part of the Notes It lesson. Mr. Altenburg reflected back on the previous unit, showing students that they had engaged and interacted with their reading in ways that had similar qualities and purposes, such as seeking main ideas and key supporting details. However, with all of this information, decisions needed to be made about what ideas to keep for their final report. Mr. Altenburg engaged students in a group discussion about the things they had learned across the unit, finally seizing on three superordinate categories and key details. Over the course of the final 2 days of the unit, Mr. Altenburg served as scribe and led his classes in an interactive writing activity as he modeled, thought aloud, and engaged the class in the co-construction of a final essay on the Middle Ages through the support of a Writes It cue card (Figure 7.6). Through this interactive writing activity, Mr. Altenburg was able to provide explicit insight and to create access to the academic discourse of writing, including ideas such as the purpose and function of introductory paragraphs, topic sentences, devices to increase audience interest, paragraphing, and how to combine details from one's writing plan into more complex sentences. The co-construction of the writing created a text that distributed learning and expertise across the entire community of learners, resulting in a product that was beyond the reach of any individual.

As this example illustrates, ACCEL was designed to support students' language and learning needs throughout the inquiry process. This support was provided at multiple levels: building level supports, teacher supports, and student supports. Inherent in the ACCEL approach was attention to a number of well-established, evidence-based areas in the literature, including cognitive strategy instruction, metacognition, and text structure (Graham, Olinghouse, & Harris, 2009). These evidence-based interventions were often "structured up" to better accommodate bilingual learners and those students with language and learning dis-

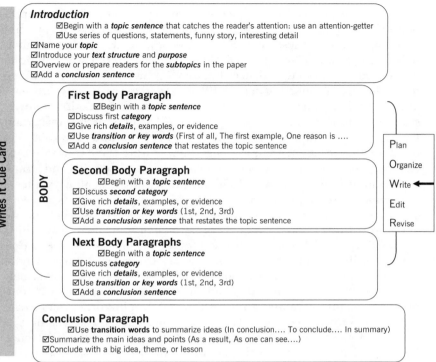

Writes It Cue Card

Introduction
☑Begin with a *topic sentence* that catches the reader's attention: use an attention-getter
☑Use series of questions, statements, funny story, interesting detail
☑Name your *topic*
☑Introduce your *text structure* and *purpose*
☑Overview or prepare readers for the *subtopics* in the paper
☑Add a *conclusion sentence*

BODY

First Body Paragraph
☑Begin with a *topic sentence*
☑Discuss first *category*
☑Give rich *details*, examples, or evidence
☑Use *transition or key words* (First of all, The first example, One reason is ....
☑Add a *conclusion sentence* that restates the topic sentence

Second Body Paragraph
☑Begin with a *topic sentence*
☑Discuss *second category*
☑Give rich *details*, examples, or evidence
☑Use *transition or key words* (1st, 2nd, 3rd)
☑Add a *conclusion sentence* that restates the topic sentence

Next Body Paragraphs
☑Begin with a *topic sentence*
☑Discuss *category*
☑Give rich *details*, examples, or evidence
☑Use *transition or key words* (1st, 2nd, 3rd)
☑Add a *conclusion sentence*

Conclusion Paragraph
☑Use *transition words* to summarize ideas (In conclusion.... To conclude.... In summary)
☑Summarize the main ideas and points (As a result, As one can see....)
☑Conclude with a big idea, theme, or lesson

Plan
Organize
Write ◄
Edit
Revise

FIGURE 7.6. Writes It cue card.

abilities, students who, we believe, benefit from more explicit instruction, greater opportunities to learn, scaffolded instruction that is reduced over time, and conscious attention to the role that language plays in the apprenticeship of academic and literate discourses.

Reflections and Future Directions

The Project ACCEL sought to provide teachers with learning tools and scaffolds that support all students while they engaged in the complex process of integrating multiple strategies before, during, and after an inquiry process. Rather than focus on learning a single strategy to mastery, the Project ACCEL sought to provide learning-to-learn and cognitive strategies across the entire inquiry process. In real contexts, it is this orchestration of multiple skills and strategies that is required for students to understand and create expository prose.

The ability to read and write fluently may mask underlying comprehension and composition challenges, especially for students who may not have appropriated these academic discourses, including those related to learning how to learn (Faltis & Coulter, 2008). In our study, middle-grade students showed evidence that they (1) had difficulty identifying main ideas and supporting details, (2) struggled to create superordinate and subordinate ideas (vs. lists of random facts) when taking notes to study for a quiz or planning their writing, (3) seldom used information from tables and graphs to add to their writing plans and essays, and (4) often abandoned their writing plans when writing their compositions. Needed are responsive teachers who can embed these skills and strategies seamlessly, intensively, and with an explicitness that allows students to become increasingly self-regulating.

In our experience with content-area middle-grade teachers, we agree with Conley (2008) that there have been some significant shifts in how these teachers use and value literacy. Schools across the nation have identified reading and writing across the curriculum as school improvement goals (including our ACCEL schools). Teachers routinely use literacy activities with their students, such as having students complete prereading vocabulary guides, fill out graphic organizers, write in science journals, complete lab reports, and engage in collaborative activity. However, we believe there is a subtle but distinct difference between having students participate in teaching activities and sociocognitive apprenticeships. In a sociocognitive apprenticeship, the instructional goals can shift to include learning how to learn as one important method for learning disciplinary content, while engaging in academic discourses that can render content meaningful (i.e., comprehension) and ways to re-present understanding (i.e., writing as a learning and cultural tool). While difficult to accomplish, when teachers raise to conscious realization their role in apprenticing students in learning how to comprehend and compose informational texts, they are creating access to goals they hope to achieve, including the processes of inquiry used by disciplinary experts (Englert & Mariage, 2003). Gaining more insight into how co-constructed knowledge in communities of practice becomes distributed within and across learners through cultural tools seems a particularly important area of study for bilingual students, ELLs, and students with learning disabilities.

Conclusion

Supporting all students in content-area writing and reading is a primary mechanism for apprenticing students into the unique academic languages that serve as markers for identity and competency as learners in these subject areas. If writing is indeed a threshold skill for career advancement in the future, then the types of expository writing (e.g., persuasion, argumentation, compare–contrast, problem–solution) and writing-to-learn strategies (e.g., note taking, highlighting, mapping, synthesizing from sources, outlining, marking) that fuel information technologies of all kinds are among the most important in intervention research. Project ACCEL has demonstrated its effectiveness in improving learning to learn, composition, and comprehension of students in comparison and control classrooms (Englert et al., 2007; Englert, Okolo, & Mariage, 2009). However, since our total number of bilingual students was insufficient to make meaningful comparisons, there remains a need to replicate these findings with this population of students in other settings. Project ACCEL may provide one way forward for future research in content-area writing and reading.

ENGAGEMENT ACTIVITIES

1. Having bilingual students, ELLs, or students with language/learning disabilities in our classrooms heightens our sensitivity to the role that language plays at all levels in constructing understanding. As practitioners, how might we raise our students' conscious realization of the unique academic discourse related to reading, composition, inquiry, and the specific content students are learning?

2. How might we as practitioners assess learning-to-learn strategies, such as note taking, highlighting, or planning to write a paper, as a window into how our students comprehend and compose?

3. The chapter argues that the unprecedented access to information may be lost on many students who do not have sufficient learning-to-learn and cognitive strategies. Without the ability to identify main ideas and key details to synthesize important information from multiple sources, or to organize information in superordinate/subordinate categories, students may struggle to benefit from the exposure to increasing amounts of information. In this chapter we have argued that students benefit from explicit instruction in these learning-to-learn and cognitive strategies. As practitioners, how can we think about how to organize this apprenticeship across the school year, especially when many students may need instruction across each of these academic discourses (i.e., learning to learn, reading, writing, disciplinary content knowledge)?

REFERENCES

Alexander, P. A., & Jetton, T. L. (2000). Learning from text: A multidimensional and developmental perspective. In M. L. Kamil, R. B. Mosenthal, P. D. Pearson, & R. Barr (Eds.), *Handbook of reading research* (Vol. III, pp. 285–310). Mahwah, NJ: Erlbaum.

Baker, S., Gersten, R., & Scanlon, D. (2002). Procedural facilitators and cognitive strategies: Tools for unraveling the mysteries of comprehension and the writing process and for providing meaningful access to the general curriculum. *Learning Disabilities Research and Practice, 17*, 65–77.

Baumann, J. F. (1984). The effectiveness of a direct instruction paradigm for teaching main idea comprehension. *Reading Research Quarterly, 20*(1), 93–115.

Brown, A., & Palinscar, A. (1989). Guided, cooperative learning and individual knowledge acquisition. In L. B. Resnick (Ed.), *Knowing, learning and instruction: Essays in honor of Robert Glaser* (pp. 393–451). Hillsdale, NJ: Erlbaum.

Chen, H.-Y. (2009). *Students' online reading comprehension strategies of informational text in general and special education classrooms.* Unpublished doctoral dissertation, Michigan State University, East Lansing.

Collins, A., Brown, J. S., & Holum, A. (1991). Cognitive apprenticeship: Making thinking visible. *American Educator, 15*, 6–11.

Conley, M. (2008). Cognitive strategy instruction for adolescents: What we know about the promise, what we don't know about the potential. *Harvard Educational Review, 78*(6), 84–106.

Delpit, L. (1995). *Other people's children: Cultural conflict in the classroom.* New York: New Press.

Deshler, D. D., Schumaker, J. B., Lenz, B. K., Bulgren, J. A., Hock, M. F., Knight, J., et al. (2001). Ensuring content-area learning by secondary students with learning disabilities. *Learning Disabilities Research and Practice, 16*(2), 96–108.

Englert, C. S., & Dunsmore, K. (2004). The role of dialogue in constructing effective literacy settings for students with language and learning disabilities. In E. Silliman & L. Wilkinson (Eds.), *Language and literacy learning in schools* (pp. 201–238). New York: Guilford Press.

Englert, C. S., Hiebert, E. H., & Stewart, S. R. (1987). Detecting and correcting inconsistencies in the monitoring of expository prose. *Journal of Educational Psychology, 79*, 221–227.

Englert, C. S., & Mariage, T. V. (2003). The sociocultural model in special education interventions: Apprenticing students in higher-order thinking. In H. L. Swanson, K. R. Harris, & S. Graham (Eds.), *Handbook of learning disabilities* (pp. 450–467). New York: Guilford Press.

Englert, C. S., Mariage, T. V., Okolo, C., Courtad, C., Shankland, R. K., Moxley, K. D., et al. (2007). Accelerating expository literacy in the middle grades: The ACCEL Project. In B. Taylor & J. Ysseldyke (Eds.), *Educational interventions for struggling readers* (pp. 138–169). New York: Teachers College Press.

Englert, C. S., Okolo, C. M., & Mariage, T. V. (2009). Content area reading and writing across the curriculum. In G. Troia (Ed.), *Instruction and assessment for struggling writers: Evidence-based practices* (pp. 132–164). New York: Guilford Press.

Englert, C. S., & Raphael, T. E. (1988). Constructing well-formed prose: Process, structure and metacognitive knowledge. *Exceptional Children, 54,* 513–520.

Englert, C. S., Raphael, T. E., & Mariage, T. V. (1998). A multi-year literacy intervention: Transformation and personal change in the community of the early literacy project. *Teacher Education and Special Education, 21,* 255–277.

Faltis, C. J., & Coulter, C. A. (2008). *Teaching English learners and immigrant students in secondary schools.* Upper Saddle River, NJ: Prentice-Hall.

Gajria, M., & Salvia, J. (1992). The effects of summarization instruction on text comprehension of students with learning disabilities. *Exceptional Children, 58,* 508–516.

Gee, J. P. (2008). *Social linguistics and literacies: Ideology in discourses* (3rd ed.). New York: Routledge.

Graham, S., & Harris, K. R. (1989). A components analysis of cognitive strategy training: Effects on learning disabled students' composition and self-efficacy. *Journal of Educational Psychology, 81,* 353–361.

Graham, S., Olinghouse, N. G., & Harris, K. R. (2009). Teaching composing to students with learning disabilities: Scientifically supported recommendations, In G. Troia (Ed.), *Instruction and assessment for struggling writers: Evidence-based practices* (pp. 165–186). New York: Guilford Press.

Graves, A. W. (1986). The effects of direct instruction and metacomprehension training on finding main ideas. *Learning Disabilities Research, 1*(2), 90–100.

Graves, A. W. (1987). Improving comprehension skills. *Teaching Exceptional Children, 19*(2), 58–67.

Graves, A. W., & Rueda, R. (2009). Teaching written expression to culturally and linguistically diverse learners. In G. Troia (Ed.), *Instruction and assessment for struggling writers: Evidence-based practices* (pp. 213–242). New York: Guilford Press.

Klingner, J. K., & Vaughn, S. (2004). Specific strategies for struggling second language readers and writers. In T. L. Jetton & J. A. Dole (Eds.), *Adolescent literacy research and practice* (pp. 183–209). New York: Guilford Press.

Klingner, J. K., Vaughn, S., Dimino, J., Schumm, J. S., & Bryant, D. (2001). *From clunk to click: Collaborative strategic reading.* Longmont, CO: Sopris West.

Ladson-Billings, G. (1992). Culturally relevant teaching: The key to making multicultural education work. In C. A. Grant (Ed.), *Research and multicultural education* (pp. 106–121). London: Falmer Press.

Malone, L. D., & Mastropieri, M. (1992). Reading comprehension instruction: Summarization and self-monitoring training for students with learning disabilities. *Exceptional Children, 58,* 270–279.

Mariage, T. V. (1995). Gaining insight into why children learn: Examining the nature of teacher talk in reading. *Learning Disability Quarterly, 18*(3), 214–235.

Meyer, B. J. F., Brandt, D. M., & Bluth, G. J. (1980). Use of top-level structure in text: Key for reading comprehension in ninth-grade students. *Reading Research Quarterly, 16,* 72–103.

Moll, L., Amanti, C., Neff, D., & González, N. (1992). Funds of knowledge for teaching: Using a qualitative approach to connect homes and classrooms. *Theory Into Practice, 31*(2), 132–141.

National Commission on Writing in America's Schools and Colleges. (2003). *The neglected "R": The need for a writing revolution.* New York: College Entrance Examination Board.

Nieto, S. (1999). *The light in their eyes: Creating multicultural learning communities.* New York: Teachers College Press.

Okolo, C. M., Ferretti, R. P., & MacArthur, C. D. (2007). Talking about history: Discussion in a middle-school inclusive classroom. *Journal of Learning Disabilities, 40,* 154–166.

Palincsar, A. S., Magnusson, S. J., Collins, K. M., & Cutter, J. (2001). Making science accessible to all: Results of a design experiment in inclusive classrooms. *Learning Disability Quarterly, 24,* 15–32.

Pearson, P. D., & Gallagher, M. C. (1983). The instruction of reading comprehension. *Contemporary Educational Psychology, 8,* 317–344.

Pressley, M., & Afflerbach, P. (1995). *Verbal reports of reading: The nature of constructively responsive reading.* Hillsdale, NJ: Erlbaum.

Purcell-Gates, V. (2002). " . . . As soon as she opened her mouth!" In L. Delpit & J. K. Dowdy (Eds.), *The skin that we speak: An anthology of essays on language, culture and power.* New York: New York University Press.

Stone, C. A. (2002). Promises and pitfalls of scaffolded instruction for students with language learning disabilities. In K. G. Butler & E. R. Silliman (Eds.), *Speaking, reading, and writing in children with language learning disabilities: New paradigms in research and practice* (pp. 175–198). Mahwah, NJ: Erlbaum.

Swanson, H. L., Hoskyn, M., & Lee, C. (1999). *Interventions for students with learning disabilities: A meta-analysis of treatment outcomes.* New York: Guilford Press.

Taylor, B. M., & Samuels, S. J. (1983). Children's use of text structure in the recall of expository material. *American Educational Research Journal, 40,* 517–528.

Taylor, B. M., & Williams, J. P. (1983). Comprehension of learning disabled readers: Task and text variations. *Journal of Educational Psychology, 75,* 743–751.

Troia, G. A., & Graham, S. (2003). Effective writing instruction across the grades: What every educational consultant should know. *Journal of Educational and Psychological Consultation, 14,* 75–89.

VanSledright, B. A. (2004). What does it mean to read history?: Fertile ground for cross-disciplinary collaborations? *Reading Research Quarterly, 39,* 342–346.

Wells, G. (1999). *Dialogic inquiry: Toward a sociocultural practice and theory of education.* New York: Cambridge University Press.

Williams, J. P. (2003). Teaching text structure to improve reading comprehension. In H. L. Swanson, K. Harris, & S. Graham (Eds.), *Handbook of learning disabilities* (pp. 295–305). New York: Guilford Press.

Williams, J. P., Hall, K. M., & Lauer, K. D. (2004). Teaching expository text structure to young at-risk learners: Building the basics of comprehension instruction. *Exceptionality, 12,* 129–144.

Williams, J. P., Taylor, M. B., Jarin, D. C., & Milligan, E. S. (1983). *Determining the main idea of expository paragraphs: An instructional program for learning disabled and its evaluation* (Technical Report No. 25). New York: Research Institute for the Study of Learning Disabilities, Teachers College, Columbia University.

Wong, B. Y. L. (1997). Research on genre-specific strategies for enhancing writing in adolescents with learning disabilities. *Learning Disability Quarterly, 20*, 140–159.

Wong, B. Y. L., & Jones, W. (1982). Increasing metcomprehension in learning disabled and normally achieving students through self-questioning training. *Learning Disability Quarterly, 5*, 228–240.

Wong, B. Y. L., & Wilson, M. (1984). Investigating awareness of and teaching passage organization in learning disabled children. *Journal of Learning Disabilities, 17*, 447–482.

PART IV

BEST PRACTICES IN ELL/BILINGUAL PROGRAMS AND APPROACHES

CHAPTER 8

From Models to Principles
Implementing Quality Schooling for ELLs

Ester J. de Jong

This chapter will:

1. Review common distinctions in program models.
2. Identify principles of quality schooling for bilingual learners.
3. Outline ways that schools can design their program policies and practices for English language learners (ELLs).

Traditionally, much debate about the schooling of bilingual learners in the United States has centered on the choice of medium of instruction: Should students classified as English language learners (ELLs) be taught exclusively in English or through a bilingual approach? While this debate might inform national policies to some limited extent, it has done little to improve our understanding of how classrooms and schools can be organized so that bilingual learners achieve academically, develop expertise in more than one language, and integrate into the classroom, school, and community. For that, we need to move away from the quest for the best model to a set of principles that underlies quality schooling for all bilingual learners (Brisk, 2006), and select approaches that are realistic for our particular teaching and learning contexts.

Programs for ELLs

Over time, a wide range of programs have been created for minority (and majority) students to develop their linguistic skills. The terminology that surrounds these various models can be confusing, especially since not everybody uses the same labels for the same practices. Although there are numerous classifications and labels, three general, basic distinctions are commonly used:

1. What are the desired (intended) language outcomes of the program? Multilingualism, bilingualism, or monolingualism in the societal language?
2. For whom is the program intended: majority-language speakers, minority-language speakers, or both groups?
3. What languages are used as the medium of instruction: one, two, or multiple languages?

Using these questions as a guideline, in the following sections I discuss program models for developing multilingual competence (additive approaches) and monolingualism in the societal language (subtractive approaches). The focus is on programs for minority-language speakers (for an overview of programs for majority-language speakers, see Genesee, 2004). The distinction between additive and subtractive bilingualism is important, because additive bilingualism has consistently been associated with higher academic achievement than subtractive bilingualism. For this reason, some scholars reserve the term *dual language* to refer only to additive bilingual programs (Howard, Olague, & Rodgers, 2003).

Additive Bilingual and Multilingual Program Models

Additive bilingual models are programs that build on students' existing language competencies and aim to add linguistic repertoires in other languages. This group of programs is also referred to under the umbrella term *dual language* to distinguish it from subtractive programs or less comprehensive programs to develop bilingual skills. Table 8.1 provides an overview of common program types that aim for bilingualism or multilingualism for majority- and minority-language speakers. Descriptions and examples of each model are provided below.

Maintenance bilingual or *heritage* language programs aim to develop, maintain, and/or revitalize Indigenous and minority languages. In the United States, language revitalization efforts are largely limited to

TABLE 8.1. Additive Programs for ELLs

Program label	Language goals	Target population	Language use and distribution
Maintenance bilingual/ heritage language education	Bilingualism and biliteracy	Minority	L1, L2 (sometimes L3)
Bilingual education for the Deaf	Bilingualism and biliteracy	Minority	L1 and L2
Integrated bilingual education: two-way immersion (TWI)	Bilingualism and biliteracy	Minority and majority (integrated)	Long-term L1 and L2 use

Native American languages. In Rough Point, Arizona, initial literacy development and content teaching is through Navajo, with some time set aside for English oral language development. Subjects are taught in both English and Navajo through second grade. As of third grade, English is used as a medium of instruction, and Navajo continues to be used as a vehicle for studying Navajo culture and citizenship (Francis & Reyner, 2002; McCarty, 2003). Internationally, language revitalization efforts can be noted in New Zealand (e.g., Spolsky, 2003), Hawai'i (e.g., Slaughter, 1997), and South America (e.g., King, 2004). It is interesting to note that maintenance bilingual education efforts in non-English-speaking countries increasingly include a multilingual component through the addition of a third, high-prestige language such as English, to the regional minority language and the societal language. Such trilingual experiments are common on the European continent in response to a multilingually defined European identity and the globalization of the world market.

Bilingual programs for the Deaf teach content through sign language and the written form of the societal language. Approaches to language (the use of different sign systems) and the curriculum vary greatly from program to program and are often constrained by teachers' lack of proficiency in sign language (LaSasso & Lollis, 2003; Strong, 1995). Deaf culture and identity is an important component of the bilingual program to counter deficit views of individuals who are deaf or hard of hearing (Allen, 2002).

Additive models of bilingual education integrate majority- and minority-language speakers, and aim for dual-language proficiency. The most developed integrated bilingual education model is *two-way immersion* (TWI) education. TWI is an integrated model of bilingual education in which native English speakers and native speakers of a minority language are educated together for most or all of the day, and receive content and literacy instruction through both English and the minority language (Howard, Sugarman, & Christian, 2003; Lindholm-Leary, 2001). According to a national database maintained by the Center for Applied Linguistics, there are currently over 300 TWI programs in the United States (see *www.cal.org/twi/directory*). The great majority of TWI programs use Spanish and English as instructional languages (93%), although Arabic, French, Korean, Mandarin, and Portuguese are also used in a few programs. Furthermore, the great majority of TWI (79%) is implemented at the elementary (K–5) level; it has been difficult to continue and/or begin programs at the secondary level. Only 13 out of the total of 338 programs are articulated K–8 or K–12. Although different models have been developed, all TWI programs share three essential features:

1. TWI programs are considered enrichment programs that aim at three interrelated goals: high levels of bilingualism and biliteracy, grade-level academic achievement, and cross-cultural competence.
2. TWI programs enroll approximately equal numbers of native speakers of English and of the minority language, and integrate these two groups of students for most or all of the day.
3. All TWI students receive content-area instruction and literacy instruction through both languages.

TWI programs are often one strand within a school, but they can also be a whole-school approach in which all students are enrolled in TWI. Two common models are the 90:10 and 50:50 model. In a 90:10 models, native English-speaking and native Spanish-speaking students are integrated for all subject areas. Spanish is the prevailing language in grades K–3 for all students, with 10% of English instruction in K–1, and 20% of English instruction in grades 2 and 3. Instruction is balanced between the two languages in grade 4 and above. The students develop their literacy skills in Spanish first, and formal English reading is introduced in third grade. The 90:10 model follows the Canadian immersion program design most closely and is implemented particularly in the Southwest (Lindholm-Leary, 2001). In a 50:50 model, native English speakers and native Spanish speakers are also integrated for all subject areas at all times. From kindergarten onwards, they receive half of their instruction in English and half in Spanish, often on a week-by-week basis (i.e., one week in Spanish, one week in English). Literacy development takes place in both languages simultaneously.

Subtractive Bilingual and Monolingual Programs

Not all programs for minority-language speakers aim for multilingualism. Subtractive models focus on developing proficiency in the societal language, with limited or no development of the students' native language(s) (refer to Table 8.2).

Specialized programs for ELLs that focus on English language development are developed specifically for speakers identified as not fluent in that language. *Submersion* is the placement of these students in a standard curriculum classroom designed for native speakers of the societal language, without any special accommodations. In the United States, since the *Lau vs. Nichols* decision (414 U.S. No. 72-6520), this kind of placement is in violation of federal law, which requires schools to take appropriate action to overcome language barriers. Not taking *any* action (i.e., submersion) is insufficient. Besides the additive bilingual approaches described earlier, districts can choose to implement subtractive models, including bilingual and monolingual models.

Subtractive Bilingual Programs

Transitional bilingual education (TBE) is the bilingual approach most commonly chosen for ethnic and immigrant languages. In TBE, the student's native language is used only for an initial period of literacy development and content learning to assist the student's transition to literacy and content learning in the societal language. Unlike the additive bilin-

TABLE 8.2. Subtractive Programs for ELLs

Program label	Language goals	Target population	Language use and distribution
Transitional bilingual education (TBE)	Proficiency in L2	Minority	L1 for limited amount of time and L2
Integrated TBE	Proficiency in L2	Minority	L1 for limited amount of time and L2
Pull-out/push-in second-language instruction	Proficiency in L2	Minority	L2 only
Self-contained English language program (immersion)	Proficiency in L2	Minority	L2 only, sometimes with L1 access

gual education models, the goal of TBE is not to maintain or develop the student's native language but to provide access to the language of school. Students are typically expected to enroll in the program for 2–3 years, then exit the program into a standard classroom or instruction in the societal language only (early-exit TBE).

A special case of TBE can be found in integrated models (integrated TBE). The purpose of these programs is not to promote bilingualism, but they are concerned with the negative impact of the segregation of minority-language students while they are becoming familiar with the new language and culture. In integrated TBE models in the United States, minority-language students are separated for some specialized instruction in their native language, then integrated with native English speakers in specific subject areas for varying amounts of time (de Jong, 2006). Brisk (1991) describes a model that integrated two fifth-grade classes, one a transitional bilingual classroom, and the other a monolingual classroom. Students were grouped by their own homeroom (the monolingual or the transitional bilingual classroom) for morning activities, social studies, and English as a second language (ESL) but were integrated for reading and language arts, math, and science. Flexible grouping practices were important to the success of the program: Students had access to Spanish-only, English-only, or bilingual instruction throughout the school day, depending on their individual linguistic and academic needs.

Despite their bilingual nature, TBE programs are in intent and design *subtractive* when this term is applied within the school context. Of course, students may continue using their native language at home and in the community, and maintain bilingual competence within that particular context. Unlike additive bilingual programs, however, TBE programs intend not to expand student repertoires in school but replace the native language with the second language.

Monolingual Programs

Nonbilingual approaches provide specialized support in second-language development without native language development. These supports can be linked to a standard curriculum classroom or exist as separate services. Pull-out second-language classes are quite common around the world to meet the needs of immigrant children. Specialist teachers take second-language learners out of their standard curriculum classroom for a specific period of time, which varies according to the proficiency level of the student, to teach the societal language. Increasingly, these teachers are asked to go into the standard curriculum classroom to provide in-class support (push-in model). The latter model is often preferred to avoid segregating students from their peers and to ensure better access to grade-level curriculum content.

Finally, there are self-contained English language programs in which students spent most of their school day. These programs are expected to teach English, as well as content matter through English, by using specific instructional strategies for language and literacy development and content teaching. Sometimes these programs are referred to as *structured immersion programs,* as a result of the restrictive language policies in California (Proposition 227), Arizona (Proposition 203), and Massachusetts (Question 2). It is important to note the difference between this type of immersion and immersion programs for language-majority speakers. Probably the best-known (foreign) language immersion programs are Canadian[1] immersion programs. French immersion programs were developed in the late 1960s in response to demands from middle-class, Anglophone parents living in predominantly French-speaking Montreal, Quebec, to provide their children with the opportunity to develop a functional level of bilingualism. In early full-immersion programs, the target (second) language, French, is introduced before the student's first language during the first 2 years of elementary school. By third grade, the student's native language (English) is formally introduced in the curriculum, and both languages are used for equal amounts of time for the rest of the program. Besides the sociopolitical context (both French and English have official status in Canada) and target population (majority-language speakers vs. minority-language speakers), the goals of the Canadian immersion and structured English immersion are thus distinctly different: Canadian immersion is an additive bilingual program (the native language is an integral part of the program), whereas majority-language immersion programs lead to monolingualism in the societal language.

It is worth mentioning a growing trend at the secondary level to establish newcomer schools. Almost half of the newcomer schools provide instruction and tutoring in the students' native languages, and they can also be classified as an example of transitional bilingual programs. Newcomer programs emerged to meet the needs of newly arrived immigrant children with no or limited English proficiency and limited literacy skills in their native language, often due to interrupted schooling (Friedlander, 1991; Short, 2002). Neither traditional ESL nor bilingual programs are typically designed to meet these students' needs, because they often assume grade-level knowledge and skills. According to a nationwide survey of newcomer programs, 77% of the newcomer programs are within schools, 17% are at a separate site, and 6% are whole-school models (Short & Boyson, 2004). Effective newcomer schools are characterized by flexible scheduling, ungraded programs, and a range of supporting services for families (for examples of specific case studies, see Short, 2002).

Best Practices in Action

Selecting a Program Model

The existence of all these different program models has invited the question: Which model is the best model? Many program evaluations comparing English-only with bilingual programs (broadly defined) have been conducted over the past 30 years to try and answer to this question. These evaluations typically set out to "prove" that one model was better than the other and the interpretation of results often depended on the ideology of the researcher. As statistical analyses have become more sophisticated, however, a consistent picture of small but significant positive effects of attending a bilingual education program on achievement (in English) emerges (Francis, Lesaux, & August, 2006; Genesee, Lindholm-Leary, Saunders, & Christian, 2006; Greene, 1998; Rolstad, Mahoney, & Glass, 2005; Willig, 1985).

One of the major drawbacks is that these program evaluations fail to take into consideration a number of contextual factors, such as teacher quality, access to resources, and student demographics. Consequently, they have not been very useful as a guideline for educators to decide what model to select for their specific local context, and how to move from ineffective to effective practices in their school setting. The tremendous variation within and among ELL populations makes it impossible to approach the schooling of ELLs with a "one size fits all" approach. Effective programs for ELLs must be developed in response to a community's specific context. For example, when a district has multiple language groups, with few speakers of each language, it becomes difficult to implement a bilingual program. If, on the other hand, much of the ELL population is from the same language background, bilingual education is a feasible option. Similarly, students with strong first language (L1) literacy skills and highly educated parents have different needs than students with interrupted schooling and/or limited L1 literacy skills. When different student populations exist side by side in the district, different programs need to be considered in recognition of these different needs. When selecting an approach for their ELLs, school and district leaders must therefore, first and foremost, find out about the strengths and needs of the ELLs in the school/district, so that they choose a program option that matches ELLs' needs with the language, academic, and sociocultural goals of school or district. Once the ELL population has been identified (e.g., through a home-language survey, language and literacy assessments, academic skills), schools and district can develop a shared vision for the education of all students that reflects the linguistic and cultural diversity in the school (Freeman, 2004).

The question ("Which is the best model?") is therefore best answered, "It depends," because you first need to know for whom you are developing this model. To avoid random or conflicting policies, it is crucial that district and school leaders make themselves familiar with their ELL population and the community. They also need to be knowledgeable about common program options for ELLs and their theoretical underpinnings, strengths, outcomes, and implementation challenges (Genesee, 1999). Random decision making can easily fragment the schooling experiences for students, send mix messages, and it may fail to provide opportunities for consistent cognitive, social, and linguistic growth.

Principles of Effective Schooling for ELLs

Program selection is only one step of a complex process of providing ELLs with optimal learning environments. Administrators and teachers also need to consider how these programs will be implemented, regardless of the particular program model chosen. They need to know what factors make a difference in providing an effective learning environment for all students, including linguistically and culturally diverse students. Studies that have looked at effective classrooms, programs, and school have pointed to a consistent picture of those policies, processes, and practices that lead to positive linguistic, academic, and sociocultural outcomes for ELLs. They can be grouped under three general principles: affirming identities, additive bilingualism, and integrated approaches. Together, these principles provide a useful background for making instructional and organizational decisions, including, but not limited to, the implementation of a particular program model (see also Brisk, 2006; Howard, Sugarman, Christian, Lindholm-Leary, & Rogers, 2007).[2]

Principle 1: Quality Schooling for Bilingual Learners Affirms Identities

Social identity construction is a fundamental aspect of schooling, and teachers and learners play active roles in this process. Through their ongoing participation in language-mediated activities at school, teachers and students (co-)construct communities of practice, and multiple identities within those communities (Freeman, 1998; Ochs & Schieffelin, 2008). The choices that educators make in organizing their programs and practices have implications for the identity options available to bilingual learners and, hence, their engagement in learning and school. Bilingual learners are complete individuals in the process of becoming bilingual and bicultural (or multilingual and multicultural), and should not be treated as deficient individuals because they don't speak English. Denying students' linguistic and cultural identities renders multilingual students invisible and inaudible, can limit their participation opportunities, and is associated with lower academic achievement (Cummins, 2001). Affirming the linguistic and cultural identities of bilingual learners can increase engagement with literacy activities and encourage investment in school (Cummins, 2006).

Affirming identities of bilingual learners at school means that educators value linguistic and cultural diversity, and draw on the linguistic and cultural resources, or "funds of knowledge" (Moll, Amanti, Neff, & González, 1992), that learners bring with them to school to support and scaffold their learning and participation in school. de Mejia (1999), for example, illustrates how a teacher enhanced student participation by using code-switching strategies during storybook reading in a second language (L2). In this case, the teacher found that the Spanish-speaking students, who were limited in English, were effectively excluded from an active learning role in her all-English-medium preschool classroom. While she carefully controlled the language input in English to make the reading as comprehensible as possible, the exclusive use of English led to teacher-dominated talk, with little engagement with the content of the story. When she decided to include Spanish, in addition to English, students were able to contribute their ideas and actively participate in constructing meaning from the story.

Critical autobiographies are another good example of practices that allow students to examine events in their lives that affect them as bilingual individuals (Brisk, Burgos, & Hamerla, 2004; Brisk & Harrington, 2000). In this project-based approach to teaching, students describe their lives as bilingual/bicultural learners and they connect their life story to social, political, economic, cultural, and linguistic events through discussion and reading of a wide range of fiction and nonfiction books. Critical autobiographies allow students to explore their own identities in multiple ways and provide authentic context for language and literacy development.

Effective teachers engage in specific practices that provide an optimal learning environment for bilingual learners. In this research, common themes are that teachers, among others,

- Maintain high expectations; they do not use limited English proficiency as an excuse for lowering standards.
- Use bilingual approaches to teaching, building on students' native language resources.
- Implement a curriculum that reflects and builds on students' cultural experiences.
- Use culturally and linguistically responsive instructional practices.

Principle 2: Quality Schooling for Bilingual Learners Promotes Additive Bilingualism

This second principle views the development of bilingualism (biliteracy, multilingualism, multilingual literacies) as an important goal and desirable outcome of schooling. We know that bilingual learners can develop the ability to use multiple languages with varying degrees of expertise for different purposes over time. It is important to acknowledge the multiple pathways to reaching these goals (Fortune & Tedick, 2008; García, Skutnabb-Kangas, & Torres-Guzmán, 2006). Not all schools can promote bilingualism and biliteracy to the same degree. In some contexts, the implementation of additive bilingual education programs, such as a TWI program, is feasible; in other schools, these programs simply are not feasible (e.g., because of a diverse, multilingual student population or restrictions imposed by state policies). However, an additive bilingual *stance* is always possible and desirable from a social justice (equity) perspective, because it aims to validate the linguistic (and cultural) resources of students and their families. Thus, in addition to selecting an additive bilingual program model, schools can make significant strides to creating additive bilingual environments. Even in English-medium classrooms, teachers can use bilingual strategies to support the multiple languages and literacies of their students and communities.

For example, Freeman and Freeman (2000) recommend the preview–view–review strategy to teach complex content-area concepts to bilingual learners. Key concepts are introduced in the students' L1 (preview). Students work with those concepts in English (view), then review those concepts in their L1. The preview and review portions of the activity/lesson/thematic unit could be facilitated by the bilingual teacher, teaching assistant, or tutor. Teachers can also structure the preview activities so that the bilingual learners works with a more competent bilingual peer to negotiate the meaning of that content-area concept in their L1. The preview can be negotiated orally, and/or it can draw on texts written in the L1; these L1 texts might be commercially made, teacher-made, student-made, or found on the Internet. For example, a unit on matter may first elicit from students oral discussion of their experiences with liquids, solids, and gases in their L1. During the view phase, the teacher can structure activities in which bilingual learners are integrated with English-speaking peers and use English to negotiate the meaning of the academic content they were learning about in segregated L1 groups. In the case of a unit on matter, the teacher may ask student to conduct experiments and write down their observations in English, using writing scaffolds for beginning writers. For the review phase, teachers group bilingual learners together again to reinforce and extend their learning in the L1. In our example, the teacher could ask students to share their understandings of what matter is, forms of matter, and how matter changes in their L1. This strategic, well-planned activity structure can simultaneously address the principles of affirming identities, promoting bilingualism, and fostering integration, and it can be used in English-medium and bilingual education contexts by monolingual or bilingual teachers.

Cummins (2006) provides another example. He suggests that teachers have students write dual-language books. He describes a multilingual literacies project implemented by monolingual English-speaking teachers working in linguistically and culturally diverse English-medium schools in Toronto, Canada. These teachers invite their students to write about topics that are aligned with the regular content-area instruction but written in English and their heritage language. Students publish their dual-language books in hard copy and on the Web, which develops a multilingual library of student-made books for the school, facilitates students' development of computer literacies, and allows the books to reach a wider audience (see *hornwood.peelschools.org/dual* for a detailed description of this process and examples of student-made, dual-language books in a variety of languages).

As illustrated, bilingual practices should not and do not have to be limited to bilingual teachers or bilingual classrooms. In addition to the strategies illustrated earlier, monolingual (and bilingual) teachers can advocate for native language tutors, acquire native language materials for their classroom, learn some basic phrases in their students' native language, ask their students to share and teach their languages, and create opportunities for students to use their native languages with each other socially, as well as for academic learning (Gravelle, 1996; Irujo, 1998). In short, program features that support bilingual outcomes include

- Sufficient material resources in both languages to implement the program (e.g., textbooks).
- A highly qualified bilingual staff proficient in the language(s) of

instruction and knowledgeable about bilingualism, L2 acquisition, and implications for teaching.

- Clear program articulation, in which curricular grade-level expectations and language use expectations for both languages are made explicit and provide a continuous experience for students for language and cognitive development.
- Teacher collaboration (within and across languages).

Principle 3: Quality Schooling for Bilingual Learners Fosters Integration

This third principle recognizes that responses to linguistic and cultural diversity in schools are embedded in a wider sociopolitical context that affects decision-making processes and outcomes at the classroom, school, and community levels. In its broadest sense, *integration* refers to bringing together different parts, on an equal basis, to make a whole (Brisk, 1991). When applied to schools, integration is a negotiated process that involves all participants, not only ELLs and their teachers. Everyone in the school is positioned as a full participant, and everyone learns to negotiate effectively in linguistically and culturally diverse situations. Thus, newcomers are provided opportunities to learn the norms of interaction and interpretation guiding behavior in their new school, and established community members (i.e., educators, students) have opportunities to interact with and learn about these newcomers without stigmatizing their culturally shaped ways of thinking, being, valuing, and interacting. In integrated communities, linguistic and cultural diversity strengthens, not threatens, the whole.

Integration is fostered equitably when the needs of all students, including those of bilingual learners, are an integral part of the school's organizational structure and decision-making processes. A study by Lucas, Henze, and Donato (1990) examined successful practices in six high schools. One of the key factors was a schoolwide commitment to biliteracy and multiculturalism. This commitment was expressed, among others, by hiring bilingual staff, by having high expectations for minority pupils, by offering advanced classes in the minority language, and by providing counseling services that encouraged pupils to go to college. The authors concluded:

> Diversity among students cannot simply be ignored. While the schools recognized the importance of integrating language-minority students with mainstream students and providing equally challenging instruction for all students, they did not try to minimize differences among mainstream and Latino students or among Latino students themselves. Approaches

to schooling that value linguistic and cultural diversity and that promote cultural pluralism were welcomed and explored whenever possible. . . . Students' languages and cultures were incorporated into school programs as part of the efforts to create a context in which all students felt valuable and capable of academic success. (p. 338)

All educators who work with bilingual learners need to understand how these students learn in and through two languages at school. When bilingual learners' strengths and needs are central, and not an afterthought, in such educational decision making, bilingual learners can achieve. A whole-school approach consist of:

- Building a strong knowledge base about bilingualism, L2 acquisition, and minority schooling across the school, not limited to a special bilingual or ESL program.
- Ensuring strong and knowledgeable leadership.
- Sharing responsibility for reaching sociocultural, linguistic, and academic goals for all learners in the school.
- Establishing a sense of community within the school, as well as the home and the wider community.

Reflections and Future Directions

Identifying a program model is an important first step for thinking about what schools need to do for ELLs. Clarity in terms of program goals and design helps to systematize language distribution, allows for shared goal setting as a community, and provides consistency in program delivery. The choice for a program model must be considered, however, in relationship to student population characteristics, available resources, and parent desires, and may need specific adaptations to respond to these contextual factors. One-size-fits-all approaches will not work for the diverse group of students that we refer to as "ELLs." Rather, the "best" model will be a schoolwide approach that allows administrators and educators to reach language, academic, and sociocultural goals for all students within the specifics of their local context.

María Estela Brisk (2006), a long-term bilingual advocate and scholar, concludes that "for too long, advocates and educators have focused on finding the ideal way to teach English. The real choice is between compensatory and quality education" (p. 14). It is time to move beyond the simple dichotomy of bilingual versus English-only program models and consider the complex set of school, program, and classroom factors that ensure ELLs equal access to quality schooling.

A principled approach that balances flexibility of implementation and an informed approach to working with ELLs also requires teachers to be active language planners. This role may be unfamiliar for some teachers, because they think language policy is something that happens in the legislature. However, teachers play an active role in shaping the educational experiences of ELLs by how they organize their school, the program models they choose (e.g., by choosing a bilingual program) and classroom practices (e.g., by taking an additive bilingual stance when planning and teaching). Each of these decisions involves language choices and ways of talking and responding to linguistic and cultural diversity. Sonia Nieto (2002) concludes, "As educators, all decisions we make, no matter how neutral they may seem, have an impact on the lives and experiences of our students" (p. 43).

Conclusion

Effective teachers of ELLs constantly weigh their own practices and those in the wider school community against a commitment to equity, affirming identities, additive bilingualism, and equal participation through integration, and work toward change when needed. When teachers see themselves as language planners, they critically analyze policies in relation to their students' strengths and needs, and they consider the extent to which the policy supports or hinders their class-room efforts to reach their language-planning goals. When they see themselves as agents of change, they think systemically and strategi-cally about the challenges they identify, and they collaborate with their colleagues to modify their approach in ways that are aligned with the principles of quality schooling for bilingual learners and appropriate for their context.

ENGAGEMENT ACTIVITIES

1. What kind of program currently exists in your school for ELLs? How are the goals, expectations, and the program model articulated to parents, students, teachers, and administrators?

2. What evidence can you find of ways that policies, programs, and practices at your school meet the criteria listed under each of the three principles?

3. What strategies can you identify that would move the policies, programs, and practices at your school more closely toward each of the three principles?

NOTES

1. Following Brisk (2006), the term *Canadian* is added to distinguish these bilingual programs from (monolingual) English immersion programs for minority students, which aim for second-language proficiency rather than bilingualism (see text).

2. The sections that follow draw from de Jong, E., & Freeman-Field, R. (in press). Bilingual approaches. In C, Leung & A. Creese (Eds.), *English as an additional language: A reader for teachers working with linguistic minority pupils.* Newcastle Upon Tyne, UK: Sage.

REFERENCES

Allen, B. M. (2002). ASL-English bilingual classroom: The families' perspectives. *Bilingual Research Journal, 26*, 1–20.

Brisk, M. E. (1991). Toward multilingual and multicultural mainstream education. *Journal of Education, 173*(2), 114–129.

Brisk, M. E. (2006). *Bilingual education: From compensatory to quality education* (2nd ed.). Mahwah, NJ: Erlbaum.

Brisk, M. E., Burgos, A., & Hamerla, S. R. (2004). *Situational context of education: A window into the world of bilingual learners.* Mahwah, NJ: Erlbaum.

Brisk, M. E., & Harrington, M. (2000). *Literacy and bilingualism: A handbook for all teachers.* Mahwah, NJ: Erlbaum.

Cummins, J. (2001). *Negotiating identities: Education for empowerment in a diverse society* (2nd ed.). Los Angeles: California Association for Bilingual Education.

Cummins, J. (2006). Identity texts: The imaginative construction of self through multiliteracies pedagogy. In O. García, T. Skutnabb-Kangas, & M. Torres-Guzmán (Eds.), *Imagining multilingual schools: Languages in education and glocalization* (pp. 51–68). Clevedon, UK: Multilingual Matters.

de Jong, E. J. (2006). Integrated bilingual education: An alternative approach. *Bilingual Research Journal, 30*(1), 23–44.

de Mejia, A.-M. (1999, Winter). Bilingual storytelling: Code switching, discourse control, and learning opportunities. *TESOL Journal*, pp. 4–10.

Fortune, W. T., & Tedick, J. (2008). *Pathways to multingualism: Evolving perspectives on immersion education.* Clevedon, UK: Multilingual Matters.

Francis, D., Lesaux, N., & August, D. (2006). Language of instruction. In D. August & T. Shanahan (Eds.), *Developing literacy in second-language children* (pp. 365–413). Mahwah, NJ: Erlbaum.

Francis, N., & Reyner, J. (2002). *Language and literacy teaching for indigenous education: A bilingual approach.* Clevedon, UK: Multilingual Matters.

Freeman, D., & Freeman, Y. (2000). *Teaching reading in multilingual classrooms.* Portsmouth, NH: Heinemann.

Freeman, R. (1998). *Bilingual education and social change.* Clevedon, UK: Multilingual Matters.

Freeman, R. (2004). *Building on community bilingualism.* Philadelphia: Caslon.

Friedlander, M. (1991). *The Newcomer Program: Helping immigrant students succeed in U.S. schools.* Washington, DC: National Clearinghouse for Bilingual Education.

García, O., Skutnabb-Kangas, T., & Torres-Guzmán, M. (2006). *Imagining multilingual schools: Language in education and glocalization.* Clevedon, UK: Multilingual Matters.

Genesee, F. (1999). *Program alternatives for linguistically diverse students.* Santa Cruz, CA: Center for Research on Education, Diversity and Excellence.

Genesee, F. (2004). What do we know about bilingual education for majority language students? In T. K. Bhatia & W. Ritchie (Eds.), *Handbook of bilingualism and multiculturalism* (pp. 547–576). Malden, MA: Blackwell.

Genesee, F., Lindholm-Leary, K. J., Saunders, G., & Christian, D. (2006). *Educating English language learners: A synthesis of research evidence.* Cambridge, UK: Cambridge University Press.

Gravelle, M. (1996). *Supporting bilingual learners in school.* Stoke-on-Trent, UK: Trentham Books.

Greene, J. P. (1998). *A meta-analysis of the effectiveness of bilingual education.* Austin, TX: Thomas Rivera Policy Institute.

Howard, E. R., Olague, N., & Rodgers, D. (2003). *The dual language program planner: A guide for designing and implementing dual language programs.* Santa Cruz, CA: Center for Research on Education, Diversity and Excellence.

Howard, E. R., Sugarman, J., & Christian, D. (2003). *Trends in two-way immersion education: A review of the research* (Report No. 63). Baltimore: Center for Research on the Education of Students Placed at Risk (CRESPAR).

Howard, E. R., Sugarman, J., Christian, D., Lindholm-Leary, K. J., & Rogers, D. (2007). *Guiding principles for dual language education* (2nd ed.). Washington, DC: Center for Applied Linguistics.

Irujo, S. (1998). *Teaching bilingual children: Beliefs and behaviors.* Boston: Heinle & Heinle.

King, K. (2004). Language policy and local planning in South America: New directions for enrichment bilingual education in the Andes. *International Journal of Bilingual Education and Bilingualism, 7*(5), 334–347.

LaSasso, C., & Lollis, J. (2003). Survey of residential and day schools for Deaf students in the United States that identify themselves as bilingual–bicultural programs. *Journal of Deaf Studies and Deaf Education, 8*(1), 79–91.

Lindholm-Leary, K. J. (2001). *Dual language education.* Clevedon, UK: Multilingual Matters.

Lucas, T., Henze, R. C., & Donato, R. (1990). Promoting the success of Latino language minority students: An exploratory study if six high school. *Harvard Educational Review, 60*(3), 315–340.

McCarty, T. L. (2003). Revitalizing indigenous languages in homogenizing times. *Comparative Education, 39*(2), 147–163.

Moll, L. C., Amanti, C., Neff, D., & González, N. (1992). Funds of knowledge for teaching: A qualitative approach to developing strategic connections between homes and classrooms. *Theory Into Practice, 31*, 132–141.

Nieto, S. (2002). *Language, culture, and teaching: Critical perspectives for a new century.* Mahwah, NJ: Erlbaum.

Ochs, E., & Schieffelin, B. (2008). Language socialization: A historical overview. In P. A. Duff & N. H. Hornberger (Eds.), *Encyclopedia of language and education* (2nd ed., pp. 3–15). New York: Springer Science+Business Media.

Rolstad, K., Mahoney, K., & Glass, G. V. (2005). The big picture: A meta-analysis of program effectiveness research on English language learners. *Educational Policy, 19*(4), 572–594.

Short, D. J. (2002). Newcomer programs: An educational alternative for secondary immigrant students. *Education and Urban Society, 34*(2), 173–198.

Short, D. J., & Boyson, B. A. (2004). *Creating access: Language and academic programs for secondary school newcomers.* Washington, DC/McHenry, IL: Center for Applied Linguistics/Delta Systems.

Slaughter, H. B. (1997). Indigenous language immersion in Hawai'i: A case study of Kula Kaiapuni Hawai'i, an effort to save the indigenous language of Hawai'i. In R. K. Johnson & M. Swain (Eds.), *Immersion education: International perspectives* (pp. 105–130). Cambridge, UK: Cambridge University Press.

Spolsky, B. (2003). Reassessing Maori regeneration. *Language in Society, 32,* 553–578.

Strong, M. (1995). A review of bilingual–bicultural programs for deaf children in North America. *American Annals of the Deaf, 122,* 84–94.

Willig, A. C. (1985). A meta-analysis of selected studies on the effectiveness of bilingual education. *Review of Educational Research, 55*(3), 269–317.

CHAPTER 9

Using Workshop Approaches to Support the Literacy Development of ELLs

Kathryn H. Au and Taffy E. Raphael

This chapter will:

1. Discuss how workshop approaches can be beneficial to English language learners (ELLs).

2. Present key concepts of authenticity underlying workshop approaches.

3. Provide practical classroom examples of routines from the writers' workshop and the readers' workshop.

In this rapidly changing, competitive world, educators who work in schools and classrooms serving English language learners (ELLs) must be concerned with issues of equity. Specifically, we must do all we can to make sure that ELLs receive the literacy instruction they need to reach the high levels of literacy required in today's world. For example, ELLs must be able to synthesize ideas gathered from a number of different sources, to determine whether the information presented is accurate or inaccurate, and to compose a summary stating and backing up their conclusions. Clearly, if students are to perform at this high level, then they must receive extensive instruction, throughout the grades, oriented toward higher level thinking with text, including the writing process and reading comprehension.

Our purpose in this chapter is to share powerful and effective approaches for accomplishing this goal, approaches framed as *workshops*. We start with key concepts underlying workshop approaches. We then visit two classrooms: Joey Inatsuka's kindergarten class, where we look in on a writers' workshop; and Elisabeth Trost-Shahata's fourth-grade ELL classroom, where we witness a readers' workshop. Students in these classrooms represent two categories typical for ELLs in the United States: (1) those who speak a nonmainstream variety of English, such as African American Vernacular English or Hawai'i Creole and (2) those who speak a language other than English, such as Spanish or Urdu.

Workshop Approaches

Workshop approaches derive from the tradition of Dewey (1944) and progressive education, although Dewey and his colleagues held views of literacy very different from those espoused here. In a workshop for artists, individuals engage in authentic practices of their craft. They do similar kinds of work, such as painting or sculpting, using their workshop time to advance their projects. They learn and apply new skills and strategies, and they practice those already learned. Despite the similarity in the kind of work the artists are doing, visitors would not expect to see everyone working on the same thing at the same time. The artists may be in different stages of completing a project or may be engaged in a similar activity but vary in how they do their work. For example, one artist may be sketching, another painting a study for a larger work, and still another putting finishing touches on a landscape. Alternatively, all may be working on paintings of landscapes, but how they approach the task, the landscapes they create, and the feelings the landscapes elicit vary according to the individual.

Similarly, in a writers' workshop, students are often in different phases of the writing process—some are planning, others are drafting, and still others are revising their pieces. The writing in which they engage is authentic, purposeful, and meaningful to each student individually. A readers' workshop similarly emphasizes authenticity of tasks. Students read, write, and talk about books to learn new ideas, argue a particular point of view, and participate as contributing members of a community of readers. As teachers prepare them to participate and engage in these activities, students learn and apply relevant reading skills and strategies.

A benefit of workshop approaches is the flexibility they offer ELLs to engage in meaningful projects, while receiving necessary supports to complete each phase of the work, what learning theorists call *legitimate peripheral participation* (Lave & Wenger, 1991). Students may move more quickly during the phases they find easy, yet more deliberately during more challenging phases, drawing on help from their teacher and peers. In workshop approaches, authenticity is reflected in the language, community, tasks, and routines teachers create and use to ensure that their students have learning opportunities that lead to a bright future.

Key Concepts

Key Concept 1. Authenticity in the Language of Literacy Practices

The first key concept we emphasize is that teachers must help ELLs learn what Gee (1990) terms a *Discourse*, which goes far beyond a linguistic code and the basic skills of reading and writing. Gee gives the following definition: "A *Discourse* is a socially accepted association among ways of using language, of thinking, feeling, believing, valuing, and of acting that can be used to identify oneself as a member of a socially meaningful group or 'social network,' or to signal (that one is playing) a socially meaningful 'role'" (Gee, 1990, p. 143, italics in the original). Gee's concept of Discourse is a good starting point, because it helps to make clear the magnitude of the challenge teachers face, and it indicates why the teacher's role is so important in the literacy learning of ELLs. Teachers must help students learn what we will call the *literate discourse* of the larger society, which involves using language in particular ways, and particular ways of thinking, feeling, believing, valuing, and acting, as Gee suggests. What we are calling literate discourse is also referred to as *essayist literacy* (Scollon & Scollon, 1981). A major reason for the poor progress shown by ELLs as a group is that they seldom receive the high-quality instruction necessary to build their knowledge of literate discourse (Au, 2008).

Key Concept 2: Authenticity in the Community of Practice

The second key concept we bring forward is that of the community of learners. If ELLs are to learn literate discourse, they must see themselves as members of what Gee (1990) describes as a socially meaningful group or social network. The teacher must bring the students together as a community of learners. In such a community, students learn from one another, as well as from the teacher, and the teacher shows an openness to learning from the students. As Vygotsky (1978, 1986) reminds us, learning first takes place on the interpersonal plane, as the more capable other guides, supports, or scaffolds the performance of the novice.

For example, when learning literate discourse, students may need many suggestions from their teacher before they can arrive at an interesting lead for a piece. Over time, the teacher gradually releases responsibility to the students, asking fewer guiding questions as students gain the ability to generate compelling leads on their own. The act of creating an interesting lead has moved from the interpersonal to the intrapersonal plane, from something between the teacher and the student to something within the student. More knowledgeable others who can scaffold students' learning include peers, as well as the classroom teacher. For example, in a readers' workshop, a student unfamiliar with colloquial English may need input from peers to understand an idiom encountered in reading. In workshop settings, a high value is placed on the ability of community members both to seek help and to provide help to others.

Key Concept 3. Authenticity of Tasks

Our third key concept involves the need for two types of learning opportunities to support ELLs in developing proficiency with literate discourse (cf. Gee's [1990] discussion of acquisition vs. learning). We call the first type of opportunity *learning that comes from engaging in the full processes of reading and writing* (Au, 2006). This type of learning occurs when students engage in reading and writing tasks for authentic purposes, ones that exist in the world outside, as well as in the classroom. Two examples of tasks that involve authentic purposes are writing to express one's feelings or opinions, such as writing a letter to the editor, and reading for pleasure, for the sheer joy of getting lost in a book. Learning by engaging in tasks that emphasize the full processes of reading and writing is essential, because all students, and especially ELLs, benefit from understanding why literacy is, or could be, important to their lives. While engaging in such authentic tasks, students have the opportunity to see reading and writing projects through, from start to finish. Some tasks, such as reading and responding to a poem, may be completed in a single class period. Others, such as conducting research using multiple sources and creating a report, may take several weeks.

We call the second kind of opportunity *learning by studying parts of reading and writing* (Au, 2006). When students are engaged in a literacy task of interest to them, for example, reading a novel, the teacher has the opportunity to teach them the concepts, strategies, and skills needed to complete the project successfully. For example, students may benefit from knowing the concept of a flashback or the strategy of comprehension monitoring. They may also benefit from analyzing previously unknown words, identifying the root word and affixes to make an educated guess about a word's meaning. Instruction in the parts of reading and writing, which includes decoding and spelling, has a greater impact on ELLs when it takes place in the context of tasks students are already motivated to complete. Students are likely to grasp skills more readily if they understand the full process of which the skill is a part. To be successful in helping ELLs acquire literate discourse, teachers must start by engaging students in the full processes of reading and writing, then following up with instruction on the parts of reading and writing that students require to complete tasks successfully.

Key Concept 4: Authenticity in Consistent Learning Routines

Our fourth key concept highlights the importance of supporting students' learning through consistent routines. We have established that the teacher's job is to help ELLs develop literate discourse within the classroom community of learners, by providing opportunities for students to learn both by engaging in the full processes of reading and writing, and by studying the parts of reading and writing. The teacher faces a significant challenge in organizing and managing a classroom in keeping with these first three key concepts. Our fourth key concept, using consistent routines, is essential to providing ELLs with an orderly, productive environment for learning. Consistent routines, such as the Author's Chair (Graves & Hansen, 1983), scaffold the participation of ELLs in workshop approaches. If the same routine is repeated on a daily or near-daily basis, ELLs will know what to expect from one moment to the next. They can focus on developing the language and social skills to participate appropriately within a familiar framework. Over time, students will be able to devote less and less attention to the routine, and more and more attention to the learning of new literacy content, strategies, and skills.

Writers' Workshop in a Kindergarten Class

Joey Inatsuka teaches kindergarten in a school in a rural community in Hawai'i. Most of her students are of Native Hawaiian ancestry, many are from low-income families, and all are speakers of Hawai'i Creole, the primary language of many individuals born and raised in Hawai'i. Joey is in her second year of teaching (pseudonyms have been used for the children in this classroom). She provides her students with an orderly, print-rich classroom environment. Near the front of the room are large charts with words the children use often in their writing: the names of their classmates; action words, such as *running, swimming,* and *eating;*

and common words, such as *mother* and *cousin*. Tables are arranged so that children can work in groups of four to six.

Joey conducts a writers' workshop every day, and by March, the date of this observation, she has firmly established the following routines: (1) daily news, (2) reflection time, (3) peer conferences for sharing story ideas, (3) writing time, (4) teacher conferences, and (5) peer conferences for sharing stories drafted that day. Our discussion focuses on the opening routine, daily news, and we consider the way Joey structures the tasks within this routine to provide authentic opportunities for the development of literate discourse within the classroom community. We also show how Joey makes the transition from the daily news to peer conferences with a brief routine devoted to reflection.

Daily News

Each morning, Joey begins with a routine called the daily news. The children sit on the carpet together and watch attentively as Joey models writing, using a sheet of chart paper everyone can see. She asks the children what day of the week it is. The children respond by saying "Friday," and they refer to the calendar, so they can say each letter in *Friday* as Joey writes the word. "What kind of day is it?" Joey asks, and the children reply that it's a cloudy day. They chorally state the letters in *cloudy* (those needing help refer to a chart of weather words at the back of the room) and Joey writes each letter. The message now reads:

> Today is Friday. It is a cloudy day.

Having established the day and the weather, Joey moves into the second part of the daily news routine, adapted from Author's Chair (Graves & Hansen, 1983), where a student is chosen to contribute a story describing an important experience. Today it is Kaleo's turn to sit in front of the class and tell his daily news story. Joey reviews for everyone the three things Kaleo will think about to create a complete story: what's happening, where it's happening, and who is there. She calls on children to ask Kaleo the following questions:

> "What's happening in your story?"
> "Where is it happening?"
> "Who is in your story?"

The children ask their questions with the confidence born of consistent practice. Kaleo responds by saying, "I am riding the roller coaster at the carnival with Jensen." Joey writes the words, *Kaleo said*, then adds

Kaleo's sentence in quotation marks. As she writes, she asks the children about the letters in each word, such as the letter with which *riding, roller coaster,* and *carnival* should start. Some of the children are able to spell common words, such as *at* and *the.* Joey asks the class to say the letters needed to spell Jensen's name, and the children know that they can refer to the chart with the names of their classmates to accomplish this task.

With Kaleo's story, the daily news text is complete. Students know that it's time to read the daily news aloud, as Joey points to the words. Joey then says to the children, "What if Kaleo wanted to extend his story? What could he ask himself?" The children reply in a chorus, "What else happened when I was riding the roller coaster at the carnival with Jensen?" Joey leaves the chart where it is, so that children can read it on their own later.

Joey makes the transition from the daily news to peer conferences using a brief but critical routine—reflection time. During reflection time, children sit with their eyes closed for a moment to encourage concentration as they prepare for their upcoming activities. The children have their eyes squeezed shut, deep in concentration about the stories they are going to be writing next. Joey closes their reflection time by saying, "I know all of you are going to write [pause]" and the children chime in, "really good stories." "Just like Kaleo," a child adds.

Authenticity and the Daily News

The daily news routine gives Joey the opportunity to teach her students much more than letters and sounds or even story elements. Her students learn to think about what they want to say and to plan their writing. They learn how to state their stories in Standard English, rather than the Hawai'i Creole they use in casual conversations. They learn how to ask one another questions about their stories. The positive effects of the daily news are seen in reflection time, when the children make the transition from watching the teacher write to thinking of the stories they will write on their own.

In the daily news, Joey reflects the four key concepts related to authenticity that we have proposed as beneficial to the learning of ELLs: (1) literate discourse, including language and concept development, (2) the community of practice, (3) meaningful tasks, and (4) routines. In terms of literate discourse, Joey carefully models this type of discourse herself, including think-alouds, so the children will understand what and why she is writing. She uses Standard English sentence structures in the writing, so the children will become familiar with these structures and be able to use them in their own writing. She teaches the children that they should share what she calls "a complete story or idea," helping them to understand the task of writing narratives: providing information about a character, setting, and action. Although she does not use these terms with the children, she believes these concepts provide important groundwork. When students are introduced to the formal language of narrative, they will have the background knowledge and experiences necessary for the language to make sense.

In terms of the community of practice, Joey makes a consistent effort to build the classroom community of learners. She has children serve as models for one another, inviting a different child to share a story with the whole class each day. She engages children in the full process of writing the daily news by having the children think first of the content of the text: the day of the week and the weather. But she also engages children in studying the parts of writing, such as when she asks them to help her spell the words correctly. Although Joey does the actual writing of the daily news, she builds children's independence in writing by familiarizing them with Standard English sentence structures and having them learn to use classroom wall charts as references for the spelling of words. As children gain these skills, they are better able to write independently, as well as help their peers.

Joey focuses on authentic tasks that help children understand the importance of developing their skills as writers. She likes modeling the use of writing through the daily news, because she finds that it shows children that "there's a reason for learning your letters and sounds." When she was a first-year teacher, Joey says, she tried teaching letters and sounds in isolation. "I didn't get anywhere with them," Joey notes. Now, as a second-year teacher, Joey finds that the children catch on much more quickly when she embeds the teaching of letters and sounds in the daily news. The modeling and scaffolding that Joey provides during the daily news contribute to the children's growing independence in drafting their own stories, beginning with reflection time. Children also gain the knowledge and skills they need to help their peers with their writing.

Joey understands the importance of consistent daily routines. She started the daily news routine on the very first day of school, at a time when many of her students knew very little about writing, letters, and sounds. Some had not had the experience of holding a pencil before. Joey faithfully conducted the writers' workshop every day, even when the schedule was changed because of special events, such as a school assembly. By March, it is clear that the children know what to expect within each routine and the flow of the morning from one routine to the next. They often are able to chime in to complete Joey's sentences, such as when she reminds them that peer conferences are important, because your classmate can help you "write really good stories." The routines provide scaffolding for the children's successful participation in the classroom community and for their learning of literate discourse. Research shows that implementation of the writers' workshop can lead to improved writing performance results for ELLs, such as those in Joey's classroom, whose primary language is Hawai'i Creole (Au & Carroll, 1997).

Readers' Workshop in a Fourth-Grade Classroom

Elisabeth Trost-Shahata teaches fourth-grade ELLs in a school that is a veritable United Nations. About 70% of the students live in homes where the first language is not English and in many cases, English is not spoken in the home at all. Over 35 different languages are spoken in the children's homes. The school's poverty level—measured by the number of children who qualify for free or assisted lunch—is about 50%, although in Elisabeth's classroom, the percentage almost doubles. In the class featured in this chapter, the students are in various stages of learning English, with 11 different language groups represented.

Elisabeth follows a format for readers' workshop adapted from Book Club (Raphael, Florio-Ruane, & George, 2001; Raphael, Pardo, Highfield, & McMahon, 1997). She organizes her readers' workshop using the five core routines from the Book Club framework: (1) opening community share, (2) reading time, (3) personal response time, (4) book club discussion, and (5) closing community share. Through these routines, students learn and use the written and oral language of a literate discourse community as they write in response to what they read, share their thoughts within peer-led discussion groups, and make their ideas public for constructive critique and analysis within the whole class (George, Raphael, & Florio-Ruane, 2003). Our discussion focuses on opening community share, the first routine in the readers' workshop in Elisabeth's classroom. The description below is of an adaptation of opening community share developed by Elisabeth to enhance vocabulary learning, a critical area for ELLs.

Opening Community Share

When Elisabeth announces they are starting Book Club with opening community share, there is a very brief commotion as students either slide their desks together or swap chairs so that they will be seated with the three or four other members of their book club discussion groups. Students know that they will be participating in the full reading process, regardless of their proficiency in English. Elisabeth's first task requires that the students collectively determine six focus words from the chapters of the novel assigned for the day.

Students are now familiar with this part of the routine. Each book club group has large sticky notes and a shared pen or pencil. Students look expectantly at Elisabeth, who stands holding a marker near an easel with chart paper. At the top of the otherwise empty chart is the phrase "Today's Words." In preparation for this morning's routine, students are supposed to have read through the day's assigned chapters at least three times, with the purpose of identifying words that present challenges or interest them in some way. Elisabeth asks for a show of fingers so the students can indicate how many times they "read" their text (to themselves, a family member, or a community member). Students know the cultural norms for this particular part of the day: Showing fewer than three fingers is a sign of having shirked their responsibility.

Most of the students have come in with lists of words and corresponding page numbers. Based on her experience with the text, Elisabeth has anticipated words the students will list: Some will refer to unfamiliar content, others to words in their oral vocabulary but not recognized in print, and occasionally, lists of words from only the first few pages of the chapter, if the students found it to be particularly difficult. Thus, she draws words from their lists, but she also seeks new ones that she believes students will find interesting or puzzling. The six words or phrases are chosen on the basis of these criteria:

- Centrality of the word to comprehension.
- Repeated exposure in the text.
- General utility of the word.

Elisabeth has students work within their book clubs to agree upon a group list of six words that they think it is important to understand. Students write their group's chosen words on the sticky note, indicating the number of the page where the word appears, as well as check marks corresponding to the number of students who had that word on their individual lists. Soon, a sticky note from each book club group is pasted to the chart.

Elisabeth reads the words aloud, does a brief think-aloud (e.g., "What an oddly spelled word!"; "Oh, this word is one we use a lot"; "This word looks a lot like a Spanish word I know") as she writes candidate words or phrases onto the large chart, then circles the six "finalists" that will serve as that day's focus. As Elisabeth writes the word and corresponding page number on the chart, students copy that information into their reading logs. Over the course of reading a chapter book, students eventually study in depth approximately 50–75 words and phrases.

Once the words have been selected and entered into each student's reading log, Elisabeth moves the class from the opening community share to the next routine, reading time. Elisabeth has found that the vocabulary work during this routine is critical to providing background on which students will draw when they reread the chapter the next day in preparation for their student-led book club discussion. Today, during reading time, students work within their book club groups on the vocabulary words or phrases just identified. Students locate the word or phrase, then take turns reading aloud the paragraph before and after the word. Each book club member offers an inference about the word's meaning, and the group decides which inference makes the most sense. In their reading logs, students write in their own words what the word means. In this community, everyone knows to ask, "Does it (the inference) make sense?" Elisabeth hears this question often as she circulates through the room. "Think about what is happening in the story," Elisabeth reminds them. "Does it make sense when you substitute your inference for the unknown word?"

Authenticity and Opening Community Share

As with Joey's use of the daily news, Elisabeth's use of opening community share shows the application of the four key concepts related to authenticity, valuable in the teaching of literate discourse to ELLs. In terms of language and concept development, Elisabeth understands the importance of giving her fourth-grade students access to the same texts that their English-speaking peers are reading in mainstream classrooms. She was attracted to the Book Club framework because it aligns with her belief that ELLs must be given the opportunities to hear, think about, and respond to texts designed for their age group (Brock & Raphael, 2005; Kong & Fitch, 2003). This exposure to, and interaction with, grade-level texts is important to students' acquisition of literate discourse at the levels of performance needed to close the achievement gap.

In terms of the community of practice, Elisabeth structures her classroom to give students every opportunity to learn literate discourse by modeling literacy activities, and by encouraging students to work together and to help one another. Book Club centers on the reading of chapter books, which allows Elisabeth to engage students in the full process of reading. She also has students study the parts of reading through the vocabulary activity during opening community share. Students read the assigned section of the chapter book three times and independently identify vocabulary words and phrases. Under Elisabeth's guidance, they work with the other students in their book clubs to decide upon the words they want to study. Instead of deciding upon the vocabulary words herself, or following the common practice of preteaching vocabulary words, Elisabeth makes the selection of vocabulary for in-depth study a collaborative venture, carried out within the classroom community of readers.

Elisabeth is well aware of involving her students in meaningful, authentic literacy activities. For ELLs, literate discourse is often elusive, because the bulk of their reading instruction typically involves skills in isolation, outside the context of authentic texts (Fitzgerald, 1995). Elisabeth provides an authentic context for the learning of vocabulary skills by having students engage with new vocabulary as part and parcel of their reading of chapter books. She enhances the meaningfulness of vocabulary learning by having students make and share their inferences about the words' possible meanings. Students' understanding of new vocabulary drawn from novels is enhanced as they participate actively in decision-making discussions with their peers.

Elisabeth, like Joey, understands the benefits of consistent daily routines in helping ELLs learn literate discourse. In terms of classroom organization and management, as well as cognitive demands, Elisabeth's twice-weekly vocabulary activity is far from simple. Students must assemble in their book clubs, share the vocabulary choices made independently, and negotiate with their peers about the words their group will recommend to the class. Elisabeth took the time to establish this routine and carefully prepare students to participate successfully in every part of it. Elisabeth's students know the flow of activities in the readers' workshop and move smoothly from one activity to the next. Little or no academic learning time is lost due to confusion on the part of the students about what they should be doing, so they can devote their attention to learning literate discourse. Time is of the essence to Elisabeth, who notes that she sees her commitment to routines as a way of "helping my students run a little faster as they attempt to catch the moving train."

Closing Comments

Elisabeth's metaphor provides a good starting point for our closing comments. We find that many teachers of ELLs have similar feelings: Trying to help their students reach grade-level expectations for literacy is like having them run after a moving train. Most ELLs must make more than a typical year's progress in a year's time, if they are to have a chance of reaching grade-level expectations in literacy. We advocate powerful instruction, such as workshop approaches, as a means of closing the gap between the literacy achievement of ELLs and their mainstream peers.

We have suggested that authenticity involves four key concepts related to the language of literacy practices, the classroom community of practice, meaningful tasks, and routines. These key concepts are captured in the following four guidelines for teachers of ELLs, as illustrated in the descriptions of workshop approaches presented in this chapter.

1. Think broadly of promoting your students' ability to understand and use literate discourse.
2. View your classroom as a community of practice in which your modeling of literacy serves as scaffolding for students' ability to support one another and gain independence as readers and writers.
3. Build instruction around literacy tasks that students find meaningful and that have value in the real world beyond the classroom, and teach skills in the context of these tasks.
4. Establish consistent routines, so that students know what they are expected to do and can focus on gaining proficiency with literate discourse within these familiar frameworks.

Workshop approaches following these guidelines offer the promise of helping educators to address persistent issues of equity involving ELLs. Whether they enter school speaking a nonmainstream variety of English, or a language other than English, ELLs come to the classroom with rich resources from the home and community. Our challenge as educators is to hold high expectations for the literacy achievement of ELLs in our classrooms, and to use the most powerful forms of instruction we know to help students reach these expectations.

ENGAGEMENT ACTIVITIES

1. Taking a child's point of view, describe what it would be like to be an ELL student in either Joey's or Elisabeth's class. How do you, as a student, feel about participating in the writers' or readers' workshop? What features of the workshop support your learning?

2. Reread the description of one of the routines highlighted in this chapter, either the daily news in Joey's class or the opening community share in Elisabeth's class. Identify the concepts, strategies, and skills the students have the opportunity to learn during the routine you chose.

3. Think about how you might implement a writers' or readers' workshop in your classroom. Which routines would you include? Which of these routines are you already well prepared to use? Which of these routines would take some time for you to figure out?

4. Make a list of the pros and cons of using workshop approaches, from your own point of view.

5. What do you see as the main barriers to the use of workshop approaches? How might these barriers be overcome?

ACKNOWLEDGMENTS

We wish to thank the teachers featured in the classroom examples—Joey Inatsuka and Elisabeth Trost-Shahata—for allowing us to observe in their classrooms and study their practice.

REFERENCES

Au, K. (2006). *Multicultural issues and literacy achievement.* Mahwah, NJ: Erlbaum.
Au, K. (2008). If can, can: Hawai'i Creole and reading achievement. *Educational Perspectives, 41*(1), 66–76.
Au, K., & Carroll, J. (1997). Improving literacy achievement through a constructivist approach: The KEEP Demonstration Classroom Project. *Elementary School Journal, 97*(3), 203–221.
Brock, C., & Raphael, T. (2005). *Windows to language, literacy, and culture.* Newark, DE: International Reading Association.
Dewey, J. (1944). *Democracy and education: An introduction to the philosophy of education.* New York: Free Press.
Fitzgerald, J. (1995). English-as-a-second-language reading instruction in the United States: A research review. *Journal of Reading Behavior, 27,* 115–152.
Gee, J. P. (1990). *Social linguistics and literacies: Ideology in discourses.* London: Falmer Press.
George, M., Raphael, T., & Florio-Ruane, S. (2003). Connecting children, culture, curriculum, and text. In G. García (Ed.), *English learners: Reaching the highest level of English literacy* (pp. 308–332). Newark, DE: International Reading Association.
Graves, D., & Hansen, J. (1983). The Author's Chair. *Language Arts, 60*(2), 176–183.
Kong, A., & Fitch, E. (2003). Using Book Club to engage culturally and linguistically diverse learners in reading, writing, and talking about books. *Reading Teacher, 56*(4), 352–362.
Lave, J., & Wenger, E. (1991). *Situated learning: Legitimate peripheral participation.* Cambridge, UK: Cambridge University Press.

Raphael, T. E., Florio-Ruane, S., & George, M. (2001). Book Club Plus: A conceptual framework to organize literacy instruction. *Language Arts, 79*(2), 159–168.

Raphael, T. E., Pardo, L., Highfield, K., & McMahon, S. I. (1997). *Book Club: A literature-based curriculum.* Littleton, MA: Small Planet Communications.

Scollon, R., & Scollon, S. (1981). *Narrative, literacy, and face in interethnic communication.* Norwood, NJ: Ablex.

Vygotsky, L. (1978). *Mind in society: The development of higher psychological processes* (M. Cole, Trans.). Cambridge, MA: Harvard University Press.

Vygotsky, L. (1986). *Thought and language* (A. Kozulin, Trans.). Cambridge, MA: MIT Press.

CHAPTER 10

A Bilingual Perspective on Writing Assessment

Implications for Teachers of Emerging Bilingual Writers

Lucinda Soltero-González, Kathy Escamilla,
and Susan Hopewell

This chapter will:

1. Provide a rationale for why it is necessary to change the current prevailing paradigm about emerging bilinguals from that of parallel monolingualism to that of a holistic bilingual perspective.

2. Illustrate how the utilization of a holistic bilingual framework when examining the writing of emerging bilingual children can yield more robust information about the writing strengths and needs of these children.

3. Illustrate how the use of a holistic bilingual lens to evaluate the writing of emerging bilingual children can change teachers' perceptions about these children.

The population of emerging bilinguals in the United States is growing quickly. We employ the term *emerging bilinguals*, instead of the more common term *English Language Learners,* (ELLs), to refer to students who speak a language other than English at home and are growing up as simultaneous bilinguals. While this population in its entirety is diverse, nearly 80% of emerging bilinguals speak Spanish as a first language. Furthermore, 60% are from Mexico, and most attend schools that are highly segregated (Kindler, 2002; National Center for Education Statistics, 2006). Literacy development and, in best case scenarios, development of biliteracy are at the forefront of discussions and debates about how to plan, implement, evaluate, and assess effective instructional programs for Spanish–English bilinguals.

While much has been written about literacy and biliteracy for emerging bilinguals, we argue in this chapter that literacy in the United States, both for native English-speaking children and for emerging bilinguals, has largely been focused on reading, with scant attention to writing instruction or writing assessment. In their recent research synthesis, August and Shanahan (2006) state,

> Research on the development of writing skills in English Language Learners is extremely sparse, and research on cross-linguistic influences in the acquisition of writing skills by English Language Learners is even more sparse. Thus, much more research that focuses on the relationship between English Language Learners' first and second language skills in the context of learning to write for academic purposes in English is necessary. (p. 169)

In a seminal work on language and literacy, Wilkinson (1970) proposed that language acquisition consists of acquiring receptive and productive skills, with receptive skills being listening and reading, and productive skills being speaking and writing. In this work, some 38 years ago, Wilkinson offered a critique of U.S. literacy practices as being too narrowly focused on the development of receptive skills (listening and reading), with too little attention placed on teaching the productive skills of speaking and writing. We argue that literacy instruction in the United States is still heavily focused on teaching listening and reading, and we further argue that effective literacy programs for emerging bilingual students must expand existing instruction and assessment practices to include greater attention to speaking and writing. For emerging bilinguals, this must include the teaching of productive skills in both the home language and English.

In addition to the teaching of productive skills, we believe that effective writing instruction and assessment practices for emerging bilinguals must move from the prevailing monolingual framework to what we call *holistic bilingualism*. Much can be learned about how to improve instruction in writing for emerging bilingual children through simultaneous examination of their written work in both English and Spanish. As the chapter demonstrates, however, the key to using children's written work to improve instruction is not dependent solely on what children produce; rather, it is equally reliant on teachers' interpretations of children's written work. We argue that there is a need to prepare teachers to evaluate the writing of emerging bilingual children in ways that both challenge and expand their current frames of reference, and we use findings from a recent 5-year intervention study titled Literacy Squared® (Escamilla & Hopewell, 2009; Escamilla, Soltero-González, Butvilofsky, Hopewell, & Sparrow, 2009) to provide a foundation for these claims.

The Need for a Holistic Bilingual Perspective on Writing Assessment

The coexistence of two or more languages in young children contributes to a uniquely endowed human being whose experiences and knowledge can never be measured or understood as independently constrained by each language separately. Thus, we propose the concept of *holistic bilingualism* to examine the writing of Spanish-English emerging bilingual children in elementary school. Holistic views of bilingualism (Grosjean, 1989; Valdés & Figueroa, 1994) consider the totality of the bilingual experience as a unique and unified whole rather than as a fractional representation that perpetuates the idea that the bilingual resembles two monolinguals in one person. It embraces the notion that a student's communicative competencies can only be evaluated by observing the myriad of ways in which the bilingual child expresses him- or herself. The totality of a person's literacy skills and knowledge may, in fact, be distributed across languages and cultures.

Research on authentic writing assessment with bilingual students (Escamilla, 2000; García, Bravo, Dickey, Chun, & Sun-Irminger, 2002; Gort, 2006; Valdés & Anloff Sanders, 1999) and research on biliteracy development from a bilingual perspective (Dworin, 2003; Dworin & Moll, 2006; Martínez-Roldán & Sayer, 2006; Reyes, 2006; Valdés, 1992) support the notion that emerging bilinguals draw on all of their linguistic resources as they learn to read and write in two languages. The concept of holistic bilingualism in this chapter is contrasted to the more common and pervasive theories of parallel monolingualism that view bilingual/biliterate development as separate cognitive and linguistic processes.

Table 10.1 provides a contrast between notions of *parallel monolingualism* and *holistic bilingualism* applied to writing assessment.

Besides advocating for a framework of holistic bilingualism applied to writing assessment and instruction, we also emphasize the role that perceptions about bilingual writing development play in the ways that

TABLE 10.1. Characteristics of Parallel Monolingualism and Holistic Bilingualism

Parallel monolingualism	Holistic bilingualism
Lack of understanding that simultaneous development of two languages is mutually reinforcing. Writing abilities that are carried over to the other language are not recognized, or are seen as random errors.	The linguistic resources in emerging bilinguals are mutually reinforcing, and children are capable of bidirectional transfer. Errors that result from bidirectional transfer often reflect systematic approximations to conventional writing. These errors are seen as predictable patterns that are part of the interlanguage development process.
Assessment is administered and analyzed in English and in the student's first language separately. Looking at writing in each language separately only gives a limited understanding of a bilingual child's learning. This assessment practice denies teachers opportunities to see how children work across languages.	Assessment is administered in English and in the students' first language, and analyzed *concurrently* for cross-language comparison. The totality of what bilinguals know and can do is distributed across languages.
Assessment instruments are mere translations from English into the other language.	Assessment takes into consideration features of language, organization, and/or discourse style that are unique to each language.
Bilinguals are expected to perform all linguistic tasks equally well in both languages.	Bilinguals may be able to perform one set of tasks well in one language and a different set of tasks well in the other language.
Bilingual strategies such as code switching, lexical borrowing, and bidirectional phonetic, syntactic, and rhetorical structure transfers are viewed as markers of low language proficiency in both languages.	Bilingual writing strategies are seen as part of the process to learn to write in two languages. They have been demonstrated to provide cognitive advantages.
Second-language writing development is measured against standards developed for monolingual speakers.	Second-language writing development is measured against English language development standards created for emerging bilinguals.

teachers evaluate children's writing. Previous research by Escamilla (2006) and Escamilla and Coady (2001) on teachers' perceptions of emerging bilingual children's writing found that emerging bilingual children have many strengths in writing; however, teachers focused on their perceived weaknesses. In particular, perceived weaknesses were generally articulated as language interference caused by behaviors such as code switching and using Spanish phonetic principles to write English words. The researchers concluded that teacher perceptions of emerging bilingual children's writing have been heavily influenced by parallel monolingual frameworks and monolingual assessment rubrics, both of which have exacerbated deficit notions about emerging bilinguals and their abilities in both of their languages.

To restate, this chapter posits that the utilization of a holistic bilingual lens in evaluating the writing of Spanish–English emerging bilingual children in both languages simultaneously is a more robust and valid means of understanding language and literacy development in bilingual children. Moreover, the development of a holistic bilingual lens can also be useful in changing teacher perceptions about children's writing, thereby enhancing instruction.

Utilizing a Holistic Bilingual Writing Assessment to Assess Biliterate Writing Development

We suggest that holistic bilingual assessment can better enable us to approximate a student's trajectory toward biliteracy.[1] Creating this profile requires the use of an instrument that captures the blossoming biliteracy development of emerging bilingual children. A writing rubric developed as a part of the Literacy Squared research project is used throughout this chapter to illustrate the concept of holistic bilingual writing assessment and to demonstrate its usefulness in examining student writing and in changing teacher perceptions. This rubric is included in Appendix 10.1 of this chapter. Its primary use in the Literacy Squared research project is to compare and contrast students' writing trajectories in Spanish and English throughout the elementary grades. To document students' bilingual writing trajectories, Spanish and English writing samples are evaluated side by side, and the scores from the two writing samples are reported on the same scoring sheet (see Appendix 10.1). The writing rubric is meant to be a tool to determine how a Spanish–English emerging bilingual child who attends a bilingual program is progressing as a writer in both languages. The writing rubric can be used both to document student growth and to inform instruction.

The writing rubric includes two main sections: a quantitative evaluation and a qualitative evaluation. The quantitative portion comprises three areas for consideration: content, punctuation, and spelling. A unique aspect is that this writing rubric does not assign equal weight to each of the three areas. Instead, it distributes the scores in a way that does not penalize students for errors or approximations that are due to the acquisition of two writing systems simultaneously. A maximum score on the rubric is 14 (content = 7; punctuation = 3; and spelling = 4). The qualitative portion comprises a three-column chart that asks teachers to identify and categorize students' use of bilingual strategies and linguistic approximations. The left and right columns of this chart ask teachers to record linguistic approximations. These approximations are divided into those typical of monolingual English-speaking students, and those that are unique to emergent bilinguals. These separations help teachers analyze the linguistic hypotheses children are utilizing as they gain bilingual writing competencies, so that they can better address them through instruction. The middle column asks teachers to note and to categorize students' bilingual behaviors and approximations. In particular, this part of the rubric asks raters to record bilingual strategies that children use as they write in either Spanish or English. This task requires focused attention on cross-language analysis. The bilingual strategies included in the rubric are described as follows:

1. Intrasentential code switching: code switching that occurs within the boundaries of a sentence (e.g., *no puedo hablar* in just one language/I can't speak in just one language).
2. Intersentential code switching: code switching that occurs at sentence boundaries (e.g., See you later! *Me voy a la tienda*/See you later! I'm going to the store).
3. Bidirectional syntax transfer: Second language (L2) syntax applied to first language (L1) writing, as well as L1 syntax applied to L2 writing (e.g., the bike of my sister).
4. Bidirectional phonics transfer: Phonetic principles unique to the L2 being used to encode L1 words, as well as phonetic principles unique to the L1 being used to encode L2 words (e.g., *japi*/happy; *jebaron/llevaron*).
5. "Others": Because the list of bilingual strategies is not exhaustive, a space for teachers to make note of "other" strategies is also provided.

To reiterate, the Literacy Squared writing rubric tool is used to determine how emergent bilinguals are progressing as writers. We have used this instrument over the past 5 years with over 2,000 children and 120 teachers to deepen our understanding of how emerging bilingual children develop as writers, and to document how teachers' observational skills across languages can be expanded.

Results of our work suggest that the use of this rubric provides teachers an opportunity to see their students in unique ways and windows to understanding simultaneous bilingual development that are not available in current assessment systems that examine each language independently.

Holistic Bilingual Assessment: Lessons Learned

We have learned that bilingual children have and utilize multiple skills and strategies when they write in Spanish and English. These strategies are cognitive, linguistic, and academic strengths that first must be recognized by classroom teachers, then utilized to create effective writing instruction to enhance and expand cross-language transfer. General findings from our studies include the following:

- Emerging bilingual writers positively transfer what they know across languages.
- Bilingual living produces bilingual writing. Bilingual living creates the need for, and the use of, code switching in written expression.
- The employment of bilingual strategies across languages is rule-governed.
- There is a high correspondence across languages with regard to approach, content, and punctuation.
- Bilingual writers use multiple strategies to express themselves in Spanish and English.

This final bullet deserves further explication. In the study we present in this chapter, we used a conceptual lens of holistic bilingualism to look carefully at students' use of bilingual strategies. We intentionally analyzed, side by side, students' writing in Spanish and English. We noticed a much richer repertoire of bilingual strategies than we had originally anticipated. As a result of this analysis, we grouped the newly identified bilingual strategies into three main categories:

1. *Discourse-level bilingual strategies*. This category includes the use of rhetorical structures and punctuation across languages. An example of cross-language rhetorical structures is the use of questioning in both

writing samples to engage the reader (e.g., concluding with a question: "*¿Quién es tu mejor amigo?*"/"Who is your best friend?" and "So, what do you think?"). Additionally, punctuation was noted when the conventions unique to one language were used while writing in the other (e.g., "¡It was the best day ever!").

2. *Sentence-level bilingual strategies.* This category includes the use of cross-language syntax, literal translations, and code switching. Cross-language syntax consists of using syntactic structures unique to one language when writing in the other language, such as word order (e.g., "The bike of my sister") and subject omission (e.g., "Is my favorite toy to play with").

3. *Word-level bilingual strategies.* This category includes the use of code switching, loan words, and nativized words. Code switching at the word level was observed when children inserted a word in the other language within a sentence (e.g., "*Yo juego en la snow*"/"I play in the snow"). Students also used loan words that have language-specific equivalents, but have been incorporated into day-to-day language use (e.g., the use of the name "Spiderman" or the word *movies* while writing in Spanish). Furthermore, loan words were sometimes nativized so that words originating in one language were changed morphologically to incorporate the structure of the other language (e.g., *spláchate*/to splash yourself).

4. *Phoneme-level bilingual strategies.* At the phoneme level, we noted that students did not always restrict themselves to the sound–symbol correspondences of only one language. They often combined spelling conventions from each language to approximate a single word (e.g., *lecktura, jappy*). We referred to these as *within-word mixing of phonetic codes*.

To compare and contrast how a student's text may be evaluated from parallel monolingualism and holistic bilingualism perspectives, we present the following example. The writing samples used herein were created in Spanish and English by a second grader in one of the participating Literacy Squared schools, in response to the Spanish writing prompt "Write about what you like to do when you are not at school. Tell us why," and to the English writing prompt "What do you like to do at recess?" A transcription of both texts is provided below (the original texts are included in Appendices 10.2 and 10.3).

Spanish Sample

"*Escribe lo que te gusta hacer cuando no estás en la escuela. Y dí por qué*"

A mi me gsta jugar saqer porque es mu divirdido para mi. A mi megusta jugar sager con mi hermano. Tavien me gusta jugar con mi hermana. Aveses guego con mi Mamá y Papá. Aveses juego sola a mi me gusta jugar sager mocho es como un deporte mi hermano me ensella aveses y tavien mihermana. luego me voy al parque yo juego sola. El sacer es muy dirverdido porque es como jugar pelota el saqueres como patear la pelota abeses juego sacer con mis hermanas y con mi amiga. El saquer es mui dirvedido para mi es muy dirverdido mucho mas dirverdido. A me me gusta cugar a la visiqleta porque me gusta a ser careras con mihermano. y con mi hermana. abeses yo voy sola en la bisiqleta yo sola por la caretera voy arededor de mi casa. Aveses voy a la montaña con mi bisigleta.

English Translation Maintaining Child's Use of Conventions

I like to play soccer because is a lot of fun for me. I like to play soccer with my brother. I also like to play with my sister. Sometimes I play with my Mom and my Dad. Sometimes I play alone I like to play soccer a lot it's like a sport my brother teaches me sometimes and also my sister. Then I go to the park and play by myself. Soccer is a lot of fun because is like playing with a ball soccer is like kicking the ball sometimes I play soccer with my siblings and with my friend. Soccer is a lot of fun for me it's a lot of fun a lot more fun. i like to ride my bike because I like to race with my brother. and with my sister sometimes I go alone in my bike I go alone on the road I go around my house. Sometimes I go to the mountain in my bike.

Same Student—English Sample

"What do you like to do at recess? Why?"

Ai like to play in the pleicroun because is so fun. At recess ai like tu play in the snou because ai cud du snou enllols. At recess ai liake to play wut ai llapbrop because is so fun.

Standard English Orthography (or Standard Form)

I like to play on the playground because it is so fun. At recess I like to play in the snow because I could do snow angels. At recess I like to play with a jump rope because it is so fun.

Using a *parallel monolingual* lens to interpret this girl's writing, one might evaluate each writing sample separately, without attending to evidence of cross-language transfer. When analyzing the English writing sample, the evaluator might be tempted to find evidence of Spanish language literacy interfering with English language development. The unusual spelling and awkward syntax in the English writing sample do not reflect that of a monolingual English-speaking child. If the "norm" is the monolingual child, this bilingual child appears to be developing "abnormally." Evidence for this conclusion begins with the weak spelling she has used. The monolingual English-speaking reader may not be able to interpret words like ENLLOLS and LLAPBROP. Being restricted to a parallel monolingual lens limits and inhibits the reader from understanding that the child is using phonetic principles from both of her languages to spell words. In fact, the child is quite adept at cross-language invented spelling, facilitated by using phonetics transfers from the L1 to the L2. Furthermore, the omission of words results in unusual phrasing that some teachers may interpret as a sign of a cognitive processing disorder. In short, this writing could be seen as evidence of language as a problem and be used to mount an argument that the child is developing abnormally (for a discussion of how to distinguish between language acquisition and learning disabilities, see Klingner, Baca, & Hoover, 2008).

Using the writing rubric developed for Literacy Squared (see Appendix 10.1) to interpret the writing through a *holistic bilingual* lens, however, we would come to a very different conclusion. We propose that the child is transferring writing abilities, such as concept of word-ness and sentence separation, across languages. Additionally, this child is using some very powerful strategies to express herself in both languages. When writing in English, she uses the Spanish phonetic system to write many of the words (e.g., AI for *I*, PLEICROUN for *playground*, and ENLLOLS for *angels*). This illustrates knowledge that sounds can be heard in our minds and then recorded on a page. She is using what she knows in one language to communicate in a second language. Furthermore, she has learned enough English to use standard spelling for many of the high-frequency words (e.g., *because, is, the,* and *so*). In other words, while she continues to draw on her Spanish phonetic knowledge when encoding words, she does not yet know how to spell conventionally in English. She displays clear evidence that she has internalized that many English words are spelled with patterns unique to that language. She is beginning to apply language-specific conventions.

Her lack of the pronoun *it* before the word *is* is likely the application of Spanish syntax to English phraseology. In fact, her Spanish sample contains the sentence, "*A mi me gusta jugar saqer* (soccer) *porque es mui divirdido (muy divertido)*" (I like to play soccer because it is very fun.) In Spanish, there is no need to use a pronoun to reference the antecedent. The sentence structure *es muy divertido* is clear and the verb tense carries reference to the indicated subject. There is no need to state the pronoun *it* explicitly. Interestingly, this illustrates knowledge that language is rule-governed and the fact that this knowledge transfers across languages.

Cross-language transfer is also observed in the Spanish sample. Note that this sample contains the word *soccer,* which is spelled in several different ways (e.g., *saqer, sager, sacer, saquer*). The use of this "loan word" provides evidence that bilingual students code-switch in a variety of ways, because their knowledge and experiences are distributed across languages. Furthermore, the different spellings of this English word in the Spanish text is an example of how emerging bilinguals draw from their two languages to generate hypothesis about how to represent, in one language, the sounds and clusters they hear in words in the other language. The invented spelling for the word *soccer* reveals the incorporation of phonetic and orthographic patterns from both languages (e.g., *sacer* and *saquer*), which we interpret as a sign of bidirectional phonetics transfer and as a characteristic of an interlanguage development stage.

Using Holistic Bilingual Writing Assessment to Change Teachers' Perceptions

This section deals with the need to change teachers' perceptions about emerging bilinguals' writing. Our belief about this need is based on a study by Soltero-González, Escamilla, and Hopewell (2009). In this study, we found that teachers did not recognize, analyze, and capitalize on the uniquely bilingual strategies their students were demonstrating. We believe this is due partially to a lack of professional development opportunities designed to hone these skills. Our experience has been that teachers' perceptions of bilingual students' writing were influenced by the training they received from us. They noticed only what we underscored. For instance, rather than emphasizing cross-language strategies at the word, sentence, and discourse levels, we focused on bidirectional phonetics transfer and code switching. It should have come as no surprise, therefore, when we discovered that teachers seemed to hyperfocus on only two types of bilingual strategies: L1–L2 phonics transfer and intersentential code switching. When they did note other strategies, such as the presence of syntax transfer, they were likely to underrepresent how often students actually employed it. Teachers rarely noted any bilingual strategy that was not explicitly listed on the rubric. This finding is important, in that it suggests that teachers absorb and apply what we teach them, but our staff development sessions must also improve. As a field, we must continually expand our understandings and the manner in which we disseminate such information.

In short, we have learned that emerging bilingual students use multiple cross-language strategies when learning to write in Spanish and English. The three main categories and subcategories we used to describe these strategies allowed us to not only fine-tune our analysis but also recognize the limited ways we had originally conceived of students' use of bilingual strategies. We realized that while we had emphasized bidirectional phonetics transfer and code switching (which was reflected in our study of teachers' evaluation of bilingual writing), we had neglected the fact that cross-language strategies also occur at the word, sentence, and discourse levels. Another important finding is that the teachers' perceptions of students' bilingual writing was clearly influenced by the training they received as part of the Literacy Squared intervention. These findings reveal to us that our limited conceptions most likely influenced teachers' perceptions and interpretations. They also reflect the important role that professional development can have in changing teachers' perceptions and knowledge about bilingual writing and, more importantly, how that can impact instructional decisions. Overall, we suggest that holistic bilingual assessment is a tool that can be used to change teachers' perceptions about emerging bilingual children's writing.

When using the Literacy Squared writing rubric, teachers are to read and score quantitatively the Spanish language sample followed by the English language sample. Using the previous example, we illustrate how one teacher scored the student's writing and compare her analysis to our reevaluation of the same pair of writing samples. The content score for both the Spanish language and the English language samples was a 4. A score of 4 indicates that the student expressed more than two ideas, that there was a discernable main idea, and that the story may not be complete. The punctuation score was also identical for each sample, with a score of 2. A score of 2 indicates that the punctuation was mostly correct, but that there were some errors. Finally, the teacher evaluated the student's Spanish spelling as meriting a score of 2 (many spelling errors, but the meaning is not affected) and the student's English spelling as meriting a score of 1 (many spelling errors, and the meaning is sometimes affected). These scores mirror a pattern that we have seen when analyzing thousands of pairs of bilingual student writing. There is a high correspondence with regard to bilingual students' ability to express content and utilize punctuation in their two languages, but a lesser correspondence with regard to spelling. When we compared our analyses of this student's writing to the teacher's analyses, we concurred with these numerical quantifications of the student's writing.

The next step in the analysis is to compare the writing side by side to identify and categorize students' use of bilingual strategies and linguistic approximations. We saw discrepancy between our analyses of this student's writing and the teacher's analyses in the ensuing qualitative analysis. The teacher's evaluation did not include anything from the Spanish language sample. Additionally, there was no explicit indication that the teacher noticed the use of bilingual strategies. What she did note was that, in the English language sample, the student had spelling approximations that were representative of common grade-level errors, as well as some that could be attributable to bilingualism. In total, she identified and listed four words. As common to grade level, she listed only one word: CUD for *could*. As common English language development errors she listed: PLEICRAUN/*playground*, AI/*I*, and SNOU/*snow*. The categorization of these words as attributable to bilingualism seems to indicate that the teacher recognizes that the student is applying Spanish language phonetics, especially the encoding of vowel sounds, to English writing; however, she did not mark this as a bilingual strategy on the score sheet. Overlooked or omitted were observations regarding loan words (*soccer/fútbol*) and the application of Spanish syntax to English writing (because is so fun/*porque es muy divertido*). Furthermore, while the words listed by the teacher indicated a use of Spanish phonetic principles, there was evidence in the Spanish sample of the reverse. Finally, it is not at all clear why the unusual spellings of the words *jump rope* and *angels* were not recorded. Was the teacher unable to discern the child's intent?

Assessment should inform instruction. If teachers cannot recognize and name the strategies students are employing, they will not be able to reinforce the uniquely bilingual competencies being developed. Writing assessment that requires teachers to examine student work in English and Spanish side by side, using a holistic bilingual lens, has the potential to increase and change teachers' perceptions and efficacy.

Reflections and Future Directions

Our ongoing research in Literacy Squared has convinced us that teachers must overcome deficit notions about biliterate writing development that view the students' home language as a barrier, and acknowledge that it is a source of support and a scaffold to literacy development.

Even in English-only classrooms, teachers should find ways to evaluate, through authentic assessment methods, emerging bilinguals' literacy abilities in both of their languages and to develop lessons that build on students' strengths and needs. Evaluating students' skills and knowledge in the two languages facilitates identifying both the abilities students have been able to transfer across languages and those that do not transfer. This information can help teachers to target instruction to meet students' specific needs.

Furthermore, in addition to using authentic writing assessment, teachers must know that there are important differences in the literacy learning of monolinguals and emerging bilinguals. Therefore, writing assessment for emerging bilinguals should consider the unique features in the development of writing for these students and abstain from penalizing them for not writing like native English speakers. Writing assessment should also consider how the language being assessed works and develops (e.g., in Spanish, we should assess the use of punctuation, accents, dieresis, spelling, and nonlinear discourse patterns, that are unique to the Spanish language).

Notions of universal assessment practices that assume that the same writing assessments developed for monolingual English speakers can be used to assess the English literacy development of emerging bilinguals should be challenged. We must question the simplicity with which English language assessments are often adopted to assess other languages without appropriate modifications. Furthermore, we advocate for the development of assessment tools that have been validated for the population with which they are to be used.

In settings where students have opportunities to develop literacy in both of their languages, they should be assessed in both languages simultaneously. It is only when we look at the bilingual child as a whole that we can better understand how he or she can work across languages, and how the languages reinforce each other. As Escamilla and Coady (2001) point out, "Assessment practices that look at second language learners only in English often underestimate the cognitive and academic strengths of students" (p. 43). In addition, we need to evaluate emerging bilinguals' writing beyond the identification of L1 to L2 phonetics transfers (phomeme-level analysis) and consider how they employ bilingual strategies at the word, sentence, and discourse levels.

This reinforces our belief that we need holistic bilingual assessment to further our knowledge about biliterate writing development in emerging bilingual children. Beyond this, however, we assert that the use of a bilingual framework can be useful to change teachers' perceptions of emerging bilingual children. We believe that teachers are willing and eager to learn new theories that better serve their emerging bilingual students. We further believe that teacher perceptions can be influenced by professional development.

Since the inception of the Literacy Squared project, teachers and researchers have had the benefit of learning to look at children's nascent biliteracy via a holistic bilingual lens and from a strengths-based perspective. As a result, the teachers' evaluations of children's writing have changed in significant ways. Their evaluations focus much more on how the children are using writing conventions and spelling patterns across languages, thereby suggesting that teachers' perceptions can be influenced by professional development.

Our work has also taught us that emerging bilinguals use a wide variety of bilingual strategies at the word, sentence, and discourse levels. Based on these observations, we have started to revise and refine the writing rubric presented in this chapter. We are hopeful that additional research, combined with more opportunities for professional development, will result in not only improved children's writing in Spanish and English but also improved ability on the part of teachers and researchers to move beyond theories of language transfer, toward more robust theories of emerging biliteracy.

Concluding Remarks

Evaluations of emerging bilingual children's writing depend not just on what children produce but, more importantly, on teachers' interpretation of the written work. Furthermore, teachers' interpretations lead to judgments about whether children's literacy is developing as expected, and what concepts or skills should constitute the focus of instruction. If teachers have deficit notions about biliterate writing development, including the bilingual strategies used by emerging bilingual children, then their instruction may be less than effective.

The findings from this study reaffirm for us the need for teachers to use a holistic bilingual lens when interpreting the writing of emerging bilingual children. They have helped us realize the importance of evaluating and teaching writing as an integrated system rather than as discrete pieces. Moreover, they emphasize the need to look at Spanish writing and English writing side by side to get a "big picture" view of the developing biliteracy of the children. The development of a holistic bilingual lens for writing evaluation should be a major focus of teacher education and staff development for teachers of emerging bilingual children.

ENGAGEMENT ACTIVITIES

1. Appendix 10.4 includes the Spanish and English writing samples of one of our students from the Literacy Squared research project. Using the Literacy Squared writing rubric in Appendix 10.1, analyze this student's writing from a parallel monolingual lens and then from the holistic bilingual lens discussed in the chapter. What cross-language strategies is the student employing? What can be said about the student's trajectory toward biliteracy? What are the implications for teaching this child?

2. Collect writing samples in both English and Spanish from children in your own school (if possible) at a variety of grade levels. Using the Literacy Squared writing rubric in Appendix 10.1, analyze these samples using a holistic bilingual frame. Choose one writing sample and create a mini-lesson for this student in English and Spanish.

3. Design and try out a different series of writing prompts for your students. Elicit student comments on the different prompts. Strive for culturally relevant prompts, as well as the more standard prompts. Assess and examine whether different prompts yield different quantitative and qualitative scores.

4. Show students writing samples and ask them to give feedback about the writing sample with regard to content, punctuation, and spelling. Note what aspects of writing the students are able to observe and discuss, and use their comments to generate mini-lessons about writing.

NOTE

1. In the Literacy Squared research study that undergirds this chapter, the concept of a trajectory toward biliteracy is used to measure a child's growth in Spanish and English literacy. Children's academic achievement is expressed in terms of biliterate development rather than by grade levels or other normative measures that look at two languages separately. The trajectory toward biliteracy documents patterns of development and growth that are distinctive to emerging bilingual children, and in essence document each child's unique biliteracy blueprint (Escamilla et al., 2009).

REFERENCES

August, D., & Shanahan, T. (2006). *Developing literacy in second-language learners: Report of the National Literacy Panel on Language-Minority Children and Youth.* Mahwah, NJ: Erlbaum.

Dworin, J. E. (2003). Insights into biliteracy development: Toward a bidirectional theory of bilingual pedagogy. *Journal of Hispanic Higher Education, 2,* 171–186.

Dworin, J., & Moll, L. (2006). Guest editors' introduction. *Journal of Early Child-hood Literacy, 6*(3), 234–240.

Escamilla, K. (2000). Bilingual means two: Assessment issues, early literacy and two language children. In *Research in literacy for limited English proficient students* (pp. 100–128). Washington, DC: National Clearinghouse for Bilingual Education.

Escamilla, K. (2006). Semilingualism applied to the literacy behaviors of Span-ish- speaking emerging bilinguals: Bi-illiteracy or emerging biliteracy? *Teachers College Record, 108,* 2329–2353.

Escamilla, K., & Coady, M. (2001). Assessing the writing of Spanish-speaking students. Issues and suggestions. In J. Tinajero & S. Hurley (Eds.), *Hand-book for literacy assessment for bilingual learners* (pp. 43–63). Boston: Allyn & Bacon.

Escamilla, K., & Hopewell, S. (2009). Transitions to biliteracy: Creating positive academic trajectories for emerging bilinguals in the United States. In J. Petrovic (Ed.), *International perspectives on bilingual education: Policy, prac-tice, and controversy* (pp. 60–94). Charlotte, NC: Information Age.

Escamilla, K., Soltero-González, L., Butvilofsky, S., Hopewell, S., & Sparrow, W. (2009). *Transitions to biliteracy: Literacy squared.* Boulder: University of Colorado, BUENO Center for Multicultural Education.

García, E. E., Bravo, M. A., Dickey, L. M., Chun, K., & Sun-Irminger, X. (2002). Rethinking reform in the context of cultural and linguistic diversity: Creat-ing a responsive learning community. In L. I. Minaya-Rowe (Ed.), *Teacher training and effective pedagogy in the context of student diversity.* Greenwich, CT: Information Age.

Gort, M. (2006). Strategic codeswitching, interliteracy, and other phenomena of emergent bilingual writing: Lessons from first grade dual language classrooms. *Journal of Early Childhood Literacy, 6*(3), 323–354.

Grosjean, F. (1989). Neurolinguists, beware!: The bilingual is not two monolin-guals in   one person. *Brain and Language, 36,* 3–15.

Kindler, A. (2002). *Survey of the states' limited English proficient students and avail-able educational programs and services: 2000–2001 summary report.* Wash-ington, DC: National Clearinghouse for English Language Acquisition. Retrieved August 18, 2008, from *www.ncela.gwu.edu/policy/states/reports/seareports/0001.*

Klingner, J., Baca, L., & Hoover, J. (2008). *Why do English language learners struggle with reading?: Distinguishing language acquisition from learning dis-abilities.* Thousands Oaks, CA: Corwin Press.

Martínez-Roldán, C. M., & Sayer, P. (2006). Reading through linguistic border-lands: Latino students' transactions with narrative texts. *Journal of Early Childhood Literacy, 6*(3), 293–322.

National Center for Education Statistics. (2006). *The condition of education 2006: Indicator 7: Language minority school age children.* Washington, DC: U.S. Department of Education: Institute of Education Sciences. Retrieved May 10, 2008, from *nces.ed.gov/pubsearch/pubsinfo.asp?pubid=2006071.*

Reyes, I. (2006). Exploring connections between emergent biliteracy and bilin-gualism. *Journal of Early Childhood Literacy, 6*(3), 267–292.

Soltero-González, L., Escamilla, K., & Hopewell, S. (2009, April). *A bilingual perspective on writing assessment: Implications for teachers of emerging bilingual writers.* Presentation at the annual meeting of the American Educational Research Association.

Valdés, G. (1992). Bilingual minorities and language issues in writing: Toward professionwide responses to a new challenge. *Written Communication, 9,* 85–136.

Valdés, G., & Anloff Sanders, P. (1999). Latino ESL students and the development of writing abilities. In C. R. Cooper & L. Odell (Eds.), *Evaluating writing: The role of teachers' knowledge about text, learning, and culture.* Urbana, IL: National Council of Teachers of English.

Valdés, G., & Figueroa, R. A. (1994). *Bilingualism and testing: A special case of bias.* Norwood, NJ: Ablex.

Wilkinson, A. (1970). The concept of oracy. *The English Journal, 59*(1), 71–77.

APPENDIX 10.1.

Literacy Squared Writing Rubric

Literacy Squared® Scoring Rubric: Grades 1, 2, 3, 4, & 5   *(Please Circle Grade)*

SPANISH SCORE	CONTENT	ENGLISH SCORE
7	Superior/Excellent Writing: Creativity that reflects children's literature	7
6	Highly Competent Writing: Varying sentence patterns	6
5	Competent Writing: Sense of completeness	5
4	Transitioning Intermediate Writing: More than two ideas, main idea discernable, may be incomplete	4
3	Beginning Writing: Two ideas	3
2	Emerging Writing: One idea	2
1	Prewriting: Not readable or incomplete thought (also, written in language other than the prompt)	1
0	The student did not prepare a sample	0

SPANISH SCORE	ENGLISH SCORE	PUNCTUATION	SPANISH SCORE	ENGLISH SCORE	SPELLING
			4	4	Accurate spelling
3	3	Accurate punctuation	3	3	Some spelling errors; mostly correct
2	2	Some punctuation errors; mostly correct	2	2	Many spelling errors, meaning not affected
1	1	Many punctuation errors—meaning not affected, or minimal punctuation used	1	1	Many spelling errors; sometimes affects meaning
0	0	Punctuation errors affect meaning, or no punctuation	0	0	Spelling errors affect meaning

Common ELD Errors	Bilingual Strategies	Common Grade-Level Errors
	Intersentential code switching (I love my new *ropa*)	
	Intrasentential code switching (begins in one language and ends in the other)	
	"" inserted to indicate knowledge that a word is borrowed from another language (*Vimos el* "jellyfish")	
	Bidirectional phonetics transfer (*japi*/happy)	
	Bidirectional syntax transfer (the bike of my sister)	
	Other?	

Literacy Squared®
Grades 1, 2, 3, 4, & 5 Writing Descriptors

Level	CRITICAL DESCRIPTORS	Category
7	Complete story or summary that demonstrates consistency, creativity, and reflects grade-level literature.	Superior writing
6	Complete story using varied sentence structures and/or descriptive vocabulary.	Highly competent writing
5	Sense of completeness Has connecting or transitioning words Logical sequence	Competent writing
4	More than two ideas The main idea can be inferred or stated explicitly. Story or summary may be incomplete.	Transitioning intermediate writing
3	Two ideas (not necessarily separate sentences) Logical order	Beginning writing
2	One idea within a story or summary (not necessarily within the same sentence).	Emergent writing
1	The sample does not have complete thoughts that can be easily understood. The sample may have letters, syllables, and/or various words, but it does not have a complete thought. Written in a language other than the prompt.	Prewriting
0	The student did not prepare a sample.	No writing

ASSUMPTIONS:

• Critical descriptors are cumulative. To receive a 7, the student must exhibit all of the relevant indicators listed in the previous levels.
• Students should write to the prompt.
• "Logical" order means any order that would be appropriate in EITHER Spanish or English. A monolingual reader may need to consult a bilingual colleague to determine whether or not the order is logical.
• Spelling should be analyzed by a bilingual person.

Note. ELD, English language development.

What do you like to do at recess and <u>why</u>?

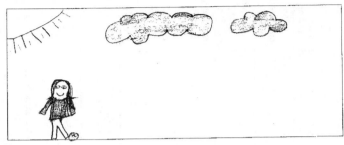

A mi me gsta jugar sager porque es mudivikdido param. A mi megusta jugar sager con mi hermana. Tavien me gusta jugar con mi hermana. Aveses quego con mi Mamá y Papá. Aveses juego sola a mi me gusta jugar sager mucho escomo und deporte mi hermano me ensella aveses y tavien mi hermana. luego me voy al parque yn juego sola. El sacer es muy dirverdido e porque es como jugar pelota el sagerres como patear la pelota aveses juego saerscon mis hermanosycom mi amiga. El saguerres mui dirvedido param mi es muy dirverdido mucho mas dirverdido.

a me me gusta cugar a la visiqleta porque me gusta a ser carreras con mihermana.

y con mihermana aveses kvoysola

en labisiqleta yo solapos lacarelera

voy arededor de mi casa. Avesesvoy a lamontaña com mi bisicleta.

English Writing Sample

What do you like to do at recess and <u>why</u>?

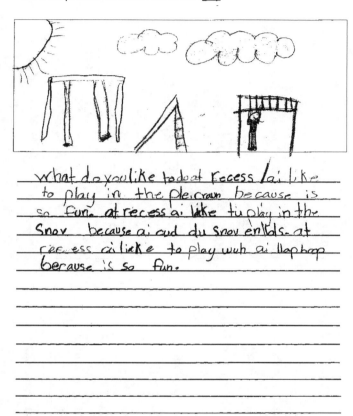

what do you like to do at recess /ai like
to play in the pleicroun because is
so fun. at recess ai like tu play in the
Snov because ai cud du Snov enkds. at
recess ai like to play wuh ai hop hop
berause is so fun.

Spanish and English Writing Samples of a Student
in the Literacy Squared Research Project

06-07 5709-S

12-11-06

Si no nos roban la esuela
yo me dormia poque tiaen
uste descansan mu mente y cuando
melevanto voy a ver la
television poque mi mente
quiere ver algo somilo
algo y luego vamos a
jugar afuera jugamos
en mi resvaladero y unos
monki bars y suings y
yo quiero jaer eso eso
cosas poque mi mente
lo quiere oser

1-4-07

06-07

5709-E

En recees y play with a frends
her name is Jennefer wy
play tog and ay am
ete and the we play
en the moncky bors
and howe ever fols
wens and ay won and
Jennefer is a fastr fond
and ay am to boy we
ress and Jennefel wens
en the ress and then
we gow back en side.

PART V

CRITICAL ISSUES CONCERNING ELL INSTRUCTION

CHAPTER 11

Meeting the Needs of ELLs with Disabilities

A Linguistically and Culturally Responsive Model

Alba A. Ortiz and Alfredo J. Artiles

The chapter will:

1. Describe characteristics of schools conducive to the success of English language learners (ELLs).

2. Present an overview of differentiated instruction and early intervention for ELLs experiencing academic difficulties.

3. Suggest ways to adapt special education processes to better serve the needs of ELLs.

4. Describe characteristics of effective instruction for ELLs in general and special education.

Setting the Context: Implications of the Convergence of Demographic and Policy Trends

Enrollment data show dramatic changes taking place in the nation's public schools. Although White students comprise 57% of the student population, U.S. Census Bureau (2009) projections indicate that by 2023, the majority of students will be members of traditionally under-represented groups. In 2005, students of color made up almost 43% of the school population: Hispanics comprised 19% of the country's students in grades PreK–12, African Americans 17%, Asian American/Pacific Islanders 5%, and Native American Indian/Alaskan Natives

1% of the student population (National Center for Education Statistics [NCES], 2005). These racial/ethnic groups represent other types of diversity: 17% live in poverty, 19% are immigrants, and many are English language learners (ELLs), that is, students with limited English proficiency (NCES, 2005).

The approximately 5,100,000 ELLs in U. S. schools represent 400 different language groups (Office of English Language Acquisition [OELA], 2008). The proportion of students that speak a language other than English is sizable in states such as California (43%), Texas (32%), Arizona (> 20%), Florida (> 20%), Nevada (> 20%), New Jersey (> 20%), New Mexico (> 20%), New York (> 20%), and Rhode Island (> 20%) (U.S. Census Bureau, 2003). ELLs represented over 10% of the students population in 12 other states (U.S. Census Bureau, 2003). Over 40% of all U.S. teachers had at least one ELL in their classrooms (U.S. Department of Education [USDOE] & National Institute of Child Health and Human Development [NICHD], 2003); however, Zehler and her colleagues (2003) found that most ELLs were educated in a relatively small number of districts. It is predicted that about 40% of the student population will speak English as a second language by 2030 (USDOE & NICHD, 2003). Over three-fourths of ELLs speak Spanish as their first language (Zehler et al., 2003).

The education of ELLs is characterized by widespread under-achievement; high rates of social promotion, retention, and school attrition; and disproportionate representation in remedial, compensatory, and special education programs (Artiles & Ortiz, 2002; Artiles & Klingner, 2006; Klingner, Artiles, & Barletta, 2006). Results of the 2005 National Assessment of Educational Progress showed that almost 73% of ELLs in fourth grade and 71% of those in eighth grade scored below basic levels on measures of English reading (Fry, 2007). Of all racial/ethnic groups, Latinos, who comprise the majority of the ELL student population, have the highest dropout rates; those who are immigrants leave school at rates nearly double those of native-born peers (43 vs. 15%, respectively; NCES, 2004).

The evidence on ELLs with special needs is alarmingly scarce. Over half of ELLs with disabilities have learning disabilities (LDs), with reading difficulties as the main problem; about one-fourth of ELLs with disabilities have speech and language impairments (USDOE & NICHD, 2003). Special education identification has important consequences for ELLs. For instance, ELLs with special needs receive fewer language support services, are more likely to be placed in English immersion programs, and tend to be educated in more segregated programs than are ELLs without disabilities (Artiles et al., 2005; Zehler et al., 2003). These trends are troubling given that general and special education teachers are underqualified to address the needs of ELLs.

ELLs are not overrepresented in special education at the national level. However, there is evidence in some states and districts that ELLs are indeed overrepresented, particularly in the mild disability categories (Artiles, Rueda, Salazar, & Higareda, 2005; Artiles, Klingner, Sullivan, & Fierros, 2010). The lack of an information infrastructure represents a major barrier in the assessment of this problem. For instance, it is difficult to trace placement trends for ethnic/minority students by language proficiency across disability categories. This barrier prevents the production of knowledge about intragroup diversity in disproportionate representation patterns.

The identification of special needs in ELLs is complicated by several factors that include the lack of a knowledge base on the intersection of second-language acquisition and disabilities (Artiles & Klingner, 2006; Donovan & Cross, 2002), procedural ambiguities (e.g., timing of referrals, appropriateness of assessment tools, stages of language acquisition; Harry & Klingner, 2006), and technical inadequacies (e.g., lack of data-collection infrastructures for criticval variables; Klingner & Artiles, 2006). Moreover, population and contextual factors complicate the disability identification process with ELLs. For example, students learning a second or additional language exhibit characteristics that may parallel traits of students with learning or language disabilities (Ortiz, 1997). It is feasible that some ELLs' academic difficulties are due to lack of opportunity to learn, produced by institutional factors such as inadequate instruction or low teacher quality. Certain behaviors associated with LDs may be customary practices for members of certain cultural groups or be produced by acculturation processes (Collier & Hoover, 1987).

The policy context further complicates work with this population. For example, the No Child Left Behind Act (NCLB; 2001) requirement that states and school districts document student academic progress by subgroup has focused attention on closing the gap between the achievement of ELLs and native English speakers, and students with disabilities and their nondisabled peers. Accommodations can be used in assessment practices for ELLs, though there is growing confusion about how to report, interpret, and use these accountability data (Forum on Educational Accountability, 2007). Local education agencies must also implement policies and practices that prevent inappropriate referrals of culturally and linguistically diverse (CLD) learners to special education, and that appropriately identify CLD students with disabilities (Individuals with Disabilities Education Act [IDEA], 2004). Compliance with these mandates requires linking special language (i.e., bilingual education and English as a second language [ESL]), general education, and special education programs and services into a coherent education system for ELLs. Such a system incorporates three major elements: (1) prevention of academic failure, (2) early intervention for struggling learners, and (3) special education processes specific to CLD students (Artiles & Ortiz, 2002; García & Ortiz, 2008; García & Ortiz, 2004; Linan-Thompson & Ortiz, 2009; Wilkinson, Ortiz, Robertson, & Kushner, 2006). How to ensure that these elements are culturally and linguistically responsive for ELLs is the focus of this chapter.

Prevention of Academic Failure

School Climate Conducive to the Success of ELLs

Research on school climate has identified several key factors that promote student learning, including a clear and focused mission, a climate of high expectations for all learners, frequent monitoring of student progress, a safe and orderly school environment, positive home–school relations, opportunities to learn, and student time on task (Lezotte, 1991). Several other elements are critical to the success of ELLs, including strong leadership by school principals; a shared knowledge base specific to, and shared responsibility for, the education of ELLs; and well-implemented bilingual education and ESL programs (Ortiz, 2002). We outline the features of these aspects of school climate in the next subsections.

School Principals

School principals play important roles in creating school climates conducive to the success of ELLs. They lead school personnel, parents, and community members in the adoption of a common philosophy and special language program model(s) that reflect an enrichment, not a compensatory or remedial, approach to the education of ELLs (Montecel & Cortez, 2002). Principals garner resources essential to program implementation, including highly qualified teachers; mentors for novice teachers; professional development opportunities; and curricula, texts, and related instructional materials for native language and ESL instruction. They continuously monitor implementation of the ELL curriculum, programs, and services to ensure that these are consistent with the school's articulated philosophy and program models. Principals are central to creating a welcoming school environment for the families of ELLs and community members. These actions facilitate the full integration of special language programs in the school culture. When large numbers of ELLs experience academic difficulties, principals focus the school community on identifying factors contributing to failure and lead school improvement efforts to ensure that ELLs meet high academic standards (Ortiz, Robertson, & Wilkinson, 2009).

Philosophy and Program Models

The amount of formal native language instruction that students receive is the strongest predictor of their achievement (Thomas & Collier, 2002). Thomas and Collier found that when ELLs exited special language programs, those schooled in all-English programs (e.g., ESL) initially outperformed ELLs schooled in bilingual education programs on measures of English achievement. However, students in bilingual education programs reached the same levels of achievement as peers schooled in all-English programs by the middle school years, and outperformed them in the high school years. Only in 90:10 and 50:50 two-way bilingual immersion and one-way developmental bilingual education programs did students reach the 50th percentile in both their native language and English in all subject areas. These programs allowed students to maintain that level or higher levels of achievement through the end of their schooling. On the other hand, the students at the lowest end of the achievement continuum were those whose parents refused bilingual education or ESL support. These ELLs showed large decreases in reading and math achievement by grade 5 compared to peers who participated in language support programs, and the largest number of dropouts came from this group. Parent refusal of bilingual education or ESL support also has significant implications for special education. Research shows that ELLs who receive the least language support are more likely to be referred (Artiles et al., 2005). These data should be carefully considered in choosing special language program models. Schools should select model(s) that meet the needs of their specific ELL population. When this is not possible, for example, as in states that operate under English-only laws and prohibit instruction in the native language, school personnel must find ways to increase the likelihood of student success. Creating a shared knowledge base and a shared responsibility for student learning is a beginning point.

Shared Knowledge about ELLs

Student academic achievement is correlated with the knowledge, skills, and practices teachers bring to the classroom and with teacher efficacy (Gruber, Wiley, Broughman, Strizek, & Burian-Fitzgerald, 2002). Yet although 41% of the nation's teachers reported that they had taught

ELLs, only 13% indicated they had received 8 or more hours of training on how to teach this population of students over a 3-year period. Thus, the lack of highly-qualified teachers to serve ELLs may be the single greatest barrier to closing the achievement gap between these students and their native English–speaking peers.

All teachers should have expertise related to second language acquisition, the relationship of the native language (L1) to development of English (L2) proficiency; the link between language proficiency and academic achievement; native language and ESL teaching methodology; sociocultural influences on learning; assessment of language proficiency; and effective instruction, progress monitoring, and working with families of ELLs (Ortiz, 2002; García & Ortiz, 2008). This shared knowledge base can facilitate collaboration between special language programs and other general education programs, making transitions easier for ELLs, for example, from native language to English instruction and from special language programs to general education classrooms, where instruction is provided entirely in English. Collaboration among teachers, along with an understanding of their respective roles and responsibilities, is also important to these transitions.

Collaboration and Shared Responsibility

The goals of bilingual education and ESL programs are to ensure that children with limited English skills become proficient in listening, speaking, reading, and writing English, that they achieve high levels of academic attainment in English, and that they meet the same challenging state content and achievement standards as their English-proficient peers (NCLB, 2001, Section 3102). Special language program teachers are key players in implementing bilingual education and ESL curricula, and in providing instruction that reflects high academic standards for native language and ESL instruction (Linan-Thompson & Ortiz, 2009). Bilingual education teachers provide language, literacy, and content-area instruction in the native language; both bilingual education and ESL teachers provide a systematic, structured program of instruction to ensure that students acquire conversational and academic English proficiency. They analyze assessment data from standardized and classroom-based assessments to plan instruction that is consistent with students' language proficiency and performance levels. And, they track student progress over time, so they can identify students who are not making expected progress in acquiring English, or who are experiencing achievement difficulties in the native language and/or in English. Teachers help to collect data to corroborate, or refute, the result of standardized language and achievement tests and to inform the decision that students have the requisite English skills before they exit from bilingual education or ESL programs (Linan-Thompson & Ortiz, 2009; Montecel & Cortez, 2002; Ortiz et al., 2009).

Like bilingual education and ESL teachers, general education teachers are critical players in the education of ELLs. Available data suggest that ELLs are taught in programs that provide instruction entirely or primarily in English (Zehler et al., 2003). In addition to ESL students, general education teachers have primary responsibility for meeting the language needs of several other categories of ELLs and bilingual students. These include ELLs whose parents deny them placement in bilingual education or ESL programs, and students whose English proficiency assessment scores are above those required for special language program eligibility, but who have not yet developed English comparable to their native English–speaking peers. General education teachers also provide ESL support critical to the continued success of ELLs who are prematurely exited from special language programs. Absent ESL support, many ELLs and bilingual students do not achieve native-like English skills, which compromises their future academic achievement.

Effective Curriculum and Instruction

An effective core curriculum for ELLs is based on academic standards specific to bilingual education and ESL programs (Linan-Thompson & Ortiz, 2009) and prepares students for success in general education classrooms where instruction is provided entirely in English. To that end, native language and/or ESL curricula and instruction must have appropriate scope and sequence across grade levels (Montecel & Cortez, 2002). And teachers' implementation of the curriculum must be consistent with the school's articulated philosophy, program model, and academic standards.

Effective instruction for ELLs includes direct, explicit skill instruction in the context of higher-order skills. For example, literacy instruction focuses on both skills and meaning, and incorporates components that have been shown to be determinants of literacy achievement for both monolingual students and ELLs: phonemic awareness, phonics, fluency, vocabulary, and comprehension, as well as study strategies (Snow, Burns, & Griffin, 1998; Goldenberg, 1998). Teachers draw on students' prior experiences, linking what they already know to what they need to learn (Leinhardt, 1992). They ensure that curriculum and instruction are culturally responsive by drawing on students' *funds of knowledge* (Moll, Amanti, Neff, & González, 1992), the culturally based knowledge and skills children acquire through their interactions with family and community members. Teachers organize instruction around themes that connect subject areas so that students have multiple opportunities to review previously learned concepts and to apply these to new tasks (Leinhardt, 1992).

Curriculum and instruction provide opportunities for students to develop the conversational and academic language proficiency needed to understand classroom language use (e.g., teacher talk and the language of texts and related materials) across the content areas (Gersten et al., 2007). Instruction is guided by results of assessments of students' native language and English language skills; these results also guide the transition from native language to English instruction and exit decisions that move students from special language to general education programs (Linan-Thompson & Ortiz, 2009). Both transition and exit decisions are based on students' language proficiency and achievement status, not simply on their age, grade, or the number of years they have been in special language programs (Linan-Thompson & Ortiz, 2009). Exiting students from special language program indicates that students have the requisite skills to succeed in classrooms where instruction is provided entirely in English (Montecel & Cortez, 2002).

Teachers' effective instruction is guided by continuous progress monitoring, using results of standardized and curriculum-based assessments to ensure that students are making expected progress. Assessment programs typically involve eligibility assessments (e.g., language proficiency tests to determine eligibility for special language programs and to monitor student progress in acquiring English), screening and teacher assessments designed to monitor progress in relation to the actual curriculum being taught and to identify struggling learners (e.g., benchmark tests, reading inventories, end-of-unit examinations), and accountability assessments to determine whether students have met content and achievement standards (e.g., district- or state-mandated achievement tests). Teachers must be able to interpret the results of these assessments and use these data to plan and deliver instruction. When students are struggling, assessment should help them determine the nature of difficulties and to redirect instruction. As skilled assessors and consumers of assessment data, teachers should consider whether assessments are appropriate for their particular student population, and whether they are consistent with recommended procedures for assessing ELLs, including the following (Ortiz & Yates, 2002): (1) Use instruments and procedures designed for ELLs or that include representative samples in the tool development process; (2) ensure that assessment tools are valid and reliable; (3) use equivalent assessments in the native language and in English; (4) correlate results of formal assessments with informal, curriculum-based measures; and (5) interpret results in relationship to students' level of native language and English proficiency.

Early Intervention

IDEA (2004) includes provisions for "early intervening services" to support struggling learners and to address the disproportionate representation of culturally and linguistically diverse learners in special education [34 C.F.R. 300.226(a)]. In response, most states and school districts have adopted what are commonly referred to as response to intervention (RTI) programs, designed to identify students at risk of academic or behavioral problems and to prevent problems from occurring in the first place and/or from becoming more serious over time. Regardless of the number of tiers in the particular model adopted, RTI approaches typically (1) apply universal design principles in planning core instructional programs and services to accommodate the broadest possible range of student background characteristics and needs, and to prevent problems from occurring in the first place; (2) differentiate instruction for students who are not making expected progress; and (3) provide a system of tiered interventions to help students who continue to struggle despite differentiated instruction (National Joint Committee on Learning Disabilities, 2005).

Differentiated Instruction

Differentiated instruction accommodates the variability in students' characteristics and experiences (Kilgore, 2004; Tomlinson, 2003), instead of simply providing whole-group instruction and hoping that most students will learn the content. Perhaps more than for other students, differentiation is critical for ELLs who demonstrate diversity in skills, abilities, and interests, and along a multiplicity of other factors, such as native language and English proficiency, native language and English achievement levels, cultural characteristics, immigration status, and socioeconomic background. Differentiated instruction accommodates individual differences by targeting instruction according to *which* students need to learn *what* content, in *which* ways (Tomlinson, 2003). This may include, for example, varying the nature and complexity of tasks and products, using multiple levels and kinds of texts and materials, modifying the pace and level of instruction, utilizing flexible grouping strategies, and allowing for alternative modes of responses or ways for students to show what they learn (Kilgore, 2004). If differentiated instruction does not resolve difficulties, teachers should use progress data to determine whether students can be maintained in the general education curriculum, or whether they need more intensive intervention than teachers can provide. In such cases, schools should have alternative programs and services that are culturally and linguistically responsive.

Problem-Solving Teams

RTI approaches typically involve standard protocols and/or problem-solving teams (Marchand-Martella, Ruby, & Martella, 2007). Standard protocol approaches include universal screenings to identify students experiencing achievement difficulties, then provide interventions using specific programs or "packaged" interventions, many of which are scripted. Because ELLs represent such diverse backgrounds, including differences in native language and English proficiency, cultural background and experiences, and school history and outcomes, it is difficult to design standard protocols that accommodate this diversity. Because of this, problem-solving approaches may be more effective for struggling learners (García & Ortiz, 2008). In the problem-solving approach, campus-based teams, referred to by a variety of names (e.g., intervention assistance teams, teacher or student assistance teams, student support team), meet with the teacher requesting assistance to discuss a student's problems and to select or design interventions, to address identified needs. Teachers implement interventions and a follow-up meeting is held to evaluate progress. If problems are resolved, the student returns to the general education core curriculum; if not, the team may also refer the student to alternative programs and services (Ortiz et al., 2009).

Participation of individuals with expertise specific to the education of ELLs is critical to the success of a problem-solving team approach to early intervention (García & Ortiz, 2008; Ortiz et al., 2009). Individuals with such expertise can ensure that data related to students' language proficiency and achievement are considered and appropriately interpreted; for example, level of achievement must be examined in relation to current levels of native language and English proficiency, and in relation to the amount of instruction provided in each language. Experts can also speak to the cultural and linguistic appropriateness of classroom interventions that have been already tried and ensure that additional interventions are responsive to these variables. The student's parents and/or other family members are among the experts who should serve on problem-solving teams. The information they provide about their child's development, performance, and behavior in the home and community is invaluable in helping to identify factors contributing to student difficulties. For example, "problem" behaviors may be explained by differences in norms and expectations of the home versus the school cultures (Kalyanpur & Harry, 1999), or by significant life events, such as illness or trauma, or emotional issues, such as divorce (Wilkinson et al., 2006).

Alternative Programs and Services

Schools often have support programs staffed by literacy and/or other instructional specialists to support struggling learners who need more intensive interventions than can be provided in the general education classroom. ELLs are sometimes denied access to these programs, because supplemental instruction is provided in English only, or because students receive inadequate support due to instructional specialists' lack of expertise related to ELLs. This problem can be avoided by including instructional specialists in professional development activities designed to build a shared knowledge base among educators who serve ELLs. Professional development focused on ELLs increases the likelihood that services provided by instructional specialists are consistent with the ELL curriculum, and with native language and ESL instruction. Instructional specialists are also in a better position to help special language program and general education teachers differentiate instruction and design increasingly intensive interventions for ELLs who continue to struggle despite differentiation.

An additional benefit of specialized knowledge is that data about interventions provided by instructional specialists can help referral committees determine whether an ELL should be assessed for special education eligibility. To that end, alternative programs and services must be linked with problem-solving processes (Ortiz et al., 2009). Teams should share information with instructional specialists about interventions that have already been tried, and data documenting the success (or lack thereof) of these interventions. Team members and instructional specialists should work together to determine how to evaluate the effectiveness of supplemental services. Instructional specialists should report student progress to the problem-solving team. If the interventions are working, the student can continue receiving supplemental support; if the problems are resolved, the student can be returned to the core curriculum. If problems persist, though, the problem-solving team can consider whether a referral to special education is needed.

Adapting the Special Education Process for ELLs

Referral Committees

Referral committees are the gatekeepers to special education placement. Thus it is important that these committees examine available data supporting the referral of ELLs, including present levels of performance in the native language and/or in English, and results of classroom and supplemental interventions. As is the case for problem-solving teams, referral committees should obtain family input to determine whether presenting problems are evident across home, community, and school contexts. In reviewing data, committee members should ask whether these problems can be explained by linguistic or cultural differences, lack of opportunity to learn, or other significant events (Wilkinson et al., 2006). The committee should carefully weigh the appropriateness and effectiveness of general education interventions, particularly in terms of whether these directly addressed the concerns identified by teachers or problem-solving teams. If these efforts are insufficient or not well documented, additional interventions should be designed and implemented in general education, and student progress should be monitored before a full and individual evaluation (FIE) is recommended (Wilkinson et al., 2006). In such cases, the referral committee follows steps similar to those used by campus-based problem-solving teams (Ortiz et al., 2009): (1) select or design linguistically and culturally responsive intervention(s); (2) determine data to be collected to evaluate effectiveness and fidelity of implementation; and (3) implement interventions and document progress. If problems are resolved, the student continues in the core or supplemental program, with ongoing progress monitoring. If problems persist, the referral committee may request a FIE. Such a request is more likely to be appropriate when based on extensive data collected by general classroom teachers describing results of differentiated instruction, and by teachers, problem-solving teams, and instructional specialists in relation to increasingly intensive interventions. Students who do not make expected progress despite these supports are likely to need special education services (García & Ortiz, 2008; Wilkinson et al., 2006). The referral committee should guide the assessment process by generating questions and identifying problems that remain unexplained even after present levels of performance, other contributing factors, and results of general education interventions have been considered (Wilkinson et al., 2006).

Full and Individual Evaluations

The FIE must be provided and administered in the language and form *most likely to yield accurate information* on what the child knows and can do academically, developmentally, and functionally, unless it is not feasible to do so (IDEA, 2004). Assessment personnel should select both formal and informal instruments, and procedures that address the specific concerns articulated by the teacher, problem-solving teams, referral committees, or parents (Wilkinson et al., 2006). The same guidelines delineated for classroom assessments apply to the FIE; that is, skills and abilities must be assessed in both languages, using valid and reliable instruments and procedures, and informal, curriculum-based measures should corroborate results of norm-referenced measures. Because of the lack of availability of appropriate special education assessments for ELLs, evaluators must determine alternative measures and/or acceptable adaptations of standardized measures. If instruments or procedures are adapted, scores should not be reported; instead, data should describe students' strengths and needs (Ortiz & Yates, 2002).

The FIE should yield data that allow comparison of skills the student possesses in the native language and in English. For each of the student's languages, the language assessment should describe both conversational and academic language skills, because both types of data are essential for planning the language of instruction and language intervention strategies (Ortiz & Yates, 2002). Achievement measures, supplemented by curriculum-based assessments, should describe performance as a result of instruction. If students have been taught in their native language, achievement measures should describe the outcomes of that instruction; in a similar vein, progress in ESL acquisition and achievement should also be reported. In calculating assessment results, the assessor should give students credit for correct responses in either language (Ortiz & Yates, 2002). This is not to say that assessors should violate the publisher's guidelines for test administration, but that they should describe patterns, strengths, and needs based on what students know and are able to do, regardless of the language in which they demonstrate knowledge and skills. Not to do so underestimates students' abilities and increases the likelihood they will meet eligibility criteria for special education.

The assessment report should describe nature and circumstances of evaluations (e.g., they were conducted by a bilingual professional, assessments were administered only in English, or the assessor used an interpreter) and any adaptations of instruments or procedures (e.g., use of translated instruments). Assessors should correlate results of standardized assessments with other data (e.g., that obtained from informal assessments) and with outcomes of early intervention efforts (Wilkinson et al., 2006; Ortiz & Yates, 2002). Most importantly, they should correlate results with the referral reasons, the student's schooling history (e.g., language proficiency characteristics and how these have changed over time; academic progress within and across grades), and the questions posed by the referral agent (Wilkinson et al., 2006). The basis for a recommendation that the student qualifies for special education should go beyond simply documenting test results. This is particularly important when assessment results do not corroborate the original reasons for referral. If they are recommending special education services, then assessors should also recommend for instructional strategies and approaches, including accommodations and adaptations to increase the likelihood of student success.

Eligibility Determinations

Special education eligibility determinations should be made by a multidisciplinary team (MDT) that includes representatives with expertise in the education of ELLs (Ortiz & Yates, 2002). The team should include personnel who have been key players in the student's instructional program, and who have participated in early intervention activities designed to resolve student difficulties (Ortiz et al., 2009; Ortiz & Yates, 2001). For example, if the student has been in an ESL program, both the general education and the ESL teachers should serve on the MDT. The instructional specialists who provided supplemental instruction should also be invited to participate. If assessment personnel have not been trained to assess ELLs, someone who can interpret assessment data from the perspective of CLD would be an important addition to the team. Parents should also be invited to attend, and an interpreter should be provided, if needed, to allow family members to participate meaningfully in team meetings.

FIE data, along with documentation of results of general education instruction and early intervention efforts, should be the basis of special education eligibility determinations (Wilkinson et al., 2006). The MDT must ensure that the FIE represents best practices in assessment of ELLs, and that the team has the data needed to rule out limited English proficiency, cultural, or other background characteristics, or lack of appropriate instruction as the cause of student difficulties. If the student is eligible, then an individualized education plan (IEP) is developed, and the least restrictive environment for serving the student is selected.

Individualized Education Plans

ELLs with disabilities are held to the same high academic standards as their general education peers, although it is recognized that they may not make progress toward meeting those standards at the same rate or pace as nondisabled peers (NCLB, 2001; IDEA, 2004). For most students with special needs, goals and standards remain the same, but the sequence of objectives is modified, and specialized teaching strategies and materials are developed to meet their specific educational needs

(Christensen, Thurlow, & Wang, 2009; Seppanen, Schaefer, & Julian, 1995). For students with severe disabilities, additional standards may have to be developed to meet their needs. For example, standards may be extended to include goals related to independent living, community integration, and school-to-work transition. In all cases, indicators that students have met expected standards would likely vary according to students' ages, grades, developmental levels, and disabilities. Instructional programs for ELLs with disabilities must additionally consider how to implement performance standards, while addressing students' cultural characteristics and language needs, as well as identified disabilities (Cloud, 2002). In addition to content standards, these students also are assessed on progress toward meeting ESL standards, which include learning to use English for social and academic purposes, and in culturally appropriate ways (Short, 2000).

ELLs, including those with disabilities, are vastly heterogeneous in terms of their language proficiency in both English and the native language as they acquire communicative abilities typical of their homes and communities (Kushner & Ortiz, 2000). Thus, IEPs should (1) identify the student's level of language proficiency in the native language and in English; (2) specify language of instruction; (3) provide for language intervention; (4) include a language use plan indicating who will use which language, for what purpose, and for which skills; and (5) provide instructional recommendations consistent with principles of first- and second-language acquisition, native language, and ESL instruction (Ortiz et al., 2009; Ortiz & Yates, 2001; Yates & Ortiz, 1998).

Educators should not assume that ELLs who have language-related disorders should be taught in English. If students have not acquired the language of their parents or caretakers through the normal process of language acquisition, it is unlikely that they will be able to acquire English skills more easily (Ortiz & Yates, 2001). Students need to develop their native language foundation as a basis for skills development in English. Thus, ELLs with disabilities should receive instruction in their native language with ESL instruction, as appropriate. The language of instruction decision is, of course, driven by current data about students' native language dominance and proficiency.

Parents are important participants in the design and implementation of IEPs. They are an important resource for supporting native language acquisition and development. Educators should reinforce parents' continuing use of the native language at home are critical to building the foundation for English acquisition (Krashen, 1982; Coelho, 2004). IEPs should incorporate strategies for involving parents in their children's education. This may include, for example, talking to children, telling them stories, reading or looking at books, visiting libraries, help-ing with homework, and modeling reading and writing.

Effective Instruction for ELLs with Disabilities

ELLs who are eligible for special education services do not lose their right to bilingual education (Ortiz & Yates, 2001). Exceptional ELLs have the right to participate in pedagogically sound programs that not only meet needs associated with their disabilities but also accommodate their language status. Compared with instruction for general educa-tion students, instruction for students with disabilities by design is more direct, intensive, and structured; is delivered with greater precision; and is more carefully monitored for outcomes (Kauffman, 1999).

To provide ELLs access to the general education curriculum, spe-cial education teachers must understand both bilingual education and ESL curricula and instruction. They must also have the skills to teach and/or support native language development, ESL acquisition, native and/or English literacy development, and mastery of the content areas. Such knowledge and skills also facilitate their roles as consultants to bilingual education, ESL, and general education teachers, so that ELLs are successfully integrated into their classrooms.

The characteristics of effective instruction for ELLs, described earlier in this chapter, also apply to special education instruction. In addition, though, teachers must be able to provide appropriate modifi-cations, accommodations, and adaptations of instruction that are con-sistent with students' disability-related needs (Council for Exceptional Children, 2009). This includes implementation of goals and objectives related to transition from home to school, across school contexts, and from school to community and postsecondary settings.

Least Restrictive Environments for ELLs

Once the IEP has been designed, the MDT must determine the *least restrictive environment* (LRE; IDEA, 2004). Several principles guide the selection of the LRE (IDEA, 2004). The first is that students should be educated with general education peers to the maximum extent possi-ble. Nondisabled students, including nondisabled ELLs, are the general education peer group of ELLs with disabilities; thus, students should be maintained in the bilingual education and/or ESL program in which they were served prior to being diagnosed as having a disability (Ortiz & Yates, 2001). As is required by federal and state laws governing special language programs, students should also have access to native English–

speaking peers. A second principle in selecting the LRE is that students should be moved only as far away from the general education classroom as is necessary. For example, if a student's needs can be met in either a special education resource room or in a self-contained special education class, the resource room constitutes the LRE. A third principle is that special education services ensure access to the general education curriculum (IDEA, 2004). In the case of ELLs in bilingual education programs, special education services must provide access to both native language and ESL curricula. Those in ESL programs must access both the English core curriculum and the ESL curriculum. Special education services that ignore special language program curricula and instruction, and that focus solely on the curriculum taught to monolingual English speakers, violate the principle of access to the general education curriculum for ELLs (Ortiz & Yates, 2001).

School districts have two important obligations to ELLs with disabilities. One is to develop strategic personnel development plans to address teacher shortages, including recruiting qualified bilingual special educators and/or special educators with ESL expertise. The second is to assess their current resources and determine how they will modify instructional services in the short term to meet the needs of ELLs with disabilities. This requires an extensive, continuing professional development program to ensure that all personnel have the requisite skills to serve ELLs in general and special education. Special educators must be able to plan instruction that accounts for not only individual learning differences and functional levels but also a range of language diversity, in which each student demonstrates a different pattern of proficiencies across at least two languages.

Bilingual Education Models for Special Education

The following instructional arrangements support students in bilingual education programs by providing native language and ESL instruction for ELLs with disabilities. These models require that special educators be bilingual and have expertise in providing native language and/or ESL instruction. In other words, teachers must be bilingual special educators.

Inclusive Bilingual Education Classroom

The bilingual education teacher teaches academic skills in the students' native language and also provides a structured ESL program to facilitate the acquisition of English. The special education teacher helps the teacher modify native language and ESL instruction to accommodate students' disabilities.

Bilingual Special Education Resource Program

In this model, ELLs spend the majority of the day in the bilingual education classroom, where they receive native language and ESL instruction. The bilingual special education teacher also provides instruction in the native language and/or uses ESL strategies, as specified in the IEP. The special education and the bilingual education teacher coordinate instructional activities and the language in which these are conducted. For example, if the student is being taught to read in his or her native language in the bilingual education classroom, the special educator also teaches reading in the native language; if the student has been transitioned into English reading, the special educator uses ESL strategies to teach English reading.

Self-Contained Bilingual Special Education Classroom

Some ELLs with severe disabilities may be served in a bilingual special education program on a full-time basis. The bilingual special education teacher delivers instruction in the native language and/or uses ESL strategies, as delineated in the IEP. Instruction also targets skills that facilitate integration of these students into classrooms with nondisabled peers, and the transition from school to community and/or postsecondary settings.

LRE for ELLs in ESL Programs

Most ELLs are not served in bilingual education programs; instead, they are in general education programs and receive supplemental ESL instruction (Zehler et al., 2003). ESL students should be served by special education teachers with ESL certification (i.e., special education/ESL teachers). Because ESL teachers do not have to be bilingual, all special educators can become skilled in providing scaffolded instruction using ESL strategies. When a school district has a bilingual education program but does not have bilingual special education teachers, special education/ESL teachers serve an important role in meeting the needs of bilingual education students with disabilities.

Inclusive General Education with ESL Instruction and Special Education/ESL Consultation

This instructional arrangement is for ESL students who are served in the general education classroom but are also taught by ESL teachers. The ESL teacher consults with the general education teacher, so that instruction in English is adapted to make it understandable to ELLs. The special education teacher consults with *both* the general education and the ESL teachers to ensure that they adapt instruction to address students' disability-related needs in their respective classrooms.

Special Education/ESL Resource Program

In this arrangement, the special education teacher uses ESL strategies in delivering instruction for ELLs, who receive the majority of their instruction in the general education classroom. The special education/ ESL teacher also works with general education and ESL specialists to ensure that the instruction they provide accommodates the student's disabilities. As indicated previously, special education/ESL teachers can also serve special education students in bilingual education classrooms. The bilingual educator addresses both native language and ESL goals and objectives; the special education/ESL teacher addresses the IEP goals and objectives that should be implemented using ESL strategies.

Self-Contained Special Education/ESL Classroom

The special education/ESL teacher provides special education instruction on a full-time basis using ESL techniques. The teacher also works toward integrating ELLs with disabilities with their nondisabled peers.

Special education/ESL and general education teachers who are monolingual can be supported by bilingual paraprofessionals (Yates & Ortiz, 1998). The assistant, however, should serve in a *support* role, for example, by previewing lessons in the native language that will then be taught by the teacher using ESL strategies. The assistant reviews the lesson content with the student in the native language. In this way, lessons taught in English are anchored by native language support. More importantly, though, this "preview/ESL lesson/review" sequence ensures that teachers retain primary responsibility for instruction.

Reflections and Future Directions

An important message in this chapter is that ELLs with special needs require the coordination of multiple service delivery systems and types of expertise to address their unique educational needs. The model proposed in this chapter is a response to this imperative. However, as we outlined in the beginning of the chapter, efforts on multiple fronts are required to make significant improvements in the design of responsive educational systems for this population. Next, we outline a few areas in need of sustained attention in future efforts.

1. The following question is often posed in research and policy debates: "Do ELLs struggle with academic literacy because of their limited proficiency in English or because of LDs?" A significant deterrent in offering meaningful responses to this question is the lack of research knowledge. Thirteen years ago, August and Hakuta (1997) raised many basic research questions about second-language acquisition and literacy that remain largely current today:

> What is the nature of the relationship between language proficiency and literacy skills? Is that relationship the same across and within languages? Is there a level of oral language knowledge that is prerequisite to successful literacy acquisition? Is the level the same for learners of different first-language backgrounds, of different ages, of different levels of first-language literacy? . . . Is literacy knowledge represented the same way for monolingual and bilingual populations? Are literacy skills and deficits acquired in the first language directly transferred to the second, and, if so, under what conditions? (pp. 71, 128–129)

It is urgent to mobilize resources and political will to support the design and implementation of a long-term research program on these basic questions and to add an ability-difference dimension to these studies. The findings from such a research program can inform the refinement of policies and practices that ultimately would benefit ELLs with and without disabilities.

2. The multiple contextual, technical, and institutional dimensions that play roles in the education of ELLs with disabilities require that policymakers, practitioners, and researchers remain equally focused on questions of over- and underrepresentation in special education. Both placement patterns have significant implications for the educational futures of these students. There has been a historical inclination to track overrepresentation patterns; however, given the inherent uncertainties and ambiguities in the identification of ELLs for special education, a concern with underrepresentation is equally critical to ensure access to services for students who need specialized supports.

3. RTI is becoming the model of choice for special education identification, particularly in the LD field. Nevertheless, it is alarming that major changes are being made in policy and practice toward an RTI model given its lack of attention to issues of cultural and linguistic difference. This is disconcerting when we consider the substantial proportion of racial and linguistic minority students that historically has been

placed in special education (Donovan & Cross, 2002). Therefore, it will be critical to refine RTI models, so that explicit and systematic attention is given to ELLs. The model proposed in this chapter is a step in that direction.

Conclusions

In an effective education system for ELLs, administrators oversee program implementation and provide needed resources, so that school climates are conducive to the success of ELLs. Teachers help students meet high academic standards in the native language and/or ESL. They know how to differentiate instruction for struggling learners and more accurately identify those who should be referred to supplemental and/or special education programs. Early intervention services are provided to determine whether students' needs can be met in the general education context before a special education referral is made. When students are referred for an FIE, assessment personnel utilize instruments and procedures that help distinguish between linguistic and cultural differences, and disabilities. And when students are eligible, special educators provide IEPs that simultaneously address the language- and disability-related needs of eligible students. IEPs are implemented in the LRE, so that ELLs can access the general education curriculum and interact with nondisabled peers.

To implement the essential elements of this comprehensive service delivery system (prevention, early intervention, and nondiscriminatory special education processes), bilingual education, ESL, general education, and special education personnel share a knowledge base about ELLs, and coordinate their programs and services. The beneficiaries of this shared expertise and collaboration are ELL students who receive programs and services that help them meet high academic standards, reducing their disproportionate representation in remedial and special education programs.

ENGAGEMENT ACTIVITIES

1. Brainstorm a list of questions that teachers can ask themselves to determine whether they have the skills meet the needs of ELLs in their classrooms.

2. Examine the special education representation of ELLs in your school. Assume that the number of students in special education, and in each disability category, should be the same as the percentage of ELLs in the school. In which

categories are ELLs most commonly served? In which are they least commonly served? How would you explain these patterns?

3. Describe three ways to assess a student's academic language proficiency.

4. Each of the following represents misconception about ELLs. Explain why they are misconceptions:

   ▪ ELLs with severe disabilities should be taught in English.

   ▪ There is no harm in putting ELLs who do not have disabilities in special education, where they will get specialized instruction to resolve achievement difficulties.

   ▪ Parents of ELLs should speak English at home, so that their children will not be confused by exposure to two languages, and to help ensure that students learn English as quickly as possible.

5. Most teachers do not have the knowledge and skills needed to serve ELLs effectively. If you were a school principal, how would you design and implement a professional development program to develop these skills and competencies? How would you gain the commitment of teachers and other professionals (e.g., speech therapists and school psychologists) to participate in this training? Why is obtaining this commitment more effective than simply requiring participation?

6. Visit *www.equityallianceatasu.org* to identify various resources for teachers and principals about the intersection of cultural and linguistic differences and special needs.

ACKNOWLEDGMENT

Alfredo J. Artiles acknowledges the support of the Center for Advanced Study in the Behavioral Sciences (CASBS) at Stanford University and the National Center for Culturally Responsive Educational Systems (NCCRESt) under Grant No. H326E020003 awarded by the U.S. Department of Education (USDOE), Office of Special Education Programs. Endorsement of CASBS and USDOE of the ideas expressed in this chapter should not be inferred.

REFERENCES

Artiles, A. J., & Klingner, J. K. (Eds.). (2006). Forging a knowledge base on English language learners with special needs: Theoretical, population, and technical issues. *Teachers College Record, 108,* 2187–2194.

Artiles, A. J., Klingner, J., Sullivan, A., & Fierros, E. (2010). Shifting landscapes: English learners' special education placement in English-only states. In P. Gándara & M. Hopkins (Eds.), *Forbidden language: English learners and restrictive language policies.* New York: Teachers College Press.

Artiles, A. J., & Ortiz, A. A. (Eds.). (2002). *Identification and instruction of English language learners with special education needs.* Washington, DC: Center for Applied Linguistics & Delta Systems.

Artiles, A. J., Rueda, R., Salazar, J., & Higareda, I. (2005). Within-group diversity in minority disproportionate representation: English language learners in urban school districts. *Exceptional Children, 71,* 283–300.

August, D. L., & Hakuta, K. (Eds.). (1997). *Improving schooling for language-minority children: A research agenda.* Washington, DC: National Academy Press.

Christensen, L. L., Thurlow, M. L., & Wang, T. (2009). *Improving accommodations outcomes: Monitoring instructional and assessment accommodations for students with disabilities.* Minneapolis: University of Minnesota, National Center on Educational Outcomes.

Cloud, N. (2002). Culturally and linguistically responsive instructional planning. In A. J. Artiles & A. A. Ortiz (Eds.), *Identification and instruction of English language learners with special education needs* (pp. 107–132). Washington, DC: Center for Applied Linguistics & Delta Systems.

Coelho, E. (2004). *Adding English: A guide to teaching in multilingual classrooms.* Toronto: Pippin.

Collier, C., & Hoover, J. J. (1987). Sociocultural considerations when referring minority children for learning disabilities. *Learning Disabilities Focus, 3*(1), 39–45.

Council for Exceptional Children. (2009). *What every special educator must know: Ethics, standards, and guidelines.* Arlington, VA: Author.

Donovan, S., & Cross, C. (Eds.). (2002). *Minority students in special and gifted education.* Washington, DC: National Academy Press.

Forum on Educational Accountability. (2007). *Assessment and accountability for improving schools and learning: Principles and recommendations for federal law and state and local systems.* Retrieved December 20, 2009, from *www.edaccountability.org/AssessmentFullReoportJune07.pdf.*

Fry, R. (2007, August). *The changing racial and ethnic composition of U.S. public schools.* Washington, DC: Pew Hispanic Center.

García, S. B., & Ortiz, A. A. (2004). Preventing disproportionate representation: Culturally and linguistically responsive prereferral intervention. Denver, CO: National Center for Culturally Responsive Educational Systems (NCCRESt). Retrieved July 30, 2009, from *www/nccrest.org.*

García, S. B., & Ortiz, A. A. (2008). A framework for culturally and linguistically responsive design of response to intervention models. *Multiple Voices, 11*(1), 24–41.

Gersten, R., Baker, S. K., Shanahan, T., Linan-Thompson, S., Chiappe, P., & Scarcella, R. (2007). *Effective literacy and English language instruction for English learners in the elementary grades: A practice guide* (NCEE No. 2007-4011). Washington, DC: National Center for Education Evaluation and Regional Assistance, Institute of Education Sciences, U.S. Department of Education.

Goldenberg, C. (1998). A balanced approach to early Spanish literacy instruction. In R. Gersten & R. Jiménez (Eds.), *Promoting learning for culturally and linguistically diverse students: Classroom applications from contemporary research* (pp. 3–25). Belmont, CA: Wadsworth.

Gruber, K. J., Wiley, S. D., Broughman, S. P., Strizek, G. A., & Burian-Fitzgerald, M. (2002). *Schools and Staffing Survey, 1999–2000: Overview of the data for public, private, public charter, and Bureau of Indian Affairs elementary and secondary schools* (NCES Report No. 2002-313). Washington, DC: National Center for Education Statistics. Retrieved July 6, 2009, from *nces.ed.gov/pubsearch/pubsinfo.asp?pubid=2002313.*

Harry, B., & Klingner, J. K. (2006). *Crossing the border from normalcy to disability: Minorities and the special education process.* New York: Teachers College Press.

Individuals with Disabilities Education Act of 2004 (IDEA), Public Law No. 108-446, 20 U.S.C. § 1400 et seq. (2004).

Kalyanpur, M., & Harry, B. (1999). *Culture in special education: Building reciprocal family–professional relationships.* Baltimore: Brookes.

Kauffman, J. M. (1999). How we prevent the prevention of emotional and behavioral disorders. *Exceptional Children, 65*(4), 448–468.

Kilgore, B. (2004). *Differentiation: Simplified, realistic, and effective.* Austin, TX: Professional Associates.

Klingner, J., & Artiles, A. J. (Eds.). (2006). ELLs struggling to learn to read: Emergent scholarship on linguistic differences and learning disabilities. *Journal of Learning Disabilities, 39,* 99–156; 386–398.

Klingner, J. K., Artiles, A. J., & Barletta, L. M. (2006). ELLs who struggle with reading: Language acquisition or learning disabilities? *Journal of Learning Disabilities, 39,* 108–128.

Krashen, S. D. (1982). *Principles and practice in second language acquisition.* New York: Pergamon Press.

Kushner, M. I., & Ortiz, A. A. (2000). The preparation of early childhood education to serve English language learners. In *New teachers for a new century: The future of early childhood professional preparation* (pp. 123–154). Washington, DC: Department of Education, Office of Educational Research and improvement, National Institute on Early Childhood Education.

Leinhardt, G. (1992). What research on learning tells us about teaching. *Educational Leadership, 49*(7), 20–25.

Lezotte, L. (1991). *Correlates of effective schools: The first and second generation.* Okemos, MI: Effective School Products, Ltd.

Linan-Thompson, S., & Ortiz, A. A. (2009). Response to intervention and English language learners: Instructional and assessment considerations. *Seminars in Speech and Language, 30*(2), 105–120.

Marchand-Martella, N. E., Ruby, S. F., & Martella, R. C. (2007). Intensifying reading instruction for students within a three-tier model: Standard-protocol and problem-solving approaches within a response-to-intervention (RTI) system. *TEACHING Exceptional Children Plus, 3*(5) Article 2. Retrieved July 18, 2009, from *escholarship.bc.edu/education/tecplus/vol3/iss5/art2.*

Moll, L. C., Amanti, C., Neff, D., & González, N. (1992). Funds of knowledge for teaching: Using a qualitative approach to connect homes and classrooms. *Theory Into Practice, 31*(2), 132–141.

Montecel, M. R., & Cortez, J. D. (2002). Successful bilingual education programs: Development and dissemination of criteria to identify promising and exemplary practices in bilingual education at the national level. *Bilingual Research Journal, 26*, 1–21.

National Center for Educational Statistics (NCES). (2004). *The condition of education*. Washington, DC: U.S. Department of Education.

National Center for Educational Statistics (NCES). (2005). *Digest of educational statistics*. Washington, DC: U.S. Department of Education, Institute of Education Sciences.

National Joint Committee on Learning Disabilities. (2005). Response to intervention and learning disabilities. Retrieved July 19, 2009, from *www.ncid. org/images/stories/resources/NJCLDReports/njcld_rti2005.pdf*

No Child Left Behind Act of 2001 (NCLB), Public Law No. 107-110, 115 Stat. 1425, 20 U.S.C. § 6301 et seq. (2001).

Office of English Language Acquisition (OELA). (2008). *Biennial Report to Congress on the Implementation of the Title III State Formula Grant Program, School Years 2004–06*. Washington, DC: Author. Retrieved July 15, 2009, from *www.ed.gov/about/offices/list/oela/title3biennial0406.pdf*.

Ortiz, A. A. (1997). Learning disabilities occurring concomitantly with linguistic differences. *Journal of Learning Disabilities, 30*, 321–332.

Ortiz, A. A. (2002). Prevention of school failure and early intervention for English language learners experiencing achievement difficulties. In A. Artiles & A. A. Ortiz (Eds.), *Identification and instruction of English language learners with special education needs* (pp. 31–48). Washington, DC: Center for Applied Linguistics and Delta Systems.

Ortiz, A. A., Robertson, P., & Wilkinson, C. Y. (2009, June). *Second language acquisition and assessment*. Presented at the Bilingual Exceptional Students: Early Intervention, Referral, and Assessment (BESt ERA) Training of Trainers Conference, Austin, TX.

Ortiz, A. A., & Yates, J. R. (2001). A framework for serving English language learners with disabilities, *Journal of Special Education Leadership, 14*(2), 72–80.

Ortiz, A. A., & Yates, J. R. (2002). Considerations in the assessment of English language learners with disabilities. In A. Artiles & A. A. Ortiz (Eds.), *Identification and instruction of English language learners with special education needs* (pp. 65–85). Washington, DC: Center for Applied Linguistics & Delta Systems.

Seppanen, P., Schaefer, R., & Julian, N. R. (1995). *Matching state goals to a model of outcomes and indicators for grade 4*. Minneapolis: University of Minnesota, National Center on Educational Outcomes.

Short, D. (2000). *The ESL standards: Bridging the academic gap for English language learners*. Washington, DC: Center for Applied Linguistics. Retrieved June 15, 2009, from *www.cal.org/resources/digest/0013eslstandards.html*.

Snow, C. E., Burns, M. S., & Griffin, P. (1998). *Preventing reading difficulties in young children*. Washington, DC: National Academy Press.

Thomas, W., & Collier, V. (2002). *A national study of school effectiveness for language minority students' long-term academic achievement: Final report*.

Retrieved June 1, 2009, from *crede.berkeley.edu/research/crede/research/llaa/1.1_final.html*.

Tomlinson, C. A. (2003). *Fulfilling the promise of the differentiated classroom: Strategies and tools for responsive teaching.* Alexandria, VA: Association for Supervision and Curriculum Development.

U.S. Census Bureau. (2003, February 25). *U.S. Census Bureau, Population Division.* Retrieved March 26, 2003, from *www.census.gov/population/www/cen2000/phc-t20.html*.

U.S. Census Bureau. (2009). *2008 National Population Projections: Projected change in population size by race and Hispanic origin for the United States.* Retrieved December 20, 2009, from *www.census.gov/population/www/projections/summarytables.html*.

U.S. Department of Education (USDOE), & National Institute of Child Health and Human Development (NICHD). (2003, June). *Key indicators of Hispanic student achievement: National goals and benchmarks for the next decade.* Retrieved June 27, 2003, from *www.ed.gov/pubs/hispanicindicators*.

Wilkinson, C. Y., Ortiz, A. A., Robertson, P., & Kushner, M. (2006). English language learners with reading-related learning disabilities: Linking data from multiple sources to make eligibility determinations. *Journal of Learning Disabilities, 39*(2), 129–141.

Yates, J. R., & Ortiz, A. A. (1998). Developing individualized education programs for exceptional language minority students. In L. Baca & H. Cervantes (Eds.), *The bilingual special education interface* (pp. 188–213). Upper Saddle River, NJ: Prentice-Hall.

Zehler, A., Fleischman, H., Hopstock, P., Stephenson, T., Pendzick, M., & Sapru, S. (2003). *Policy report: Summary of findings related to LEP and SPED-LEP students* (Submitted by Development Associates, Inc., to U.S. Department of Education). Washington, DC: Office of English Language Acquisition, Language Enhancement, and Academic Achievement of Limited English Proficient Students, U.S. Department of Education.

CHAPTER 12

Best Practices for Native American Language Learners

Mary Eunice Romero-Little

> *This chapter will:*
>
> 1. Increase awareness and contribute to the development of a clearer understanding of this nation's Indigenous school-age learners and their language-learning needs—of both their Indigenous languages and English.
>
> 2. Help educators working with Native students and their communities to develop a knowledge base of best practices to create a more meaningful and equitable education for Native Americans.

It may be surprising for some readers to learn that the average Native American (NA) student does not fit the definition of a typical English language learner (ELL). The latter usually enters school speaking a primary language other than English and is acquiring English as a second, third, or even fourth language. In contrast, the majority of NA children enter school as primary speakers of English. At the same time, they are likely to speak a variety influenced by the grammar, sound system, and use patterns of the Indigenous language, which may still be spoken by parents and grandparents in their communities. Sociolinguists refer to this as *Indian English, Reservation English,* or in the case of the English spoken in Alaskan Native communities, *Village* or *Bush English,* although more accurate terms reference specific Indigenous languages and speech communities (e.g., *Navajo English*, *O'odham English*; Leap, 1993). Although the differences between these dialects and Standard English are seldom great enough to interfere with communication between speakers, they are often misunderstood or rejected in school, leading NA students to be characterized by educators as "alingual," "semilingual," or "limited English proficient." Grim statistics bear testimony to the negative educational consequences that ensue from these labeling practices: NA students are more than twice as likely as their White peers to score at the lowest level on the National Assessment of Educational Progress reading assessments, are heavily overrepresented in special education programs, and up to 40% will not graduate from high school (Castagno & Brayboy, 2008; Romero-Little, McCarty, Warhol, & Zepeda, 2007). As Castagno and Brayboy wrote in a recent review of the literature, "Schools are clearly not meeting the needs of Indigenous students and change is needed if we hope to see greater parity in . . . measures of academic achievement" (2008, p. 942).

Although NA children may not possess competency in their heritage language, they are likely to be exposed to it in a variety of ways. For instance, in my community of Cochiti Pueblo, New Mexico, it is music to the ears of adults to hear a young child speak in our Native language Keres; it is also a rarity. There have been virtually no young native speakers of Cochiti Keres for over 30 years. Except for a few homes and communities, young native speakers of Indigenous languages are few and far between all across Native America. When the youngest members of a speech community are not speaking the community language, it is also an unambiguous sign that more than the Native language is endangered; because language and culture are so closely intertwined, when a language dies, much of the cultural knowledge it encodes is also in jeopardy of being lost. Consequently, NA families and communities today are engaged in language maintenance and renewal initiatives to ensure that their children learn their heritage language as they acquire fluency and literacy abilities in English.

A close examination of the teachers of NA learners reveals that the majority are non-Natives who, in many cases, know little about Native children, families, communities, and language(s). A recent national study found, for example, that just 1% of the teachers of Native students are NA (Stancavage et al., 2006). This chapter focuses on NA language learners (American Indian, Alaskan Native, and Native Hawaiian), in full recognition of that situation. It rises out of a concern that although there may be a genuine interest and desire to learn about America's original inhabitants, the average U.S. citizen, including many educators, has little, if any, credible knowledge and understanding of NA

students' situation or the dilemma facing their communities, or educational needs, including the best practices for teaching them. Thus,
the first goal of this chapter is to increase awareness and contribute
to the development of a clearer understanding of this nation's Indigenous school-age learners and their language learning needs—both in
their Indigenous languages and English. Second, this chapter aims to
assist educators and school leaders in recognizing, valuing, and accom-
modating the rich intellectual, sociocultural, and linguistic traditions
and abilities of NA learners. Third, this chapter provides some practical strategies that educators and others can use to learn about Native
Americans, in general, and NA students, in particular. The ultimate
goal is to support educators in working with Native students and their
communities to create a more equitable education for all learners in a
multicultural and democratic society.

Because each country has its preferred terminology when referring
to its original citizens, which sometimes creates confusion, I take this
opportunity to clarify the terminology for this chapter. In Australia,
for instance, *Aboriginal* is an acceptable term, whereas *tribal* is not. In
Canada, *First Nations* is preferred over *tribal* or *Native nations* to refer
to its original citizens, and is always capitalized. In the United States,
Indian, American Indian, Native American, and *Native* all refer in general
to its Indigenous population. For this chapter, the various U.S. terms
will be used interchangeably and should be considered inclusive of the
three main groups of Indigenous peoples in the United States: American Indians, Alaska Natives, and Native Hawaiians.

This chapter begins with a brief overview of Indigenous peoples
of the United States, then moves to a discussion of NA language learners and the diversity that exists among them. This is followed by a brief
examination of English-language instruction that took place during
early English-only schooling, and the problems that arose from such
practices, as means for understanding critical issues today in the education of NA students. The chapter concludes with an examination of
best practices for teaching NA language learners, supported by recent
language education research, and community- and school-based efforts
to retain heritage languages and cultures, while promoting children's
full acquisition of English. Lessons from the past and contemporary initiatives provide valuable insights into best practices for teaching English
and English literacy, while strengthening and revitalizing the heritage
language. Moreover, these lessons help us better understand the social
justice and human rights issues of Indigenous learners and communities in light of ongoing pressures for English-only, standardization, and
high-stakes testing.

Indigenous Peoples and Languages of the United States

Presently in the United States there are 4.5 million American Indians and Alaska Natives, and 1,118,00 Native Hawaiians, who together represent 1.5% of the total population (De Voe, Darling-Churchill, & Snyder, 2008, p. 8; U.S. Office of Health and Human Services, 2009, p. 1). Politically, Native Americans represent 564 federally recognized tribes, 245 federally nonrecognized tribes (most of whom are currently petitioning the U.S. government for recognition), and over 100 state-recognized tribes. The delineations of "federally recognized, "nonfederally recognized," and "state-recognized" refer to the unique legal and political status of Native peoples in the United States—a status unlike that of any other U.S. ethnolinguistic group. From the first encounters between Native peoples and Europeans, the two groups have operated on a government-to-government basis (Snipp, 2002, p. 2). At the heart of that relationship is the right of tribal sovereignty—"self-government, self-determination, and self-education" (Lomawaima & McCarty, 2006, p. 10), whereby the federal government has a trust responsibility to "represent the best interests of the tribes and their members," including education (American Indian Policy Center, 2002, p. 1). As we will see, this distinctive legal–political relationship has had and continues to have important implications for the schooling of NA students.

In addition to their political status, each Native nation has its own specific name for itself—for example, Chippewa, Lakota, Jemez Pueblo (Walatowa), Cochiti Pueblo, Diné (Navajo), Inuit, Eastern and Western Cherokee, Tohono O'odham, Caddo, Eastern Pequot, Seminole, Oneida, and so forth—and its own genesis theories. The two largest tribes are the Cherokee Nation of Oklahoma, with 729,533 citizens, and the Navajo Nation, with approximately 298,000 citizens (U.S. Census Bureau, 2002). Each Native nation has its own historical, political, governance, economic, cultural, sociolinguistic, and linguistic characteristics and context. What all Native communities have in common is their singular status as tribal sovereigns and the fact that they have undergone enormous sociocultural and linguistic change since the arrival of Europeans to the continent. Early on, the colonizers deemed that schooling was necessary to bring Native peoples into their society by "civilizing" and "Christianizing" them (Adams, 1995). A key consequence of the colonizing experience has been Native language attrition.

Before European contact, it is estimated that over 750 NA languages were spoken in North America (Silver & Miller, 1997). Today, just 175 distinct NA languages are still spoken in the United States, each with varying degrees of vitality. For example, Navajo, found in the Four Corners area where Arizona, New Mexico, Utah, and Colorado meet, is still spoken by over 100,000 tribal citizens, whereas Coeur d'Alene, found in Northern Idaho, has fewer than five speakers out of a population of 800 tribal members (Grimes & Grimes, 2000).

Understanding NA Learners and Their Language(s)

In 2006–2007, 645,601 American Indian and Alaska Native students—or 1% of the U.S. student population—attended K–12 schools. In addition, there were 132,052 Native Hawaiian children between birth and age 17, a substantial proportion of which attended K–12 schools (National Caucus of Native American State Legislators, 2008). Over 90% of NA students attend public schools, and the remaining 10% attend federally funded schools operated by the Bureau of Indian Education or parochial schools (Moran, Rampey, Dion, & Donahue, 2008). These figures reflect the increasing number of NA learners and families residing in urban areas, with myriad educational, social, and economic experiences among them.

This diversity is also reflected in the range of linguistic competencies among Native learners even with respect to English. For example, some children may come to school speaking the Indigenous language as a first language; these children are acquiring English as a second language. In some cases, as in the Indigenous communities in the Southwest, where Spanish is prominent, English is acquired as a third language. These young speakers of Indigenous languages, as noted earlier, are scarce, and although they enter mainstream schools with sound primary language competencies, many are in great danger of losing their mother tongues as they acquire English, as a consequence of the highly subtractive process[1] of second-language learning (Lambert, 1974, 1981) found in American school systems. Most Native students who retain any knowledge of their Indigenous languages at all are English-dominant with, at most, receptive (listening) or limited production (speaking) abilities in the Native language. Altogether too many Native students have no Native language exposure at all and know nothing of their heritage languages. "Students with each of these language profiles (or some combination) may be present in a single classroom or school," emphasizing the point that a uniform, "one-size-fits-all" approach is untenable for this population of students (McCarty, 2009, pp. 9, 11).

Data from a recent, large-scale study of Native American language practices in the Southwest illustrate these diverse linguistic repertoires (McCarty, Romero-Little, Zepeda, & Warhol, 2007; Romero-Little et al., 2007). This study found that even in communities in which Native languages are not being acquired as first languages, children are nonetheless exposed to multiple varieties of the Native language(s), English, and in some cases, regionally significant languages such as Spanish. Furthermore, the study found that Native American

> children may have more Native language proficiency than they manifest; although they may lack academic proficiency in English and/or proficiency in the Native language, children in these communities are not "a-lingual." . . . Their sociolinguistic repertoires reflect multiple types of bi-/multilingualism and "mono"-lingualism across a range of academic, conversational, receptive, and literate codes, modes, registers, genres, and domains. (McCarty et al., 2007, p. vi)

In other words, whether or not they are able to speak the languages of their heritage, many Native American children, by virtue of their home environments and cultures, bring with them to school rich sociolinguistic and intellectual resources that reflect multidimensional proficiencies and ways of knowing and learning. However, these resources are typically not well understood, appreciated, or recognized in the school setting. As a result, NA students are judged strictly on the basis of whether they have the background the school believes they should have, and not only are their resources overlooked, but they are also seen in terms of deficiencies, and are likely to be tracked into remedial programs.

"No Indian Talk": English-Only Schooling of Native Americans

So she [teacher] told me that anytime anyone speaks their language, their Indian language in the schoolyard, they were going to be punished. . . . She told me "You spoke Indian language in back of school; I heard about it and now you have to go into the little room." There I would be strapped. Well, I just couldn't help it; I talked my language.
—TESTIMONY OF FRANCES JACK, HOPLAND BAND POMO
(quoted in Hinton, 1994, p. 179)

Understanding the complexity of teaching language and literacy to contemporary Indigenous children begins with an understanding of their educational history. Framed in the 19th century, when assimilative education for Indigenous children aimed at eradicating any signs of their indigeneity, including their identities, languages, cultural practices, religions, and cultural affinities, this history reveals the process by which Indigenous children in the United States began formally (and forcibly) to learn English as a second language. From this early era emerged a paradigm of English-language instruction created from the trial-and-error efforts of teachers and others responsible for carrying out the government's education policies. The majority of these European American teachers (like many today) knew very little of the language, culture, and abilities of the children they were responsible for teaching and, consequently, they struggled to find effective strategies of second-language instruction at a time when there were few teaching aides to guide them. Beginning in the 1870s, NA children were forcibly taken from their families and placed in boarding schools, often at great distances from their tribal communities, for the purpose of "civilizing" and teaching them English. The 1868 report of the "Peace Commission," which had been given the task of deciding the fate of Native peoples after removal from their homelands, describes the goals of that policy: "Schools should be established, which children should be required to attend; their barbarous dialects should be blotted out and the English language substituted" (from the Report of the Commissioner of Indian Affairs; Atkins, 1887).

Between 1887 and 1900, some 500 government boarding schools were established, enrolling more than 100,000 NA children, some as young as 4-years of age. The schools were located far from the children's homelands and families, the intention being to keep them from the influence and comfort of their families and communities. As Frances Jack, a member of the Hopland Band of Pomo (California) Indians, testified in the opening epigraph to this section, "No Indian talk" was the policy in these enforced and oppressive English-language acquisition environments, where children who spoke the only language they knew—their Native language—were publicly humiliated and physically abused (Spack, 2002). In retrospect, these horrible acts, whether done with good or bad intentions, were a result of the Anglo-American ethnocentric ideology of the time. It was a flawed belief with long-lasting consequences that are still being felt today (Adams, 1995).

In this early era of Indian education, although the true intention for teaching English to NAs was always to curtail the continued use of Indigenous languages and cultures, a number of early educators did perceive the advantages of bilingualism. For example, John P. Williamson, a missionary to the Yankton Sioux during the 1870s, argued that English was not the way to teach Indian children; ideas and truths, he believed, were best learned in the mother tongue (Spack, 2002). Likewise, Superintendent of Indian Schools William N. Hailmann, in 1890, understood that the "possession of one language, far from being a hindrance in the acquisition of another, rather facilitates it" (quoted in Spack, 2002, p. 26); he prescribed a curriculum that emphasized meaningful conversation and the use of subject matter of relevance to

Native children. Cora Folsom, a teacher of English during this early era, found that if NA students were already literate in their own language, it facilitated their learning of English (Spack, 2002). Interestingly, Virginia Collier and Wayne Thomas's (1997) national study of school effectiveness for language-minority students found that the amount of primary language schooling a student receives is the strongest predictor of second-language student achievement. In further evidence of these findings, many Native students who had the benefit of the type of bilingual schooling described were "high achievers" who went on to become bilingual educators themselves. Thomas Wildcat Alford (Shawnee) became a teacher and school principal in the Indian service, Sarah Winnemucca (Pauite), a speaker of five languages (three Native languages, Spanish, and English), became a government interpreter and teacher; Luther Standing Bear (Oglala Lakota) became a teacher and critic of the English-only educational policy and promoter of bilingual education (Spack, 2002).

In the next section, we will look at current approaches to educating Native children, and in so doing, begin to identify practices that have developed in reaction to the assimilative processes of the past. This examination focuses attention on aspects of school culture that are in sharp contrast to cultural practices in Native communities, as a way of defining what culturally responsive language instructional programs should look like.

Teaching Contemporary
Native American Language Learners

In the previous section, we learned that learning English is not new to NAs; they have been learning English since the time of European contact, albeit under linguistically and culturally repressive conditions. Unfortunately, historically, learning English has come at the cost of the Native languages and cultural identities of countless numbers of NA school children. The result of these subtractive educational policies and practices has been catastrophic for the Native peoples of North America. Of 175 Indigenous languages still spoken in the United States today, only 20 (11%) are still being acquired by children through intergenerational transmission as a first language (Krauss, 1998). Moreover, 97% of NA fourth through eighth graders, whether they are speakers of Indigenous languages or not, receive instruction entirely in English (Stancavage et al., 2006), which puts the few remaining languages that are still being spoken in further danger. To reverse this situation, a number of innovative programs have been designed to help students master the Native language and culture alongside English and mainstream academic content. A growing body of research documents the effectiveness of the "promising practices" used in these programs. All of this has led to a new paradigm for Indigenous language education. Although the approaches and methods differ depending on the local context, a central aim of all of these initiatives is the creation of a new generation of young adults that is equally proficient in the heritage language and English.

In a review of the research on promising practices for American Indian, Alaska Native, and Native Hawaiian students, McCarty (2009) argues that the best practices are those that facilitate learners' self-efficacy, critical capacities, and intrinsic motivation; such practices, she adds, also "support teachers' professionalism and invest in the intellectual resources present in local communities" (p. 22). These practices, designed to enable Native students to achieve full educational parity with their White peers, contribute to building strong academic and cultural identities and promote positive school–community relationships (McCarty, 2009).

Practices with these goals are often grouped together under the rubric of *culturally responsive schooling* (CRS), also called *culturally based education* (CBE). In their review of the CRS/CBE literature, Castagno and Brayboy state that these approaches assume "a firm grounding in the heritage language and culture indigenous to a particular tribe is a fundamental prerequisite for the development of culturally-healthy students and communities . . . and thus is an essential ingredient for . . . educators, curriculum, and schools" (2008, p. 941). David Beaulieu (2006) describes CBE as education that is both academically effective and locally meaningful, adding that whole-school approaches that use the Native language as the medium of instruction are more effective than "add on" or "pull-out" programs. In her study of language and culture instruction at three Ojibwe-serving schools in the Great Lakes region, Mary Hermes (2005) validates these points, noting the problems of trying to teach Native cultural content in English. She argues instead for schoolwide restructuring and implementation of heritage-language immersion, which provides the "complete meaning-making context for cultural content" (p. 53).

Heritage-language immersion, whereby all or most content is delivered in the Native language, is an increasingly popular and proven pedagogy for achieving CRS/CBE goals. In the sections that follow, I provide examples of the heritage-language immersion approach. A key tenet underlying this approach is that NA students, like their non-Native peers, have the right to learn their community/heritage languages, and that this can be done without diminishing their English-language learning or excluding the Native child and culture from the school context. However, immersion is not always feasible or appropriate in settings in which there are children of diverse language and cultural backgrounds. In these settings, other types of CBE/CRS may be implemented, including the use of culturally appropriate materials and teaching styles. In the subsections below, I provide examples of these approaches. All of them are based on an "additive" or enrichment philosophy that values the maintenance of the children's heritage language and culture as essential components of curriculum and pedagogy.

Indigenous Language Immersion: Promising Practices in Two Navajo Schools

Tsehootsooi Diné Bíoltá

Located on the eastern edge of the Navajo Nation in Arizona, Tsehootsooí Diné Bíóltá (TDB, or the Navajo School at the Meadow between the Rocks or the Fort Defiance Navajo Immersion School), offers Navajo (Diné) immersion in grades K–8. Ninety-nine percent of the students at TDB are Navajo, but they enter school with English as a primary language and only passive knowledge of Navajo. At the same time, many of these students struggle with Academic English and are identified as limited English proficient (Arviso & Holm, 2001). In the lower grades, all instruction, including initial literacy, is in Navajo. Time spent in English, introduced in second grade, is gradually increased until a 50:50 distribution is attained by grade 6. According to educators close to the program, the TDB curriculum is presented from a Diné perspective. Innovative features of this curriculum include:

- Incorporation of both Diné cultural standards and state standards in reading, writing, and mathematics.
- A Diné language and culture-rich environment, including the use of "situational Navajo" activities designed to create real-life situations, and of Navajo verbs in real conversations.
- Strong parent involvement, including school-sponsored training on acquiring the heritage language as a second language.
- Technology training for teachers and parents, and the use of technology for language learning.
- A "total program" approach with high expectations for high levels of both Diné and English language mastery. (Johnson & Legatz, 2006, pp. 29–31)

Longitudinal data show that TDB students consistently outperform their Navajo peers in mainstream English classes on local and state tests of English reading, writing, and mathematics. Meanwhile, they are developing Navajo oral language and literacy skills as well.

Puente de Hózhó Dual-Immersion School

In another public school in northern Arizona, immersion approaches are also showing great success. The name of this school represents its vision and honors its linguistic heritage—Spanish and Navajo. The K–8 Puente de Hózhó Dual-Immersion School (*Puente de* for the Spanish "bridge of" and *Hózhó* for "beauty" in Navajo) provides two parallel bilingual programs in which native Spanish-speaking and native English-speaking students are taught jointly for a half-day in their primary languages, and spend the rest of their time alongside English-dominant Navajo students in a one-way Navajo immersion program. As in the TDB model (discussed earlier), Navajo kindergartners at this dual-language school receive 90% of their instruction in Navajo, with English instructional time gradually increased to 80:20 in first grade and 60:40 by third grade. In grades 4–8 these students receive 50% of their instruction in English and 50% in Navajo. All state standards are taught in Navajo and English, or Spanish and English (McCarty, 2009). In English language arts, English reading and mathematics Puente de Hózhó students outperform their peers in monolingual English programs by as much as seven points. Equally important, although not always quantifiable, are increased pride, confidence, and motivation in the students (Fillerup, 2005).

Notably, data from these two heritage-language immersion schools show that children acquire the heritage language as a second language without "cost" to their English-language development or academic achievement, as measured by local and national standardized tests. Moreover, these heritage-language learners outperform their English mainstream peers, who tend to lose whatever heritage-language ability they had upon entering school (McCarty, 2009).

Promising Practices in Indigenous Homes and Communities

So far, this discussion has focused on lessons learned from contemporary language initiatives in the context of schools that reveal most effective instructional programs and practices for promoting high levels of Academic English and Native language retention. Yet Native societies have their own ways of educating their children, and although our focus tends to be on mainstream education and schools, it is important to remember that knowledge is acquired outside of school in children's homes and communities, and through various mediators, such as grandparents, siblings, and peers (Gregory, Long, & Volk, 2004). Additionally, it is vital to recognize and understand the goals that each Native society has for its own children. In mainstream U.S. society, for example, ensuring that children start school "ready to learn" is crucial for school (and life) success, and is viewed as a prime responsibility of schools and families. "Readiness" in the minds of mainstream parents, educators, and policymakers includes parental preparation of young children for literacy and school learning by reading to them; working with them on number, letter, and shape recognition; engaging them in verbal expression, and so forth—in English.

While the vast majority of NA parents concur that preparing young children for school is a fundamental obligation and priority, for many, the goals for children extend far beyond those promoted by mainstream schools. They include experiences designed to teach their children *cultural literacy,* the essential knowledge, skills, competencies, and beliefs fundamental for ensuring their participation in the Native society. Like mainstream parents and educators, Native parents also dedicate enormous amounts of time and energy to teach their children the competencies and knowledge required for participation in the Native world during the preschool years. The teaching methods and strategies of this early socialization process are framed by long-held traditions and beliefs about human relations and abilities. In the Pueblo communities of New Mexico, for example, participation is a crucial form of learning one's role and responsibilities as a contributing member of one's family and community, as well as learning the language children need for life in the Pueblo world, a world that involves continual linguistic and social interaction with many caretakers–teachers (Romero, 2003).

These Pueblo teaching methods, in sharp contrast to the teaching practices followed in the school world, are noncoercive and much more child-centered than teacher-centered. Children are included in all family and community functions but are not required to take an active part until they are ready. They observe, and through their observations, learn about the relationships and bonds that are key to existence and communal life.

When a person—young or old—desires to participate in an activity and is physically able, he or she is encouraged to do so (except for certain reserved esoteric activities). However, neither children (nor adults) are forced to do things, including participation in the community's activities, if they do not wish to participate. It is more often the case that children simply decide to participate in communal activities, often ones requiring extraordinary skills, stamina, and effort, to the astonishment of outsiders. The following observations of children's participation during the winter dance at Cochiti Pueblo is a case in point.

It had snowed during the night but the snow has been cleared in the center of the plaza for today's buffalo dance. The plaza is filled with dancers, singers, and people who have come to watch the dance. Gray puffs of air stream from the singers' mouths into the chilled air. Along with the adult singers and buffalo dancers are sixteen children and youths dressed as deer, antelopes, and rams encircling the adult dancers who are in the center. Among the "animals" are two tiny rams; one is a little taller than the other. The taller ram is around five years of age, and the smaller one is perhaps three. This tiniest ram appears to be wearing his pajamas under his dance attire. Both of the rams take their role in the performance seriously and do not miss a beat as they dance. After the first verse of the buffalo song, people come down from their seats and begin giving gifts to the dancers. Several women attach bags of chips, popcorn and candy on the two little rams' horns. The tiniest ram loses his balance with the weight of the goodies dangling from his horns. A singer comes over just in time to remove them and the tiny ram returns to his place and continues dancing. Amazingly, these tiny dancers dance the entire day. (Romero, 2003, pp. 187–188)

Such behavior is bewildering to outsiders, who find it hard to believe that children as young as the 3 or even 5 years old would ever do what these children are doing without coercion! But there is none. In the Pueblo world, children would never be forced to undertake or to learn anything they did not want to do, and in fact, it is even difficult to imagine how it could be done.

It is not uncommon to witness children as young as 2 years of age taking part in the communal events, such as the one described, at a powwow, or at fish camp, an important summer activity for Native Alaskans. In all these instances, young novices are integral participants in the event and, depending on the Native culture, may be rewarded by the community in direct (praise or little gifts) or indirect ways (smiles of approval) for their efforts. In such ways, the community acknowledges that the children are active members or apprentices being guided by more experienced members, who have scaffolded and co-constructed the learning of skills needed for participation in the community (Rogoff, 1990). In contrast to the teaching that goes on in traditional communities, where children decide when they are ready to learn new skills and to participate in the work of the community, the teaching at mainstream schools is structured around a curriculum and the school's schedule, and the model of instruction is of students being taught skills and information by teachers according to that curriculum; learners are viewed as passive recipients of adult teaching. As we have seen in the previous vignette of a Pueblo winter dance, learning and teaching in Indigenous homes and communities exists in a context of dynamic and meaningful interaction with others. Lave and Wenger (1991) refer to this process involving "relations among persons, activity, and world, over time and in relation with other tangential and overlapping" (p. 98) as *communities of practice*. Such experiences of learning require an expansion of our understanding of language and literacy learning as an essential means for improving education for NA children.

Discourse Patterns in Native Communities

Native children come to school with well-established ways of communicating, and particular forms of knowing and learning framed through their languages, cultures, and early socialization experiences. In Hawai'i, for example, people engage in what is commonly known as *talk story*. In these informal conversations, people share a story with others, who add to it—a collaborative talking process. Educators of Native Hawaiian children have found talk story to be a powerful tool for teaching. In typical mainstream classrooms, dialogue patterns represent a teacher–learner relationship, one in which a teacher controls the sociolinguistic interactions of the classroom. In Native Hawaiian classrooms, "children are expected to master not only the content of curriculum material presented by the teacher, but also the socially appropriate use of communicative resources through which such mastery is demonstrated" (Philips, 1983, p. 73). In mainstream schools, raising one's hand, or providing the "correct" answer only after the teacher has called upon the student, is a way the learner can demonstrate mastery (Cazden, 1972). But, in Hawai'i, where talk story has been incorporated as a strategy, learners are encouraged to collaborate through communication, or talk, as the following example (story) demonstrates:

> A 5th grade teacher . . . gives her students daily opportunities to practice talk story in small groups in which topics are discussed freely and at length. Sometimes she asks open-ended questions or provides story prompts, while other times students determine the discussion topic. The level of her students' engagement is "amazing," she says. Clearly, students really do have a voice in talk story. (Taosaka, 2002, p. 9)

In addition to serving as an example of culturally responsive practices, namely, teaching practices that recognize, respect, value, and use students' identities and background for creating optimal learning environments, talk story also reflects the oral teaching, learning strategies, and methods that continue to guide families and communities on how children are inculcated and socialized into the world of their families and cultural communities.

We know that many Native children find school to be an unwelcoming and alienating environment for learning, and this has deeply affected their ability to learn what they really should be learning in school. As noted earlier, Native children have done more poorly in school than all other minority groups. I argue that it is essential to look for conflicts between the instructional practices and methods of mainstream school culture and those that are fairly common across Native cultures. I have attempted to do so in Table 12.1, which compares practices and methods according to approach, curricular organization and emphasis, teaching methods, instructional organization, and participant structures in classroom discourse.

As Table 12.1 shows, the instructional world of mainstream schools in our society differs sharply from the instructional world in many, if not most, Native communities and homes in nearly every respect, providing at least one possible explanation why so many Native children fail to thrive academically in our schools. Since the passage of No Child Left Behind (NCLB) in 2001, the contrast shown in Table 12.1 has increased as schools put a greater and greater premium on evidence of instructional outcomes, as assessed by standardized testing of discrete skills and subject matter. If there ever was much inclination to make school more hospitable to children whose preferred ways of learning are collaborative, noncompetitive, and mutually supportive, there is little support for such approaches now.

At hearings held by the National Indian Education Association (NIEA; 2005) on how NCLB is affecting the educational progress of Native children, Indian elders and leaders testified on mostly negative consequences of such approaches. They testified that the reliance on standardized testing on just two subjects, English language arts and mathematics, has been especially harmful to instructional programs that have tried to be responsive to the cultural and linguistic needs of Native learners and communities. Not only have the one-size-fits-all programs promulgated under NCLB been counterproductive educationally, but they have also undermined the efforts of many communities and schools to revitalize Indigenous languages by using them at school. The following remarks by leaders at the Green Bay, Wisconsin, hearing sum up the consensus of Native educators concerning "the incredible mismatch between the programs NCLB supports, and what we know works with Native American children." As one speaker put it:

> The No Child Left Behind has facilitated a back-door standardized curriculum which amounts to teaching to the test. As a result of the law there is a backlash in Indian Country which amounts to an aggressive, forced assimilation of our Indian children into a white middle class culture. In

TABLE 12.1. Comparing Modes and Methods of Instruction

	Frequent practices in U.S. mainstream schools	Frequent Indigenous practices
Instructional organization	Curriculum determines what skills and elements are taught at each level, and for each knowledge domain or discipline. Instruction is divided into 1-year segments for each area. Learning is assumed to be accretional, with basic skills taught first, and more complex skills and applications taught later.	Curriculum is organized around life cycles (age of learners, traditional expectations) and spiritual and natural calendars: seasons and ceremonial. Teaching and learning are integrated into family or communal activities of life. Relationships, differentiated domains, individual desires, as well as family and communal connections, are considered.
Instructional focus	Teaching discrete concepts, information and skills within a subject area that are reductionist, measurable, decontextualized. Individual mastery of materials is encouraged.	Teaching focuses on holistic learning, skills, and practices in context. Connected, contextualized, collaborative learning is encouraged.
Modes of instruction	Formal teaching events, explanations, demonstrations, and discussions led by teachers. Written texts augment teaching or serve as primary means of learning. Individual work assignments are assigned for practice on skills taught, or written work is required to provide evidence of learning.	Teaching is by oral modes, demonstrations, explanations, and stories. Additional instruction is provided as needed. Private practice is preferred to public practice in some communities. In some communities, a skill is revealed only after it has been mastered.
Activity and participant structure in instructional activities	Teacher-centered and -directed activity (teacher is authority figure), and teacher determines what gets taught and how activities are structured. Activities are often leveled (i.e., students are grouped for activities by ability). Main participant structures: teacher to class; teacher to group; individual activities, and peer work groups. Evaluations are based on individual efforts and outcomes, and competition between individuals is promoted.	Informal, one-on-one instruction, beginning with participant observations in activities, in which learners take in the entire process of such activities; participation as apprentices when learners are ready. Instruction is informal and provided as needed by learners. Collaborative, mutually supportive learning is encouraged, and interdependence between learners and experts is stressed, since outcomes are seen as beneficial to community.

(cont.)

TABLE 12.1. *(cont.)*

	Frequent practices in U.S. mainstream schools	Frequent Indigenous practices
Instructional discourse	Instructional discourse in classrooms is most often structured as IRE events: Teacher initiates (I), students are called on to respond (R), and teacher evaluates (E) students' contribution.	Depending on situation and event: There are times, as in storytelling instructional events when one individual—the storyteller—holds the floor and others listen; in other situations, where the discourse is more collaborative, participants are free to contribute to the event. In general, these events are more open and flexible than classroom discourse generally is.

classrooms across the reservation there is serious conflict of cultural values. Native languages and cultures are no longer taught because Indian children are drilled all day long in reading and math in preparation for the state standardized assessments.

The standards and practices are not sound for the teaching of Indian children. Our children see and order their world very differently from most other children, and, as a result, demonstrate their knowledge in deepening and unique ways. The current push to meet the academic standards set out in the No Child Left Behind law rejects the need to provide culturally competent instruction. (quoted in NIEA, 2005, pp. 16–18)

It should be noted that whereas there is a broad consensus among leaders and educators in Indian Country concerning the need to teach Native children the languages of their communities and heritage, and to support those languages at school, there is also universal recognition of the need for Native children to have strong English language skills. But can English be taught and even emphasized at school without overwhelming the Indigenous language skills that have been taught at home or in the special programs designed to revitalize them? In the case of children who speak varieties of English such as so-called "Reservation English" or "Indian English," can support for learning the standard variety of English valued in school be provided without disparaging the English they already speak, or the sense of belonging represented by that language? As Fillmore (1996) has argued, the varieties of English spoken in many Indian and Alaskan Native communities have a special meaning for their speakers. These "Englishes" evolved to replace the languages lost to the assimilative process that took place in schools Native children were forced to attend:

> They [the children] created from the English they heard at school,
> a language that worked for them; they then added their own spin to it
> and molded it until it allowed them to express who they were, what they
> believed in, and what they valued. The language they devised allowed
> them to establish relationships with one another, and a community for
> mutual support. (Fillmore, 1996, p. 442)

While speakers of these varieties of English do have to learn the standard variety in order to make educational progress, they should not have to give up the vernaculars that enable them to communicate easily with others in their home communities, any more than Native children who speak Indigenous languages should have to give up the language of their communities for the sake of learning English. The way to avoid turning English instruction into a zero-sum game is by turning to culturally responsive language instruction where Native children are concerned. To discover what culturally responsive language instruction for Native children might comprise, I now turn to Indigenous communities in rural Alaska.

Aspects of Culturally Responsive Practices

One effort to address the needs of Native students and community by integrating Native knowledge and systems exists in rural Alaska. In Alaska's public school system, 26% of the 41% minority students are Alaska Native, and more than half of Alaska's schools are in remote villages (Klump & McNeir, 2005). Through the Alaska Rural Systemic Initiative (ARSI), rural school districts are developing programs and projects that integrate Indigenous knowledge with educational policies (Barnhardt & Kawagley, 2005). After 10 years, ARSI is showing impressive results, including an increase in student achievement scores, lower dropout rates, and an increase in college-bound students. One of ARSI's impressive programs is found in Russian Mission, a tiny village in one of the remotes parts of Alaska in the Yukon Delta National Wildlife Refuge. The majority of Russian Mission residents support themselves with subsistence activities, such as hunting and fishing. Recognizing that only a few of its young members would go on to college, village members worked with school personnel to rethink and to recreate a curriculum that was more responsive to the needs of their children and community. This included the designing a "Yup'ik model of education—which has been carried out for 10,000 years" (Klump & McNeir, 2005, p. 16) outdoors. The curriculum tapped into Native knowledge and skills, while integrating mainstream U.S. academic standards. For example, the berry-picking unit

> asks students to study and identify five types of berries, learn where these berries are traditionally harvested, and then use the berries to create traditional Yup'ik foods. The berry picking activity incorporates benchmarks from science, health, and personal/social skills standards. Students then demonstrate what they have learned through writing assignments and use technology to create a PowerPoint presentation about making traditional foods. (p. 17)

In the each of the Native examples of culturally responsive practices presented in this section, key to their successes were the partnerships between schools and the communities they served. Just as critically, the recognition and incorporation of time-honored pedagogical approaches provide Native children with rich social and communicative learning experiences that serve as precepts for English-language and literacy learning in schools. Although these home experiences and processes may not resemble the language and literacy practices of mainstream families and schools, they are nonetheless a means by which NA children begin to develop their sociolinguistic repertoires, and self- and collective identity foundations. Thus, in a deep sense, coupling Native students' first (home and community) socialization with their second socialization (school), when balanced, is key to ensuring their development into competent and compassionate bilingual and bicultural adults.

Best Practices: What Do We Know?

> So we went to school to copy, to imitate; not to exchange languages
> and ideas, and not to develop the best traits that had come out of
> unacountable experiences of hundreds and thousands of years living
> upon the continent. Our annual, all happenings of human import,
> were storied in our song and dance rituals, our history differing in
> that it was not stored in books, but in the living memory. So, while
> the white people had much to teach us, we had much to teach them,
> and what a school could have been established on that idea.
> —LUTHER STANDING BEAR (quoted in Spack, 2002, p. 107)

Contemporary research, practical teaching experiences, and thousands of years of Indigenous intellectual traditions and pedagogical practices have provided a treasure trove of best practices for teaching NA learners. In this chapter we have learned that what is taught in school, including the acquisition of English and English literacy, is only a small part of what Native children must learn if they are to be successful in and beyond their own communities. Although misunderstood (or misdirected) in the early education of NA children, we know, as Luther Standing Bear (Oglala Lakota), one of the first NA learners of English in the 19th century, alluded, that there are academic benefits of approaches that systematically *include* home and community language(s), and cultural practices as integral to the school curriculum. Research consistently concludes that teaching principles promoting the maintenance of the Native language and culture, while teaching English, are far more effective and successful in creating an optimal environment for learning that results in higher academic achievement. This involves instructional practices that do the following:

• Recognize that NA learners bring to the classroom and their learning a vast array of linguistic and cultural resources, experiences, perspectives, values, and proficiencies in both the Native/heritage language and English. If viewed as a resource, this diversity has a critical and positive impact on Native students' learning in the classroom and on their own cultural and school identities. Thus, it is important that teachers find ways to learn about their NA learners and the Native/heritage and English language and literacy practices of the home and community. Some Native communities, for instance, may not have a history of mother tongue literacy; most, however, have strong oral traditions that serve as vital avenues for language and cognitive development. These oral traditions include forms of collaborative narrative discourse, such as talk story in Hawai'i. This information can be used to create meaningful and relevant language learning and literacy practices in the classroom, such as small-group discussion, storytelling, songs, poems, and so forth, that incorporate local or other Native languages and cultures.

• Foster a classroom (and school) climate of caring, respect, and valuing of NA learners' cultures and languages. In such classrooms, children are treated respectfully and supportively. In such a school climate, teachers value students' prior knowledge, experiences, and understandings, and seek ways to bridge these aspects of instruction in their Native world with academic learning, to encourage students to speak and write in the Native language (if mother tongue literacy exists), as well as in English. A substantive and growing body of research from diverse cultural–linguistic settings, including NA language education contexts, has shown that providing students with opportunities to use and think in their mother tongue significantly contributes to their acquisition and learning of another language. This transfer can be encouraged and nurtured through prediction, analyzing and contrasting strategies through oral discourse and literacy activities. Fundamentally, through reflection in their language(s), NA learners are focusing on how meaning is expressed and validated in their own Native/heritage languages systems, as well as English.

• Incorporate culturally responsive teaching and a challenging NA curriculum to make learning meaningful and relevant for NA learners. Additionally, this additive approach to learning enriches learning for all learners, including non-NA classmates. Several examples of CRS/CBE were illustrated earlier.

We know, as well, that culturally responsive teachers are

> inherently and consistently engaged in cultural production and reproduction. The transmission of dominant cultural knowledge and norms occurs on a daily basis in U.S. schools, but the consistent message in much of the research on culturally responsive education is that successful teachers of Indigenous youth *also* work to transmit values, beliefs, knowledge, and norms that are consistent with their students' home communities. (Brayboy & Castagno, 2008, p. 37)

In an effort to demonstrate the power and possibilities to transform the practices and approaches to teaching language and literacy to NA students, I have emphasized the critical role that educators play in this transformation. Specifically, today's teachers of NA learners, in addition to knowing the fundamentals of teaching English literacy, also need to become familiar with the language backgrounds and cultural experiences of their students. If they recognize that language and culture are part and parcel of a people, they can uncover the language and literacy knowledge and practices, the literacies (Street, 1984), as well as the learning pedagogy of Indigenous families and communities. This in turn leads them to the realization that they are important mediators of language and literacies in the classroom and in other contexts. In a deeper sense, teachers can provide NA learners (including parents and others) space to articulate and celebrate their intellectual traditions, practices, and views in meaningful and powerful ways. Of course, all of this requires a close partnership between teachers and community members. On this note, I conclude with a few recommendations and best practices for educators, policymakers and teachers who are striving to understand better and improve education for Native children and youth.

Implications for Practice

• Promote understanding and acceptance of different forms of literacy and ways to achieve meaningful literacy, and recognize that NA children have relevant, valuable, and diverse language and literacy experiences that have framed their understandings in general, and their identities in particular.

• Recognize and value the various linguistic and cultural "gifts" children bring from their homes and communities to the school context. Sometimes schools tend to look at NA children in less favorable ways, because they do not exhibit mainstream educators' expectations of "good learners." These misconceptions originate from misinformation or lack of information and/or understanding about NA children and their cultures. Such misconceptions can be refuted by beginning with the belief held by many Indigenous people that "all children have gifts to contribute" to the classroom (and the world).

• Recognize that learning is a two-way street. As Luther Standing Bear advised earlier, societies have much to learn from and contribute to each other. Educators should learn about the local Native families and communities served by the school, and about their practices, goals, and challenges, if they want the children of the community to learn what the school expects them to learn.

• Recognize and understand the challenges that Indigenous communities are facing as they work toward the maintenance and renewal of their languages; become their allies with NAs by making a commitment to the maintenance of NA children's Indigenous language, if it is their primary language, or the acquisition of their heritage language, if they are learning it as a second language.

ENGAGEMENT ACTIVITIES

1. Observe Native children and community members in their own world. For example, when you are invited to attend community events, such as ceremonial dances or powwows, it would be instructive to attend and learn as much as possible about life and the concerns in Native communities. In many instances you will get a glimpse of the important home and community mediators (teachers), such as parents, grandparents, uncles, aunts, siblings, Native leaders, and others who are directly and indirectly involved in the lives of the Native children. Moreover, in this way, you can interact with NA children, and families in a language and literacy context in which they are the "experts," and are most comfortable and confident.

2. Incorporate Indigenous literacies and forms of communicating with mainstream classroom and home practices. For example, the use of multicultural and bilingual texts, music, or stories to honor the diverse cultures and language communities of which learners are a part can be a way to show that the school–family respects and honors the learners' world.

3. As a means for developing a deeper understanding of language and literacy experiences of Indigenous people, first ask yourself the questions below. Reflect on your answers before asking a Native adult the same questions (i.e., American Indian, Alaskan Native, Native Hawaiian):

- Where do you hear your local/Native language(s) being spoken today?
- Where do you see your local/Native language(s) in print today?
- Do you believe that the Native language is important for children to learn today? Why or why not?
- Should schools teach the Native language? Why or why not?
- Is reading and writing important in the teaching of Native languages? Why or why not?
- Should Indigenous children learn their Native cultures? Why or why not?
- What ideas do you have to improve the education of NA children?
- What are some ways that Native languages can be preserved or perpetuated? What role, if any, do you have in this effort?

NOTE

1. This is the process in second-language learning in which the second language replaces the learner's first language, in contrast with additive second-language learning, where a second language is added to the first. This happens in societal situations where the second language is afforded a higher status than the learner's primary language, which is not valued and supported.

REFERENCES

Adams, D. W. (1995). *Education for extinction: American Indians and the boarding school experience, 1875–1928*. Lawrence: University Press of Kansas.

American Indian Policy Center. (2002). *American Indian tribal sovereignty primer*. Retrieved July 30, 2006, from *www.airpi.org/pubs/indiansov.html*.

Arviso, M., & Holm, W. (2001). Tséhootsooídí Diné Bizaad Bíhoo'aah: A Navajo immersion program at Fort Defiance, Arizona. In L. Hinton & K. Hale (Eds), *The green book of language revitalization in practice* (pp. 203–226). San Diego: Academic Press.

Atkins, J. D. C. (1887). "Barbarous dialects should be blotted out . . . ": Excerpts from the 1887 Report of the Commissioner of Indian Affairs. Retrieved

January 29, 2008, from *ourworld.compuserve.com/homepages/Jwcrawford/ atkins.htm.*

Barnhardt, R., & Kawagley, A. O. (2005). Indigenous knowledge systems and Alaska Native ways of knowing. *Anthropology and Education Quarterly, 36*(1), 8–23.

Beaulieu, D. (2006). A survey and assessment of culturally based education programs for Native American students in the United States. *Journal of American Indian Education, 45*(2), 50–61.

Brayboy, B. M. J., & Castagno, A. (2008). Self-determination through self-education: Culturally responsive schooling for Indigenous students in the USA. *Teacher Education, 20*(1), 31–53.

Castagno, A., & Brayboy, B. M. J. (2008). Culturally responsive schooling for Indigenous youth: A review of the literature. *Review of Educational Research, 78*(4), 941–993.

Cazden, C. B. (1972). Functions of language in the classroom. In C. B. Cazden, V. P. John, & D. Hymes (Eds.), *Child language and education* (pp. 370–394). New York: Teachers College Press.

Collier, R., & Thomas, W. P. (1997). *School effectiveness for language minority students* (Resource Collection Series A, No. 9). Washington, DC: National Clearinghouse for Bilingual Education.

DeVoe, J. F., Darling-Churchill, K. E., & Snyder, T. D. (2008). *Status and trends in the education of American Indians and Alaska Natives: 2008.* Washington, DC: U.S. Department of Education, National Center for Education Statistics, Institute of Education Sciences.

Fillerup, M. (2005, September/October). Keeping up with the Yazzies: The impact of high stakes testing on Indigenous language programs. *Language Learner,* pp. 14–16.

Fillmore, L. W. (1996). What happens when languages are lost?: An essay on language assimilation and cultural identity. In D. I. Slobin, J. Gerhardt, A. Kyratzis, & J. Guo (Eds.), *Social interaction, social context, and language: Essays in honor of Susan Ervin-Tripp* (pp. 435–446). Mahwah, NJ: Erlbaum.

Fishman, J. (2001). *Can threatened languages be saved: Reversing language shift, revisited, a 21st century perspective.* Clevedon, UK: Multilingual Matters.

Gregory, E., Long, S., & Volk, D. (Eds.). (2004). *Many pathways to literacy: Young children learning with siblings, grandparents, peers and communities,* New York: Routledge/Falmer.

Grimes, B. F., & Grimes, J. E. (2000). *Ethnologue: Languages of the world, 14th edition.* Dallas, TX: SIL International.

Hermes, M. (2005). "Ma'iingan is just a misspelling of the word wolf": A case for teaching culture through language. *Anthropology and Education Quarterly, 36*(1), 43–56.

Hinton, L. (1994). *Flutes of fire: Essays on California Indian languages.* Berkeley. CA: Heyday Books.

Johnson, F. T., & Legatz, J. (2006). Tséhootsooí Diné Bióltá. *Journal of American Indian Education, 45*(2), 26–33.

Klump, J., & McNeir, G. (2005). *Culturally responsive practices for student suc-*

cess: A regional sampler. Retrieved June 17, 2009, from *www.nwrel.org/ request/2005june/textonly.html.*

Krauss, M. (1998). The condition of Native North American languages: The need for realistic assessment and action. *International Journal of the Sociology of Language, 132,* 9–12.

Lambert, W. E. (1974). Culture and language as factors in learning and education. In F. E. Aboud & R. D. Meade (Eds.), *Cultural factors in learning and education* (pp. 91–122). Bellingham: Western Washington State University.

Lambert, W. E. (1981). Bilingualism and language acquisition. In H. Winitz (Ed.), *Native language and foreign language acquisition* (pp. 9–12). New York: New York Academy of Sciences.

Lave, J., & Wenger, E. (1991). *Situated learning: Legitimate peripheral participation.* Cambridge, UK: Cambridge University Press.

Leap, W. L. (1993). *American Indian English.* Salt Lake City: University of Utah Press.

Lomawaima, K. T., & McCarty, T. L. (2006). *"To remain an Indian": Lessons in democracy from a century of Native American education.* New York: Teachers College Press.

McCarty, T. L. (2009). The impact of high-stakes accountability policies on Native American learners: Evidence from research. *Teacher Education, 20*(1), 7–29.

McCarty, T. L., Romero-Little, M. E., Zepeda, O., & Warhol, L. (2007). *The impact of Native language shift and retention on American Indian students' English language learning and school achievement: Final report submitted to the U.S. Department of Education Institute of Education Sciences* (Grant No. R305T030007). Tempe: Arizona State University.

Moran, R., Rampey, B. D., Dion, G., & Donahue, P. (2008). *National Indian Education Study 2007 Part I: Performance of American Indian and Alaska Native students at grades 4 and 8 on NAEP 2007 reading and mathematics assessments (NCES 2008-457).* Washington, DC: National Center for Education Statistics, Institute of Education Sciences, U.S. Department of Education.

National Caucus of Native American State Legislators. (2008). *Striving to achieve: Helping Native American students succeed.* Denver, CO: National Conference of State Legislatures.

National Indian Education Association. (2005). *Preliminary report on No Child Left Behind in Indian Country.* Washington, DC: National Indian Education Association. Retrieved March 5, 2008, from *www.niea.org.*

Philips, S. U. (1983). *The invisible culture: Communication in the classroom and community on the Warm Springs Indian reservation.* Long Grove, IL: Waveland Press.

Rogoff, B. (1990). *Apprenticeship in thinking: Cognitive development in social context.* Oxford, UK: Oxford University Press.

Romero, M. E. (2003). *Perpetuating the Cochiti way of life: Language socialization and language shift in a Pueblo community.* Unpublished dissertation, University of California at Berkeley.

Romero-Little, M. E., McCarty, T. L., Warhol, L., & Zepeda, O. (2007). Language policies in practice: Preliminary findings from a large-scale study of Native American language shift. *TESOL Quarterly, 41*(3), 607–618.

Silver, S., & Miller, W. R. (1997). *American Indian languages: Cultural and social contexts*. Tucson: University of Arizona Press.

Snipp, C. M. (2002). *American Indian and Alaska Native children in the 2000 Census*. Baltimore/Washington, DC: Annie E. Casey Foundation/Population Reference Bureau.

Spack, R. (2002). *America's second tongue: American Indian education and the ownership of English, 1860–1900*. Lincoln: University of Nebraska Press.

Stancavage, F. B., Mitchell, J. H., Bandeira de Mello, V., Gaertner, F. E., Spain, A. K., & Rahal, M. L. (2006). *National Indian Education Study Part II: The educational experiences of fourth- and eighth-grade American Indian and Alaska Native students*. Washington, DC: U.S. Department of Education Institute for Education Sciences. Retrieved July 22, 2009, from *nces.ed.gov/nationsreportcard/pubs/studies/2007454.asp*.

Street, B. V. (Ed.). (1984). *Literacy in theory and practice*. Cambridge, UK: Cambridge University Press.

Taosaka, S. (2002, March). Let's talk story: Nonthreatening instructional strategy encourages student participation. *Pacific Educator, 1*(1), 8–10. Retrieved July 23, 2009, from *www.prel.org/products/paced/mar02/re_.pdf*.

U.S. Census Bureau. (2002). *The American Indian and Alaska Native population: 2000* (Census 2000 Brief). Washington, DC: U.S. Department of Commerce Economics and Statistics Administration.

U.S. Office of Health and Human Services. (2009). *Native Hawaiian and other Pacific Islanders profile*. Washington, DC: U.S. Office of Health and Human Services, Office of Minority Health. Retrieved July 14, 2009, from *www.omhrc.gov/templates/browse.aspx?lvl=2&lvlID=71*.

CHAPTER 13

Supporting Literacy Learning in Families for Whom English Is an Additional Language

Jeanne R. Paratore, Barbara Krol-Sinclair, Mariela Páez, and Kristen Paratore Bock

---

This chapter will:

1. Examine and interpret evidence of best practices when supporting literacy development within families for whom English is an additional language.

2. Review theory and research that informs planning and implementation of programs and practices intended to bring parents, children, and teachers together in literacy learning.

3. Describe a program that grew out of such evidence, and share lessons learned as we planned, implemented, and evaluated these efforts.

4. Describe an example of a new model for working with families.

The importance of involving families in children's learning is supported by decades of research (e.g., Henderson & Mapp, 2002; Jeynes, 2003; Meidel & Reynolds, 1999); and the particular claim that parents make an important contribution to children's success in literacy learning has also received substantial research support (e.g., Baker, Mackler, Sonnenschein, & Serpell, 2001; Clark, 1976; de Jong & Leseman, 2001; Durkin, 1966; Sénéchal & LeFevre, 2002; Sénéchal, LeFevre, Thomas, & Daley, 1998). Evidence consistently supports a relationship between parents' own reading and interest in books, parent–child storybook reading, and parents' general interactions with their children around print and children's success in early reading. Moreover, the importance of and inclination toward parent involvement in children's learning does not vary in relation to first language, culture, ethnicity, or socioeconomic status (e.g., Fan & Chen, 2001; González-Dehass, Willems, & Holbein, 2005; Jeynes, 2003; Weiss et al., 2003).

In response to such evidence, policymakers, administrators, and teachers often turn to home–school partnerships as a solution to the learning problems experienced by children who are acquiring English as an additional language. These initiatives are often categorized as "family literacy interventions," and despite frequently being implemented in urban settings with a high incidence of immigrant families, there is often little attention to the influence language and culture may have on family literacy traditions and practices. As a result, attempts to engage parents in the types of literacy practices that are likely to support children's school success often fall far short of expectations (e.g., Vasquez, Pease-Alvarez, & Shannon, 1994).

Rationale

Our work with families is grounded in sociocultural theory that posits that literacy development and use cannot be separated from social and cultural contexts. Within this perspective, literacy is defined as more than the ability to read and write. Rather, as explained by Pérez (1998), theoreticians working within a sociocultural perspective strive "to understand the cultural context within which [individual people] have grown and developed" (p. 4) and "to understand how [people] interpret who they are in relation to others, and how [they] have learned to process, interpret, and encode their world" (p. 4). Furthermore, according to Pérez, sociocultural theoreticians hold that "there are *multiple literacies* and reading, writing, and language are embedded in and inextricable from *discourses*" (p. 23). In other words, a person's ability to demonstrate *literacy* depends on the specific purposes and contexts for literacy use (e.g., Pérez, 1998; Rogers, 2003).

In our work as family literacy researchers and practitioners, these ideas have been fundamental as we have sought to understand the ways that family routines and experiences contribute to the development and practice of literacy. In the remainder of this section, we summarize related research within two areas of focus: (1) studies of the ways parents and children use literacy in home and community settings; (2) studies that explore the outcomes of family literacy intervention programs.

What Do We Know about How Families Use Reading and Writing?

A common perception described in the literature on family literacy is that all families incorporate some form of literacy in their family and community routines (e.g., Street, 1995). Despite the apparent clarity of this claim, making sense of it in terms of the types of literacy experiences that prepare children for success in school often causes a good deal of tension among literacy researchers and practitioners. As noted by Taylor (1997):

> There are many kinds of literacy and many kinds of families, and the use of reading and writing within family contexts does not necessarily reflect the teaching of reading and writing in classroom settings. In many societies, children are encultured into the most common and evident forms of literacy in their homes and communities before they even begin school. The accumulated ways of knowing and funds of knowledge of family members—their local literacies—are complexly structured and are intricately woven into their daily lives. (p. 3)

Nonetheless, however rich and varied these "local literacies," there is ample evidence that not all literacy experiences and practices effectively or easily align with the literacy demands of early childhood classrooms and curricula (e.g., Heath, 1983; Purcell-Gates, 1995, 1996). We know, for example, that children who experience early success in American schools typically have many preschool experiences with storybook reading (e.g., Durkin, 1966; Clark, 1976; Bus, van IJzendoorn, & Pellegrini, 1995); opportunities to develop phonological awareness through the recitation of rhymes and songs, playing with and learning to name alphabet letters, and being encouraged to spell and write (e.g., Baker, Fernandez-Fein, Scher, & Williams, 1998; Sénéchal & LeFevre, 2002); exposure to sophisticated vocabulary and complex language structures (e.g., De Temple & Beals, 1991; Weizman & Snow, 2001; Wells, 1985); and opportunities to develop "world" knowledge through books and experiences about complex and interesting topics (e.g., Neuman, 2006; Tabor, Beals, & Weizman, 2001; Weizman & Snow, 2001).

Many researchers have examined the extent to which these types of experiences occur in various home contexts. In a study of the relations between home background and preschool children's literacy development, Teale (1986) described the extent and nature of children's print literacy experiences across different participant structures and domains of activity. He found substantial variation in the frequency of children's print literacy experiences: Children participated in reading and writing from five to 53 times a day and spent an average of 40 minutes to 7.5

hours a day in such activities. However, Teale also found that frequency of children's print literacy experiences could not be reliably linked to common explanations:

> Our analysis indicated that the answer does not lie in explanations which make use of variables like ethnicity, sex of the child, level of education, or family size. . . . Rather, in order to understand why there is considerable literacy activity in some homes and little in others and why the functions and uses of literacy vary across families, we must "unpackage" terms such as SES [socioeconomic scale] and ethnicity and keep at the forefront of our considerations that literacy is a social process and a cultural practice. (p. 193)

Teale's findings of differences in frequency and type of print literacy interactions are supported by numerous other studies (e.g., Purcell-Gates, 1996; Taylor & Dorsey-Gaines, 1988). Some researchers have suggested that, in immigrant families, this variation is at least in part associated with differences in parents' beliefs about their role in educating their children, often citing a disconnect between what goes on in nonmainstream homes and what goes on in school. For example, in a case study of 10 Latino families, Valdés (1996) found that parents consistently attended to children's behavior, monitoring children's activities in and out of the home setting and modeling "good" behavior. They did not, however, "engage in ritualistic activities involving reading and writing, and they did not teach their children school concepts and ideas" (p. 192). Valdés explained that these parents did not "see themselves as their children's adjunct schoolteachers or responsible for their children's cognitive development" (p. 193).

Likewise, in their study of 11 Latino families, Delgado-Gaitan and Trueba (1991) reported that parents were deeply interested in their children's school success but did not see themselves as qualified or capable of supporting their academic learning. Thus, they emphasized appropriate behavior and respect for teachers and adults. They rewarded school achievement (i.e., good grades) as a way to "seal a common understanding between the children and their parents that doing well in school was important" (p. 134).

However, findings such as these are not universal. Other studies have found that Latino parents take an active educational role in supporting the academic learning of their children. For example, Gillanders and Jiménez (2004) reported that parents demonstrated this responsibility formally through writing, completing workbooks, taking dictation, writing numbers, and writing names of family members; as well as informally through playing with words while skipping rope, finding the first letter of a word, inventing stories before going to bed, reading advertisements, playing school, and writing letters to family members in Mexico. Likewise, Vasquez et al. (1994) argued that the "discontinuity perspective" represents an oversimplification of the complex array of factors (e.g., school climate, teaching styles, individual learning rates) that influence the school success of minority youngsters, and by so doing, "draws attention away from accurate descriptions" (p. 9) of the ways minority parents support their children's school success. In their analysis of data from three separate studies of Mexican immigrants who had lived in the United States for fewer than 20 years, they found the families deeply involved in their children's learning:

> Parents see themselves as responsible and deliberate participants in their children's language learning process. Like middle-class Anglo parents, some follow their children's lead and accommodate their speech to their children. Many claim to involve their children in language teaching exchanges that focus on a particular skill and that are reminiscent of the kind of direct instruction that goes on in schools. Most also recounted how they had provided experiences and obtained materials that they felt would lead to or enhance their children's language and literacy development (e.g., providing trips to the library, purchasing crayons and paper, reading aloud to their children, engaging a third party to tutor their children). (p. 77)

Smith (2006), too, found that common home activities among Latino immigrant families were diverse: Parents supported their children's learning by offering emotional support; participating in both culture-based activities and school-like activities, and monitoring homework and written communications from school. Activities included playing games (in Spanish and English) and watching television together (often about the native country in an effort to establish/maintain some connection or familiarity with the native culture); also, parents created activities to supplement what children were doing in school or to resemble activities that parents had done as students.

Yet other researchers caution that the types of academic support parents give is not always consistent with the school's ideas about what is most effective. In a study aimed at determining the school's effects on children's home literacy experiences, Goldenberg, Reese, and Gallimore (1992) found that "repetition and lack of attention to print-meaning characterized children's [home] literacy experiences with school materials" (p. 514). The authors speculated that the reason for this behavior is that many Latino parents' knowledge of how children learn to read, often based on their own school experiences, suggests that repetition of sounds is most effective. Accordingly, in this study, if parents perceived activities as being school-related, they focused on copying and repetition. But if they perceived activities as fun for kids, they focused on content and meaning making (p. 518).

In summary, available evidence suggests no single characterization of the ways that children from immigrant families experience literacy before school entry, or the ways parents attempt to support their children's success in school. However, what does seem to be nearly universal among studies of immigrant parents is parents' belief that education is critically important, as well as parents' willingness to support their children in the ways about which they are knowledgeable.

What Are the Effects of Family Literacy Intervention Programs?

Recognition that not all children share the same *literacy heritage* (i.e., enculturation into the types of literacy practices that prepare children for success in American schools) has led to the development of programs designed to help increase children's exposure to school-like language and literacy, and to make this exposure more intentional. Several such programs begin by grounding the "new" literacy practices within parents' existing knowledge, beliefs, and cultural models (Auerbach, 1989; Paratore, 2001; Pérez, 1998; Rodríguez-Brown, 2003; Roser, 2008). As Paratore (2001) noted, "We have learned that affirming and valuing the many ways in which families share literacy are just as important as introducing new uses of literacy" (p. 13). Likewise, Roser (2008) stated, "It seems essential that the literacy practices and beliefs of nonmainstream parents be well understood as a base for socially, culturally, and historically responsive schooling" (p. 11). Throughout the literature, researchers highlight the need to focus on "authentic" activities that occur naturally as parents and children go about their daily lives (Purcell-Gates, Degener, Jacobson, & Soler, 2002). These may include direct child–parent interactions around literacy tasks or reading with or listening to children read. They may also include parents reading and writing independently, using literacy to address family and community problems, addressing child-rearing concerns through family literacy class, supporting the development of the home language and culture, and interacting with the school system (Auerbach, 1989; Paratore, 2001; Purcell-Gates, 2000; Rodríguez-Brown, 2003). In the next section, we examine research related to the outcomes of such family intervention efforts.

Overall, research on the effects of family literacy interventions is limited and largely qualitative. However, in a recent review, Sénéchal and Young (2008) identified 16 experimental or quasi-experimental studies of the effects of parent involvement in children's acquisition of early literacy. They delimited the examined studies to those that included at least five participants and either effect sizes or data that would allow the calculation of effect sizes. Based on a combined sample of 1,340 families of children in kindergarten to grade 3 and meta-analytic procedures, they found that parent involvement had a moderately large effect ($d = 0.65$). They then analyzed the focal studies according to three types of parent interventions: read to child, listen to child read books, or tutor specific literacy skills with activities. Training parents to tutor specific literacy skills (7 studies) yielded the strongest outcomes ($d = 1.15$). Training parents to listen to their children read books (6 studies) yielded moderate positive outcomes ($d = 0.52$). Parents reading to children (3 studies) yielded an effect size of only 0.18, indicating no effect. Subsequent analyses revealed no differences in effects based on children's grade levels and reading status (at or below grade level), or families' SES (working class or middle–high economic class).

As Sénéchal and Young (2008) acknowledged, their finding of no effect of parents reading to children conflicts with correlational evidence of statistically significant positive effects (Bus et al., 1995). They acknowledge that the singular focus on a reading outcome measure (and no oral language measure) may have failed to capture "indirect" effects; that is, reading aloud to children may enhance oral language and improve comprehension (e.g., Morrow & Temlock-Fields, 2004; De Temple & Snow, 2003), neither of which was captured in the outcome measure; book reading likely increases children's knowledge of literate discourses, which may facilitate reading later but may not be evident in early measures (Paris, 2005). As well, book reading in kindergarten may increase children's motivation to read, which may in time result in more frequent reading for pleasure. More frequent reading, in turn, is likely to boost reading achievement (Stanovich, 1986).

Understanding the effects of home literacy activities is also complicated by evidence that simply participating in particular literacy activities is not necessarily associated with positive outcomes. Several additional factors, including read-aloud conditions, the talk that surrounds the text, and the types of texts read may also influence outcomes. Each of these is addressed in turn.

Read-Aloud Conditions

Read-aloud conditions have consequential effects on children's language knowledge. In studies by Sénéchal and Cornell (1993), a single reading of a storybook increased children's receptive, but not expressive, vocabulary, while repeated readings and questions were more likely than a single reading to increase receptive vocabulary ($d = 1.06$; Sénéchal, 1997). Answering questions during repeated readings (three) resulted in greater word learning than a single reading or rereadings without questioning (Sénéchal, 1997).

Text Talk

One of the most consistent findings in the literature on read-alouds is the idea that reading aloud includes more than just reading the words in the text (Deckner, Adamson, & Bakeman, 2006; Hindman, Connor, Jewkes, & Morrison, 2008; Karass & Braungart-Rieker, 2005; Morrow & Temlock-Fields, 2004; Reese, Cox, Harte, & McAnally, 2003; Snow & Ninio, 1986; van Kleeck & Vander Woude, 2003). It also includes the talk that happens before, during, and after the actual reading, and this talk shapes the effects of storybook reading. For example, a collection of studies by Whitehurst and colleagues (Arnold & Whitehurst, 1994; Valdéz-Menchaca & Whitehurst, 1992; Whitehurst et al., 1994) provides evidence that when children take an active role in shared reading, and parents or teachers provide feedback through expansions, modeling, corrections, and praise, children learn substantially more words. These results hold across groups of children of different SES and with children scoring below average on language measures.

Weizman and Snow (2001) also studied effects of conditions of talk surrounding book reading. Specifically, parental utterances, characterized as instructive or helpful, "explained as much variance in word learning as did the density of sophisticated words" (p. 27). As explained by De Temple and Snow (2003), "Children can start to establish a lexical item in their memory after one or two exposures—fast-mapping—but full specification of the item's phonology, meaning, and usage may require many exposures" (p. 20). Word understanding is less likely to occur from passive encounters, and word knowledge is likely to increase from opportunities to connect and link new words to other words and concepts (Nagy & Scott, 2000).

Adding yet another layer to the complexity is evidence that effects of interactional styles during book reading are mediated by children's initial vocabulary knowledge. Children who begin with higher levels of vocabulary knowledge benefit when mothers emphasize text comprehension, whereas children who begin with lower levels of vocabulary knowledge benefit when mothers emphasize word learning (e.g., labeling and describing objects and ideas; e.g., Haden, Reese, & Fivush, 1996; Reese et al., 2003). Data from studies such as these have been used to support a conclusion that for children with larger vocabularies, conversations need not be related to the word itself, but can be more broadly related to the context in which the word appears (De Temple & Snow, 2003), whereas children with smaller vocabularies need more direct support in learning new words.

Text Type

Interactional styles are also affected by text types. In a study of effects of narrative and expository book sharing between middle- to upper-middle SES parents and their preschool children, Price, van Kleeck, and Huberty (2009) found that text genre affected the amount of talk (parents and children talked more when reading expository text); types of talk (i.e., parents uttered more extratextual utterances when reading expository text); and the linguistic complexity of talk (parents used significantly more varied vocabulary and significantly longer utterances when reading expository text). The type of adult talk prompted by different types of texts is important, because adults' use of rare and sophisticated vocabulary, interesting and unfamiliar topics, and complex syntax is positively associated with children's language development (e.g., Huttenlocher, Vasilyeva, Cymerman, & Levine, 2002; Tabors et al., 2001; Pan, Rowe, Singer, & Snow, 2005).

Of particular relevance to the immigrant population that is the focus of our work here, Roberts (2008) studied the influence of first-language and English-language home storybook reading on English-language vocabulary development when combined with English-language storybook reading in classroom settings. In a sample of 33 preschool children from low SES families and two different language groups, Roberts found that after a brief intervention (6 weeks), children who engaged in first-language storybook reading at home learned statistically significantly more target English vocabulary words than did their peers who read books at home in English. Of importance is her finding that home reading by itself had no discernable effect. Rather, it was home reading in the primary language in combination with classroom reading in English that yielded higher vocabulary scores. Roberts noted that "this pattern is compatible with the idea that children were developing primary-language vocabulary and concepts that became available in the second-language context of the classroom lessons and supported acquisition of the related English vocabulary" (p. 119).

Other researchers have explored the extent to which texts suggested by schools or family literacy programs are culturally relevant and culturally appropriate. For example, in a study of the ways in which literacy program participants from immigrant cultures acquired and used literacy information and procedures offered to them by their host culture, Janes and Kermani (2001) noted:

> The fact that storybooks were in Spanish and often beautifully illustrated was not sufficient to make them familiar: children's literature is far less available in Latin America, and therefore its conventions, tone, and intent may well be obscure to some new Latino immigrants. Furthermore, there can be a danger for educators who . . . seek out "culturally relevant" texts. Latin America is very diverse, and sometimes what is culturally relevant to one group of immigrants makes little sense to another. (p. 463)

Summarizing What We Know

Our review of related literature leads us to the following principles to guide planning and implementation of family literacy intervention efforts with immigrant families:

1. Parents' interest and disposition toward supporting their children's school success does not vary by SES, ethnicity, language, or culture.

2. Most families use literacy to get things done in the course of their daily lives. However, the particular forms of literacy may differ from those that are commonly practiced in preschool and early elementary classrooms, and these differences have consequences in children's preparation for school-based literacy. Effective family literacy interventions explore with families the existing literacy practices, and help them to add to these the types of literacy routines and events that will help children experience success in early and later literacy.

3. The particular ways parents interact with children is not a function of language or culture, so we cannot make assumptions about home practices or routines on the basis of the dominant language or culture. Instead, getting to know families, and understanding individual circumstances and practices are most effective in determining the types of interventions that are beneficial.

4. Empirical studies of the effects of various family literacy interventions indicate that training parents to tutor specific literacy skills (e.g., letter name knowledge, phonemic awareness) has the strongest effects. However, this may be a function of the timing (preschool and early primary grades) and type (code knowledge) of evaluation measures; that is, interventions that emphasize code knowledge are likely to have an effect on early literacy evaluation tasks; while those that emphasize vocabulary and language learning in the preschool years are likely

to have their greatest influence in later elementary grades, when the texts that children read are more difficult and comprehending them demands higher levels of language and conceptual knowledge.

5. Parent–child shared book reading is more likely to have positive effects on children's literacy and language learning when parents engage children in multiple readings of a text; when parents encourage children to respond to text through questioning and elaborating; and when the texts read include both narrative and expository genres (e.g., Sénéchal & Young, 2008; Bus et al., 1995; Scarborough & Dobrich, 1994).

6. Of particular importance to the instruction of English language learners, first-language shared book reading at home provides background and conceptual knowledge that seems to "bootstrap" English-language learning. Although untested, it is reasonable to assume that encouraging families to incorporate their first language into intervention activities will also support children's concept learning, and as such, provide a resource for English-language learning.

7. Children's vocabulary and language knowledge grows in relation to parents' use of language. When parents talk more and use more sophisticated words and grammatical structures, children's language knowledge varies accordingly. As well, the types of books parents share influence the types of language children hear. Expository texts typically introduce children to more rare and content-bearing words, and they also prompt more explanatory and extratextual talk about the topic.

Research to Practice: Applying the Evidence

In this section, we describe two initiatives developed with attention to these guiding principles. The first is a family literacy program that has a long history, having just celebrated its 20th year of implementation. The second is an initiative that offers promising new directions for systematically connecting literacy development at home and at school. The programs are similar in that both focus on parent–child reading as a core activity. Given the evidence that training parents in literacy skills is likely to yield more rapid, immediate effects, one might ask why creators of these two projects chose to take this approach. The answer is simple: Our reading of the evidence of code knowledge acquisition at home and at school convinces us that focused, intensive, and explicit instruction can mediate children's lack of code knowledge reasonably quickly. However, gaps in vocabulary and world knowledge are far less easily closed (e.g., Neuman, 2006; Whitehurst & Lonigan, 2002) and so we chose to focus our attention on practices that might prevent the gap from forming. We first describe the ideas and routines that frame each of the two programs, and then we articulate our shared understandings.

The Intergenerational Literacy Program

The Intergenerational Literacy Program (ILP) has served immigrant parents and their children for two decades. The program, housed in Chelsea, Massachusetts, is a collaboration of Boston University and the Chelsea Public Schools.

Chelsea, a geographically small, densely populated city adjacent to Boston, is among the most diverse communities in the Commonwealth. Increasingly, the community comprises families who speak a first language other than English, a demographic that has grown from 71% of the PreK–12 student population in 1999, to 84% in 2008.

The goals of the ILP are many: to help parents strengthen their own reading and writing in English; to introduce adult family members to the ways that their children learn in U.S. schools; to familiarize parents with the expectations that schools typically have of parents (e.g., monitoring homework, participating in parent–teacher conferences); to introduce parents and children to high-quality children's literature and effective read-aloud strategies; and to reinforce parents' efforts in reading and writing with their children at home.

In addition to adult literacy classes, the ILP offers language- and literacy-based instruction for children who are not in school while their parents are in class. Each children's classroom is staffed by a teacher and five to six tutors. In the morning, the children's classroom serves children ages 6 months to 5 years (children under age 6 months stay with their parents in class); the average age of participating children is 2 years old. In the evening, we offer two classes: one for children ages 6 months through kindergarten, and the other for children in first through sixth grades.

Participants are primarily parents (and mostly mothers), although grandparents and uncles and aunts also attend classes, if they can demonstrate that they are closely involved with at least one preschool- or school-age child. On average, adult learners have attended formal schooling for 8 years, although this ranges widely: At any given time, a few learners have had some university education, and others have never attended school before coming to the ILP.

Classes meet four mornings or three evenings per week throughout the year, for a total of 40 weeks. We expect daily attendance, and learners respond with an overall attendance rate of 80%. Classes are deliberately multilevel and multilingual, allowing us to build on the wide range of experiences, educational levels, and English proficiency levels of the adults who participate. To work effectively with such diverse groups, intensive staffing is necessary. Each class of 25 adult learners is taught by a team of two teachers and supported by three or four tutors. For the most part, morning teachers are graduate students in education at Boston University, and evening instructors teach in PreK–12 classes in the Chelsea Public Schools during the day. Most tutors are Boston University undergraduate and graduate students who receive Federal College Work–Study. (This is crucial to our ability to staff our classes fully, because the tutors' salaries are fully supported through the America Reads Program.) We also employ parent tutors (adults who were formerly learners in the classroom) when funds are available.

Since the inception of the ILP, our connections to PreK–12 instruction have been strong. In addition to ILP staff who also work within the school system, the program is located in an early learning center, which houses all public school PreK and kindergarten classes. Reports, flyers, and newsletters from the school system frequently serve as instructional material in the adults' classrooms, and ILP staff work closely with administrators in each school to ensure that we are accurately portraying school policies and routines.

Adult literacy classes are both structured and responsive to families' needs. Approximately 60% of the instructional day is devoted to supporting family literacy practices, while the other 40% focuses on adult literacy interests. Typical family literacy lesson units include strategies for monitoring and supporting children's homework (whether or not parents can understand the homework themselves); storybook reading techniques; the importance of supporting first-language use at home; strengthening home–school communication; author studies (most recently, Tomie dePaola); understanding children's performance on the state assessments; and local resources (e.g., museums and library programs). Adult literacy lesson units focus on topics such as fire safety, seeking jobs, tenant rights and responsibilities, and reading children's and young adult novels with messages that resonate with adults (recent selections include *Seedfolks* by Paul Fleischman [1997], *Sadako and the Thousand Paper Cranes* by Eleanor Coerr [1993], and *My Name Is Maria Isabel* by Alma Flor Ada [1993]).

We select instructional materials that learners are likely to encounter in their daily lives, such as children's books, parent brochures and flyers, report cards, job applications, informational bulletins, and websites. Teachers develop lesson plans for a week at a time, in response to participating parents' questions or concerns in the community. As a result, while certain topics tend to be repeated every year (e.g., planning for parent–teacher conferences), the actual information that learners read, discuss, and write about in class changes to reflect current research, policies, and specific community issues.

Although lesson content is flexible and evolving, our instructional practices and routines are more structured. To meet the many goals we have set, each day incorporates reading, writing, discussion, and opportunities for parents to work individually, in pairs or small groups, and as a whole class. On a daily basis at the beginning of class, parents complete *literacy logs*, two-sided documents in which they share the previous day's literacy activities at home, both those of personal interest and those shared with children. We explain to learners that literacy logs allow us to see how families are using literacy at home and help us focus our future lessons; they give parents a chance to reflect on ways they engage in reading and writing on a daily basis and (because a few minutes each day is devoted to sharing literacy logs) to learn about literacy activities their classmates use that they might adapt to their own families. (See Figures 13.1 and 13.2 for examples of both sides of a current learner's literacy log.)

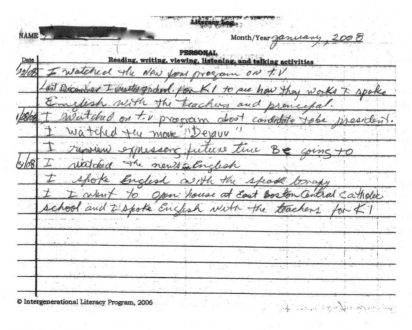

FIGURE 13.1. Literacy log detailing a parent's personal literacy activities.

FIGURE 13.2. Literacy log detailing a parent's literacy activities with her child.

Following the completion of literacy logs, the class reads the "book of the week," which is done daily in the children's classroom and helps parents to connect with the themes and stories their children are sharing. Early in the week, the two teachers introduce the day's topic by reviewing and asking about the previous day's lesson, presenting the title of the day's reading, and asking learners to discuss with tutors in small groups what they think they will be reading about and what they know about the subject. After a few minutes, the class members reconvene to share their thoughts, and the teachers introduce four or five key vocabulary words. A teacher or a tutor then reads the day's reading passage aloud, while learners follow along on their own copies. (See Figure 13.3 for a typical article read in class.) Tutors support learners who need help in tracking the print. After a short discussion comparing their predictions to what they actually read, the class members split into small, homogeneous groups to reread the passage.

How much and how closely a group works through the passage depends on the English literacy proficiency of the parents in that group; we do not expect that all learners will end up with the same knowledge at the end of the class period. A high-level literacy group may read the passage silently and reread in pairs; this is followed by a discussion of

Tips for Supporting Reading Fluency

You can help them read more quickly and accurately. Schools call this reading fluency. Your kids will call it fun!

When kids can read fluently, it's easier for them to understand what they're reading. And they read aloud easily and with expression. Needless to say, this makes reading a lot more enjoyable.

Less fluent readers read more slowly and word by word. Their attention is focused on sounding out each word; so, they pay less attention to understanding what they've read. Their comprehension and their motivation can suffer. Of course, beginning readers aren't fluent yet, but by the end of first grade, kids should be reading books at their grade level with ease and expression.

Choose the right books.

Help your child choose books that he or she can comfortably read. The "five-finger test" is a useful guideline for beginning readers. As your child reads, count the number of words he or she cannot read per page. In general, there should be five words or fewer that give him or her trouble on each page. If a book contains several pages on which you count more than five words that he or she can't read, consider reading that book to your child until he or she develops more reading skill.

Listen every day.

Once you've found a collection of books that your child can read, listen to your child read every day. Be patient—new readers often read slowly! Offer help when your child gets stuck, and always give lots of praise and encouragement.

Read it again, Sam.

Encourage your child to reread favorite books, and make it fun! Repeated readings improve children's fluency and comprehension. They also provide opportunities to practice reading with expression. Children will enjoy giving the wolf a scary growl or using a squeaky little voice for a mouse.

Read to your kids every day.

Model your own fluent reading as you read and reread books with your child. Even though your child may be able to read on his or her own, continue to find time each day to read books that are just beyond his or her reading level. The child will enjoy listening to more advanced stories, and he or she will hear a great example of fluent reading.

FIGURE 13.3. Typical adult reading selection. Adapted from *www.readingrockets.org/article/1605*.

the material presented and the learners' written reactions or personal connections to the topic. A mid-level literacy group may complete the same passage by reading a paragraph chorally and discussing key information presented, before class members move on to the next paragraph and complete a graphic organizer when they've finished. A group of parents with limited print literacy experience may focus mostly on the bold topic headings, echo reading them, talking about what they mean, and sounding out and writing key words and paraphrasing main ideas in writing.

In the last few minutes, the whole class reconvenes and each group shares thoughts and opinions on what the members have read and discussed. This serves not only to reinforce the material read and discussed, but also to build community, because all learners have the opportunity to share what they have learned from the text and how they relate it to their own lives.

What We Have Observed

Since the ILP began in 1989, we have had the opportunity to see parents and children adjust to life in Chelsea, grow, and move forward. Over the years, we have documented positive outcomes of ILP instructional practices on children's literacy learning (e.g., Paratore, 1993, 2001; Paratore et al., 2008; Paratore, Krol-Sinclair, David, & Schick, 2010) and the importance of both home literacy activities and school instructional practices in children's literacy development (Paratore, Melzi, & Krol-Sinclair, 1999). We have also demonstrated the positive effects on parent–child shared reading of training parents as classroom storybook readers (Krol-Sinclair, 1996) and of using home literacy portfolios to increase the incidence of print literacy at home and increase parents' awareness and understanding of classroom literacy (Krol-Sinclair, Hindin, Emig, & McClure, 2003; Paratore, Hindin, Krol-Sinclair, & Duran, 1999; Paratore et al., 1995). More informally, our observations have both affirmed and deepened our understanding of the immigrant parents with whom we work and their stance toward supporting their children's school success. In this regard, we have reached three important understandings.

First, we cannot claim an increase in motivation or interest in supporting children's school success as an outcome of our work with parents. Rather, like the parents represented in other published studies, at the outset, ILP parents are eager to participate in their children's learning. On program intake forms, we have consistently documented immigrant parents' high expectations for their children and interest in their children's academic progress. Often, though, they do not readily attend school activities, such as open house or parent–teacher conferences, and are hesitant to ask questions of their children's teachers. When they are "given the code," that is, when we share with them what American schools expect parents' roles to be and teach them ways to carry out those roles, most become active participants.

Second, the practice of shared storybook reading is new to most of our adult learners when they enroll in the ILP, largely because they have had little access to books in their home languages or in their home settings. Nearly all families, however, have preexisting literacy routines that support not only the completion of daily goals and routines but also their children's academic learning. For the latter, homework support and storytelling are the most common activities, but some parents choose to provide educational activities based on their own learning as children.

Third, some types of literacy are more easily incorporated than others into families' lives. From the beginning of the program, parents have shown interest and enthusiasm in learning about shared book reading. They enjoy learning about and practicing how to share children's books in their adult classes, and they readily apply at least some read-aloud strategies modeled by teachers and tutors. Our parents, too, are consistent in monitoring their children's homework and have a strong understanding of the importance placed on homework by the schools. Supporting the practice of shared writing, though, develops less readily, and requires consistent and deliberate emphasis in our adult classrooms.

In summary, over the past 20 years, the ILP's core mission and instructional rationale have not varied, and our focus has remained steadfast on supporting parents' and children's literacy development. At our recent 20th anniversary celebration, this was brought home to us by visiting former staff and learners, who immediately identified with the messages presented by current learners in their speeches. As one former teacher noted, the faces may have changed, new languages and ethnicities may have been added, but the essence of the program continues unchanged. As they have since 1989, parents who attend classes report communicating more effectively with teachers; reading more with their children at home, learning strategies for supporting their children, becoming more confident in using English in their daily lives, and feeling secure in their ability both to maintain their rich home languages and cultures, and build customs that reflect their new lives.

At the same time, the ILP is never the same from one semester to the next. The frequent turnover of teachers, tutors, and families mandates that we constantly revisit our practices, justify our approaches, and refine how we teach literacy as we learn from each new participant.

We have learned that our parents and children, as well as our staff, come to the ILP with tremendous bodies of experience and knowledge that not only help us support their development but also add to the ways we use literacy in our classrooms and our lives, and allow us to view literacy through a variety of lenses.

A Promising New Model: *Lectura en Familia*

The Kindergarten Language Study (KLS), a 5-year longitudinal research project, comprises the design, implementation, and assessment of an intervention aimed at improving the language skills of Spanish–English bilingual kindergarten students. The intervention focuses on improving vocabulary and extending discourse skills, aspects of children's oral language that research has identified as areas of weakness related to literacy outcomes for young bilingual students. Using a quasi-experimental design, the study will yield evidence of the effects the intervention in three conditions (home, classroom, and home and classroom) on children's oral language development. The hypothesis for KLS is that the condition linking Spanish-language enrichment in the home to English development in the classroom will be the most effective way to develop and sustain English reading skills for students in kindergarten throughout second grade. Schools and classrooms with a high density of Spanish–English bilingual children are participating in this intervention.

The classroom and home interventions are parallel, and the goals and target vocabulary words are the same for both interventions; the home component was developed in Spanish and the classroom component, in English. Vocabulary words were chosen because they are key to understanding the stories used, are not too difficult, can be found in the productive vocabulary of most second-grade children, and are high-frequency words in the text to which children are exposed in school.

In this chapter, we focus only on the home intervention, *Lectura en Familia*, which was informed by Project EASE (Early Access to Success in Education; Jordan, Snow, & Porsche, 2000) and two family literacy programs, the Intergenerational Literacy Program (Paratore, 2001) and Project FLAME (Rodríguez-Brown, 2003). Although *Lectura en Familia* builds on many of the ideas in these programs, it differs from them in that, by using the same children's books in both home and classroom contexts, it matches English language and literacy development in classrooms with Spanish language and literacy development at home. Parents are informed of the program through flyers, letters, phone calls, and conversations with teachers and school administrators. As an incentive to participate in workshop and data-collection activities, parents receive gift certificates for attending each workshop and for participating in the pre- and postintervention questionnaires (i.e., a total of $150 for participation in all project activities).

Intervention Materials

Both the classroom and home interventions are structured as 5-month-long units, each addressing four essential literacy domains: phonological awareness and word study, vocabulary, narrative retelling, and extended discourse. Each unit includes four or five books; three are the same titles used in the classroom, in Spanish rather than English. The additional books are culturally relevant and differ from the others in length and difficulty. The unit packet also includes (in Spanish) text summaries, prompts suggested for use with each text, and suggested activities that parents may do with their children. Each unit is introduced with a training session that explains its goals and activities. Teachers and parents attend separate sessions; teacher sessions are conducted in English and parent sessions, in Spanish.

Intervention Training Sessions

Sessions last approximately 1 hour and take place at the school site. Each session begins with a focus on the unit theme, and the session leader invites parents to share their personal knowledge, experiences, and questions about the topic. The leader then distributes the unit books and encourages parents to browse through them, asking questions and sharing their reactions to the text and illustrations. Next the session leader presents between three and six concepts pertaining to theme. Following explanation and modeling by the session leader, parents practice reading aloud, using the focal strategies to develop their children's conceptual knowledge and to guide comprehension. The session leader invites parents to comment on how these strategies are consistent with what they are already doing with their children. Each session closes with an opportunity for parents to discuss anything they noticed during the group work, to ask questions, or to voice concerns. After the initial meeting, each session begins with an informal reflection on the previous month's activities. The final session reviews the concepts introduced in the previous four sessions.

Data collection includes the administration of a short demographic questionnaire at the beginning of the intervention and a follow-up interview in the spring. Additionally, at the end of each week, parents are asked to complete and return a short evaluation of the week's activities and readings. A parent liaison calls each family every 2 weeks to offer assistance with these evaluations. In addition, following each training session, session leaders record detailed observations of parents' conversation and engagement at each workshop.

What We Have Observed

We have now completed the first year of a 5-year initiative, and our observations allow us to draw three preliminary conclusions about this work and the likelihood that it will make a difference in the literacy learning of the children in these families.

First, parents eagerly seek support to use Spanish at home. Providing parents first-language resources, Spanish, in this case, allows them to draw on their rich language knowledge to continue to introduce children to complex and sophisticated language structures that are likely to transfer to and support their children's English-language learning. Additionally, by deliberately connecting home texts and activities to classroom learning, we introduce or expand parents' knowledge of "classroom literacy" (Corno, 1989), making it more likely that parents will initiate related and supportive activities on their own. Moreover, because parents may bring a different store of knowledge to the focal topic, children stand to learn more about the topic than they may have learned from the teacher and classroom resources alone.

Second, preliminary evidence indicates that parents have increased the frequency of parent–child shared reading. Preintervention questionnaires indicate that 75% of all participating parents read to their children at least once a week in English, and 45% read to their children at least once a week in Spanish. Data from weekly evaluations show that 100% of participants read in Spanish with their children at least once a week. Additionally, these evaluations indicate that all parents who participated in the workshops read the same books multiple times (number of readings ranges from one to seven). As noted previously, rereadings of the same book increases the likelihood that children will improve their vocabulary and language knowledge.

Third, the school appreciates and supports the intervention. The principals and teachers demonstrate enthusiasm about the collaboration by encouraging children to share and talk about home reading and writing, and display the products of literacy activities done at home. Additionally, at one site, the principal attends the workshops.

In summary, early anecdotal evidence indicates that supporting parents and children in the use of Spanish at home is an effective strategy for encouraging home literacy practices. We look forward to the examination of more formal data to test the effectiveness of these informal observations and to expand our understanding of *Lectura en Familia* on students' oral language skills in English and Spanish.

Reflections and Future Directions

Taken together, both the ILP and *Lectura en Familia* demonstrate the importance of providing support for families where they are, rather than where we, as educators, think they should be. Both programs offer additive approaches that build on parents' and children's knowledge and experiences in their first language, while providing scaffolding that increases their access to specific and critical school literacies. In both settings, parents are enthusiastic in supporting their children's learning when they have the opportunity to become familiar with effective and easily adapted strategies. The emphasis of both ILP and *Lectura en Familia* on reading at home allows families to adapt effective and appropriate learning tools in ways that can be easily integrated into home routines. Parents' collaboration with the school communities legitimizes their beliefs that they can and should be active partners in their children's education, and they are able to feel confident about their ability to facilitate their children's literacy development at home. In short, we believe that programs such as these are not the answer to setting children who typically experience high rates of school failure on a path to success, but, combined with excellent classroom instruction, such programs may be part of the answer.

Both the ILP and *Lectura en Familia* are ongoing initiatives that continue to evolve. As we reflect on our actions and lessons learned to this point, we remain committed to strengthening home–school activities as two-way partnerships. Our work clearly indicates that parents have multiple ways of supporting their children's learning, long before children enter school, and that home literacy and language can complement and strengthen school learning. Moving forward, we hope to facilitate parents' communication with schools in ways that help teachers understand and apply lessons from children's literate lives at home, while continuing to strengthen parents' ability to foster children's school learning. Identifying strategies and materials that can be adapted easily for both home and school use (e.g., books read in English at school and in the first language at home) can help build a seamless connection between home and school, and provide children with increased understanding of the roles literacy can play in their daily lives.

ENGAGEMENT ACTIVITIES

1. *Examining parent–child storybook reading: Lectura en Familia* emphasizes the importance of extending school reading by providing classroom books in children's first languages for reading at home. To examine the effects of such an intervention for the children you teach, start by selecting just a few children whose parents you think would be willing to participate. Obtain copies of books and stories read in class (or even stories that are similar) in the first languages of students, and invite two or three parents to meet with you. During the meeting, explain why you have chosen these books for at-home reading, and describe the ways you would like them to share the books with their youngsters. Over the course of the next 3 or 4 weeks, send home one or two books a week for at-home reading. At the end of each week, interview parents and children about their at-home reading experiences, asking them if they enjoyed it, what they learned from it, and so forth. You might also observe the children in the classroom. When they return to stories that were shared at home, do they read them with greater interest, understanding, and fluency? If you find positive outcomes, consider how you might expand this work for a longer period of time and include more families. If you find limited evidence of positive effects, try to determine what the stumbling blocks might have been: Were the books too difficult for parents to read on their own? Were the books insufficiently interesting to engage both parents and children and motivate them to read together? Were parents and children unable to establish a consistent time for at-home reading? Can you think of ways to help overcome or diminish the challenges that you observed?

2. *Deepening understanding of ways to build home–school congruence*: As explained in this chapter, even among parents schooled in the United States, there is sometimes a disconnection between the ways they learned in school and the classroom instruction in which their children engage. For parents who have attended school in different countries and speak languages other than English, the knowledge gap is much wider. To deepen your understanding of the ways such differences can influence parents' interactions with their children about school and learning, interview the parents of children in your classroom about their own school experiences and their perceptions of their roles and responsibilities in their children's schooling. Based on what you learn, plan a series of workshops that will give parents a hands-on look at what their children are doing in school. Provide ample time during the workshop for discussion, giving parents a chance to compare their experiences to those of their children, to ask questions, and to describe the types of tasks and activities that will both "fit in" with the families' daily routines and activities and also support children's school learning.

3. *Learning about home literacies*: One of the principles drawn from research and theory is that in almost all families, parents and children use various forms of literacy to accomplish daily tasks and activities. However, it can be difficult for

us, as teachers, to understand precisely what parents and children do together at home. One way that you might try to gain a better understanding of the ways individual families use literacy at home is by inviting parents and children to assemble home literacy portfolios that provide examples of the ways they read and write at home. To do so, try these steps: Introduce portfolios in the class- room by giving children a pocket folder or accordion file, and encourage them to personalize it. Reinforce the value of these portfolios by encouraging parents to become co-investigators into their children's literacy learning by collecting examples of the ways their children read and write at home. Then, refer to the portfolios on a frequent basis in class and at pick-up/drop-off time, and invite parents to share their children's home portfolios at parent–teacher conferences. As you view the samples in the family literacy portfolio, consider the similarities and differences in the ways children use literacy at home and at school. Does the family literacy profile confirm what you already know, or does it suggest strengths and needs different from those that are evident in the child's reading and writing at school? How can you use the information in the family literacy portfolio to make meaningful connections between parents' family and school literacy connections?

REFERENCES

Ada, A. F. (1993). *My name is Maria Isabel*. New York: Aladdin Paperbacks.

Arnold, D. S., & Whitehurst, G. J. (1994). Accelerating language development through picture book reading: A summary of dialogic reading and its effects. In D. K. Dickinson (Ed.), *Bridges to literacy: Children, families, and schools* (pp. 103–128). Cambridge, MA: Blackwell.

Auerbach, E. R. (1989). Toward a socio-cultural approach to family literacy. *Harvard Educational Review, 59*, 165–181.

Baker, L., Fernandez-Fein, S., Scher, D., & Williams, H. (1998). Home experi- ences related to the development of word recognition. In J. L. Metsala & L. C. Ehri (Eds.), *Word recognition in beginning literacy* (pp. 263–288). Mahwah, NJ: Erlbaum.

Baker, L., Mackler, K., Sonnenschein, S., & Serpell, R. (2001). Parents' interac- tions with their first-grade children during storybook reading and rela- tions with subsequent home reading activity and reading achievement. *Journal of School Psychology, 39*, 415–438.

Bus, A., van IJzendoorn, M. H., & Pellegrini, A. (1995). Joint book reading makes for success in learning to read: A meta-analysis in intergenerational transmission of literacy. *Review of Educational Research, 65*(1), 1–21.

Clark, M. (1976). *Young fluent readers: What they can teach us*. London: Heine- mann.

Coerr, E. (1993). *Sadako and the thousand paper cranes*. New York: Putnam.

Corno, L. (1989). What it means to be literate about classrooms. In D. Bloome (Ed.), *Classrooms and literacy* (pp. 29–52). Norwood, NJ: Ablex.

Deckner, D., F., Adamson, L. B., & Bakeman, R. (2006). Child and maternal contributions to shared reading: Effects on language and literacy development. *Applied Developmental Psychology, 27*, 31–41.

de Jong, P. F., & Leseman, P. M. (2001). Lasting effects of home literacy on reading achievement in school. *Journal of School Psychology, 39*(5), 389–414.

Delgado-Gaitan, C., & Trueba, H. (1991). *Crossing cultural borders: Education for immigrant families in America.* New York: Falmer Press.

De Temple, J. M., & Beals, D. E. (1991). Family talk: Sources of support for the development of decontextualized skills. *Journal of Research in Childhood Education, 6*, 11–19.

De Temple, J. M., & Snow, C. E. (2003). Learning words from books. In A. van Kleeck, S. A. Stahl & E. B. Bauer (Eds.), *On reading books to children: Parents and teachers* (pp. 16–36). Mahwah, NJ: Erlbaum.

Durkin, D. (1966). *Children who read early.* New York: Teachers College Press.

Fan, X., & Chen, M. (2001). Parental involvement and students' academic achievement: A meta-analylsis. *Educaptional Psychology Review, 13*(1), 1–22.

Fleischman, P. (1997). *Seedfolks.* New York: HarperCollins.

Gillanders, C., & Jiménez, R. T. (2004). Reaching for success: A close-up of Mexican immigrant parents in the USA who foster literacy success for their kindergarten children. *Journal of Early Childhood Literacy, 4*, 243–267.

Goldenberg, C., Reese, L., & Gallimore, R. (1992). Effects of literacy materials from school on Latino children's home experiences and early reading achievement. *American Journal of Education, 100*, 497–536.

González-DeHass, A. R., Willems, P. P., & Doan Holbein, M. F. (2005). Examining the relationship between parental involvement and student motivation. *Educational Psychology Review, 17*(2), 450–470.

Haden, C. A., Reese, E., & Fivush, R. (1996). Mothers' extratextual comments during storybook reading: Stylistic differences over time and across texts. *Discourse Processes, 21*, 135–169.

Heath, S. B. (1983). *Ways with words: Language, life, and work in communities and classrooms.* Cambridge, UK: Cambridge University Press.

Henderson, A. T., & Mapp, K. L. (2002). *A new wave of evidence: The impact of family, school, community connections on student achievement.* Austin, TX: Southwest Educational Development Laboratory.

Hindman, A. H., Connor, C. M., Jewkes, A. M., & Morrison, F. J. (2008). Untangling the effects of shared book reading: Multiple factors and their associations with preschool literacy outcomes. *Early Childhood Research Quarterly. 23*, 330–350.

Huttenlocher, J., Vasilyeva, M., Cymerman, E., & Levine, S. (2002). Language input and child syntax. *Cognitive Psychology, 45*, 337–375.

Janes, H., & Kermani, H. (2001). Caregivers' story reading to young children in family literacy programs: Pleasure or punishment? *Journal of Adolescent and Adult Literacy, 44*(5), 458–466.

Jeynes, W. H. (2003). A meta-analysis: The effects of parental involvement on minority children's academic achievement. *Education and Urban Society, 35*(2), 202–218.

Jordan, G. E., Snow, C. E. & Porsche, M. V. (2000). Project EASE: The effect of a family literacy project on kindergarten students' early literacy skills. *Reading Research Quarterly, 35,* 524–546.

Karass, J., & Braungart-Rieker, J. M. (2005). Effects of shared parent–infant book reading on early language acquisition. *Applied Developmental Psychology, 26,* 133–148.

Krol-Sinclair, B. (1996). Connecting home and school literacies: Immigrant parents with limited formal education as classroom storybook readers. In K. A. Hinchman, D. J. Leu, & C. K. Kinzer (Eds.), *Literacies for the 21st century: Research and practice* (pp. 270–283). Chicago: National Reading Conference.

Krol-Sinclair, B., Hindin, A., Emig, J., & McClure, K. (2003). Using family literacy portfolios as a context for parent–teacher communication. In A. DeBruin-Barecki & B. Krol-Sinclair (Eds.), *Family literacy: From theory to practice* (pp. 266–281). Newark, DE: International Reading Association.

Meidel, W. T., & Reynolds, A. J. (1999). Parent involvement in early intervention for disadvantaged children: Does it matter? *Journal of School Psychology, 37,* 379–402.

Morrow, L. M., & Temlock-Fields, J. (2004). Use of literature in the home and at school. In B. H. Wasik (Ed.), *Handbook of family literacy* (pp. 83–100). Mahwah, NJ: Erlbaum.

Nagy, W. E., & Scott, J. A. (2000). Vocabulary processes. In M. L. Kamil, P. B. Mosenthal, P. D. Pearson, & R. Barr (Eds.), *Handbook of reading research* (Vol. III, pp. 269–284). Mahwah, NJ: Erlbaum.

Neuman, S. B. (2006). The knowledge gap. In D. K. Dickinson & S. B. Neuman (Eds.), *Handbook of early literacy* (Vol. 2, pp. 29–40). New York: Guilford Press.

Pan, B., Rowe, M., Singer, J., & Snow, C. (2005). Maternal correlates of growth in toddler vocabulary production in low-income families. *Child Development, 76*(4), 763–782.

Paratore, J. (1993). Influence of an intergenerational approach to literacy on the practice of literacy of parents and their children. In C. Kinzer & D. Leu (Eds.), *Examining central issues in literacy, research, theory, and practice: Forty-second yearbook of the National Reading Conference* (pp. 83–91). Chicago: National Reading Conference.

Paratore, J. R. (2001). *Opening doors, opening opportunities: Family literacy in an urban community.* Needham Heights, MA: Allyn & Bacon.

Paratore, J. R., Hindin, A., Krol-Sinclair, B., & Duran, P. (1999). Examining parent–teacher discourse during conferences based on home literacy portfolios. *Education and Urban Society, 32,* 58–82.

Paratore, J. R., Homza, A., Krol-Sinclair, B., Lewis-Barrow, T., Melzi, G., Stergis, R. et al. (1995). Shifting boundaries in home–school responsibilities: Involving immigrant parents in the construction of literacy portfolios. *Research in the Teaching of English, 29,* 367–389.

Paratore, J. R., Krol-Sinclair, B., Cassano, C., Leighton, C., O'Brien, L., Smock, J., et al. (2008, December). *Effects of a family literacy intervention on the vocabulary and literacy growth of children in prekindergarten to grade two.*

Paper presented at the annual meeting of National Reading Conference, Orlando, FL.

Paratore, J. R., Krol-Sinclair, B., David, B., & Schick, A. (2010). Reading the next chapter in family literacy: Long-term effects on children's academic experiences. In D. Fisher & K. Dunsmore (Eds.), *Family literacy* (pp. 265–288). Newark, DE: International Reading Association.

Paratore, J. R., Melzi, G., & Krol-Sinclair, B. (1999). *What should we expect of family literacy?: Home and school literacy experiences of Latino children whose parents participate in an intergenerational literacy project.* Newark, DE: International Reading Association.

Paris, S. G. (2005). Reinterpreting the development of reading skills. *Reading Research Quarterly, 40*(2), 184–202.

Pérez, B. (1998). *Sociocultural contexts of language and literacy.* Mahwah, NJ: Erlbaum.

Price, L. H., van Kleeck, A., & Huberty, C. J. (2009). Talk during book sharing between parents and preschool children: A comparison between storybook and expository book conditions. *Reading Research Quarterly, 44*(2), 171–194.

Purcell-Gates, V. (1995). *Other people's words: The cycle of illiteracy.* Cambridge, MA: Harvard University Press.

Purcell-Gates, V. (1996). Stories, coupons, and the *TV Guide*: Relationships between home literacy experiences and emergent literacy knowledge *Reading Research Quarterly, 31*(4), 406–428.

Purcell-Gates, V. (2000). Family literacy as the site for emerging knowledge of written language. In B. H. Wasik (Ed.), *Handbook of family literacy* (pp. 101–116). Mahwah, NJ: Erlbaum.

Purcell-Gates, V., Degener, S. C., Jacobson, E., & Soler, M. (2002). Impact of authentic adult literacy instruction on adult literacy practices. *Research Reading Quarterly, 37*, 70–92.

Reese, E., Cox, A., Harte, D., & McAnally, H. (2003). Diversity in adults' styles of reading books to children. In A. van Kleeck, S. Stahl, & E. B. Bauer (Eds.), *On reading books to children* (pp. 37–57). Mahwah, NJ: Erlbaum.

Roberts, T. A. (2008). Home storybook reading in primary or second language with preschool children: Evidence of equal effectiveness for second-language vocabulary acquisition. *Reading Research Quarterly, 43*, 103–130.

Rodríguez-Brown, F. V. (2003). Family literacy in English language learning communities: Issues related to program development, implementation, and practice. In A. Debruin-Parecki & B. Krol-Sinclair (Eds.), *Family literacy: From theory to practice* (pp. 126–146). Washington, DC: International Reading Association.

Rogers, R. (2003). *A critical discourse analysis of family literacy practices: Power in and out of print.* Mahwah, NJ: Erlbaum.

Roser, N. (2008, October). *Talking over books at home and in schools.* Paper presented at the Ball Foundation Family Literacy Symposium, Chicago, IL.

Scarborough, H. S., & Dobrich, W. (1994). On the efficacy of reading to preschoolers. *Developmental Review, 14*, 245–302.

Sénéchal, M. (1997). The differential effect of storybook reading on preschoolers' acquisition of expressive and receptive vocabulary. *Journal of Child Language, 24*, 123–138.

Sénéchal, M., & Cornell, E. H. (1993). Vocabulary acquisition through shared reading experiences. *Reading Research Quarterly, 28*, 360–374.

Sénéchal, M., & LeFevre, J. A. (2002). Parental involvement in the development of children's reading skill: A five-year longitudinal study. *Child Development, 73*, 445–460.

Sénéchal, M., LeFevre, J. A., Thomas, E. M., & Daley, K. E. (1998). Differential effects of home literacy experiences on the development of oral and written language. *Reading Research Quarterly, 33*, 96–116.

Sénéchal, M., & Young, L. (2008). The effect of family literacy interventions on children's acquisition of reading from kindergarten to grade 3: A meta-analytic review. *Review of Educational Research, 78*(4), 880–907.

Smith, J. (2006). *Immigrant Latino parents' perspective of parent engagement.* Unpublished doctoral dissertation, Boston College, Chestnut Hill, MA.

Snow, C. E., & Ninio, A. (1986). The contracts of literacy: What children learn from learning to read books. In W. H. Teale & E. Sulzby (Eds.), *Emergent literacy: Writing and reading* (pp. 116–138). Norwood, NJ: Ablex.

Stanovich, K. (1986). Matthew effects in reading: Some consequences of individual differences in the acquisition of literacy. *Reading Research Quarterly, 21*, 360–407.

Street, B. (1995). *Social literacies: Critical approaches to literacy development.* New York: Longman.

Tabors, P. O., Beals, D. E., & Weizman, Z. O. (2001). You know what oxygen is: Learning new words at home. In D. K. Dickinson & P. O. Tabors (Eds.), *Beginning literacy with language: Young children learning at home and at school* (pp. 93–110). Baltimore: Brookes.

Taylor, D. (1997). *Many families, many literacies.* Portsmouth, NH: Heinemann.

Taylor, D., & Dorsey-Gaines, C. (1988). *Growing up literate: Learning from inner-city families.* Portsmouth, NH: Heinemann.

Teale, W. H. (1986). Home background and young children's literacy development. In W. H. Teale & E. Sulzby (Eds.), *Emergent literacy: Writing and reading* (pp. 173–207). Norwood, NJ: Ablex.

Valdés, G. (1996). Con respeto: *Bridging the differences between culturally diverse families and schools.* New York: Teachers College Press.

Valdéz-Menchaca, M. C., & Whitehurst, G. J. (1992). Accelerating language development through picture book reading: A systematic extension to Mexican day care. *Developmental Psychology, 28*, 1106–1114.

van Kleeck, A., & Vander Woude, J. (2003). Book sharing with preschoolers with language delays. In A. van Kleek, S. Stahl, & E. B. Bauer (Eds.), *On reading books to children* (pp. 58–92). Mahwah, NJ: Erlbaum.

Vasquez, O. A., Pease-Alvarez, L., & Shannon, S. M. (1994). *Pushing boundaries: Language and culture in a Mexicano community.* Cambridge, UK: Cambridge University Press.

Weiss, H. B., Mayer, E., Kreider, H., Vaughan, M., Dearing, E., Hencke, R., et al. (2003). Making it work: Low-income working mothers' involvement in their children's education. *American Educational Research Journal, 40,* 879–901.

Weizman, Z. O., & Snow, C. E. (2001). Lexical input as related to children's vocabulary acquisition: Effects of sophisticated exposure and support for meaning. *Developmental Psychology, 37*(2), 265–279.

Wells, G. (1985). *The meaning makers: Children learning language and using language to learn.* Portsmouth, NH: Heinemann.

Whitehurst, G. J., Arnold, D. S., Epstein, J. N., Angell, A. L., Smith, M., & Fischel, J. F. (1994). A picture book reading intervention in day care and home for children from low-income families. *Developmental Psychology, 30,* 679–689.

Whitehurst, G. J., & Lonigan, C. J. (2002). Emergent literacy: Development from prereaders to readers. In S. B. Neuman & D. K. Dickinson (Eds.), *Handbook of early literacy research* (Vol. 1, pp. 11–29). New York: Guilford Press.

CHAPTER 14

"It's Just Like Telling Them They Will Never Be Scientists"

A White Teacher's Journey Transforming Linguistic and Racial Categories

Cynthia H. Brock, Julie L. Pennington, Eleni Oikonomidoy, and Dianna R. Townsend

> We see what we believe. To challenge my own mental paradigm,
> I need to change my perception. . . . When I believe that
> my students are future scholars, doctors, dentists, lawyers,
> [scientists]—whatever their hearts and minds desire, then I will
> see it. I will see them. When I believe that they can do anything,
> then I will see it. . . . It all has to do with expectations.
> —HELEN (July 22, 2005)

This chapter will:

1. Present one White teacher's (Helen's) journey as she learned to engage in best practices for educating her children from nondominant backgrounds.

2. Present questions to ponder as you read about Helen's conceptual growth regarding best practices for educating children from nondominant backgrounds.

3. Provide a theoretical framework for understanding Helen's conceptual growth regarding best practices for educating children from nondominant backgrounds.

---

4. Describe what others have learned in the process of exploring best practices for working with children from nondominant backgrounds.

5. Propose a mind-set and a series of questions to ponder as you strive to enact best practices for working with children from nondominant backgrounds.

Helen is a fourth-grade teacher at an inner-city school that serves primarily children from nondominant backgrounds.[1] At the time Helen made the opening comment, she had been a teacher for a year and was taking the first in a three-course professional development sequence that focused on racial and linguistic diversity. Like almost 90% of the teachers in American public schools, Helen is a White, monolingual, English-speaking woman (Wiggins & Follo, 1999). Also, similar to the experiences of her White colleagues, many of the children in Helen's classroom are from nondominant backgrounds. Nationally, there are large and growing numbers of children from nondominant backgrounds in U.S. schools (August & Hakuta, 1997). As one example, it is projected that between 2000 and 2020, the Hispanic population in the United States will increase by 47% (Santa Ana, 2004). Clearly, there is a significant difference between teachers teaching in U.S. schools and the children attending U.S. schools (Riegelhaupt & Carresco, 2000). Do these differences matter, however? Scholars (e.g., Marx, 2004; Marx & Pennington, 2003) assert that White teachers—at all educational levels—must attend carefully and thoughtfully to issues of racial and linguistic diversity and the ways White teachers' perceptions of race and language can impact their work with children from nondominant backgrounds. One important way that White educators can seek to teach children from nondominant backgrounds more effectively is to explore their own racial and linguistic "situatedness"—including the ways they categorize themselves and others—in their work as teachers (Cross, 2003; McIntyre, 1997; Ndura, 2004).

The purpose of this chapter is to explore Helen's learning about racial and linguistic diversity during the first course in a three-course professional development sequence as she examines her own racial and linguistic identity and how her understanding of her own racial and linguistic identity impacts her work with students in her classroom. In particular, we explore Helen's learning with respect to the ways she categorizes herself and others linguistically and racially. This chapter is framed in the following manner: First, we explicate the theoretical framework on which we draw in our work to explore Helen's learning, and we discuss related studies that have explored issues of diversity and teacher learning. Second, we discuss the methods we used to study Helen's learning. Third, we present our findings. Finally, we discuss the implications and significance of this work for our broader field of literacy.

Exploring Helen's Understanding of Best Practices: A Theoretical Foundation

We begin this section of our chapter with a thought experiment. Please engage with us in this activity before reading on. We use this thought experiment to make our conceptual focus for this chapter—and our reasons for this conceptual focus—clearer to you. Look at the items in Figure 14.1. How would you categorize them? Why?

We speculate that you may have categorized these items in one of the two following ways. First, you may have put the fish and the whale together, because both fish and whales live in water. Second, you may have put the mouse the whale together, because both the whale and mouse are mammals.[2] Several questions emerge for us. First, did you find the activity of categorizing items an odd request? (We speculate that you did not, although you may have found *what* we asked you to categorize odd!) Second, how and why did you learn to categorize the items as you did? Third, what does this thought experiment have to do with the focus of our chapter? We address each of these questions in turn.

First, we conjecture that you did not find the activity of categorizing items odd, because categorization is one of the main ways that we, as humans, make sense of our experiences (Lakoff, 1987). For example, you may recall learning in high school biology that species of organisms are classified according to the following categories: **k**ingdom, **p**hylum, **c**lass, **o**rder, **f**amily, **g**enus, **s**pecies. (In fact, you may remember your high school biology teacher teaching you a mnemonic device, such as

FIGURE 14.1. A fish, a whale, and a mouse.

"King Philip came over from Geneva, Switzerland," as a way to remember the first letters in the classification scheme for categorizing species of organisms.) Thus, conceptual systems—like the conceptual system to classify the species of organisms—are organized in terms of categories. While the categorization of species of organisms is something we must learn, most "categorization is automatic and unconscious. . . . In moving about the world, we automatically categorize people, animals, and physical objects, both natural and man-made" (Lakoff, 1987, p. 6).

Second, how and why do we learn to engage in the process of categorization? Our example from high school biology illustrates that the categorization used in some conceptual systems is taught and learned explicitly. However, we wish to reiterate that most of the categorization we do in our lives is done automatically and unconsciously (Lakoff, 1987). Thus, we are socialized to categorize in particular ways, and this socialization process is mostly "below the radar" of conscious awareness. Why might this matter? If most of the categorization in which we, as humans, engage is done automatically and unconsciously, then most of the categorization in which we engage is not subject to scrutiny. If categorization is a primary means of thinking, and "our behavior is dependent on how we think" (Lakoff, 1987, p. 337), then many of our behaviors may not be subjected to sufficient scrutiny. This matters most, of course, if our behaviors negatively impact the lives of others.

This brings us to our third question: What does all this have to do with our chapter? As mentioned earlier, we, as humans, categorize many things—including people. If much of our categorization of people is unconscious and not subject to scrutiny, and if our behavior is dependent on how we think, then we may be categorizing people, and acting on those categories, in ways that are problematic. Studies have long shown that categorizing children in negative ways impacts negatively their learning opportunities (e.g., Rist, 1970; Oakes, 1985). Returning to the focus of our chapter, then, if White, monolingual, English-speaking teachers are categorizing their children from nondominant backgrounds in nonproductive ways, and these categorization schemes are not subject to scrutiny, then their teaching actions are likely to be nonproductive, too.

In this chapter, we explore Helen's conceptual shifts across time with respect to how she categorized herself as a White, monolingual, English-speaking teacher, and how she categorized the children, teachers, and families with whom she worked. Just as categorization can be acquired unconsciously as we are socialized in our own sociocultural communities, it can also be learned explicitly (e.g., with the classification of species of organisms in biology we discussed earlier). An explicit focus of the course in which Helen enrolled was a careful examination of racial and linguistic diversity. In the following section we explore what others have learned from their work as they, too, have studied teachers' experiences in learning about racial and linguistic diversity.

Evidence-Based Best Practices

In this section, we explore what several scholars have learned about best practices for pre- and inservice teachers who seek to learn to work with students from nondominant backgrounds. We end this section with a list of ideas derived from this literature. Gallego (2001) asserts that in order for teachers from the dominant culture really to understand the children from nondominant backgrounds that they serve in their classrooms, they must do more than read information about different cultures and ethnicities. Somehow, either vicariously through narratives (e.g., Florio-Ruane, Raphael, Glazier, McVee, & Wallace, 1997) or through lived experiences, White teachers must experience social and cultural differences and reflect carefully and thoughtfully upon those experiences. Gallego (2001) argues that meaningful experiences, and careful and thoughtful reflection on those meaningful experiences, can lead to a transformation and growth in understanding about racial and linguistic diversity.

Merryfield (2000) studied 80 educators who engaged in long-term cultural immersion outside of the United States. Many educators involved in her study told her that they often, "went away and made sense of home" (p. 435). Informants in Merryfield's study noted that their lives were forever changed as a result of the powerful racial, cultural, and linguistic experiences they had outside of the United States. As one example, many informants saw for the first time what it is like to be perceived as "the Other" (p. 434). Merryfield (p. 440) was careful to point out, however, that it was not the cross-cultural experiences alone that led to informants' greater understanding of racial, cultural, and linguistic awareness; rather, informants who made the greatest gains in their understanding of racial, cultural, and linguistic diversity reflected deeply about the meaning of their experiences cross-culturally. In essence, then, understanding others' perspectives and life experiences does not happen without deep conceptual reflection and a disposition of *empathy* (i.e., an inclination to strive to understand others' lives, experiences, and worldviews).

Clark and Medina (2000) studied a graduate-level course designed to explore key issues about literacy and multiculturalism. A central goal of the study was to examine how students' understandings of literacy and multiculturalism were mediated through acts of reading and writing literacy narratives. The researchers found that the process of becoming sensitive and aware racially, linguistically, and culturally was a very personal process for class participants. Most class participants engaged in personal questioning of their own beliefs, and many participants began constructing new identities as multicultural educators. Clark and Medina argued that educators must examine closely their personal ideologies; moreover, becoming multiculturally aware and sensitive requires an intense revision of one's own identity in relation to racial, linguistic, and cultural experiences.

Our review of the work of other scholars (e.g., Clark & Medina, 2001; Merryfield, 2000) illustrates the positive benefits that can accrue when White teachers engage in powerful, identity-changing experiences with respect to racial and linguistic diversity—whether they are vicarious experiences (e.g., Clark & Medina, 2001) or actual cross-cultural experiences in other countries, as in the work of Merryfield (2000). We conclude this section by listing several ideas/experiences in which White teachers can engage as they learn to work more effectively with children from nondominant backgrounds:

- Long-term cultural experiences and deep reflection on those experiences can help White teachers learn to work effectively with children from nondominant backgrounds.
- White teachers can become more sensitive and aware racially, culturally, and linguistically by reading and writing narratives that help them to reflect deeply and thoughtfully on the lives of others from different cultural, linguistic, and racial backgrounds.

Setting the Context
for Exploring Helen's Understanding of Best Practices

Helen

Helen describes herself as a White, monolingual, English-speaking woman. She was born and raised in Reno, Nevada. She attended public schools and graduated from high school in Reno. After high school, Helen attended the University of Nevada, Reno. She majored in teacher education as an undergraduate. Immediately after earning her undergraduate degree, Helen got a position teaching fourth grade at a local elementary school. After earning her undergraduate degree, Helen also started taking classes to work toward her master's degree in Literacy Studies without delay. Helen had been teaching for a year when she took this summer course. She was teaching at a year-round school, so the beginning of her second year started in June 2005. Helen was in her early 20s during the summer course.

The Summer Course in Which Helen Enrolled

The summer graduate seminar in which Helen enrolled was geared toward teachers who wanted to explore issues pertaining to literacy instruction and diversity. This course was the first in a three-course professional development sequence sponsored by our local school district. (The three-course sequence was called the Multiliteracies Teacher Institute Program—M-TIP, for short.) The primary emphasis of the first course was the exploration and implementation of current conceptions of quality literacy instruction for children from diverse backgrounds in mainstream classrooms. Major themes and issues addressed in the course were (1) teachers' own backgrounds, beliefs, and practices relative to serving children whose backgrounds and experiences may differ significantly from theirs; (2) background information about the needs of children from linguistically and culturally diverse backgrounds; (3) the lived experiences of individuals from diverse cultural and linguistic backgrounds, who, as guest speakers, could provide powerful commentary on the complexities of crossing linguistic and cultural boundaries in U.S. public schools; and (4) studies of autobiographies by authors from diverse ethnic and linguistic backgrounds to explore how insights from those authors could help course participants think about new ways to craft literacy instruction in their classrooms better to meet the needs of all children in their classrooms. Required texts included Heath's (1982) *Ways with Words: Language, Life and Work in Communities and Classrooms*; Edwards, Pleasants, and Franklin's (1999) *A Path to Follow: Learning to Listen to Parents*; Florio-Ruane's (2001) *Teacher Education and the Cultural Imagination: Autobiography, Conversation, and Narrative*; Frankenberg's (1997) *Displacing Whiteness: Essays in Social and Cultural Criticism*; Howard's (1999) *We Can't Teach What We Don't Know: White Teachers, Multiracial Schools;* and Santa Ana's (2004) *Tongue-Tied: The Lives of Multilingual Children in Public Education*. Students also chose one of the following narrative texts to read and discuss in small online Book Club groups (Florio-Ruane, 2001): Angelou's (1993) *I Know Why the Caged Bird Sings;* Hoffman's (1989) *Lost in Translation: A Life in a New Language;* Rodríguez's (1982) *Hunger of Memory: The Education of Richard Rodríguez;* Rose's (1989) *Lives on the Boundary: A Moving Account of the Struggles and Achievements of America's Educationally Underprepared;* and Tan's (1991) *The Kitchen God's Wife.*

Case Study of Helen's Learning in the Summer Course

Drawing on Stake (2005), we conducted a case study of Helen's learning across the first course she took in the overall three-course professional development project. Data sources for this investigation included videotapes of all class meetings across the first professional development course. Additionally, we analyzed all of Helen's course assignments. Assignments included weekly short papers that focused on course readings, a final course paper, and weekly discussions pertaining to class activities and readings that each student, including Helen, posted to the WebCT discussion board. Finally, we conducted a reflective interview with Helen after the end of the course. During that interview, we asked Helen to identify events across the course of the class that were most significant to her learning (Erickson, 1992).

Data analysis proceeded in the following manner. First, we read through all of Helen's course assignments and her reflective interview. When Helen referred to particular class sessions or segments of class sessions, we watched those on the videotapes of class sessions to review the course experiences that Helen considered to be most significant. Finally, we analyzed these focused data sources for key themes/issues relative to Helen's learning across the course.

The Evolution of Helen's Understanding of Best Practices

Our analysis of the data pertaining to Helen's learning across the course of the summer class revealed two general themes involving how Helen saw herself and her work as a teacher. First, we identified specific shifts that occurred in Helen's learning relative to each major theme (i.e., the first theme related to Helen's understanding of herself as a teacher, and the second related to Helen's thinking about her teaching practices). Second, as a specific writing convention, we begin our discussion of each of the two major themes with one or more questions we would like you to ponder. We address these questions throughout our discussion of each theme.

The first theme we address focuses on Helen's understanding of herself as a person and a teacher. *Here's the question we would like you to ponder as you read about Helen's experiences in the M-TIP class relative to the first theme: What does Helen (or any teacher for that matter!) seek to gain from understanding herself as a person and a teacher?*

First Theme: Helen's Understanding of Herself as a Person and a Teacher

First Shift (June 23): Moving from a Focus on "Self" to a Focus on "Other"

Helen was in her early 20s and had been a teacher for a year when she enrolled in the summer class that is the focus of this work. A central component of the summer course was to invite speakers who represented a range of cultures and racial and linguistic backgrounds and experiences. Pat Edwards (an African American literacy scholar and a coeditor of this text) was one of our guest speakers. Prior to Pat's visit to our class, the students read the 1999 book that she and her colleagues wrote (i.e., *A Path to Follow*). When Pat visited our class, she spoke with the teachers in the course about her book and her many experiences studying families—especially African American families—and family literacy. That evening, the entire class joined Pat—as the guest of honor—for a potluck at Cindy's house, where folks continued their conversations with Pat in a much less formal context.

One component of the course was an online forum, where students posted their course assignments as well as their thoughts and ideas about the course, to the instructors and to one another. On June 23, shortly after Pat's visit to our class, Helen posted a reflection on Pat's visit in the form of a letter to Pat. (The course instructors encouraged Helen to actually e-mail her letter to Pat!) We include an excerpt from Helen's letter that illustrates an important first shift we noticed in Helen's understanding of herself as a teacher and how she has categorized the students with whom she works.

> "As a first-year teacher, I have been very once-sided in my teaching approach. *I have focused on making the transition from a student to a teacher, and in that process I have been rather self involved.* . . . You [referring to Pat] discussed the topic of labeling students of color as "at risk," which I am guilty of doing in the past. This passage [Helen refers here to a passage in Pat's book] struck me very personally and made me do some self-reflecting. . . . Labeling students takes the responsibility off of me and blames the family, culture, or socioeconomic level of the family. It is time to take responsibility for student achievement and work cooperatively with parents to find the best way to serve their child."

Helen's comments illustrate that she sees the need to shift from focusing on herself (i.e., being "self involved") to focusing on her students, their families, and their needs. Moreover, in the process of making this shift from focusing solely, or primarily, on herself as a teacher to focusing on her students, their families, and their needs, Helen realizes that even the way she has categorized some of her students of color in the past (i.e., as "at risk") has been "self-involved"; that is, when a White, middle-class teacher labels her children from nondominant backgrounds as "at risk," she is likely abdicating her responsibility to understand her children, their families, and their needs—which may be different (not better or worse) from White, middle-class children, their families, and their needs.

Please stop for a moment and think back to the question we asked you to ponder as you read this subsection. What do you think Helen gained in this first shift in her understanding of herself as a teacher?

Second Shift (July 8): Helen Sees Herself Racially and Linguistically

Toward the middle of the summer course, the teachers read and discussed Susan Florio-Ruane's (2001) powerful text *Teacher Education and the Cultural Imagination*. After reading the introduction and the first two chapters, Helen stated: "I connected immediately with Susan Florio-Ruane's writing as it relates to exactly what we are doing in M-TIP. It was as if she was simply another lead professor in our class." In the beginning of her book, Florio-Ruane talks about the power of story to help us understand ourselves and others. Specifically, she asserts that we can learn about language and culture by listening to, reading, and talking about the stories of others.

In her written reflection on the introduction and first chapters of Florio-Ruane (2001), Helen stated the following:

> "The terms *culture, race, ethnicity,* and *racism* have been thrown around and talked about in one class after another, all the way through my undergraduate studies. Never have I actually felt as though it was something I could grasp and truly connect with. The terms and their effects have been a gray area, always looming above everything we do as teachers, but never tangible to me."

As this statement illustrates, throughout her undergraduate work, and in her early graduate courses, Helen understood racial and linguistic diversity in a decontextualized manner. As a result of participating in M-TIP, however, Helen no longer sees racial and linguistic diversity as something detached from her and "out there." Rather, Helen is starting to see racial and linguistic diversity in an embodied manner; this new "seeing" on Helen's part gives her a much deeper and personal understanding of racial and linguistic diversity. Lakoff and Johnson (1999) argue that bodily experiences are the "primal basis for everything we can mean, think, know, and communicate" (p. xi). In other words, we must engage in educative encounters in meaningful contexts that are experiential and deeply engage the body. Thus, deep, rich conceptual learning does not evolve as just a "thinking" activity; rather, it is a thinking–doing–feeling activity. In summary, as a result of taking this summer class in general, and of reading the Florio-Ruane (2001) text in particular, Helen has become "emotionally involved" in the process of understanding herself and others in an embodied manner. Helen realizes that she must engage in the process of identifying her own racial and linguistic identity; this understanding has important implications for her work with others. Notions of racial and linguistic "situatedness" are now becoming contextualized in Helen's own story, the stories of her classmates, and the stories that she read in class texts.

In essence, then, Helen is learning to categorize herself racially and linguistically. Whereas, in the past, she categorized the "other" (i.e., people of color) racially and linguistically, Helen is now seeing that she, too, can be categorized racially and linguistically. Left unexamined, Whites can view their "place" or category in American society as the default "norm" against which all others (i.e., people of color) are categorized (Florio-Ruane, 2001; Frankenberg, 1997; Howard, 1999). This is problematic, of course, because this default categorization goes unexamined and unquestioned (Cherryholmes, 1989).

Please stop for a moment and think back to the question we asked you to ponder as you read this subsection. What do you think that Helen gained in this second shift in her understanding of herself as a teacher?

Third Shift (July 11 and August 1): Helen Sees Her Own White Privilege

As the summer class progressed, Helen continued to shift in her thinking. Recall that earlier in the summer she shifted from a focus on herself to a focus on others. Next, she began to situate herself racially and linguistically with respect to others; that is, not only did others (i.e., people of color) have unique racial, cultural, and linguistic identities, but, as a White, monolingual, English-speaking woman, she also had a unique racial, cultural, and linguistic identity. Finally, toward the end of the summer class, she began to see her place in American society differently; she began to see her own White privilege. During the week of July 11, Helen posted the following comment on the WebCT discussion board:

> "This experience has really given me perspective on who I am, not only as a teacher, but the position that I hold in society. I want you all to know that you are helping me to see myself more clearly (the things I take for granted my language, my power, and even the possibility of how I might be a dominant force in my classroom)." [July 11, 2005]

Helen made this comment on the discussion board in response to several comments that her classmates had made. In particular, Helen said that the life story of another person in class (whom she did not identify) made her feel "guilty, ashamed, and reflective" [about being White in America].

A few weeks later, Helen made the following observation on the WebCT discussion board:

> "I have had difficulties in standing up for what I believe when an argument arises. I have always been a pleaser in the way that I react to others. I would rather not cause disturbances or argue with others; however, this class has taught me that being silent is allowing racism and White dominance to continue. I have to break my habit of silence, or else I, too, am guilty of not standing up to change wrongs done to others." [August 1, 2005]

Helen's August 1st comment on the WebCT discussion board illustrates the following: Now that Helen realizes that she, too, as a White, monolingual, English-speaking woman in America, can be categorized racially and linguistically, she "sees" that the category in which she finds herself affords her power and privilege that others (i.e., people of color) are not afforded. Essentially, then, she not only sees her own White privilege, but she also realizes that this "seeing" carries with it a responsibility to speak up when she sees instances of racism and White dominance (Frankenberg, 1997; Howard, 1999).

Before moving to the next theme, let's revisit the question we asked you to ponder as you read this subsection. *What did each shift in Helen's thinking reveal about what she had to gain by examining herself as a person and a teacher?* We share our answers to this question with you. Please compare what we think with your own thinking as you read through Helen's learning relative to the first theme. Helen's first shift in thinking resulted in a shift from a focus on herself as a teacher to a focus on her students as learners. This shift is crucial for fostering student learning; if teachers wish to foster student learning, they must focus not on what they are doing as teachers but on what students are learning as a result of what teachers ask them to do (Lave, 1996). Additionally, Helen shifted her understanding of how she categorized her students. As a result of her work with Pat Edwards, Helen realized that categorizing her students and their families as "at risk" could make it easier for her, as a teacher, to use her White privilege to abdicate her responsibility to work effectively with her children and their parents. The next two shifts in Helen's thinking revealed that she began to categorize herself racially and linguistically, and to see the privileged role that she is afforded in American society as a White, English-speaking woman. Why do both of these insights matter? By categorizing herself as a White, English-speaking woman in American society, Helen is now open to seeing herself and others differently. And, because our actions and behaviors are facilitated by our thinking (Lakoff, 1987), Helen is open to different (and possibly more productive) courses of action relative to herself and her students and their families.

Second Theme: Helen's Evolving Identity as a Teacher Changed the Way She Saw Her Teaching

As you read through the shifts in Helen's thinking below relative to how she sees her teaching, ask yourself the following questions: Who stands to benefit as Helen changes the ways that she sees her teaching? Why? How? Additionally, before reading about the first shift in Helen's thinking below, please think about how you would respond if you heard a fellow teacher make the following statement about the student population at another school: "Their demographics are worse than ours."

First Shift: Helen Begins to See "Other" Differently

On Saturday, June 18, 2005, Helen and her classmates participated in a M-TIP class activity called "The Privilege Walk" available online at *www.whatsrace.org/images/privwalk-short.pdf*. Here's how the activity worked. The entire class of 17 teachers went outside and formed a long line in the grass outside the building. Each student stood side by side, initially holding hands, a full arm's length apart. The instructor began asking questions. If the answer to the question was "Yes," students took a step forward. If the answer to the question was "No," students took a step backward. There were approximately 20 questions. Here are two examples of the types of questions asked: "Was someone at home to help you with your homework when you arrived from school every day, yes or no?" and "Were you ever told that you could not succeed at something because of your race, yes or no?"

Try to visualize 17 teachers lined up at arm's length from one another, and moving forward and backward depending on their personal answers to the questions posed to them. By the end of the 20 questions, the 17 teachers in class were spread out across the lawn. When the instructor stopped reading the list of questions, she asked students to look at their locations and the locations of their fellow classmates. She asked folks what they noticed. Then she asked everyone to walk quietly back to the classroom. As teachers returned to the classroom and sat down, it was clear that some of them were holding back tears. As the instructor debriefed with the class, teachers mentioned that this experience presented a stark visual image of the often unacknowledged "privilege" of some. Here is what the group saw. The teachers of color were at the very back of the entire group. The White upper- and middle-class teachers were at the very front of the group. The remainder of the folks in class were distributed between these two groups. The activity (and the discussion of the activity) ended with class participants noting that America is not a level playing field. Some people in the United States begin, and move through, life with privileges that others do not have. Even putting forth the same amount of effort, White, monolingual, English-speaking people are going to be way ahead of people of color and individuals who do not speak English as a first language. It takes significantly more effort and determination for English learners and individuals from nondominant backgrounds to reach the same level of privilege to which White, English-speaking individuals are born.

Recall that Helen teaches at an inner-city school. Approximately 80% of the children at her school are Latino and speak Spanish as their first language. Because Helen was teaching at a year-round school, she started her second year of school in June 2005. Thus, shortly before our M-TIP class engaged in "The Privilege Walk," Helen had begun to work with a new group of fourth-grade children. The evening after "The Privilege Walk," Helen posted the following comment on the WebCT discussion board:

> "I am beginning to catch on to attitudes held by others about the population at my school. One individual who was speaking at our [staff] meeting was talking about another school whose "**demographics are worse than ours**." Talk about seeing our students' culture as a problem and not a resource. I was amazed. I even glanced around to see if anyone else caught it. I felt a surge of mixed emotions. Angry that he would say, or rather, unconsciously think that, and I also felt somewhat excited that I heard it and caught it, that I hear it now and it has come to the surface for me." [June 18, 2005]

Helen's words illustrate that not only has she begun to see and categorize herself differently racially and linguistically, but she also has begun to see and categorize others around her differently. Helen acknowledges that in the past a comment like the one made by her White colleague about the children at another school (i.e., the "demographics there are worse") may not have even registered with her. Now, she is paying attention to derogatory and racist comments, such as the one made by her colleague at her school. Helen now understands that when her White colleague is talking about "bad demographics," he is talking about children who are not White, and who do not speak English as a first language.

Helen also realizes something else. Her comments below, made a month after the previous comment reveal that she realizes we must reflect on our ourselves and the situations in which we live and work if we wish to recognize (and subsequently act on) issues of racism and prejudice.

> "We [as teachers] are not always objective, which is why it is so important to reexamine ourselves and our realities. . . . I need to begin letting down my walls and really listening to not only my students, but their families and the community in order to know best how to serve them—instead of assuming that since I went through the teacher program, that I know best. Apparently there was much I did not learn in the undergraduate program." [July 15, 2005]

Helen wrote this comment in response to a reading in Florio-Ruane's (2001) *Teacher Education and the Cultural Imagination*. Helen's comment is a reflection on the following comment by Florio-Ruane: "The images and narratives we hold, unexamined, penetrate our thinking and indeed, come to be our experience." Later in the same reflective WebCT entry, Helen acknowledges that her own thinking has been significantly shaped and formed by reading Florio-Ruane's book, by reading about and listening to family stories shared by Edwards, and by Howard's (1999) narrative about his own journey in learning about linguistic and racial diversity. Helen's words illustrate that she realizes the importance of listening deeply and carefully to important "others" including students, their families, and the members of the community of which her school is a part. Helen acknowledges that to listen carefully and reflect "changes what I think and know, and who I am" (July 15, 2005).

At the beginning of our discussion of this second major theme, we asked you, as the reader, to contemplate the following questions: *Who stands to benefit as Helen changes the ways that she sees her teaching? Why? How?* Please consider these questions now. We will talk more about them at the end of our discussion of this second theme. We also asked you to consider what your own reaction would be if you heard a colleague make the following statement about the children at a local school: *"Their demographics are worse than ours."* We hope that, like Helen, you "see" the derogatory and racist nature of this comment. A further question merits consideration. *How might you have responded had you heard a colleague make that comment at a staff meeting?*

Second Shift: Helen Begins to Value "Other" Differently

Much as Helen was shifting in the ways she categorized herself linguistically and racially, she was also shifting in how she saw her work as a teacher. As indicated by our discussion of her first shift, seeing her teaching differently, Helen noticed inappropriate language that her White colleague used about children from nondominant backgrounds. Helen knew that it was wrong to categorize children from nondominant backgrounds in this way. In addition to noticing the inappropriate language of a colleague and realizing that her children and other children from nondominant backgrounds deserved better, Helen began to wonder how she could make more of a difference in her own classroom by valuing and honoring the languages, cultures, and experiences her children brought to her classroom. For example, Helen read a poem in the text *Tongue-Tied: The Lives of Multilingual Children in Public Education* (Santa Ana, 2004, p. 11). After reading the poem about the poet's experiences as a 5-year-old, non-English-speaker in school, Helen stated:

> "It is so sad that this young child has been hurt by not knowing English, and by not being validated in her own language. One interesting point was her struggle between school and home. . . . What if this were a student in my room? How would I help her, not knowing her language?" [July 11, 2005]

In a comment posted on the WebCT discussion board a week later, Helen continued expressing her concern about valuing and honoring her children's home languages and cultures. As well, she acknowledged the importance of valuing and honoring children's home literacy practices. Helen made the comment below after reading Heath's (1982) book *Ways with Words*. Helen had been reading Heath's account of families' different home literacy practices in the cities of Roadville and Trackton, whereby the home literacy practices of children from African American families and poor White families were significantly different from those of White children in middle-class homes, on whom the local schools based their literacy practices. Helen wrote:

> "I liked thinking about my classroom in that light. Not just that my students each have cultural and ethnic characteristics to be considered, but that their home literacy experiences must be acknowledged in the classroom as well." [July 18, 2005]

Even though Heath's work was done approximately a quarter-century ago, more current research illustrates that similar home–school literacy mismatch problems still exist today. For example, exploring the home and school literacy practices of Chinese Canadian children in Canadian schools, Li (2006) found that home literacy practices and expectations differed significantly from school literacy practices relative to a host of different factors, including unfamiliar instructional methods, different expectations around homework, and poor communication between home and school. While the mismatches between home and school literacy practices continue to plague schools and communities in the United States and Canada, there are examples of schools that have made changes to connect with, honor, and value the races, languages, and home literacy practices of community members. For example, the work of Moll, Amanti, Neff, and González (1992) illustrates the powerful home–school bonds that can be forged when schools seek to understand and draw on the home languages, cultures, and literacy practices of families in the local community. Now that Helen recognizes the value and importance of home literacy practices, she can draw on the work of scholars such as Moll et al. and Edwards et al. (1999) as models for how she might draw on those home literacy practices in her classroom.

At the beginning of our discussion of this second major theme, we asked you, as the reader, to contemplate the following questions: *Who stands to benefit as Helen changes the ways that she sees her teaching? Why? How?* As you have just finished reading about Helen's second shift relative to her reflections on her teaching, we ask you to consider these questions again. We will talk more about them at the end of our discussion of this second theme.

Third Shift: Helen Begins to See Broader Institutional Contexts Differently

The last major shift we noticed in Helen's thinking about her work as a teacher is related to her understanding of her work situated within broader institutional contexts. Her comments below from the WebCT discussion board indicate that she understands that factors outside of her classroom have an impact on what happens inside her classroom. Commenting on a classmate's discussion of accountability measures for teachers and their children, Helen states the following:

> "Ella, I completely agree with you that standardized testing and No Child Left Behind have created a more 'seeable' aspect of institutionalized racism. Why do we never hear stories of a child who has come to America in second grade, speaking no English and makes wonderful progress in learning a new language and excelling in academics? Why was [my school's] student not in the news for tak-

ing a first place ribbon on the regional science fair? (They were not recognized at all.) It makes me so sad that our children are learning at such quick rates and jumping over language barriers to do it. True, they may be slightly behind students who are English proficient, but does the public realize that it takes up to 7 years to learn English, or any language, fluently enough to learn academics in it? The public and politicians just want things to look good on paper. They should come into my room sometime and meet the faces whose statistics they are so concerned about. They should meet the fifth graders who come into our classes not knowing a word of English, but who are willing to come, day in and day out, to try to learn a language and succeed in school. . . . Treating each student as being gifted is a terrific reminder as a teacher about how our attitudes and responses should be." [July 25, 2005]

Helen's comments reveal the following: Not only does Helen understand that forces outside her classroom influence what happens to her children in terms of testing, and so forth, but she also understands that the accountability measures used to "measure" her children do not reveal the tremendous strides they make in their daily learning in her classroom. Nor do the external accountability measures reveal her children's tremendous heart and effort as they come to school day after day, striving to learn English and learn through English.

In the comment below, Helen also discloses her understanding that children from nondominant backgrounds in schools that serve families with low socioeconomic status are often overlooked at the community/ district levels. Helen shares the following story with her classmates:

"Recently the region had a science fair. Kids at my school actually took first place in the regional fair. Instead of being recognized like they deserved to be, there were passed over and forgotten. The ceremony was changed at the last minute, and these children, who were in first place in the region, did not even get their ribbons, much less the savings bonds and recognition that they were promised. How devastating. I am still so angry about that. It is just like telling them they will never be scientists. Their accomplishments were unimportant and unvalued." [August 5, 2005]

At the beginning of our discussion of this second theme about Helen's shifts in learning about herself as a teacher, we asked you to ponder the following questions: *Who stands to benefit as Helen changes the ways that she sees her teaching? Why? How?* We revisit these questions with you now. Helen's first two conceptual shifts involved "seeing" and "valuing" others differently. By Helen's own admission, she started to see racist and derogatory comments made by fellow White teachers. She also saw more clearly the importance of valuing children's home literacy practices, in addition to their races, cultures, and home languages. Helen's third major conceptual shift revealed that she saw unfair treatment of her children from the broader contexts in which her classroom and school were embedded. Here Helen talked about unfair testing practices and children from her school not receiving the recognition they were due for their achievements at the regional science fair. Her conceptual shifts reveal that Helen recognized that she should not only scrutinize her own words and actions but also the words and actions of others within and outside her school context.

Returning to the initial question we posed (i.e., *Who stands to benefit as Helen changes the ways that she sees her teaching? Why? How?*), the first and most obvious answer is that the children stand to benefit as Helen changes the ways she sees her teaching. For example, the children benefit as Helen and her colleagues fight for more fair testing practices for English learners, and as they fight to make sure that their children receive the recognition they are due for winning the science fair contest. However, others stand to benefit as well. For example, the children and their families from nondominant backgrounds stand to benefit when teachers like Helen recognize and honor their home languages, cultural practices, and literacy practices, and make instructional decisions that draw, and build upon, the rich backgrounds children bring to their classrooms. The children and their families from dominant backgrounds stand to benefit, too, as their teachers help them to learn about the rich backgrounds and experiences that those from nondominant backgrounds bring to classroom contexts. Finally, Helen, and her fellow teachers and community members, stand to benefit, as well, when they are made aware of unfair and racist words and actions that are hurtful to children from non-dominant backgrounds and their families. In short, everyone stands to benefit when we learn to recognize and value others (Trueba, 1999).

Reflections and Future Directions

We began this chapter asking you to think about categorization. Categorization is important, because it is a central way that we, as humans, make sense of our experiences (Lakoff, 1987). Throughout the chapter, we have been exploring how Helen shifted in the ways that she categorized herself and her work as a teacher with respect to issues of racial and linguistic diversity. Figure 14.2 provides a brief overview of the ways

FIRST THEME: Helen's understands herself as a person and a teacher.	SECOND THEME: Helen's evolving identity as a teacher changed the way she saw her teaching.
First shift (June): Helen moves from a focus on "self" to a focus on "other."	First shift (June): Helen begins to see "other" differently.
Second shift (early July): Helen sees herself racially and linguistically.	Second shift (early July): Helen begins to value "other" differently.
Third shift (later July and early August): Helen sees her own White privilege.	Third shift (later July and early August): Helen begins to see broader institutional contexts differently.

FIGURE 14.2. Helen's conceptual shifts across time.

Helen's categorization of herself and her work as a teacher shifted conceptually across time during the summer course.

Several points are worth noting in terms of how Helen categorized herself and others. First, notice that initial shifts in both thematic categories started with the individual and moved to broader social categories. For example, regarding the first theme, Helen first came to understand her own racial and linguistic "situatedness" before she saw the broader White privilege she is afforded as a White, English-speaking woman in American society. Regarding the second theme, Helen first noticed a racist comment made by a fellow teacher before she started seeing racism on a larger, societal level in terms of unfair testing practices and unfair treatment of children from nondominant backgrounds. This conceptual movement from the more individual to the more social makes sense. According to Trueba (1999, p. xxvii), "Making sense of our own personal life is the first step in a series of efforts to articulate meaningfully our existence and define ourselves."

Second, notice the kinds of categorical shifts that Helen made. For example, one of Helen's first insights was that as a White, monolingual, English-speaking woman, she herself belonged in racial and linguistic categories. Like many other White Americans, Helen initially saw "the Other" (i.e., people from nondominant backgrounds) in categories, but not herself (Howard, 1999). Why is this dangerous? Because the category—White, English-speaking—becomes the "norm," the default category that goes unexamined; that is, it is the unexamined "norm" against which all "Others" are evaluated and categorized (Howard, 1999). Moreover, only by "seeing" and categorizing herself racially and linguistically did Helen first come to see the existence of White privilege. As an additional example, regarding the second theme, Helen came to see and to value more clearly the children in her classroom from nondominant backgrounds. This increased "seeing" and "valuing" also opened her eyes to broader institutional/societal forms of racism.

Concluding Remarks

We end our chapter with applause for Helen and other teachers like her, as well as some cautions and questions. As Helen herself points out, rethinking the ways we categorize ourselves and others racially and linguistically is an important, albeit messy and often confusing, enterprise. Helen states:

> "I must admit that the process of understanding culture, ethnicity, and racism has been so overwhelming at times that I have . . . shut it out completely. I can't honestly claim that I wish to continue on this road, but I already know too much to turn back. In order to offer my students the quality of education that they deserve (which also means the kind of life that they deserve), I must come to terms with my own stubbornness and continue the process of identifying and trying to define my own culture first, and then the culture, and implications of that culture, on those around me. . . . Being vulnerable requires honestly looking at your own beliefs and identifying experiences that may be painful and hard to understand." [July 8, 2005]

As those of us from the dominant culture rethink the categories in which we place ourselves and others, we would do well to examine our personal and professional goals and dispositions in the process. As a White teacher of predominantly Black, inner-city children, Fecho (2004, pp. 7–8) argued:

> My role was not about "saving" Black children. Such a concept, so prevalent in mainstream media, is entirely too problematic. First of all, what would I be saving them from? Certainly not their culture. The richness of the working-class Black community was and remains a wonder to me, replete with an honesty, directness, sense of acceptance for those it enfolds, and sense of connectedness to its beliefs.

The Latino scholars, Paulo Freire and Donald Macedo (1996, p. xvi), echo, and extend, Fecho's (2004) caution to Whites who work with individuals from nondominant backgrounds:

Tolerance for different racial and ethnic groups as proposed by some White liberals not only constitutes a veil behind which they hide their racism, it also puts them in a compromising racial position. While calling for racial tolerance, a paternalistic term, they often maintain the privilege that is complicit with the dominant ideology. In other words, the call for tolerance never questions the asymmetrical power relations that give them their privilege.

Fecho (2004, p. 8) suggests that an important goal for us as educators should be to "provide a framework upon which other individuals can outwardly build their own frameworks for learning"; we should not strive to "save students"; rather, we ought to "assist students toward self-actualization and self-empowerment." We can do this by becoming teachers as educational inquirers about racial, cultural, and linguistic diversity and equality on the local level in our classrooms and schools, and on broader societal and institutional levels as we strive to identify and name the visible and invisible institutional mechanisms that perpetuate linguistic, racial, and cultural intolerance (Fecho, 2004).

ENGAGEMENT ACTIVITIES

1. Form a small study group with other teachers. Discuss the following questions that we, as educational inquirers, might address to help us achieve the kinds of goals we have just proposed in this chapter:

   - What do we, as educators, stand to gain from exploring the ways in which we categorize ourselves and others?
   - How can we come to understand, and examine carefully, the ways we categorize ourselves as individuals and teachers?
   - What instances of prejudice in racial, linguistic, and cultural categorizations can we identify in our own classrooms and schools?
   - How can we work to mitigate these different forms of prejudice and intolerant categorizations in our classrooms and schools?
   - What instances of prejudice in racial, linguistic, and cultural categorizations can we identify at the societal and institutional levels?
   - How can we work to mitigate these different forms of prejudice and intolerant categorizations in our classrooms and schools?

2. Engage in a professional book club with your teacher study group. Focus specifically on connections between the authors' ideas and your own learning journey, with a special emphasis on connections between the authors' ideas and your work with children at your school. We highly recommend starting with *Tongue Tied*, by Otto Santa Anna, and *We Can't Teach What We Don't Know: White Teachers, Multiracial Schools*, by Gary Howard.

NOTE

1. We borrow the term *nondominant* from Gutierrez (2008). *Nondominant* refers to individuals who are not White, monolingual, English-speaking, and middle-to-upper class.

2. Credit for this activity goes to Dr. Jim Gavelek, who used this activity in one of his graduate seminars at Michigan State University to help illustrate to students the difference between Vygotsky's notion of everyday and scientific concepts. While we use this activity in a slightly different way, we wish to credit Jim for his development of the idea.

REFERENCES

August, D., & Hakuta, K. (1997). *Improving schooling for language-minority children: A research agenda.* Washington, DC: National Academy Press.

Angelou, M. (1993). *I know why the caged bird sings.* New York: Bantam.

Cherryholmes, C. (1989). *Power and criticism: Post-structural investigations in education.* New York: Blackwell.

Clark, C., & Medina, (2000). How reading and writing literacy narratives affect preservice teachers' understandings of literacy, pedagogy, and multiculturalism. *Journal of Teacher Education, 51*(1), 61–76.

Cross, B. (2003). Learning or unlearning racism: Transferring teacher education curriculum to classroom practices. *Theory Into Practice, 42*(3), 203–209.

Edwards, P., Pleasants, H., & Franklin, S. (1999). *A path to follow: Learning to listen to parents.* Westport, CT: Heinemann.

Erickson, F. (1992). Ethnographic microanalysis of interaction. In M. D. LeCompte, W. L. Millroy, & J. Preissle (Eds.), *The handbook of qualitative research in education* (pp. 201–223). New York: Academic Press.

Fecho, B. (2004). *"Is this English?": Race, language, and culture in the classroom.* New York: Teachers College Press.

Florio-Ruane, S., with Detar, J. (2001). *Teacher education and the cultural imagination: Autobiography, conversation, and narrative.* New York: Erlbaum.

Florio-Ruane, S., Raphael, T., Glazier, J., McVee, M., & Wallace, S. (1997). Discovering culture in discussion of autobiographical literature. Transforming the education of literacy teachers. In C. Kinzer, K. Hinchman, & D. Leu (Ed.), *Inquiries in literacy theory and practice* (pp. 452–464). Chicago: National Reading Conference Yearbook.

Frankenberg, R. (1997). *Displacing whiteness: Essays in social and cultural criticism.* Durham, NC: Duke University Press.

Freire, P., & Macedo, D. (1996). A dialogue: Culture, language, and race. In P. Leistyna, A. Woodrum, & S. Sherblom (Eds.), *Breaking free: The transformative power of critical pedagogy* (pp. 199–228). Cambridge, MA: Harvard Educational Review.

Gallego, A. M. (2001). Is experience the best teacher?: The potential of coupling classroom and community-based field experiences. *Journal of Teacher Education, 4*, 312–325.

Guttierrez, K. (2008, April–June). Developing a sociocultural literacy in the third space. *Reading Research Quarterly, 43*(2), 148–164.

Heath, S. (1983). *Ways with words: Language, life, and work in communities and classrooms.* New York: Cambridge University Press.

Hoffman, E. (1989). *Lost in translation: A life in a new language.* New York: Penguin Books.

Howard, G. (1999). *We can't teach what we don't know: White teachers, multiracial schools.* New York: Teachers College Press.

Lakoff, G. (1987). *Women, fire, and dangerous things: What categories reveal about the mind.* Chicago: University of Chicago Press.

Lakoff, G., & Johnson, M. (1999). *Philosophy in the flesh: The embodied mind and its challenge to Western thought.* New York: Basic Books.

Lave, J. (1996). Teaching as learning, in practice. *Mind, Culture, and Activity, 3*(3), 149–164.

Li, G. (2006). *Culturally contested pedagogy: Battles of literacy and schooling between mainstream teachers and Asian immigrant parents.* Albany: State University of New York Press.

Marx, S. (2004). Regarding whiteness: Exploring and intervening in the effects of white racism in teacher education. *Equity and Excellence in Education, 37*, 31–43.

Marx, S., & Pennington, J. L. (2003). Pedagogies of critical race theory: Experimentations with white preservice teachers. *International Journal of Qualitative Studies in Education, 16*(1), 91–110.

McIntyre, A. (1997). *Making meaning of whiteness.* Albany: State University of New York Press.

Merryfield, M. (2000). Why aren't teachers being prepared to teach for diversity, equity, and global interconnectedness?: A study of lived experiences in the making of multicultural and global educators. *Teaching and Teacher Education, 16*, 429–443.

Moll, L., Amanti, C, Neff, D., & González, N. (1992). Funds of knowledge for teaching: Using a qualitative approach to connect homes and classrooms. *Theory Into Practice, 31*(2), 132–141.

Ndura, E. (2004). ESL and cultural bias: An analysis of elementary through high school textbooks in the Western United States of America. *Language, Culture, and Curriculum, 17*(2), 143–153.

Oakes, J. (1985). *Keeping track: How schools structure inequality.* New Haven, CT: Yale University Press.

Riegelhapt, F., & Carrasco, R. L. (2000). Mexico host family reactions to a bilingual Chicana teacher in Mexico: A case study of language and culture clash. *Bilingual Research Journal, 24*(4), 405–421.

Rist, R. (1970). Student social class and teacher expectations: The self-fulfilling prophecy in ghetto education. *Harvard Education Review, 40*(3), 411–451.

Rodriguez, R. (1982). *Hunger of memory: The education of Richard Rodríguez.* New York: Bantam.

Rose, M. (1989). *Lives on the boundary: A moving account of the struggles and achievements of America's educationally underprepared.* New York: Penguin Books.

Santa Ana, O. (Ed.). (2004). *Tongue-tied: The lives of multilingual children in public education.* New York: Rowman & Littlefield.

Stake, R. (2005). Case studies. In N. K. Denzin & Y. S. Lincoln (Eds.), *The handbook of qualitative research* (2nd ed., pp. 435–454). Thousand Oaks, CA: Sage.

Tan, A. (1991). *The kitchen god's wife.* New York: Ivy Books.

Trueba, E. (1999). *Latinos unidos: From cultural diversity to the politics of solidarity.* New York: Rowman & Littlefield.

Wiggins, R. A., & Follo, E. J. (1999). Development of knowledge, attitudes, and commitment to teach diverse student populations. *Journal of Teacher Education, 50*(2), 94–105.

CHAPTER 15

Best Practices in Professional Development for Teachers of ELLs

Guofang Li and Maria Selena Protacio

This chapter will:

1. Present research and best practices of professional development for teachers in general.

2. Summarize specific principles for conducting professional development for teachers of English language learners (ELLs).

3. Describe an ongoing ELL professional development practice that applies the principles.

4. Suggest directions for future research and practice.

The number of immigrant students in the United States has been constantly increasing. It is estimated that by 2015, 30% of the school-age population will be language minorities (Kindler, 2002); however, the teaching force has remained virtually unchanged, with most teachers still coming from White, middle-class backgrounds. The changing demographics in U.S. schools have highlighted an ill-prepared teaching force that is struggling to deal with the cultural and linguistic diversity these new students bring to the schools. Many researchers (e.g., González, Yawkey, & Minaya-Rowe, 2006; Gutiérrez, 2002; Migliacci & Verplaetse, 2008; Walqui, 2008) have pointed to the underpreparedness of the teaching force to meet the demands of the rapid growing English language learner (ELL) population. According to a national survey of K–12 public school teachers by the National Center for Education Information in 2005, 85% of the teaching force are middle-class, White, monolingual teachers, and 87.5% have little or no training in teaching linguistically diverse students (NCELA [National Clearinghouse for English Language Acquisition] Newsline Bulletin, 2005). In a survey in California on the needs of teachers of ELLs, Gándara, Maxwell-Jolly, and Discoll (2005) found that many ELL teachers have had little or no professional development to help them teach these students, and the quality of training has been uneven. For example, during the 5 years before the survey, 43% of teachers with 50% or more ELLs in their classrooms had received no more than one inservice program focused on the instruction of ELLs. For those teachers with 26–50% ELLs in their classes, 50% had had no, or only one, incident of professional development. Furthermore, only 50% of the new teachers in the sample, those required by law to participate in some ELL-focused inservice as part of their induction and progress toward a credential, had done so. Furthermore, professional development for these ELL teachers often comprised poorly planned and executed presentations by uninformed presenters; often professional development did not meet teachers' needs and was not applicable to ELLs or practical. Not surprisingly then, these teachers cited multiple teaching challenges, including inability to connect with parents, and to inform them of standards, expectations, and ways to help; insufficient time to teach ELL students all of the required subject matter, including English language development; frustration with the wide range of English language and academic levels often found in their classrooms; and the lack of tools to teach, including appropriate assessment materials and instruments. Similar feelings of unpreparedness were also observed among the 279 teachers surveyed by Reeves (2006): 81.7% believed that they did not have adequate training to work effectively with ELLs, and 53% wanted more preparation.

The alarming underpreparedness of our teaching force for culturally diverse students suggests that there is an urgent need to prepare teachers of ELLs to meet the double-challenge of teaching both content and English as a second language (ESL) literacy to ELLs, particularly in low-income and urban areas. But how can we help inservice teachers who suddenly find their classrooms filled with culturally and linguistically diverse students? Teachers are realizing how difficult it is to meet the needs of the ELLs in their classrooms (Truscott & Watts-Taffe, 2003). González and Darling-Hammond (1997) have argued that with the increasing number of immigrant students in American schools, professional development for teachers must be revamped and veer away from traditional inservice training.

Another important consideration is the standards movement that has overtaken the American educational system. Teachers are pressured to ensure that all students meet state standards. However, increasingly more students come from diverse and minority backgrounds, and there is a documented achievement gap between minority and mainstream students (National Assessment of Educational Progress [NAEP], 2007). How can teachers help minority students, including ELLs, when they do not feel competent to meet their needs? These problems justify the need for more professional development for not only ESL teachers but also content-area teachers. Professional development would provide teachers with ESL teaching methodologies and content development, as well as ways to implement their training in the classroom. But what kind of professional development do we need for teachers to improve their teaching of ELLs? What are the components of effective professional development for teachers in order to improve instruction with ELLs? Does it depend on the duration of the professional development program? Does it depend on the level of involvement of the teachers in the professional development program? Or does it depend on the focus of the professional development program? Though sufficient attention has been drawn to ELLs' achievement crisis, little guidance or effort in research has been offered to address effective professional development practices to help teachers meet the varied and challenging academic, cultural, and linguistic needs of ELLs (Short & Fitzsimmons, 2007). Teachers of ELLs must be prepared to differentiate instruction for all students within the classroom, including students with special needs, students working beyond classroom expectations, students with poor motivation, or those who face challenges of poverty. Such students—along with ELLs—come to school with a variety of needs, thus providing a challenge to even the best-trained teachers.

In light of these challenges, in this chapter, we first review research on effective professional development practices for all teachers, followed by a review of guiding principles for effective professional development practices for teachers of ELLs, especially those for content-area teachers. We also highlight successful models for teachers of ELLs and describe an effective professional development project in action. We conclude with future directions for research and practice about professional development for teachers of ELLs. In this chapter, *best* or *effective professional development* is defined as "that which results in improvements in teachers' knowledge and instructional practice, as well as improved student learning outcomes" (Wei, Darling-Hammond, Andree, Richardson, & Orphanos, 2009, p. 3).

Effective Practices of Professional Development for Teachers of All Students

With the push required by No Child Left Behind (NCLB), professional development continues to be a driving force within schools to improve student outcomes (Buxton, Lee, & Santau, 2008). Researchers have begun to explore the best ways to conduct this specialized training, so that there are positive results for student learning. However, despite the heavy financial investment in teacher training, professional development continues to be "fragmented, intellectually superficial and does not take into account what teachers learn" (Borko, 2004, p. 3).

What are the common essential elements of effective professional development? A large body of literature concludes that effective professional development must be sustained, content-focused, and collaborative in order to effect change in teacher practice in ways that ultimately improve student learning (Hawley & Valli, 1999; Wei et al., 2009). Specifically, the following four principles of effective professional development are considered essential: (1) the content of professional development must focus on specific classroom strategies; (2) the structure of professional development must engage teachers in active learning; (3) collaboration is key in professional development; and (4) professional development must be sustained.

Professional Development Content Must Focus on Specific Classroom Strategies

Studies have shown that the content of professional development is a key factor in its effectiveness (Darling-Hammond & McLaughlin, 1995; Richardson & Anders, 2005; Wei et al., 2009). Professional development influences teaching practices when the content includes specific pedagogical practices, instructional inquiry, and specific content areas (Wei et al., 2009). A focus on a specific content area or a particular pedagogical strategy enables teachers to take this new knowledge from the professional development session and integrate it with their classroom practice.

Desimone, Porter, Garet, Yoon, and Birman (2002) conducted a longitudinal study to examine the extent to which 207 mathematics and science teachers' instructional practices changed because of their engagement in professional development activities. In terms of content, they analyzed the effects of three focus areas of professional development—technology use, instructional methods, and student assessments that teachers often use in their classroom practices. They found that professional development activities that focused on these particular practices increased teachers' use of those practices, independent of their prior use of these practices, as well as subject matter and grade level being taught. However, they found that the effect of professional development that focused on a set of similar practices rather than just one specific practice alone did not increase teachers' use of a specific practice within that area. This finding by Desimone et al. suggests that professional development intended to increase a specific instructional practice must "focus squarely on that specific practice" (p. 91).

Similar findings have also been observed in other studies of the effects of professional development on teacher practices. For example, in their analyses of a national sample of 1027 mathematics and science teachers' professional development, Garet, Porter, Desimone, Birman, and Yoon (2001) found that professional development activities that give greater emphasis to content and that are better connected to teachers other professional development experiences and reform efforts are more likely to produce enhanced knowledge and skills. Such substantially enhanced teacher knowledge and skills, in turn, have a significant impact on change in their teaching practices. The Garet et al.'s findings suggest that professional development activities must not only be content focused, they must also be designed to improve teachers' knowledge and skills in the content area.

In sum, the content of professional development programs must focus on specific content areas and strategies to be effective in increasing teachers' knowledge and transforming their classroom practices.

Professional Development Structure Must Engage Teachers in Active Learning

The structure of professional development influences its effectiveness. Increasingly, researchers and practitioners have recognized that the traditional one-day workshop model aimed at teacher mastery of prescribed skills and knowledge is ineffective, since it has failed to effect positive teacher change (Clarke & Hollingsworth, 2002; Stein, Smith, & Silver, 1999; Wei et al., 2009).

Due to the ineffectiveness of the traditional one-shot workshops, teacher professional development in recent years has increasingly moved toward a reform-oriented model that focuses on providing opportunities for teacher professional learning. These reform-oriented professional development activities often include being mentored or coached; participating in a committee, study group, or networks; engaging in an internship; or being involved in resource centers (Desimone et al., 2002; Penuel, Fishman, Yamaguchi, & Gallagher, 2007). These reform-oriented professional development activities provide both formal and informal forums for teacher professional learning. According to Wei et al. (2009), teacher professional learning is a product of both externally provided and job-embedded activities (e.g., common planning time, shared opportunities to examine student work, or tools for self-reflection) that increase teachers' knowledge and change their instructional practice in ways that support student learning. Thus, the structure of effective professional development must include a wide range of experiences that may result in professional learning—both formal and informal.

One important aspect that differentiates effective from ineffective professional development is opportunities for teachers to participate in active, engaging learning activities and take an active role in learning during the professional development program (Desimone, 2008). According to Garet et al. (2001), active learning allows teachers to engage in meaningful analyses of teaching and learning, and may include four dimensions: observing and being observed teaching (the opportunity for teachers to observe expert teachers and to be observed teaching in their own classroom); planning for classroom implementation (the opportunity to link the ideas introduced during professional development to their teaching context); reviewing student work (opportunities to develop skills in diagnosing student problems and to design appropriate lessons); and presenting, leading, and writing (the opportunity for teachers to delve more deeply into the substantive issues that are introduced).

Researchers have found that professional development activities that encourage active learning increase the impact of the program (Desimone et al., 2002; Garet et al., 2001; Hawley & Valli, 1999; Wei et al., 2009). For example Desimone et al. (2002) found that professional development that uses "active learning"—where teachers are not passive recipients of information—increases the impact of the professional development activities and deepens teachers' understanding of how their students learn. Similarly, in a study on the impact of professional development programs in which teachers engaged in a structured dialogue to solve problems of literacy learning, Hollins, McIntyre, DeBose, Hollins, and Towner (2004) found that through these kinds of problem-solving professional development activities, teachers ultimately researched and adopted new practices that influenced student achievement. Therefore, professional development programs must eliminate prescriptive, linear approaches that may limit teacher growth; instead, they must take into consideration teachers' agency in professional learning (Clarke & Hollingsworth, 2002; Richardson & Anders, 2005). Hawley and Valli (1999) suggest that effective professional development should also involve teachers in the identification of what they need to learn and in the development of their own learning opportunities. Such active involvement will encourage more engagement and motivation for teachers to participate in professional development programs.

Collaboration Is Key in Professional Development

Consistent with the need to promote active learning, the importance of teachers' collaborative learning through learning communities formed in professional development programs has been emphasized in research (Desimone, 2008; Wei et al., 2009). *Learning communities* are "teams that meet on a regular basis . . . for the purposes of learning, joint lesson planning, and problem solving" (National Staff Development Council, 2001, p. 8). Effective professional development should not only address individual needs but also provide opportunities for teachers to come together in learning communities to engage in professional activities, such as action research groups, study groups, lesson study, and curricular development planning, so that teachers can come together to address issues of concern and discuss potential solutions to these problems (Hawley & Valli, 1999). Garet et al. (2001) suggest that collective participation of teachers should involve smaller groups of teachers from the same school, department, or grade level rather than involving many individual teachers from a large number of schools. When teachers from the same grade level, department, or school participate in shared professional development, it provides a broader base for understanding and support at the school level that would not be present if only a few teachers from a particular setting participated (Wei et al., 2009). In addition to the activities listed earlier, group activities can also be used to promote teachers' active learning. Examples of such activities include being mentored or coached; participating in a committee, study group .or networks; peer observation; planning for classroom implementation; reviewing student work; and presenting, leading, and writing. As Richardson and Anders (2005) note, these kinds of learning communities help "move the group to a place where teacher participants are allowed or pushed toward deep investigations and critiques of their own and each other's practices" (p. 214).

In addition to school-based collaboration, researchers have also recognized the importance of teacher collaborative learning beyond the school (Darling-Hammond & McLaughlin, 1995). Such collaboration can be done via a variety of methods. For example, teachers from different schools can attend summer institutes, seminars, and workshops, or participate in courses to learn specific knowledge and skills (see Lieberman & Wood, 2002, on the summer institute of the National Writing Project). They can also bring in experts from outside the school to enrich school-based programs with knowledge, ideas, and an outside perspective, and to work with individual teachers or professional learning teams (Department of Education and Training, 2005).

Professional Development Must Be Sustained

Effective professional development should be ongoing and continuous (Hawley & Valli, 1999). Since one-shot workshops or seminars are not as effective in advancing teachers' knowledge compared to sustained professional development, time span and teacher contact hours are critical to sustain professional development. Research has shown that the duration or time span of professional development is a factor that contributes to the effectiveness of professional development (Desimone et al., 2002; Garet et al., 2001; Hawley & Valli, 1999; Wei et al., 2009).

Smith, Hofer, Gillespie, Solomon, and Rowe (2003) found that one of the most important factors that influenced teacher change was the number of hours of professional development attended by the participants. From their review of studies of the effects of program time span and teacher contact hours on teacher change, Wei et al. (2009) conclude that whereas substantial contact hours of professional development (ranging from 30 to 100 hours in total, with an average of 49 hours) spread out over 6–12 months showed a positive and significant effect on student achievement gains, programs with a limited amount of professional development (ranging from 5 to 14 hours in total) showed no statistically significant effect on student learning (see also Yoon, Duncan, Lee, Scarloss, & Shepley, 2007). Therefore, when developing professional development programs for teachers, organizers must consider the duration and frequency of contact and avoid 1-day workshops that will not further teacher learning. Instead, professional development programs should have a longer duration (at least a year) and greater frequency (at least 30 contact hours) in a well-designed program.

Specific Principles of Professional Development
for Teachers of ELLs

The alarming underpreparedness of our teaching force to teach culturally and linguistically diverse students has pointed to two solutions to the problem: One is to prepare content-area teachers to meet the double challenge of teaching both content and literacy to ELLs; the other is to train ESL teachers to master content-area instruction. Research to date, however, has shown that neither solution is easy. Since the latter is almost impossible, most efforts in research have been devoted to content-area teacher training. To date, little guidance or effort in research has addressed effective ways to help content-area teachers meet the varied and challenging academic needs of ELLs (Short & Fitzsimmons, 2007).

As we discussed earlier, content-area teachers' training has mostly been geared toward working with mainstream or native English–speaking students. Because the demographics of America's schools are rapidly changing, teacher education and professional development are critical to narrow the disparity between the needs of ELLs and the knowledge and skills of their teachers (Ballantyne, Sanderman, & Levy, 2008). Working with an increasing number of culturally and linguistically diverse students requires a different set of knowledge, skills, tools, dispositions, and abilities. As de Jong & Harper (2005) point out, although good teaching practices for native English speakers are often relevant for ELLs, they are insufficient to meet their specific linguistic and cultural needs. For example, there is a gap between good teaching practices for fluent English speakers and for ELLs in terms of facilitating language and literacy development, and a lack of explicit attention to the linguistic and cultural needs of ELLs in most training for mainstream teachers (de Jong & Harper, 2005). Therefore, professional development for teachers of ELLs must attend to the specific knowledge and skills needed to teach ELLs, in addition to the general principles of effective practices for all teachers outlined in the previous section.

Based on our review of the literature, we have summarized the following specific principles: (1) professional development for teachers of ELLs must include language-related knowledge and skills, and effective teaching strategies; (2) professional development for teachers of ELLs must promote collaboration between mainstream content-area teachers and ESL specialists; (3) professional development for teachers of ELLs must help teachers address cultural diversity; and (4) professional development for teachers of ELLs must promote inquiry-based professional learning.

Professional Development for Teachers of ELLs Must Include Language-Related Knowledge and Skills and Effective Teaching Strategies

Motivating mainstream content-area teachers to change the way they have traditionally taught and to include literacy instruction for ELLs in their lesson designs is a slow process that takes a great deal of support (Short & Fitzsimmons, 2007). Short and Fitzsimmons argue that teachers of ELLs need sustained professional development and job-embedded practice if they are to implement new interventions or substantially change their instructional approaches. To become effective teachers of ELLs, teachers must gain knowledge bases in first- and second-language acquisition theory, ESL and sheltered instruction methodologies, content-area language and discourse, linguistic and cross-cultural contexts, curriculum development, and assessment, in addition to their content-specific knowledge. As Wong-Fillmore and Snow (2000) maintain:

> [Teachers of ELLs] need to help children learn and use aspects of language associated with the academic discourse of the various school subjects. They need to help them become more aware of how language functions in various modes of communication across the curriculum. They need to understand how language works well enough to select materials that will help expand their students' linguistic horizons and to plan instructional activities that give students opportunities to use the new forms and modes of expression to which they are being exposed. Teachers need to understand how to design the classroom language environment so as to optimize language and literacy learning and to avoid linguistic obstacles to content area learning. (p. 7)

To help teachers of ELLs meet these needs, the content of professional development for these teachers must focus on language-related knowledge, skills, and strategies for teaching ELLs (de Jong & Harper, 2005; Lucas & Grinberg, 2008; Wong-Fillmore & Snow, 2000).

In terms of language-related knowledge and skills, researchers agree that all teachers, especially content-area teachers with no prior training in first- and second-language acquisition, must master a basic knowledge of educational linguistics and know how to attend to both oral and written language development of ELLs (de Jong & Harper, 2005; Lucas & Grinberg, 2008; Lucas, Villegas, & Freedson-González, 2008; Wong-Fillmore & Snow, 2000). According to Lucas and Grinberg (2008), language-related qualities that teachers need to teach ELLs include four aspects: language-related experiences, attitudes and beliefs, knowledge, and skills. Language-related experiences for teaching ELLs can be achieved through studying a foreign/second language or contact with people who speak a language other than English. Language-related attitudes and beliefs needed for teaching ELLs include affirmation of views of linguistic diversity and bilingualism, awareness of sociopolitical dimensions of language use and language education, and the inclination to collaborate with colleagues who are language specialists. Language-related knowledge for teaching ELLs includes the language backgrounds, experiences, and proficiencies of their students; second-language development; the connection between language, culture, and identity; and language forms, mechanics and uses. Language-related skills for teaching ELLs include skills for conducting basic linguistic analyses of oral and written texts, for participating in cross-cultural and cross-linguistic communication, and for designing instruction that helps ELLs learn both language and content.

In specific relation to second-language development, Lucas et al. (2008, p. 363) summarized the following essential understandings of second-language learning for teachers of ELLs:

1. Conversational language proficiency is fundamentally different from academic language proficiency, and it can take many more years for an ELL to become fluent in the latter than in the former.
2. Second-language learners must have access to comprehensible input that is just beyond their current level of competence, and they must have opportunities to produce output for meaningful purposes.
3. Social interaction in which ELLs actively participate fosters the development of conversational and Academic English.
4. ELLs with strong native language skills are more likely to achieve parity with native English–speaking peers than are those with weak native language skills.
5. A safe, welcoming classroom environment, with minimal anxiety about performing in a second language, is essential for ELLs to learn.
6. Explicit attention to linguistic form and function is essential to second-language learning.

In addition to language-related knowledge and skills, teachers of ELLs also need a repertoire of teaching strategies and techniques from which they can draw to teach ELLs with diverse cultural and linguistic needs effectively. Migliacci and Verplaetse (2008) posit that effective pedagogy for teachers of ELLs in both elementary and secondary schools must inhibit the following four characteristics:

1. Teachers hold high expectations for all students, including ELLs.
2. Teachers consciously work to make content comprehensible.
3. Teachers engage ELLs in an abundance of interaction, both written and oral.
4. Teachers create tasks, assignments, and assessments that are authentic in nature. (p. 318)

Since ELLs often have different levels of English proficiency and different experiences with prior schooling, these four qualities of effective practices serve as good guidelines when teachers of ELLs utilize a wide variety of teaching strategies and techniques in their classroom. Although many strategies are available, researchers have found the following key strategies and techniques to be most effective with ELLs (see Alliance for Excellent Education, 2005; de Jong & Harper, 2005; Lucas et al., 2008; Meltzer & Hamann, 2005; Migliacci & Verplaetse, 2008; Walqui, 2008):

1. Engage students in the construction of a culture that values the strengths of each person and respects his or her interests, abilities, and languages.
2. Use meaning-based context and universal themes, such as students' experiences and language backgrounds, as a point of departure and an anchor to explore new ideas.
3. Attend to vocabulary and language that are key to substantive ideas and concepts.
4. Use modeling, graphic organizers, and visual aids to help ELLs recognize essential information and its relationship to supporting ideas, as well as text features.
5. Use explicit instruction or direct teaching of core concepts, academic language, learning strategies, reading comprehension strategies, and sociocultural expectations needed to complete classroom tasks.
6. Provide guided interaction through complex and flexible forms of collaboration to maximize students' opportunities to work together to understand what they read—by listening, speaking, reading, and writing collaboratively about the academic concepts in the text.
7. Scaffold ELLs' learning by supplementing and modifying written and oral texts.

Based on these studies, if professional development is to be effective, the focus should be on these key practices that teachers can implement into their classrooms. These language-related knowledge and skills, and effective ELL teaching strategies, must become the core content of the professional development for teachers of ELLs.

Professional Development for Teachers of ELLs Must Promote Collaboration between Mainstream Content-Area Teachers and ESL Specialists

To help ELLs succeed in content learning and language learning, content-area teachers need to make contents comprehensible to ELLs and to teach the high-level reading and writing skills required to succeed in the content-area courses that are the bulk of the school curriculum, especially at the secondary level (Alliance for Excellent Education, 2007). Having trained as content-area specialists, most content-area teachers (in math, science, social studies, English, or other fields) know little about how to make mainstream content comprehensible to ELLs, nor do they know how to teach reading and writing to ELLs. Furthermore, content-area teachers do not necessarily see it as their job to teach literacy or English-language skills (Alliance for Excellent Education, 2007). On the other hand, most ELL specialists are trained in language teaching and know little about how to teach content-area knowledge. Often there exists a deep schism between ELL specialists and mainstream content-area teachers, and there is little interaction or collaboration between the two groups of teachers (Hamann, 2008).

Researchers have noted that traditional professional development has failed to engage content-area teachers as active participants in utilizing existing ELL resources (i.e., ELL specialists; Alliance for Excellent Education, 2007; Clair, 1998; Hamann, 2008; Gándara et al., 2005). Typically, professional development of teachers of ELLs has been conducted in lectures or workshops in which teachers are passive receivers of knowledge transmitted from experts. In addition, these workshops typically separate content-area teachers and ELL specialists. These traditional approaches are problematic given the well-known drawbacks of passive learning and the need for content-area teachers to leverage available ELL resources, which are always sparse, especially in inner-city contexts. This approach has been found to be de-contextualized from teachers' instructional reality. Therefore, content-area teachers must work collaboratively with ELL specialists to address the needs of ELLs' in learning both content and literacy, and professional development for these teachers must encourage collaboration between these two groups of teachers.

Several research studies that involve collaboration between content-area teachers and ELL specialists have proven successful. In Buck, Mast, Ehlers, and Franklin's (2005) study on beginning teachers' processes of establishing a classroom to meet the needs of middle-level ELL learners, the collaboration between two science teachers and an ELL educator was found to be instrumental to teachers' professional learning. Clair (1998) also found that such cross-disciplinary collaboration in a learning community with study groups, in which teachers explored together issues of teaching and learning in linguistically and culturally diverse schools, was an effective alternative to traditional teacher professional development programs. Several states, including New York, Michigan, and Minnesota (Center for Advanced Research on Language Acquisition, 2009; Saunders & Hart, 2008), that have used this school-based, team-training model, concluded that collaboration among the key members of the ELL educational community (mainstream teachers and classroom paraprofessionals, bilingual assistants, ESL or bilingual certified teachers) is critical in ensuring that ELLs succeed in school.

In addition to the ELL educational community, professional development can also help teachers of ELLs to form learning communities with other bilingual educators with cultural background knowledge, district- or state-level personnel, university faculty, or outside researchers (Ballantyne et al., 2008). Irujo (2005) further suggests that teachers should become active pursuers of knowledge by designing their own professional development that is inherently customized to meet their needs, and they can do so in conjunction with a school system, a university, or an outside organization to create professional development plans or team with researchers to investigate and improve their own teaching practices.

Professional Development for Teachers of ELLs Must Help Teachers Address Cultural Diversity

Ballantyne et al. (2008) maintain that cultural differences lie in cultural norms for nonverbal modes (e.g., body language, gestures, facial expressions, eye contact, and distance between speakers) and verbal communication (e.g., in silence, questions, and discourse styles). These sociocultural norms must be acknowledged and valued if teachers of ELLs are to be successful (Janzen, 2008). Teachers must not only be well versed in the content they are teaching and know strategies to teach that content, but they must also understand their own cultural identity, the cultural identity of their students, their attitudes toward cultural diversity, and their assumptions about ELLs. In addition to this knowledge base, they also need to have the skills to incorporate multiple cultural perspectives into their curriculum, to anticipate and adjust for students' different communication and learning styles and abilities, and to accept and value cultural differences in their classrooms (de Jong & Harper, 2005).

To do this, teachers must be provided training that focuses on how to address cultural diversity with the diverse student populations in their classrooms. For example, to help build a positive classroom culture that values differences, teachers need to learn ways to incorporate students' diverse cultural experiences, provide examples, and use artifacts to make a content area, such as science, become more relevant to the lives and cultural backgrounds of students (Lee, 2004). These skills are especially important, because some concepts in content-area subjects, such as Western science, are contrary to students' cultural beliefs and practices (Lee, 2004). Lee's study on elementary science teachers' patterns of change in teaching as they learn to connect science with students' cultural backgrounds revealed that when teachers mediate science with students' linguistic and cultural knowledge, science is more accessible and meaningful to students. Therefore, cultural congruency is important to the integration of students' culture and language in content-area and English language and literacy learning. Lee, however, points out that establishing cultural congruency in instruction is a gradual and demanding process that requires teacher reflection and insight, formal training, extensive support, and sharing. de Jong and Harper (2005) maintain that to address the gap in knowledge bases and skills in establishing cultural congruency, teachers must be prepared in three areas for effective instruction of ELLs: the cultural context of schools, the cultural foundation of literacy, and the cultural identity of ELLs.

In terms of the cultural contexts of schools, teachers must understand how to accommodate differences in classroom participation structures and incorporate students' background knowledge and experiences. For example, while active questioning and peer discussion are considered fundamental in the process of learning in effective U.S. classrooms, many ELLs come from cultures where teachers are considered to be the final authority, and where questioning the teacher is considered disrespectful. Therefore, it is important for teachers to be able to interpret student behavior in light of different cultural beliefs (Ballantyne et al., 2008). In addition to knowing how to interpret students' behavior properly, teachers also need to know appropriate strategies to elicit students' prior knowledge. Strategies such as story maps, semantic webs, or KWL (what I *K*now, what I *W*ant to know and what I *L*earned), though effective for students with high levels of proficiency, may not work effectively, especially when ELLs have limited English proficiency (de Jong & Harper, 2005). Therefore, de Jong and Harper argue that to become effective teachers of ELLs, teachers need to get to know their students at a personal level and be able to recognize ELLs' strengths (e.g., languages used by the students and their family members, the students' cross-cultural experiences, and their L1 (first language) and L2 (second language) literacy history) in areas often excluded from monolingual contexts.

In terms of the cultural foundation of literacy, different cultures have different literacy expectations, traditions, and practices, as well as different oral and written skills. These diverse traditions, practices, and skills can go unrecognized if teachers do not know how to integrate them in instruction. Li (in press) points out that though there are commonalities in literacy use across cultures; many factors, such as cultural values, family socioeconomic backgrounds, and parental educational level, influence how literacy is practiced in the home. For example, parental involvement in Hispanic families often includes providing opportunities for children to learn through observation, to achieve gradual mastery of skills, to cooperate in tasks, and to collaborate in negotiating life's everyday trials (Carger, 1996; Lopez, 2001; Valdés, 1996). These practices differ from mainstream schools' emphasis on active questioning and independent learning.

Cultural differences also shape how families make sense of their involvement in school settings. Many minority or immigrant parents, for example, consider themselves to be important home-based educators, and their role is to support their children's education with involvement in their lives in the home; they view formal education as the school's responsibility and often do not actively participate in school settings (Goldenberg & Gallimore, 1995; Li, 2006, 2008; Zarate, 2007). These culturally different perceptions of parental involvement often result in school–home cultural discontinuities. One example of the effects of such cultural discontinuities is illustrated in Li's (2006) study of mainstream teachers and middle- and upper-class Chinese parents' perspectives in their children's literacy education. The Chinese parents considered their involvement at home to be monitoring and supervising homework, and investing in their children's learning, for instance, by hiring tutors. The teachers, on the other hand, viewed parental involvement as a shared activity, a task that should be completed through parent–child interactions at home. The teachers expected the parents' academic involvement at school and considered their "parenting" roles inappropriate. These differences are important to understanding the school–home cultural conflicts between immigrants and minorities and teachers, and teachers must know how to adapt and adjust instruction to address these cultural conflicts and to involve culturally diverse families in their children's education. In addition, they must be able to access and compile community resources and be aware of the resources available at the school and district level for ELLs and their families, such as translation services or hotlines for parents who speak a specific language (Ballantyne et al., 2008). Therefore, professional development for teachers of ELLs must help teachers become cognizant of "the cultural assumptions regarding the nature of literacy, of literacy learning, and of parent involvement, and incorporate these understandings into their curriculum and instructional approaches" (de Jong & Harper, 2005, p. 114).

Finally, professional development for teachers of ELLs must help teachers understand how cultural identity affects students' learning. Learners' engagement in learning involves personal investment, in that students not only exchange information with others but also constantly reread, reflect, and revisit a sense of who they are and how they are connected through complex social relationships with others in their everyday lives (Li, in press). de Jong and Harper (2005) maintain that understanding these sociopsychological foundations of L2 learning is important, so that teachers can respond to a range of student attitudes, motivations, and behaviors.

Li (in press), in her review of the role of culture in ELLs' literacy learning, concludes that conflicts between heritage and mainstream cultures often result in cultural clashes and identity conflicts, and the clashes in values, behaviors, and attitudes between home and school cultures often produce serious internal struggles for adolescents. For example, many ELLs who may feel the pressure to assimilate at the expense of their own cultural heritage withdraw from and reject interactions with the mainstream, or act out or become apathetic to preserve their cultural identities (Suárez-Orozco & Suárez-Orozco, 2001). These antisocial behaviors can be misunderstood or misinterpreted if teachers do not have the knowledge base to understand ELLs' identity development process. Therefore, as de Jong and Harper (2005) suggest, to adjust instruction to address the cultural clashes that might arise in the classroom, teachers of ELLs must be able to draw on a broader explanatory framework, and understand that societal and school contexts influence students' attitudes toward learning the L2 and the process of acculturation. In addition, they must also be able to incorporate this knowledge and understanding into their teaching process.

Professional Development for Teachers of ELLs Must Promote Inquiry-Based, Reflective Practices

As is evident in the aforementioned three principles, professional development for teachers of ELLs is a complex and demanding process that must take into consideration teachers' own identity development and attitudes toward ELLs, their knowledge about how to integrate English-language learning in content instruction, their knowledge about their students and the sociocultural contexts of teaching and learning, as well as the skills and strategies they need to teach ELLs effectively. This complex, demanding process cannot be accomplished by the traditional workshop model of professional development that limits teachers' growth and change. Rather, professional development for teachers of ELLs should provide opportunities for teachers to exercise their agency in assessing how their students are doing, in identifying problems, in engaging in the process of their own professional development, and in planning for and monitoring change (National Research Center on English Learning and Achievement, 2009). Weinburg, Smith, and Clark (2008) recommend that reflective practices involve consistent, ongoing sessions of joint planning–teaching–reflecting, preferably between a pair of teachers. In this joint planning–teaching–reflecting process, the teachers develop a form of deep thinking in which they pose questions and solve problems. As Darling-Hammond and McLaughlin (1995) indicate, professional development should be grounded in inquiry and reflection, and should be participant driven. When teachers have opportunities to implement the skills and strategies they learn from the professional development and to think critically and deeply about their practice, they generate new realizations and beliefs about learning, content, and pedagogy (Darling-Hammond & McLaughlin, 1995).

Given the complexity of the issues of teaching ELLs, this inquiry-based reflective practice, which provides teachers the opportunity to experiment with their new learning, identify strategies that work well with students in their local contexts, and think critically about their practice, is especially essential to professional development for teachers of ELLs. Therefore, professional development for teachers should involve more than addressing a discrete set of competencies needed to teach ELLs; it must also engage teachers in a process wherein they see themselves as learners involved in discovering how their own students learn, and reflect on how they can create optimal environments for ELLs and all other students in the classroom (Milk, Mercado, & Sapiens, 1992). As Milk et al. point out, change will only occur if teachers themselves change what they are doing in the classroom; and for the change to occur, teachers of ELLs must become engaged in a reflective practice through formation of "problem-solving teams" or teachers' "learning communities."

Research to Practice: Applying the Principles

Many successful models of professional development for teachers of ELLs have adopted these principles. Among these are the well-known Project GLAD (Guided Language Acquisition Design) in California, Project MORE (Preparing Minorities to Be Outstanding Responsible Educators) in North Carolina, and Project MELL (Mathematics for English Language Learners) in Texas (for other successful models, see Hart & Lee, 2003; Meskill, 2005; Téllez & Waxman, 2005). In this section, we describe an ongoing professional development program for teachers of ELLs that has applied the principles for effective practices described earlier: content focus on language-related knowledge and skills, as well as ESL teaching strategies, structured opportunities for collaboration between content-area teachers and ESL specialists, attention to cultural diversity, and emphasis on teachers' active learning and reflective practices.

The Program and the Context

The program entitled *Scaffolding Mainstream Teachers of ELLs in Content Area Instruction through a Team Training Approach* (shortened as *The Team Training Program*) was implemented in two high schools in the Lansing School District in spring 2009, and will continue through the next academic year. About 14 teachers, including content-area teachers in social studies, mathematics, and science, and ESL teachers and bilingual specialists from the two schools participated in the program.

The Lansing School District, the fifth largest school district in Michigan, has approximately 2,000 teachers and staff members and more than 15,000 students. Among the students, 67% qualify for free or reduced price lunch and, currently, 54 foreign languages are spoken, representing 71 countries. Both participating high schools have large numbers of ELL students, with 665 ELLs in total. In one of the high schools, for example, 19.9% of its 1,365 students are bilingual, and 12.3% are bilingual LEP (limited English proficiency) students. In the other high school, 18.2% of its 1,542 students are bilingual, and 10.2% are bilingual LEP students.

The high schools are on D-Alert in Michigan's Education YES! Grades and did not meet the standards of AYP (*adequate yearly progress* defined by NCLB). Education YES! Grades are based on student performance on the Michigan Educational Assessment Program (MEAP) and Michigan Merit Examination (MME), whether performance is improving or declining, and the school's self-rating on indicators of school performance. Despite consistent efforts to add services and create classes that specifically shelter students according to their language proficiency levels, the achievements of LEP students have remained low. According to the results from the 2008 MME, among the grade 11 LEP population, only 15% (9% in 2007) were proficient or at advanced level in science, 14% in math (3% in 2007), 8% (6% in 2007) in language arts, 40% (51% in 2007) in social studies, 15% (10% in 2007) in reading, and 2% (0% in 2007) in writing.

The low academic achievement among the LEP students suggests an urgent need for the district to improve the instruction these students receive. Despite the increasing cultural and linguistic diversity within the schools, little professional development on how to teach culturally and linguistically diverse students had been offered in the district. As a result, many content-area teachers who were trained to teach their subject areas to mainstream students are not prepared to teach these students. *The Team Training Program*, with its focus on enhancing teachers' instruction with opportunities for professional learning by forming teams and learning communities among content-area teachers and ESL specialists, aimed to fulfill this need to achieve quality instruction for ELLs and other students in the two schools.

Designing Professional Development for Collaboration

As described earlier, professional development for teachers of ELLs must encourage different levels of collaboration: among content-area teachers and ESL specialists, and among different institutions (e.g., universities and the school district) and different stakeholders (e.g., teachers, administrators, and parents). *The Team Training Program* involves collaboration at two different levels. First, the program is a joint effort between the Bilingual Education Office of the Lansing School District and the Department of Teacher Education of Michigan State University (MSU). A team of researchers from MSU works closely with the Bilingual Education Office to oversee the program design and implementation. Second and most importantly, the key component of this project is structured collaboration between content-area teachers and ESL specialists. The teachers were divided into three teams, each with three to four content-area teachers and at least one ESL teacher or bilingual assistant. The teams were first asked to discuss current teaching practices and the specific challenges they face in teaching ELLs and to identify the instructional, training, and professional development needs of their ELL students. Following these discussions, each team decided to address one challenge collaboratively in their particular schools. For example, the first team decided to work on how to collect information regarding ELLs' linguistic and cultural backgrounds, and how to use the cultural data to support teaching in the classroom; the second team decided to work on how to use technology to facilitate ELLs' language and content learning; and the third team narrowed the topic down to how to teach content vocabulary instruction to ELLs.

Promoting Active Learning and Teacher Reflective Practice

Since engaging in inquiry-based reflective practice is fundamental to teachers' professional learning and pedagogical change, each team of content-area teachers and ELL specialists was asked to conduct an action research project to problem-solve their issue of concern. Each team was trained to do action research and provided references books, as well as on-site support on how to conduct the research throughout the process. Action research is considered one of the best methods to engage teachers in inquiry-based reflective practice (Farrell, 2008), because it involves utilizing a cyclical method of identifying an issue, reviewing the literature on the issue and planning a solution to address the issue, taking action on the plan, observing and evaluating (including self-evaluation) data on the implementation of the plan, and monitoring and critical reflection prior to planning the next cycle (Farrell, 2007). To work on the issues collectively identified, each team met weekly or biweekly to design the action plan and collect data and information regarding the issue. The teams also met monthly as a whole group to share their project progress, raise issues and challenges that arose during their project, and share their reflections on the process, as well as the product of their project.

To promote better professional learning and teachers' participation and activation relative to their sense of agency, an online Wikispace (ELL-professional development) was created to foster a community of practice and to facilitate teachers' information sharing and professional dialogue. The Wikispace provided teachers a community space for sharing teaching resources, as well as common concerns and issues in teaching ELLs. For example, the team that focused on ELLs' cultural and linguistic data routinely updated information and cultural tips they collected. Some of the information (e.g., the "dos" and "don'ts" of how to interact with people from certain cultures) was deemed very helpful to other teachers. The team that focused on technology also had resources about different websites and technologies that teachers could use in their classrooms. This kind of sharing created an important and nonthreatening space for peer learning.

Focus on Second-Language Learning and Strategies for Teaching ELLs

In addition to the teachers' action research project, the professional development program described here also focused on building and strengthening teachers' pedagogical content knowledge and skills in L2 learning and teaching. A university graduate-level course that focused on ESL literacy instruction, including reading and writing and oral language development in K–12 settings, was offered to the participating teachers (though not all teachers attended this course in spring 2009) through MSU. The course provided an introduction to ESL instructional approaches and methodologies, including how to plan, guide, and evaluate instruction in a variety of cultural and educational settings; how to make texts comprehensible to ESL learners; and how to develop critical thinking abilities and become a reflective practitioner. The course also took a learning-by-doing approach, wherein the teachers were asked to apply the methodologies in their own teaching throughout the course. As part of the course, the teachers also did teaching demonstrations of their use of the ELL strategies they learned from the course.

To better facilitate teachers' growth in language-related knowledge and skills, the professional development program leaders also invited external experts to conduct 2-day workshops on some of the key language teaching strategies, such as explicit instruction in key content concepts, vocabulary, and ongoing assessment and evaluation. These strategies were then further reinforced through the weekly or biweekly team meetings. The team members were also regularly observed in their classrooms to see how they tried out some of the strategies learned during the professional development process.

A third effort to help teachers master the key strategies included compiling a tool kit for the teachers. With the input of the participating teachers and the university research team, the Office of Bilingual Education compiled a tool kit that included the demographic information and cultural background knowledge of the students in the high schools, key concepts in L2 teaching, and key content-area instructional strategies and language-teaching strategies that addressed the teachers' concerns and challenges in the classrooms. This tool kit was distributed by the Office of Bilingual Education to all teachers of ELLs as a teaching resources in the coming academic year as the project continues.

Attention to Cultural Diversity

As is evident from these descriptions, cultural diversity is a constant theme in the Team Training Program. To summarize briefly, cultural diversity is an integral part of the content of the professional development program because it is the focus of one of the action research teams. The action research not only improved the teams' understanding of their students' cultural backgrounds, but it also helped other team members learn about issues concerning cultural diversity and strategies to address them. During the monthly whole-group meetings, team members often provided useful tips and strategies on how to address particular cultural values from certain ethnic groups in their instruction (e.g., gender issues in certain religious groups; possible ethnic conflicts among different groups of students in a classroom). In addition, the Wikispace and the tool kit also provide a wide range of information and instructional strategies on how to accommodate students' cultural backgrounds and prior knowledge.

Reflections and Future Directions

In this chapter, we have reviewed general principles of effective professional development programs, as well as essential principles for teachers of ELLs. We also illustrated the application of such principles in an ongoing professional development program in a local school district. These principles provide important guidelines for developing effective professional development programs for teachers of ELLs. As the principles suggest, the program for teachers of ELLs must attend to teachers' understanding of L2 development and the role of L1 and culture in learning, and their knowledge base in effective teaching strategies for ELLs. As well, professional development for teachers of ELLs must activate teachers' agency in professional learning and focus on building school-based inquiry by bringing together content-area teachers and ESL specialists, or interdisciplinary teams of teachers. As Borko (2004) indicates, professional development must provide ways for teachers to enhance their content knowledge (e.g., language-related knowledge, skills) and pedagogical techniques (effective practices for teaching ELLs) to enable them to feel more efficacious in meeting the needs of ELLs in their classrooms. Furthermore, professional development should also equip teachers with ways to implement their newly developed knowledge and skills in their classrooms. Only by allowing teachers to make connections between theory and practice can the professional development programs effect change in teaching practices.

Due to space constraint, this chapter is limited only to the discussion of professional development for inservice teachers. With the number of immigrant students in the United States constantly increasing, it is also critically important to address the issue of preparing preservice teachers in teacher preparation institutions to better educate ELLs, as well as the induction of novice teachers who have limited preparation in teaching ELLs. Similar to professional development for inservice teachers, teacher education institutions must revamp their education programs to ensure that future teachers are well-equipped to deal with multilingual and multicultural student populations in urban and diverse settings (Ladson-Billings, 1999). To effect such change, efforts must be made first to educate teacher education faculty, redesign the curriculum to infuse ELL scholarship, and reconstruct the institutional culture (Costa, McPhail, Smith, & Brisk, 2005). Only by effecting change in both teacher education programs and inservice teacher professional development programs can we transform an underprepared teaching force and close the achievement gaps between ELLs and their peers.

ENGAGEMENT ACTIVITIES

1. Conduct a short interview with a content-area teacher and an ESL teacher, and consider the challenges they face in teaching ELLs. Based on these challenges, think about what kind of professional development they need.

2. Attend a professional development program for teachers of ELLs in your local school district or school and determine (a) the program structure, (b) the program content, (c) how cultural diversity is addressed, and (d) how collaboration is promoted. Talk to a couple of teachers who have attended about the effectiveness of the program.

3. Form a learning community with one or two other colleagues to address a shared concern or issue in your experience of teaching ELLs. Design a professional development plan for your group using the principles outlined in the chapter.

4. Take another teacher as a partner (preferably an ESL specialist), observe each other's lessons, and discuss (a) what language-related knowledge and skills you already possess and what you need to know more as a teacher of ELLs, and (b) what strategies for teaching ELLs you already know and use well in your classroom, and what you need to know more about to better teach the ELLs.

5. Conduct an inventory of the cultural backgrounds of ELLs in your class. How well do you know students' cultural and linguistic backgrounds (e.g., the languages they speak, the cultures they come from, what is unique about their culture, and their family circumstances). Think about strategies to elicit sociocultural data about them and consider how to incorporate the data into your lessons.

REFERENCES

Alliance for Excellent Education. (2005). *Six key strategies for teachers of English-language learners.* Washington, DC: Author.

Alliance for Excellent Education. (2007). *Urgent but overlooked: The literacy crisis among adolescent English language learners.* Retrieved November 1, 2008, from *www.all4ed.org/files/urgentover.pdf.*

Ballantyne, K. G., Sanderman, A. R., & Levy, J. (2008). *Educating English language learners: Building teacher capacity.* Washington, DC: National Clearinghouse for English Language Acquisition. Retrieved July 23, 2009, from *www.ncela.gwu.edu/practice/mainstream_teachers.htm.*

Borko, H. (2004). Professional development and teacher learning: Mapping the terrain. *Educational Researcher, 33*(8), 3–15.

Buck, G., Mast, C., Ehlers, N., & Franklin, E. (2005). Preparing teachers to create a mainstream science classroom conducive to the needs of English-language learners: A feminist action research project. *Journal of Research in Science Teaching, 42*(9), 1013–1031.

Buxton, C., Lee, O., & Santau, A. (2008). Promoting science among English language learners: Professional development for today's culturally and linguistically diverse classrooms. *Journal of Science Teacher Education, 19,* 495–511.

Carger, C. L. (1996). *Of borders and dreams: A Mexican-American experience of urban education.* New York: Teachers College Press.

Center for Advanced Research on Language Acquisition. (2009). *TEAM UP: Teaching English language learners action model to unite professionals.* Retrieved July 24, 2009, from *www.carla.umn.edu/esl/teamup.html.*

Clair, N. (1998). Teacher study groups: Persistent questions in a promising approach. *TESOL Quarterly, 32*(3), 465–492.

Clarke, D., & Hollingsworth, H. (2002). Elaborating a model of teacher professional growth. *Teaching and Teacher Education, 18*, 947–967.

Costa, J., McPhail, G., Smith, J., & Brisk, M. E. (2005). The challenge of infusing the teacher education curriculum with scholarship on English language learners. *Journal of Teacher Education, 56*, 104–118.

Darling-Hammond, L., & McLaughlin, M. W. (1995). Policies that support professional development in an era of reform. *Phi Delta Kappan, 76*, 597–604.

de Jong, E. J., & Harper, C. A. (2005). Preparing mainstream teachers for English language learners: Is being a good teacher good enough? *Teacher Education Quarterly, 32*(2), 101–124.

Department of Education and Training. (2005). *Professional learning in effective schools: The seven principles of highly effective professional learning.* Melbourne, Australia: Author.

Desimone, L. (2008, April). *Determining the effectiveness of professional development: Substantive and methodological findings and challenges with implications for evaluations.* Paper presented at the Council of Chief State School Officers Conference, Washington, DC.

Desimone, L., Porter, A., Garet, M., Yoon, K., & Birman, B. (2002). Effects of professional development on teachers' instruction: Results from a three-year longitudinal study. *Education Evaluation and Policy Analysis, 24*(2), 81–112.

Farrell, T. S. C. (2007). *Reflective language teaching: From research to practice.* London: Continuum Press.

Farrell, T. S. C. (2008). Reflective practice in the professional development of teachers of adult English language learners (CAELA Network Brief). Washington, DC: Center for Applied Linguistics.

Gándara, P., Maxwell-Jolly, J., & Driscoll, A. (2005). *Listening to teachers of English learners.* Santa Cruz, CA: Center for the Future of Teaching and Learning. Retrieved October 1, 2008, from *lmri.ucsb.edu/publications/05_listening-to-teachers.pdf.*

Garet, M., Porter, A., Desimone, L., Birman, B., & Yoon, K. S. (2001). What makes professional development effective?: Results from a national sample of teachers. *American Educational Research Journal, 38*(4), 915–945.

Goldenberg, C., & Gallimore, R. (1995). Immigrant Latino parents' values and beliefs about their children's education: Continuities and discontinuities across cultures and generations. In M. Maehr & P. R. Pintrich (Eds.), *Advances in motivation and achievement* (Vol. 9, pp. 183–228). Greenwich, CT: JAI Press.

González, J. M., & Darling-Hammond, L. (1997). *New concepts for new challenges: Professional development for teachers of immigrant youth.* Washington, DC: Center for Applied Linguistics.

González, V., Yawkey, T., & Minaya-Rowe, L. (2006). *English-as-a-second-language (ESL) teaching and learning: Pre-K–12 classroom applications for students' academic achievement and development.* Boston: Pearson.

Gutiérrez, R. (2002). Beyond essentialism: The complexity of language in teaching mathematics to Latina/o students. *American Educational Research Journal, 39*, 1047–1088.

Hamann, E. T. (2008). Meeting the needs of ELLs: Acknowledging the schism between ESL/bilingual and mainstream teachers and illustrating that problem's remedy. In L. S. Verplaetse & N. Migliacci (Eds.), *Inclusive pedagogy for English language learners: A handbook of research-informed practices* (pp. 305–316). New York: Erlbaum.

Hart, J., & Lee, O. (2003). Teacher professional development to improve the science and literacy achievement of English language learners. *Bilingual Research Journal, 27*, 475–541.

Hawley, W. D., & Valli, L. (1999). The essentials of effective professional development: A new consensus. In L. Darling-Hammond & G. Sykes (Eds.), *Teaching as the learning profession: Handbook of policy and practice* (pp. 127–150). San Francisco: Jossey-Bass.

Hollins, E. R., McIntyre, L. R., DeBose, C., Hollins, K. S., & Towner, A. (2004). Promoting a self-sustaining learning community: Investigating an internal model for teacher development. *International Journal of Qualitative Studies in Education, 17*, 247–264.

Irujo, S. (2005). Professional development for teachers of ELLs: A "do-it-yourself" approach. Retrieved November 16, 2008, from *www.coursecrafters.com/ell-outlook/2005/nov_dec/elloutlookitiarticle3.htm.*

Janzen, J. (2008). Teaching English language learners in the content areas. *Review of Educational Research, 78*, 1010–1039.

Kindler, A. L. (2002). *Survey of the states' limited English proficient students and available educational programs and services: 2000-2001 summary report.* Washington, DC: National Clearinghouse for English Language Acquisition and Language Instruction Educational Programs.

Ladson-Billings, G. (1999). Preparing teachers for diversity: Historical perspectives, current trends, and future directions. In L. Darling-Hammond & G. Sykes (Eds.), *Teaching as the learning profession: Handbook of policy and practice* (pp. 86–123). San Francisco: Jossey-Bass.

Lee, O. (2004). Teacher change in beliefs and practices in science and literacy instruction with English language learners. *Journal of Research in Science Teaching, 41*, 65–93.

Li, G. (2006). *Culturally contested pedagogy: Battles of literacy and schooling between mainstream teachers and Asian immigrant parents.* Albany: State University of New York Press.

Li, G. (2008). *Culturally contested literacies: America's "rainbow underclass" and urban schools.* New York: Routledge.

Li, G. (in press). The role of culture in literacy learning and teaching. In M. L. Kamil, P. D. Pearson, E. B. Moje, & P. Afflerbach (Eds.), *Handbook of reading research* (Vol. IV). Mahwah, NJ: Erlbaum.

Lieberman, A., & Wood, D. (2002). From network learning to classroom teaching. *Journal of Educational Change, 3*, 315–337.

Lopez, G. (2001). The value of hard work: Lessons on parent involvement from an (im)migrant household. *Harvard Educational Review, 71*, 416–437.

Lucas, T., & Grinberg, J. (2008). Responding to the linguistic reality of the mainstream classroom: Preparing classroom teachers to teach English language learners. In M. Cochran-Smith, S. Feiman-Nemser, & J. McIntyre (Eds.), *Handbook of research on teacher education: Enduring issues in changing contexts* (pp. 606–636). Mahwah, NJ: Erlbaum.

Lucas, T., Villegas, A. M., & Freedson-González, M. (2008). Linguistically responsive teacher education: Preparing classroom teachers to teach English language learners. *Journal of Teacher Education, 59*, 361–373.

Meltzer, J., & Hamann, E. (2005) *Meeting the literacy development needs of adolescent English language learners through content area learning. Part Two: Focus on classroom teaching and learning strategies.* Providence, RI: Brown University, The Education Alliance.

Meskill, C. (2005). Infusing English language learner issues throughout professional educator curricula: The Training All Teachers project. *Teachers College Record, 107,* 739–756.

Migliacci, N., & Verplaetse, L. S. (2008). Inclusive pedagogy in a mandate-driven climate. In L. S. Verplaetse, & N. Migliacci (Eds.), *Inclusive pedagogy for English language learners: A handbook of research-informed practices* (pp. 317–342). New York: Erlbaum.

Milk, R., Mercado, C., & Sapiens, A. (1992). Re-thinking the education of teachers of language minority children: developing reflective teachers for changing schools. *NCBE Focus: Occasional Papers in Bilingual Education, 6,* 1–15.

National Assessment of Educational Progress (NAEP). (2007). *The nation's report card.* Retrieved November 13, 2008, from *nces.ed.gov/nationsreportcard.*

National Research Center on English Learning and Achievement. (2009). *Developing communities of reflective practice.* Retrieved July 29, 2009, from *cela.albany.edu/research/partnerC2.htm.*

National Staff Development Council (NSDC). (2001). *Standards for staff development: Revised.* Oxford, OH: Author.

NCELA Newsline Bulletin. (2005). *NCES survey: Over 40% of the teachers teach LEPs.* Retrieved November 21, 2007, from *www.ncela.gwu.edu/enews/2002/0611.htm.*

Penuel, W., Fishman, B., Yamaguchi, R., & Gallagher, L. (2007). What makes professional development effective?: Strategies that foster curriculum implementation. *American Educational Research Journal, 44*, 921–958.

Reeves, J. R. (2006). Secondary teacher attitudes toward including English-language learners in mainstream classrooms. *Journal of Educational Research, 99*, 131–142.

Richardson, V., & Anders, P. L. (2005). Professional preparation and development of teachers in literacy instruction for urban settings. In J. Flood & P. L. Anders (Eds.), *Literacy development of students in urban schools: Research and policy* (pp. 205–230). Newark, DE: International Reading Association.

Saunders S., & Hart, K. (2008). *Educators share strategies to help ELLs succeed: A voice for English learners.* Retrieved July 24, 2009, from *www.nysut.org/cps/rde/xchg/nysut/hs.xsl/newyorkteacher_9665.htm.*

Short, D., & Fitzsimmons, S. (2007). *Double the work: Challenges and solutions to acquiring language and academic literacy for adolescent English language learners.* New York: Carnegie Corporation of New York and Alliance for Excellent Education.

Smith, C., Hofer, J., Gillespie, M., Solomon, M., & Rowe, K. (2003). *How teachers change: A study of professional development in adult education.* Boston: National Center for the Study of Adult Learning and Literacy.

Stein, M. K., Smith, M. S., & Silver, E. A. (1999). The development of professional developers: Learning to assist teachers in new settings in new ways. *Harvard Educational Review, 69,* 237–269.

Suárez-Orozco, C., & Suárez-Orozco, M. M. (2001). *Children of immigrants.* Cambridge, MA: Harvard University Press.

Téllez, K., & Waxman, H. C. (2005). *Effective professional development programs for teachers of English language learners.* Philadelphia: Temple University Center for Research in Human Development and Education

Truscott, D. M., & Watts-Taffe, S. (2003). English as a second language, literacy development in mainstream classrooms: Application of a model for effective practice. In A. I. Willis, G. E. Garcia, R. B. Barrera, & V. J. Harris (Eds.), *Multicultural issues in literacy research and practice* (pp. 185–202). Mahwah, NJ: Erlbaum.

Valdés, G. (1996). Con respeto: *Bridging the distance between culturally diverse families and schools: An ethnographic portrait.* New York: Teachers College Press.

Walqui, A. (2008). The development of teacher expertise to work with adolescent English learners: A model and a few priorities. In L. S. Verplaetse & N. Migliacci (Eds.), *Inclusive pedagogy for English language learners: A handbook of research-informed practices* (pp. 103–126). New York: Erlbaum.

Wei, R. C., Darling-Hammond, L., Andree, A., Richardson, N., & Orphanos, S. (2009). *Professional learning in the learning profession: A status report on teacher development in the United States and abroad.* Dallas: National Staff Development Council.

Weinburg, M., Smith, K., & Clark, J. (2008). Using the reflective teaching model in a year-long professional development: A case study of a second year urban elementary teacher. *Electronic Journal of Science Education, 12*(2), 1–19.

Wong Fillmore, L., & Snow, C. (2000). *What teachers need to know about language* (Special report). Washington, DC: ERIC Clearinghouse on Languages and Linguistics.

Yoon, K. S., Duncan, T., Lee, S. W.-Y., Scarloss, B., & Shapley, K. (2007). *Reviewing the evidence on how teacher professional development affects student achievement* (Issues and Answers Report, REL 2007-No. 033). Retrieved July 23, 2009, from *ies.ed.gov/ncee/edlabs.*

Zarate, M. E. (2007). *Understanding parental involvement: Perspectives, expectations and recommendations* (Policy report). Los Angeles: Tomas Rivera Policy Institute.

Index